The Politics of Gender Justice at the International Criminal Court:
Legacies and Legitimacy

OXFORD STUDIES IN GENDER AND INTERNATIONAL RELATIONS

Series editors: J. Ann Tickner, University of Southern California, and Laura Sjoberg, University of Florida

Windows of Opportunity:
How Women Seize Peace Negotiations for Political Change
Miriam J. Anderson

Enlisting Masculinity:
The Construction of Gender in U.S. Military Recruiting Advertising during the All-Volunteer Force
Melissa T. Brown

Cosmopolitan Sex Workers:
Women and Migration in a Global City
Christine B.N. Chin

Intelligent Compassion:
Feminist Critical Methodology in the Women's International League for Peace and Freedom
Catia Cecilia Confortini

Gender and Private Security in Global Politics
Maya Eichler

Scandalous Economics:
The Specter of Gender and Global Financial Crisis
Aida A. Hozić and Jacqui True

Gender, Sex, and the Postnational Defense:
Militarism and Peacekeeping
Annica Kronsell

The Beauty Trade:
Youth, Gender, and Fashion Globalization
Angela B. V. McCracken

From Global To Grassroots:
The European Union, Transnational Advocacy, and Combating Violence against Women
Celeste Montoya

Who is Worthy of Protection?:
Gender-Based Asylum and U.S. Immigration Politics
Meghana Nayak

A Feminist Voyage through International Relations
J. Ann Tickner

The Political Economy of Violence against Women
Jacqui True

Queer International Relations:
Sovereignty, Sexuality and the Will to Knowledge
Cynthia Weber

Bodies of Violence:
Theorizing Embodied Subjects in International Relations
Lauren B. Wilcox

The Politics of Gender Justice at the International Criminal Court

Legacies and Legitimacy

Louise Chappell

OXFORD
UNIVERSITY PRESS

OXFORD
UNIVERSITY PRESS

Oxford University Press is a department of the University of Oxford. It furthers the University's objective of excellence in research, scholarship, and education by publishing worldwide.

Oxford New York
Auckland Cape Town Dar es Salaam Hong Kong Karachi
Kuala Lumpur Madrid Melbourne Mexico City Nairobi
New Delhi Shanghai Taipei Toronto

With offices in
Argentina Austria Brazil Chile Czech Republic France Greece
Guatemala Hungary Italy Japan Poland Portugal Singapore
South Korea Switzerland Thailand Turkey Ukraine Vietnam

Oxford is a registered trade mark of Oxford University Press
in the UK and certain other countries.

Published in the United States of America by
Oxford University Press
198 Madison Avenue, New York, NY 10016

© Oxford University Press 2016

All rights reserved. No part of this publication may be reproduced, stored in a retrieval system, or transmitted, in any form or by any means, without the prior permission in writing of Oxford University Press, or as expressly permitted by law, by license, or under terms agreed with the appropriate reproduction rights organization. Inquiries concerning reproduction outside the scope of the above should be sent to the Rights Department, Oxford University Press, at the address above.

You must not circulate this work in any other form
and you must impose this same condition on any acquirer.

Library of Congress Cataloging-in-Publication Data
Chappell, Louise A., 1966– author.
The politics of gender justice at the International Criminal Court :
legacies and legitimacy / Louise Chappell.
  p. cm. — (Oxford studies in gender and international relations)
Includes bibliographical references and index.
ISBN 978–0–19–992791–3 (pbk. : alk. paper) — ISBN 978–0–19–992789–0
(hardcover : alk. paper) — ISBN 978–0–19–992790–6 (ebook) —
ISBN 978–0–19–027958–5 (online resource) 1. International Criminal Court.
2. Women—Crimes against. 3. Sex discrimination against women—Law and legislation. 4. Women—Legal status, laws, etc. I. Title.
KZ7312.C42 2015
345'.01—dc23
                              2015013621

9 8 7 6 5 4 3 2 1

Printed in the United States of America on acid-free paper

Dedicated to three wise women:

To the memory
of Annette Chappell
and Helen Nelson
and for Marg Walsh.

CONTENTS

Figures, Boxes, and Tables viii
Preface xi
Acknowledgments xv
Abbreviations xix

1. The Politics of Gender Justice at the International Criminal Court 1
2. The International Criminal Court in Time and Space 29
3. Representing Gender Justice at the International Criminal Court 51
4. Recognizing Gender Justice at the International Criminal Court 87
5. Redistributing Gender Justice at the International Criminal Court 130
6. Complementing Gender Justice at the International Criminal Court 160
7. Legacies and Legitimacy of International Gender Justice 190

Appendix 207
Notes 217
Bibliography 233
Index 261

FIGURES, BOXES, AND TABLES

Figures

3.1   Percentage of candidates for judicial positions   66

3.2   Percentage of judicial positions held by male and female judges: 2003–2014   67

3.3   Percentage of judges with gender expertise: 2003–2013   68

3.4   Percentage of male and female staff in ICC organs: 2012   71

3.5   Victims formally accepted to participate in proceedings (situations and cases) up to June 30, 2013   76

4.1   Percentage of successful sexual and gender-based violence charges and other charges at different stages of proceedings, as of July 1, 2014   105

4.2   Number of sexual and gender-based violence charges at "arrest warrant/summons to appear" stage as of July 1, 2014   106

4.3   Number of sexual and gender-based violence charges at "confirmation of charges" stage as of July 1, 2014   107

6.1   Number of states parties with domestic legislation covering sexual and gender-based violence crimes against humanity in the Rome Statute   183

6.2   Number of states parties with domestic legislation covering sexual and gender-based violence war crimes in the Rome Statute   184

Boxes

2.1   The formal gender justice rules of the ICC   33

2.2   Gender legacies of international law   37

Tables

3.1 Gender justice representation: priorities, rules, and enforcement   *81*

4.1 Gender justice recognition: priorities, rules, and enforcement   *126*

5.1 Women's Caucus priorities for the ICC reparations program   *155*

6.1 Gender justice and complementarity: priorities, rules, and enforcement   *181*

PREFACE

Gracing the cover of this book is Peter Paul Rubens' *The Consequences of War*, which hangs in the Pitti Palace in Florence. In 2011, I found myself standing before this masterpiece while exploring the Palace's vast galleries with my family. Dominating the wall on which it hangs, I was arrested by its exquisite execution and immense dimensions, and by its subject matter. Although this painting was completed in 1638 it remains as relevant today as it was then, and goes to the heart of the issues that I explore in this book.

The Consequences of War was commissioned by the Medici family during Europe's Thirty Years' War and captures the turmoil that was engulfing the continent at the time. Importantly, this war ended in 1648 with the Peace of Westphalia, a series of treaties that established the foundations of the contemporary international relations system, based on the notion of state sovereignty. As discussed throughout this book, this notion continues to shape international relations, including the operation of the International Criminal Court (ICC).

The allegorical painting projects a strong antiwar message through its depiction of the devastating consequences of conflict. In this masterpiece, the central illuminated female figure, Venus, the Roman goddess of love, appears as a plaintive victim: despite her entreaties, her lover, Mars, the god of war, seems determined to continue the battle, spurred on by the wicked Alekto, the goddess of fury. The darkly draped female figure of Europa desperately looks on, while her sister, representing arts and culture, is trampled. The cowering woman clinging to her child points to the particular vulnerability of mothers and children in warfare. The near nakedness of almost all the female figures is a reminder to the viewer of the violations of women's bodies in combat, an abuse that is itself treated as an unfortunate, but incidental, consequence of war.

In illustrating the terror and destruction that comes with conflict, the painting reminds us that war has always been understood in gendered terms, represented primarily by the male warrior and the female victim—though here, with the presence of Alekto, Rubens also raises the specter of another female archetype: the furious monster.

These gendered dimensions of conflict, conveyed with such powerful imagery in Rubens' painting, have been reflected not only in art but also in conflict-related politics and diplomacy, and in the laws of war. As in this masterpiece, international humanitarian and criminal law, including the Geneva Conventions, has tended to portray men as the architects and combatants of battle—the active legal subjects of armed conflict. By contrast, women have been treated primarily as vulnerable victims, and as mothers, but rarely as independent public actors. In distinction to Rubens' depiction, women's roles as belligerents and perpetrators of violence have largely been ignored. The foundations of contemporary international law, developed at the same time as this painting, were strongly influenced by Dutch diplomat Hugo Grotius. According to international legal scholar Dianne Amann (2014, 7), Grotius's worldview depicts

> women and children as bystanders, beings not fully conscious of the world around them—not actors, but rather objects, in the tableau of the battlefield.

Importantly for this book, as many feminist legal scholars have documented (see Askin 2003; Charlesworth and Chinkin 2000; Ní Aoláin et al 2011), the law has been especially blind to the systematic and widespread use of sexual and gender-based violence—experienced by men and boys, but most notably by women and girls. For millennia, conflict-related sexual violence has largely been treated as irrelevant and inconsequential compared with other forms of conflict-related violence. Where such violence has been recognized as a crime, it has usually been considered, in Grotius's terms, "a violation of chastity." Rape and other forms of sexual violence have been treated as crimes against the honor of a woman, and of her male protectors, but not a grievous violation equivalent to other war crimes.

Given that these crimes are rarely identified, investigated, or prosecuted, the victims of conflict-related sexual violence have survived without the protection of the law, left to carry the shame and stigma of their traumatic experiences. Where the perpetrators of these crimes have been put on trial, their victims have often suffered a retraumatization in the courtroom. Facing humiliating questioning and aspersions about their character, the testimony of women victims of sexual and gender-based violence has often been met with disbelief or ridicule, while the voices of male victims of such violence are all but nonexistent. Prosecutors, relying on methods that are often inappropriate for the investigation of sexual violence crimes, have assumed that these crimes are necessarily harder to investigate and prove in a court of law, a view judges have encouraged and reinforced.

These are some of what I call the gendered legacies of international criminal law. It is these legacies that gender justice advocates have sought to contest through the design and implementation of the mandate of the Rome Statute of the ICC.

The Politics of Gender Justice at the International Criminal Court: Legacies and Legitimacy is interested in exploring how far international law has moved on from the gendered images depicted in Rubens' painting and historically codified in international criminal law. To what extent do the gender rules underpinning the "new" ICC reflect a turning point in the recognition of women and victims of sexual and gender-based violence under international law? Where and why have some of these new provisions failed to be implemented? And what are the consequences of the gender justice outcomes of the ICC for the legitimacy of the Court?

My interest in the ICC was first piqued in 2002 when the Court commenced its operations. I was drawn to it out of a curiosity about the role new institutions play in shaping gender outcomes; in this case, what the "new" Rome Statute could deliver for gender justice via the "new" ICC. Once it was established, I have also been interested in understanding how the ICC can best secure and strengthen its ongoing legitimacy. As anyone following the fortunes of the Court is aware, it is a fragile institution buffeted by the competing demands of a wide array of constituents and operating within a highly political international environment, where claims of regional bias and victors' justice are never far away. Bringing together three sets of theories—on gender justice, feminist institutionalism, and the legitimacy of international organizations—this book aims to provide a comprehensive and unique perspective on the design and implementation of the ICC's groundbreaking gender justice mandate. Its ultimate objective is to offer new ways of thinking about the transformation of the gendered practices depicted in *The Consequences of War* that have for so long prevented women and victims of sexual and gender-based violence from achieving the justice they deserve.

ACKNOWLEDGMENTS

As with many books, this one has had a long gestation and owes its existence to the support and encouragement of many people. Trained as a political scientist, not a lawyer, I have been fortunate to have been stimulated and guided by many academic colleagues working on the ICC, international criminal law, and gender justice. I have been inspired by the work of fellow political scientist Ben Schiff, whose own analysis of the ICC has provided a model for attempting to bring a nonlegal perspective to analyzing the Court, and I thank him for his encouragement with this project. I am also indebted to the many legal scholars who have directed me through the labyrinth of the international law literature, including its feminist debates. Special thanks go to Christine Bell, Andrew Byrnes, Hilary Charlesworth, Solange Mouthaan, Fionnuala Ní Aoláin, and Sarah Williams. Valerie Oosterveld deserves special mention for generously sharing with me her extensive knowledge of the gender and law canon as well as her first-hand experience of the design and implementation of the Rome Statute. Of course, all legal and other errors in this study are my responsibility.

I have been privileged to work with a number of talented research assistants/Ph.D. students during the project. Rosemary Grey, whose careful and patient research assistance and deep understanding of the Rome Statute has helped me better comprehend many of the technical aspects of the Statute and its interpretation—patiently revealing the "unknown unknowns" of the ICC's legal framework to a nonlawyer. Emily Waller has also been a pillar of strength as I progressed through the research and writing phases of this project. Emily has a sharp analytical mind, exceptional research and organizational skills, generosity of spirit, and a calm persona that in combination have enabled me to overcome the many trials and tribulations of a long-term writing project. Emily and Rosemary also contributed intellectually to the project, including through our joint exploration of the nuances and complexities of the complementarity principle. I appreciate their willingness to allow me to draw on our coauthored work on gender and complementarity in Chapter 6. I am also grateful to Rosemary for allowing me to publish findings from her groundbreaking Ph.D. research on ICC prosecutorial discretion in Chapter 4. I would also like to acknowledge the excellent research assistance of Emma Palmer and Jennifer Hunt, who supported the project at different stages, as well the insights of my other Ph.D. students Kavitha Suthanthiraraj, Chen Reis, and Natalie Galea in the areas of gender, institutions, and change.

I am indebted to Andrea Durbach, my good friend and law colleague at the University of New South Wales, for sharing her many profound insights into the area of reparations and gender justice, especially the link between the grounds of nonrepetition and transformative gender justice reparations. Chapter 5 reflects these insights and our jointly published work in the area. Throughout this project, Andrea's constructive critique, nurturing skills, and sense of humor have helped to keep me focused and smiling. As ever, Deborah Brennan has provided sustaining friendship, guidance, and endless support; her willingness to cast her intelligent, critical eye across a full draft of the book went way beyond the call of duty, but I am immensely grateful for it. I have also been exceedingly fortunate to receive Murray Goot's encouragement and advice during this project.

At the University of New South Wales, I thank James Donald, the Dean of the Faculty of Arts and Social Sciences, Deputy Dean Eileen Baldry, and Chris Walker, the Head of the School of Social Sciences, for providing a supportive academic environment in which to pursue my research.

One of the highlights of my time working on this book has been interacting with feminist institutionalist colleagues, and especially working closely with Fiona Mackay in Edinburgh and Georgina Waylen in Manchester. I have been strongly influenced by both Fiona's and Georgina's scholarship, and I am a fortunate recipient of their friendship, collegiality, and support. Fiona's willingness to read versions of the manuscript has been greatly appreciated and her sharp insights have influenced the final product. I thank Georgina for involving me as an investigator on her European Research Council grant on Understanding Institutional Change (RG123325) and am grateful to her and the Council for providing research funding and supporting my involvement in a range of grant workshops and other activities. I would also like to acknowledge the feedback and encouragement of other colleagues from Australia and beyond, including Clare Annesley, Karen Beckwith, Elin Bjarnegård, Jennifer Curtin, Alan Fenna, Francesca Gains, Mary Katzenstein, Sally Kenney, Meryl Kenny, Laura Shepherd Vivien Lowndes, Allan McConnell, Marian Sawer, Aili Tripp, Jacqui True, Laurel Weldon, and Jill Vickers.

During my research, a range of senior ICC officials have generously given me their time and insights into the operation of the Court and kindly taken an interest in this project. I thank President Sang-Hyun Song, Prosecutor Fatou Bensouda, Registrar Silvana Arbia, Justice Elizabeth Odio Benito, Alexandra Tomic, Fiona McKay, Claudia Perdomo, Kristin Kalla, Antônia Pereira de Sousa, Gloria Atiba-Davies, Mathias Hellman, and the other personnel who asked to remain anonymous for sharing their experiences and assisting me with my research. Since we first connected in the Court's early days, Brigid Inder, Executive Director of Women's Initiatives for Gender Justice and Special Gender Advisor to the Prosecutor of the ICC, has kindly shared her extensive expertise on all things related to gender justice and the ICC. I thank Brigid for her trust and openness on these topics and her willingness to be drawn into a range of activities related to this project that added further pressure to her busy schedule. I would also like to thank Carla Ferstman and Gaelle Carayon of REDRESS and Jonathan O'Donohue of Amnesty International for sharing with me their views on the ICC.

I gratefully acknowledge the funding I have received to support the research underpinning this book. This includes two Australian Research Discovery Grants (DP 0879958 and 140102274) and an Australian Research Council Future Fellowship (FT0991602), the latter of which gave me the crucial time needed to engage closely with the ICC and to write the manuscript. Other funding opportunities have also helped make this project possible, including the aforementioned European Research Council grant and a range of fellowships, including a Hallsworth Fellowship, Manchester University; an Institute for Advanced Studies in the Humanities/School of Social and Political Sciences Fellowship, University of Edinburgh; and an Australian/European University Institute Fellowship, Fioesle. I am indebted to my hosts during these visits, especially Clare Annesley and Georgina Waylen at Manchester; Fiona Mackay, Georgie Young, Christine Bell, Anthea Taylor, and Jolyon Mitchell at Edinburgh; Sarah Nouwen at Cambridge; Solange Mouthaan at Warwick; and Ruth Rubio Marin at the EUI. Their generous hospitality made these rich and rewarding experiences for both my family and me.

Angela Chnapko, my editor from Oxford University Press, has provided sage advice and endless patience while she waited for the manuscript. I thank her, Princess Ikatekit, and the team at OUP for making the publication process a seamless one, and also thank OUP's Gender and International Relations series editors J. Ann Tickner and Laura Sjoberg for supporting the inclusion of this book in the series.

I owe a debt of gratitude to my friends for sharing their interest, moral support, hospitality, and showing me many other acts of kindness while I was invested in writing the book. My thanks go to Pauline Crogan and John Bishop; Suzie and Pete Crogan; Madeleine Drake and Bill Budd; Richard Falconer and Sian Oliver; Jennifer Fleming and Jeff Forster;

Geoffrey Harrison; my "Houdini" Sisters; Lisa Hill; Liz Kirby; Rebecca Macken; Katie Mann, Bern Clancy, Ella and Lauren; Trevor Matthews and Lye Yang; Kerry and Mark McCallum; Lindsey and Chris McHugh; Leesa Moore and Chris Ridley; the Morrison-Dochertys and Bryan Kane and family in Glasgow; Aloysious Mowe; Catherine Nelson and Bart Verraest in Ghent; Brett Stone; and Vicky Tycho and David Matchett. Drs. Dave Segara and Kath Smartt have also played a crucial role in my life during this time, and I am immensely grateful to both of them.

My wonderful parents, Ray and Annette, and siblings, Maree, Linda, Carolyn, and Paul and their families, have showered me with endless love and support throughout the research and writing process. I thank my Dad for his words of wisdom, interest in my work, and patience with me at those times when I *think* I know better. I am forever grateful to Carolyn and Ben for their generosity, and looking after their nephews, at critical moments. My mother-in-law, Betty Armbruster, who stood beside me in the Pitti Palace examining Rubens' masterpiece, has been kindness personified, giving up her time to care for our boys and providing me a quiet workspace when I needed it.

Words seem inadequate for expressing my gratitude to Robert Ridley, my husband, for his enduring love, patience, and generosity. I would never have been able to start or finish this project without him. My sons, James and Angus, have reminded me on a daily basis of the most important things in life. Modeling their father, they too have been incredibly patient, giving me the time and space to work when there were many other interesting and fun things to do. I look forward to now joining them at the cinema and the beach (but may still need an excuse when it comes to camping!).

This book is dedicated to three wise and remarkable women: my beloved mother, Annette Chappell, and my friends Helen Nelson and Margaret Walsh. Sadly, both my mother and Helen died before this book was finished, but it is my hope that they both left the world understanding their profound and positive influence on me personally as well as on the direction of my work. My mother was my guiding light, demonstrating through example the importance of unconditional love, peace, family, and commitment. Helen, my mentor, lived by the principles of honesty, equality, generosity, and open-mindedness and demonstrated to me the benefits of lifelong learning. Marg, my insightful teacher, continues to show me the value of deep reflection, warmth, integrity, and balance. All three have shared in common a wonderful sense of humor; the echo of their laughter is a reminder that one should never take life too seriously. It may be an impossible task to model their collective attributes, but aspiring to this goal helps to give my life direction and purpose.

ABBREVIATIONS

ASP	Assembly of States Parties
CAH	crimes against humanity
CAR	Central African Republic
CEDAW	Convention on the Elimination of All Forms of Discrimination against Women
CICC	Coalition for the International Criminal Court
DRC	Democratic Republic of Congo
ELN	National Liberation Army (Colombia)
FARC	Revolutionary Armed Forces of Colombia
FIDH	Fédération internationale des ligues des droits de l'Homme
FPLC	Forces Patriotiques pour La Libération du Congo
HRW	Human Rights Watch
ICC	International Criminal Court
ICRW	International Center for Research on Women
ICTR	International Criminal Tribunal for Rwanda
ICTY	International Criminal Tribunal for the Former Yugoslavia
NGO	nongovernmental organization
OPCV	Office of the Public Counsel for Victims
OTP	Office of the Prosecutor
PrepCom	Preparatory Committee
SGBV	sexual and gender-based violence
TFV	Trust Fund for Victims
UN	United Nations
UN GA	United Nations General Assembly
UNSC	United Nations Security Council
UPC	Union of Congolese Patriots
VWU	Victims and Witnesses Unit
VPRS	Victims Participation and Reparations Section

WC	war crimes
WCGJ	Women's Caucus for Gender Justice
WCRO	War Crimes Research Office
WIGJ	Women's Initiatives for Gender Justice
WPS	Women, Peace and Security

The Politics of Gender Justice
at the International Criminal Court:
Legacies and Legitimacy

CHAPTER 1

The Politics of Gender Justice at the International Criminal Court

With the codification of gender-based crimes in the Rome Statute . . . the ICC is attempting a kind of legal alchemy, infusing a gender analysis into established legal concepts and practices and transforming assumptions and static legal reasoning into justice outcomes which recognise the multi-faceted nature of sexual violence as well as the gender dimensions of other forms of criminality (Brigid Inder 2014).

The International Criminal Court (ICC) offers a new and unique venue through which to pursue gender justice claims. The 1998 Rome Statute underpinning the ICC, which came into force in 2002, was considered by its architects and many international observers to mark a turning point—or, in the language of historical institutionalists, a critical juncture—in the trajectory of international humanitarian and criminal law. The Statute is pioneering in many ways: it creates the first permanent court aimed at ending impunity for genocide, war crimes, and crimes against humanity; it establishes a complementarity regime to balance international and national jurisdictional claims over the prosecution of these crimes; and it amalgamates retributive and victim-centered approaches to justice. Of central importance here, the Rome Statute gave the ICC explicit new rules capable of challenging gender distortions and inequalities in international humanitarian and criminal law.

Gender justice actors helped make history during negotiations over the Rome Statute. Working the corridors of power at the 1998 Rome Conference and the earlier preparatory meetings (PrepComs), members of the Women's Caucus for Gender Justice ("Women's Caucus" or "Caucus") convinced state delegates that longstanding gender injustices in international humanitarian and criminal law could no longer be tolerated. Drawing lessons from national and international conflicts, and from the partial and often inadequate responses to women's experiences in existing United Nations (UN) ad hoc criminal tribunals for the former Yugoslavia and Rwanda (ICTY and ICTR), Women's Caucus members called on states to transform the core institutions of international justice. Their objective was to help design a new court capable of *recognizing* gender concerns, *representing* women and men officials and victims, and providing gender just *redistribution* measures. State representatives responded by encoding some, but not all, of the Women's Caucus's demands. Nonetheless, the result was groundbreaking. The Rome Statute came to include a detailed gender justice mandate that aspired to end impunity for all atrocities, including sexual and gender-based violence; provisions to have women and gender experts represented in its deliberations; and was capable of dispensing restorative justice, including through reparations.

As with all aspirational international treaties, the challenge of realizing the Rome Statute's gender mandate lies in its implementation. In its formative years, the ICC's implementation record in regard to gender justice has been partial and inconsistent. Commentators have been most critical of the ICC's dismal prosecution record: in its first decade the ICC failed to secure a single conviction for sexual and gender-based crimes (Amann 2014). Given less attention, but of equal significance, are other gaps, including in the application of the gender aspects of ICC's victims' redress system. Yet these negative analyses do not capture the full implementation story. Certain Rome Statute gender provisions have been realized, most notably the attainment of high levels of women's representation as well as the successful incorporation of a gender approach in some of the ICC's redistributive activities—carried out primarily through the Court's TFV. Signs are also emerging that ICC personnel, especially the Court's second Prosecutor, Fatou Bensouda, are learning from initial failures and undertaking review and reform in an effort to address the implementation gaps. Time will tell, but in the next phase of Court operations, these developments may act as an important counterweight to the Court's initial negative gender justice outcomes.

The questions driving *The Politics of Gender Justice at the International Criminal Court: Legacies and Legitimacy* are these: why has it been so difficult to implement some of the Rome Statute's substantive gender justice rules and not others? And what are the consequences for the Court and for international gender justice actors of these outcomes? In answering these questions, this book does not centrally engage with the normative argument about what the focus of international law *should* be, although it does touch on some of these claims, especially in regard to the inclusion of protection of women's human rights. Rather, its core objective is to trace *what is*—the gap between the promise of the Rome Statute gender justice provisions and the reality—and to explain *why* certain outcomes have been (re)produced. In making this assessment, the book seeks to better explain the interaction between actors and institutions in an international context and to understand the potential and limits of gender justice advocates' strategies in promoting change.

The answers to the questions raised in this book have their foundation in gender politics. Gender justice actors engaged in the design and implementation phases of the ICC with a clear set of transformative objectives. At each phase, these objectives have triggered contestation and opposition. During negotiations, gender justice actors gained support for some initiatives but confronted strong resistance to others, resulting in significant compromises, and indeed losses, in some priority areas. This book argues that *gender legacies* of the law underlie this contestation. Working as *informal* rules—existing social norms, practices, and expectations—these legacies helped "rule in and rule out" reform possibilities through the Rome Statute.

The influence of these legacies did not end with the creation of the Rome Statute; it has been carried forward into the practice of the ICC, setting the temporal and spatial context in which the ICC is "nested" (Mackay 2014a). While the Rome Statute establishes a "new" framework (albeit with some important omissions) for addressing gender injustices, it operates within a context where longstanding gender legacies continue to influence its interpretation. This is especially the case where there is a degree of "constructive ambiguity" in the rules, allowing Court officials greater interpretative scope. Gender legacies of international law have helped shape the path of gender justice at the ICC; they have sometimes operated to positively reinforce the Rome Statute's progressive gender justice provisions; at other times they have undermined and displaced new formal rules, resulting in gaps in the implementation of the Statute. Working alongside, underneath, and between the formal rules and their implementation, these legacies have contributed to "locking in" some of the Statute's limitations and "locking out" potentially more progressive gender interpretations of the Statute.

Gender politics operates at the ICC at a micro level through gender legacies, as well as at a macro level through the Court's imbrication in the contemporary world of international relations. The Court is a node in a network of other international organizations, including the UN, and operates within the broader international relations environment of state actors. This spatial context in which the Court is nested has served to limit the scope of options available to the architects and enforcers of the Rome Statute. This is most apparent in relation to the complementarity principle that is at the center of the Rome Statute system, and that makes the ICC a court of last resort. As will be detailed in this book, the ongoing salience of state sovereignty norms, which are embedded in the ICC's complementarity framework and which are traditionally blind to gender justice concerns, has played an important role in influencing the operations of the ICC. While politically necessary, complementarity has served to limit the reach of the ICC's gender mandate, as well as restrict the expressive power of the Court in terms of influencing reforms to address gender discriminatory practices in national jurisdictions.

This mixed gender justice record has the potential to have profound impact on views about the *legitimacy* of the ICC. The ICC's legitimacy is fragile. Balancing the demands of multiple constituencies, each of whom has different, sometimes conflicting, expectations and demands, places the ICC in a tenuous position. It must work to satisfy each constituency without alienating others in the process. This includes the ICC's gender justice constituency, who is an important audience given the influential role it played during Rome Statute negotiations and throughout the early years of its implementation.

For the ICC to lose the support of this constituency because of poor performance would create a serious legitimacy crisis for the Court, both in a normative sense of having a "right to rule" and in a sociological sense of a core constituency *believing* it had the right to rule (Buchanan and Keohane 2006, 405). As will be discussed more fully below, to maintain the commitment of its gender justice constituency, the Court need not to meet every demand of these actors, but the ICC must be accountable for its actions, be transparent in its decision making, and especially demonstrate a willingness to respond to its limitations and revise its practices where significant implementation gaps arise. The extent to which the ICC has demonstrated an ability and willingness to meet these conditions is explored throughout the chapters of this book.

This introductory chapter outlines the key contributions of, and approaches used, in the book. Part One clarifies how the term *gender justice* is understood, demonstrating the value of Nancy Fraser's trivalent model of justice and also situating this analysis in the broader feminist scholarship on gender and the law and international relations. Part Two outlines the contours of the historical and feminist institutionalist approach that provides the conceptual framework for this study. It defines the core concepts of "formal" and "informal" rules, gender legacies, and "nestedness" that will be developed throughout the following chapters. Part Three discusses the concept of legitimacy and explains how it is understood in this analysis. Part Four details the research methods used and provides an outline of the structure of the book.

PART ONE: DEFINING GENDER JUSTICE

The notion of gender justice is at the core of this book: it is the yardstick by which the performance of the ICC is measured. But it is an ambiguous concept, used across different disciplines to refer to a range of different practices and outcomes. Feminist philosophers, political scientists, and legal scholars all conceive of the concept differently. For feminist philosophers such as Iris Marion Young (1990) and Martha Nussbaum (2006) gender justice is essentially about redistribution, about enabling women to live an autonomous life that requires securing the minimum conditions needed to do so. Anne Phillips (1995) emphasizes equal representation of men and women within democratic institutions as a determining feature of just policies and practices. Maxine Molyneux suggests that, at its core, "gender justice implies full citizenship for women," with all individuals treated as "'moral equals' in the letter and practice of law" (2007, 60). Development theorist Anne Marie Goetz defines gender justice as "the ending of—and if necessary the provision of redress for—inequalities between women and men that result in women's subordination to men" (2007, 30–31). For Goetz and Jenkins (2005, 163) addressing gender injustice requires a dualist approach, first combating "gender capture" (i.e., outright male control of the power positions through which the formal rules are formulated) and second removing "gender bias" (i.e., the "leakage" of gender norms into seemingly impartial law and policy).

Each of these definitions tackles important dimensions of gender justice, but arguably the framework that best captures its wide-ranging and intersecting elements is that advanced by social theorist Nancy Fraser.[1] For Fraser, overcoming injustice means "dismantling institutionalized obstacles that prevent some people from participating on par with others, as full partners in social interaction" (2009, 16). Fraser's model was initially a bivalent one, focused on economic *redistribution* and identity *recognition* (1997) as the core elements. Over time, the framework has come to include a third element, *representation* (Fraser 2009, 29). In her work, Fraser (1997) highlights injustices across a range of socioeconomic and political identities, including race, sexuality, and gender.

The first two elements of Fraser's model—redistribution and recognition—are directed toward justice *outcomes*. *Redistribution* focuses on overcoming the economic structures that deny some people "the resources they need to interact with others as peers" (Fraser 2009, 16; also see Fraser and Honneth 2003, 12–13). These injustices are gendered: "Insofar as the economic structure of society denies women the resources they need for full participation in social life, it institutionalizes sexist maldistribution" (Fraser 2007, 28). The remedy for the gender variant of maldistribution involves addressing women's exploitation, economic marginalization in the "pink economy," and deprivation.

Recognition is needed to address problems of "status inequality and misrecognition" (2009, 16). Again, as Fraser points out, this element of justice has a gender dimension. In her view "a major feature of gender injustice is androcentrism: an institutionalised pattern of cultural value that privileges traits associated with masculinity, while devaluing everything coded as "feminine," paradigmatically—but not only—women" (2007, 26). In Fraser's view, "Insofar ... as the status order of society constitutes women as less-than-full partners in interaction, it institutionalizes sexist misrecognition" (2007, 28). The remedy is "that institutionalized patterns of cultural value express equal respect for all participants and ensure equal opportunity for achieving social esteem" (2007, 28), with particular attention on women as equal partners, which includes also recognizing their differences to men.

Representation is, according to Fraser, the political dimension of justice and specifies the reach of the other two dimensions. Representation is "centred on membership and procedures." (2009, 17) As she argues, "[i]t tells us who is included in and who is excluded from the circle of those entitled to a just distribution and reciprocal recognition" and relates to the procedures for "staging and resolving contests in both economic and cultural" justice arenas (2009, 17). Gender representation requires achieving parity, but for Fraser this is not only about equal numbers (2007, 27–29). Rather, it is about "creating new rules of inclusion and procedure, or whole new structures of democratic decision-making" (Fraser 2009, 17; also see Williams 2012).

In selecting strategies to address these three levels of injustice, Fraser argues for *transformative* responses; these are remedies that "restructure the underlying generative framework" (1997, 23) and destabilize the gender status quo. Such responses are contrasted with affirmative remedies aimed at correcting inequitable outcomes, without disturbing the underlying framework that generates them (1997, 23). To be transformative, gender justice strategies need to work at a number of levels simultaneously. It is necessary to first develop strategies to tackle each dimension of injustice individually, as each one stems from autonomous foundations—the economic system, cultural hierarchies, and rules about who participates and how they participate. For instance, targeted strategies are needed to restructure the economy to address the sexual division of labor, or to unsettle gender hierarchies to better recognize women. However, because these three dimensions are also "thoroughly imbricated with one another" (Fraser 2007, 26), gender injustice requires addressing all three levels at once. For Fraser "changing both the economic structure and the status order of contemporary society," as well as rules around representation, must happen at the same time as "[none] alone will suffice" (2007, 26). Crucially, strategies also need to break down the other "axes of social differentiation," including race, class, sexuality, religion, and nationality, to ensure that in addressing one form of misrepresentation, another is not exacerbated (2007, 29). Finally, these changes must occur not only at and within the level of the nation-state but also within new political communities that operate trans- and internationally (Fraser 2009, 114).

Fraser's focus on the trans/international level emerges from recognition of the impact of globalization and the weakening of what she terms the "Keynesian-Westphalian" state toward a "post-Westphalian frame" (2009, 13). The shift in relations between the national and international resulting from globalization has, for Fraser, brought into sharp relief questions not only about *what* justice should deliver, but also about the *who* and the *how* of justice (2009, 29). Fraser notes the particular gender aspects of this shift—how "women's chances for living good lives depend at least as much on processes that trespass the borders of territorial states as those contained within them" (2009, 112). The inclusion of the trans/international level in Fraser's model makes it particularly applicable to this study. As detailed in Chapter 6, the emergence of the ICC has triggered debates about whether and when it is appropriate for the international criminal justice system "to pierce the veil of state sovereignty" (Coomaraswamy 2014) to bring to account individuals who have committed atrocities and who were previously protected under norms of state sovereignty (for two excellent accounts of these debates see Sikkink 2011 and Simmons 2009). A core concern for Fraser, and of this book, is to better understand the ways in which this emerging transnational legal order can address national and transnational injustices, especially those related to gender and sexual violence.

Like many feminists, Fraser is interested in the way gender operates as a process—through what she defines as androcentric practices that reinforce a masculine/feminine binary that maps onto both men and women. In her work on gender justice Fraser seems most interested in plotting how gender operates to influence injustices suffered by *women*. This is not to say she is entirely uninterested in the specific injustices men confront because of gender processes, but that her primary attention has been directed toward understanding the way gender operates to influence women's lives, and to seek to remedy the injustices arising from this process. This book adopts a similar approach. The reason that the focus of the following chapters is primarily on women is not because the analysis sees gender as unimportant to men. As feminist philosopher Moira Gatens suggests, both sexes are constrained by gender norms, although men, "by and large," benefit from them (1998, 5). This book traces the gendered experiences of women because women have been central to the efforts of those who took the lead in designing the gender justice elements of the Rome Statute, the Women's Caucus for Gender Justice, and those who have continued to hold the ICC accountable in its implementation phase, the Women's Initiatives for Gender Justice ("Women's Initiatives"), supported in both cases by feminist legal scholars, policy practitioners, and advocates in other nongovernmental organizations (NGOs). Their work has been focused on "surfacing" (SáCouto 2012) the long-ignored experiences of women in times of war and conflict, to ensure that these are represented alongside those of men, who have been the traditional subjects of international law. These advocates have been alert to the fact that the law misses the nuances in men's experiences of conflict, too, paying particular attention to male victims of sexual violence. However, the primary focus of their work, and as a logical progression of this book, is to understand and unravel the ways in which gender processes have affected *women*, and especially female victims of sexual and gender-based violence.[2]

In developing this analysis, I am alert to critiques of what might be dubbed the "international feminist legal project." The aim of this project has been seek to (re)design institutions of international justice from within; this strategy, according to some critics, risks "tinkering" at the edges rather than "staking out more transformative claims" (Nesiah 2011, 151, also see Buss and Manji 2005; Charlesworth and Chinkin 2000;). Many of these critics reflect Carol Smart's view that "law is so deaf to the core concerns of feminism that feminists should be extremely cautious of how and whether they resort to law" (1989, 2). They are also skeptical about privileging a judicialized approach to gender justice that treats courts as "the crown jewel in the transitional toolbox" (Nesiah 2011, 144). A particular concern of many critics is that the feminist legal project has tended to construe women only as victims (Nesiah 2011), disregarding women's agency, including as the perpetrators of violence (Brown 2014; Sjoberg and Gentry 2008). Critics of this project have been particularly vexed about the focus on violations of women's bodily integrity, viewing it as reductionist and dangerous (Engle 2005; Halley 2008; Nesiah 2011). In their view, by making rape victims the "privileged subjects" of the law (Nesiah 2011, 143), the international feminist legal project risks heightening the harm of such crimes. Aligning sexual violence crimes with other atrocities within the "pantheon of privileged rights violations" (Nesiah 2011, 151) suggests a level of devastation that victims themselves may not experience (Halley 2008; Nesiah 2011, 151).

This book situates itself in a middle position between those who champion and those who critique the "feminist international law project," a position that could be considered a form of "critical friendship." Critical friends are, as Mackay and Chappell define them, academics or practitioners who offer (2015, n.p.) "sympathetic critique and make contextual judgement. They celebrate the 'small wins' that feminist insiders may make against the odds, and expose the gendered obstacles and power asymmetries that blunt reformist potential." The position I take in this book is inspired by the work of Mary Katzenstein (1998) and others who recognize that engagement in institutions of power, including the law, is indeed fraught, but can produce incremental, transformative change over time. In relation to international law in particular, the position I present here is that gender justice actors through their engagement can (inadvertently) reinforce gender biases, even where their objective is to do the opposite. As Charlesworth notes (2013, 32), there is always a risk that potentially transformative sex and gender norms "can be hollowed out by bland repetition and deployed to reinforce the status quo." Yet, as in other institutional arenas through feminist engagement the law can also be "re-gendered" in ways that can shift the status quo and can produce "wins" for those previously excluded or harmed within an institutional setting. The proposition of this book is that deep contestation over gendered power relationships can stymie change, but it can also sometimes produce transformative responses; where such gains are made, they are usually incremental and discrete. To understand transformative change as the outcome of gradual change is to adopt the view of institutionalist theorist Kathleen Thelen (in Lowndes and Roberts 2013, 128), who suggests that "not all significant change has to have its source in a major exogenous shock that upends old arrangements and somehow clears the way for new ones . . . significant change often takes places gradually and through a culmination of seemingly small adjustments." Similarly, this book's argument is that although the result of gender engagement with the law can be nothing more than a "least worst outcome," sometimes such entanglements can add up over time to something more significant and transformative. However, as historical institutionalists suggest, to see such change it is necessary to take the long view.

This book speaks to the feminist literature on international law, but it also engages with and seeks to contribute to feminist international relations scholarship. The canon of feminist international relations is wide-ranging, including analyses of the gendered design and operation of international relations and organizations (Meyer and Prugl 1999; Rai and Waylen 2008; Shepherd 2008; Tickner 2001; Tripp et al. 2013), norm diffusion processes of gender policies (Keck and Sikkink 1998; Krook 2009; Krook and True 2012; Zwingel 2005), and the engagement of transnational feminist actors within the system of global governance (Caglar et al. 2013; Friedman 2003; Moghadam 2005; Stienstra 1994). This book contributes to this literature by offering a new framework for conceptualizing the influence of transnational feminist activism on gender justice outcomes. Much of the extant literature in this field has used actor-focused social movement theory to understand how gender justice advocates have made use of framing, resources, organizational forms, and access to shape international institutional outcomes to advance women's rights (Bennoune 2012; Chappell 2006a; Hawkesworth 2006; Moghadan 2005). A problem with some of this work is that it presents an overly voluntaristic (and also often a triumphalist) interpretation of the relationship between transnational actors and international institutions. While interested in understanding how actors shape the rules, this study simultaneously inverts the lens to consider how the rules—in this case the Rome Statute and informal rules of international law—have constrained and permitted the development of actors' preferences, access, and influence. It does this by applying a feminist institutionalist approach, which draws upon both historical institutionalism and gender and politics frameworks, outlined in the following discussion.

PART TWO: THE ICC THROUGH A (FEMINIST HISTORICAL) INSTITUTIONALIST LENS

New institutionalism is an umbrella term, capturing under its awning historical, sociological, rational choice, discursive, and, most recently, feminist variants. These different approaches to the study of institutions share a central premise: that institutional rules shape both the preferences and behavior of political actors and political outcomes.

As the late Nobel Laureate, Elinor Ostrom argued, institutions "operate to rule out some actions and to rule in others" (2005, 18). According to John Campbell, "institutions enable, empower and constitute actors by providing them with the principles and practices that they can use to modify existing institutional arrangements." However, as he goes on to note, "institutions also act as constraints by limiting the number of possible innovations that they can envision and make" (2004, 72). Institutional rules influence the particular type of actors that will emerge and thrive in any context, and the extent of reform possible (Mahoney and Thelen 2010, 28).

Historical institutionalism is centrally interested in the temporal dimensions of institutions and procedures, both formal and informal, which establish the "rules of the game" (Campbell 2004, 23). It "pays particular attention to when and how historical processes shape political outcomes" (Fioretos 2011, 369) by focusing on moments of institutional design and tracing how institutional legacies, including the allocation of existing power resources, become intertwined in the operation of new institutions (Pierson 2004). This book provides an intriguing case study of an important new international institutional arena. It illustrates how the legacies of international law have influenced the design process of the Rome Statute and the operation of the ICC during its early years.

Illuminating the gender dimensions of the design and operation of the Statute and the Court, and their impact on gender justice outcomes, this book aims to address the gender-blind nature of much of the existing institutionalist scholarship (Mackay et al. 2010) and demonstrate the value of a feminist historical approach. It also taps into a growing interest in international relations scholarship about historical institutionalism. International relations scholars have embraced the "institutionalist turn" in the wider field of political science represented with realist and sociological institutionalist approaches now well established in the discipline (for a discussion see Keohane and Martin 2003; Koremenos et al. 2001). But as Fioretos (2011) points out, historical institutional analysis, which has been applied in comparative domestic-level research (see Campbell 2004; Pierson 2004; Steinmo et al. 1992; Streek and Thelen 2005), is only just starting to receive attention in the international relations field.

This book argues that there are three interlinked institutional factors that have influenced the recognition, representation, and redistributive gender justice outcomes at the ICC: the formal institutional design features of the Rome Statute, informal rules, and the nested environment in which the Court operates. This section explains how these terms are conceptualized and will be applied in the following chapters.

Institutional Design: Formal and Informal Institutions

Much neo-institutionalist analysis, including its historical variant, has focused on the influence of *formal* rules on political outcomes. Formal institutions are those that are "consciously designed and clearly specified" (Lowndes and Wilson 2003, 292) and range from constitutions, statutes, and bylaws to individual contracts and operational guidelines (North 1990). Formal institutions involve rules and procedures that are "created, communicated, and enforced through channels widely accepted as official" (Helmke and Levitsky 2004, 727). It is this official enforcement, undertaken by a third party, that gives a formal institution its legitimacy (Streek and Thelen 2005). The Rome Statute, with its codified rules and enforcement by the ICC, is a good example of a formal institution.

Formal institutions play an important part in shaping the behavior and outcomes of institutional actors, but they never operate alone. They combine within informal mechanisms to constrain design options and political behavior once formal rules have been codified (Lowndes and Roberts 2013, 55). Informal institutions are harder to identify than their formal counterpart because they "shy away from publicity" (Lauth 2000, 26). By their very nature, they are hidden and embedded in the everyday practices that are disguised as standard and taken for granted (March and Olsen 1989). As a consequence, this term is often treated as a residual category, and applied to "virtually any behaviour that departs from ... the written-down rules" (Helmke and Levitsky 2004, 727). Helmke and Levitsky have developed a working definition that identifies informal institutions as "socially shared rules, usually unwritten, that are created, communicated, and enforced outside of officially sanctioned channels" (2004, 727). For Azari and Smith, informal institutions exist "when shared expectations outside the official rules of the game structure political behaviour" (2012, 39).[3]

The formal design rules and informal institutions are often coupled and closely interact. The informal can work to "weaken, substitute for, or work in parallel with" formal institutions (Radnitz 2011, 352). Informal institutions can fill in the gaps where formal institutions are incomplete, operate as "a second best strategy" when it is difficult to change formal institutions, or allow actors to pursue goals not publicly acceptable, including those that are unpopular or illegal (Azari and Smith 2012, 41; Helmke and Levitsky 2004, 730). Informal institutions can also distort and stymie formal institutions (Levitsky and Slater 2011, 6). The interaction between formal design rules and informal institutions leads to "myriad, complex and often unexpected effects: whereas some informal rules compete with and subvert democratic institutions, others complement and even help sustain them" (Helmke and Levitsky 2004, 3).

Recognizing the interaction between formal and informal rules casts a new gloss on our understanding of institutional design, challenging the notion of intentional institutional design and designers. Scholars of historical and sociological institutionalism see institutional design as central to institutional outcomes, but not in a straightforward way. Institutional design is considered by scholars in both traditions to be a "messy" process (Barnett and Finnemore 1999, 707; Goodin 1996; Pierson 2004). Institutions come about through the influence of multiple designers, whose objectives are often in conflict (Campbell 2004, 69). Moreover, an institution's design not only evolves at "heroic foundational moments," such as the drafting of a new constitution, or in this case the Rome Statute, but also through "disparate small acts of judgment by strategic actors on the ground" (Lowndes and Roberts 2013, 171).

Moreover, newly designed institutions are never entirely new but are a product of past practices. As Bob Goodin (1996, 30) explains, institutional designers "always work with materials inherited from and to some extent unalterably shaped by the past" such that the traces of the past constrain present actions and future options. William Riker (1995, 16) made a similar point when he argues that "in any new institution one should expect to see hangovers from the past. There is no reason to expect these hangovers to be internally consistent or to fit perfectly with the goals of the reformers."

Past practices and legacies can be embedded in "new" formal rules—for instance, discriminatory provisions that prohibit particular individuals from carrying out tasks, such as rules disallowing women from combat roles in the military. But legacies are primarily found in the operation of *informal* rules, working at the level of norms and practices (Lowndes and Roberts 2013, 57–59). Importantly, as Leach and Lowndes (2007, 186) argue, informal rules can serve to modify changes in the formal institutional framework, reincorporating old ways and old paths and "leaving power relationships intact." In this book, the informal rules that are carried over from the pre-Rome Statute era of international criminal law, especially specific gender legacies (see below and Chapter 2), are understood as setting the temporal context in which the ICC is nested.

Institutional Nestedness

The temporal nestedness of an institution is important to its outcomes, but so too is its "spatial nestedness." As leading historical institutionalist Paul

Pierson notes, institutions operate in "contexts of complex social interdependence" (2004, 35), which limit or bind their capacity for innovation. This is especially true for new institutions. Fiona Mackay has developed the context of "nested newness," which is useful for understanding how this process works. For Mackay, as well as being shaped by past legacies through informal rules, new formal institutions are also influenced by the "initial and ongoing interactions with already existing institutions (formal structures and rules, informal practices, norms and ideas) within which they are 'nested' and interconnected" (2014a, 567). Similarly, Lowndes and Roberts argue that institutions "interact and co-evolve within and without the political domain" in which they are situated (2013, 165). The spatial nestedness of an institution can limit institutional innovation, because each is bounded within an existing system (Streek and Thelen 2005; Thelen 2004). But the interaction between institutions within a specific environment can also be a source of change, "providing novel templates for . . . redesign or adjustment" (Lowndes and Roberts 2013, 165; also see Chappell 2002).

The tensions inherent in any institutional design, the power and persistence of informal rules and practices, and the environment in which institutions operate mean that institutional outcomes cannot be "read off" their formal design features. Rather, institutions will develop in unintended and unexpected directions. Actors obviously make a difference to the direction institutions take—institutions depend on actors "for their maintenance, defence, revision and rediscovery" (Lowndes and Roberts 2013, 136). However, importantly, it is almost never the institutional architects who become the interpreters or enforcers of the rules (Mahoney and Thelen 2010; Pierson 2004, 121). Those who inherit the rules are likely to have different aims and expectations from those of the designers, and also among themselves. Moreover, their decisions are likely to be determined by the logics appropriate to the environment in which they are operating (Lowndes and Roberts 2013; March and Olsen 1989; Pierson 2004, 110–111).

Paul Pierson makes the point that the early decisions actors take within new institutional arenas are critical to shaping their future path. Early decisions place an institution onto "distinct tracks, which are then reinforced through time" (Pierson 2004, 45). This view suggests that early decisions can "lock in" particular patterns, which become "sticky" (Pierson 2004, 44) and which influence the "logic of appropriateness" shaping the opportunities and obstacles facing institutional actors (Chappell 2006b; March and Olsen 1989).

It is also the argument of this book that actors can also "lock out" possible paths of institutional development. Formally encoded rules that do not fit neatly with an emergent path can be ignored and left to wither away due to a lack of active maintenance, blocking progressive reform (Lowndes and Roberts 2013, 185). "Lockout," as this book defines it, occurs through direct resistance to new rules, including acts of noncompliance, nonaction, and "deliberate neglect" (Lowndes and Roberts 2013, 184). As Mackay has shown in her work on the Scottish Parliament, this can include a process of "forgetting the new" (usually formal rules) and "remembering the old" (usually informal rules) (Lowndes and Roberts 2013, 184; Mackay 2014a).

Institutional Change

It has been widely acknowledged that historical and other forms of institutionalism have been better at explaining stasis rather than change, although recent theorizing and empirical research have started to remedy this imbalance. Change is sometimes, and most obviously, provoked by exogenous shocks, such as changes in government, war, or economic or environmental crises, but recent scholarship has also found that change can occur endogenously and incrementally. As Mahoney and Thelen argue, change often occurs in incremental steps through the "gaps" and "soft spots" between formal rules and their interpretation (2010, 14). Lowndes and Roberts agree, suggesting that while institutions tend toward stability, gaps and contradictions open up, creating instability and possibilities for change (2013, 134). Those actors who find these "creative spaces" (Lowndes and Roberts 2013, 134) and who select appropriate strategies for the context in which they are operating will have the best chance to bring about change (Lowndes and Roberts 2013, 136–137; Mahoney and Thelen 2010). This can involve less powerful groups bending and reinterpreting the rules where the opportunities arise (Lowndes and Roberts 2013, 176).

The term "constructive ambiguity" is useful for understanding how the gaps in formal legal rules can influence outcomes, especially for the purposes of this study. This diplomatic term relates to the use of deliberatively vague language at strategically important points in treaty and other legal contract negotiations in order to gain agreement between the negotiators; constructively ambiguous clauses ultimately leave "interpretation for another day or to other people" (Oosterveld 2014). The greater the degree of ambiguity within formal institutional rules, the more opportunity to channel rules in different directions during the implementation phase, and the less predictable the outcomes (Campbell 2009, 107).

Feminist scholars have demonstrated that this process is as true for gender justice actors as others (Beckwith 2005; Chappell 2006b; Mackay 2013). Such actors have used ambiguities to entrench new rules, practices, and norms that challenge and in some cases overturn gender biases, but equally, they have experienced slippage and regression too. An important factor identified as influencing the outcome of this process is the strength of informal gender-biased rules and practices, which are a holdover from earlier institutional settings (Chappell and Waylen 2013). As feminist institutionalists caution, and as the remaining chapters in this book highlight, such ambiguity can cut both ways: it can allow informal institutions, including gender bias legacies, to move in to fill the lacunae, or it can enable a more expansive and groundbreaking understanding of the term, opening up the possibility of transforming the gender status quo (Chappell and Waylen 2013; Mackay 2014a; Ooseterveld 2014).

Revisability

While accepting that institutional design is a messy and ongoing process, recent work has begun to pay attention to design features that may maximize success for those seeking reform. Vivien Lowndes and others have argued that in aiming to make changes "stick," institutional architects need to pay attention to both the "robustness" and "revisability" of the design. Robustness relates to the clarity of values informing institutional design, and the nature and effectiveness of "third party enforcement" (Lowndes 2005; Lowndes and Roberts 2013, 189–190). Revisability has two features. The first concerns flexibility, the capacity of an institution to adapt over time—in Lowndes' terms, "to capture the benefits of learning by doing" (Lowndes and Roberts 2013, 191). Its second feature relates to variability, the extent to which there is tolerance of different design variants in different locations. Revisability is relevant to this book, especially as it relates to an institution's capacity to learn and adapt. The ability of the Court to learn from its initial mistakes, to respond by introducing new policies and procedures, has been essential to making certain gender justice provisions of the Rome Statute "stick." Where Court personnel have failed to learn and respond, outcomes have suffered, not only in sense of the Court failing to meet the standards of the Statute, but also in terms of gender actors maintaining a sense of legitimacy of the ICC (see further below).

A Feminist Institutionalist Approach

While new institutionalist theory has made an important contribution to understanding the operation and outcomes of institutions, it has almost entirely ignored the ways gender norms and practices influence these processes. Over the past decade feminist political scientists have sought to address this deficit, developing a loosely configured "feminist institutionalist" approach to demonstrate how gender shapes institutional design, processes, and outcomes (see Gatens 1998; Krook and Mackay 2011; Lovenduski 1998, 2005; Mackay and Waylen 2009, 2014; Mackay et al. 2010). One feature of this work has been to demonstrate how institutions operate with their own "gender logic of appropriateness" (Chappell 2006b) and are structured by gendered assumptions and "dispositions" (Annesley and Gains 2010). This research highlights the ways in which the institutional status quo is so often underpinned by gender relations that work to prescribe (as well as proscribe) "acceptable" masculine and feminine forms of behavior, rules, and values. According to Gatens (1998, 5),

> Gender norms support a *status quo* in which one party is placed in a position of advantage and power in relation to the other party and this situation is itself presented as the "natural order of things" rather than as an exercise of power.

Gender underpins and works through rules, serving as a constraint on institutional design options and paths of development. It also influences institutional outcomes. The products of institutions—laws, policies, and rules—are imbued with gendered institutional values and come to shape societal norms and expectations (Beckwith 2005). In this way, gender norms and practices can become reinforcing.

Feminist institutionalist analysis has demonstrated the ways that women and men (especially those who fall outside hegemonic masculine boundaries) (Connell 1987) have sought to disrupt institutional gender logics of appropriateness by identifying and then challenging the gender foundations of taken-for-granted rules and practices within legislative, bureaucratic, and legal arenas (Chappell 2002; Kenney 2012; Kenny 2013; Lovenduski 2005). They have shown that like institutional rules existing gender norms have proven to be very "sticky." Defenders of the gender status quo—those advantaged by existing power arrangements—sometimes deliberately work to maintain the existing rules, including through the active resistance to the implementation of new formal gender justice rules. Sometimes resistance has been more subtle and less conscious; it comes about by neglecting new gender justice rules and allowing "old" ways of doing things to move in and fill the gaps. These are examples of how "lockout" of gender reforms can occur.

But there is also evidence that gendered institutional reform can take place in institutional "soft spots" or "creative spaces," often through subtle and small shifts over time and especially when there is a degree of "constructive ambiguity" in the formal rules. The existing literature suggests that certain conditions are helpful for exploiting these spaces, including the presence of feminist-minded advocates, policymakers, politicians, and judges working from inside institutions to exploit openings as they arise (see Chappell 2002); having strong external supporters who are willing and able to push to support those working internally (Weldon 2002); and identifying the right time to make a move, including at crucial moments of transition (Waylen 2007).

This book takes the position that gender operates as a set of norms and practices on and under the surface of institutions, in ways that profoundly shape their design, paths, and outcomes. It works through formal but especially informal rules and practices (see Chappell and Waylen 2013)—in the case of the ICC, the gender legacies of international humanitarian and criminal law (discussed in detail in Chapter 2). But because these gender rules are unstable and open to interpretation, advocates seeking to change the law can sometimes effect shifts in the gender order, and by implication the outcomes of the law.

This book seeks to make a contribution to feminist institutionalist scholarship. It supports the call within feminist institutionalism for more comparative research across scales of governance (Chappell 2010a; Waylen 2011) and the need to better understand the gender dimensions of institutions by looking both *horizontally* across a range of domestic-level institutions (bureaucratic, legal, legislative, and federal) and *vertically* (between local, national, and international levels) to explain gender justice outcomes. As a study of an international justice institution operating set within an international system of sovereign states, the book provides a valuable case study for the growing literature on the interconnections between multilevel governance, gender processes, and outcomes governance (Banazsack et al. 2003; Rai and Waylen 2008; Vickers 2013). It also makes a contribution by linking for the first time feminist institutionalism with the literature on institutional legitimacy, which as this book demonstrates is critical to understanding institutional actors, architecture, and outcomes.

PART THREE: LEGITIMACY AND THE ICC

Legitimacy is necessary to the evolution and survival of any institution. It is difficult to secure in any context, but especially so for institutions of global governance. In the international context, institutions cannot rely on the checks or balances provided in national democratic systems. They must also interact with multiple and disparate constituencies, leading to intensive debates and compromises about core institutional objectives, especially where these institutions have high levels of authority (Bodansky 2008)—as is the case with the ICC. Institutions of global governance provoke considerable disagreement among their various constituencies, first about how institutions should be designed and second about how they should operate (Buchanan and Keohane 2006, 410).

The literature on legitimacy and international institutions defines legitimacy in two senses. The first is as *normative* legitimacy—that is, whether an institution has strong grounds to justify its claim to exercise authority. This is a philosophical argument about whether the institution in question has the *right* to rule. Second, legitimacy is understood in a *sociological* or descriptive sense (Buchanan and Keohane 2006, 405–406). It is not whether the claim to exercise power is justified, but whether its constituents perceive it to be so (Buchanan and Keohane 2006; also see Brunnee and Toope 2010, 53). According to international law and legitimacy expert Daniel Bodansky (2012, 8), "[a]n institution is descriptively legitimate when it is socially sanctioned and when people tend to follow its decisions not due to self-interest or compulsion, but because they accept the institution's right to rule." Bodansky (2008; 2012) also reminds us that although these two concepts are distinct, they are often conflated. Institutions are unlikely to be *perceived* as legitimate unless there are good grounds supporting their claim for exercising authority in the first place. In this study, the focus is on the ICC's gender justice constituency and its view of the ICC's right to rule, based on its perception of its promise and performance.

Legitimacy questions first arise around the establishment of the "rules of the game"—these relate to whether the rules are just, and discursively justifiable. Discussing the legitimacy of international legal institutions specifically, Finnemore and Toope argue that any such institution will be perceived as legitimate "only to the extent that it produces rules that are generally applicable, exhibit clarity or determinacy, are coherent with other rules, are publicized . . . seek to avoid retroactivity, are relatively constant over time, are possible to perform and are congruent with official action" (2001, 749).

Once an institution commences operation, questions of legitimacy arise in relation to its exercise of authority. Echoing Max Weber, contemporary legitimacy theorists suggest that institutional legitimacy rests on an assessment by relevant constituencies of how well an institution's performance aligns with its objectives. As Barnett and Finnemore argue (2004, 168): "The general presumption is that organisations should be judged by what they accomplish, and if they do not deliver what they promise then their lack of effectiveness injures their legitimacy." The assessment by a constituency of institutional performance is an ongoing process and as such makes institutional legitimacy inherently unstable. Having agreed to support an institution at the design stage, institutional actors may or may not maintain this level of support over time; the social contract upon which an institution is based can easily dissolve if an institution fails to live up to expectations (Bodansky 2008, 312). Bodansky makes the related point that "[l]egitimacy cannot be created at once, it takes time to develop, because it takes time to develop a body of experience to evaluate whether an institution is producing good results" (2008, 315). The fact that the ICC is a permanent organization, in contrast to earlier ad hoc tribunals, gives it the opportunity to build up its legitimacy over time (Struett 2008, 153).

Judgments about institutional legitimacy in the international sphere cannot be based on absolute alignment with democratic standards, as the processes and systems of checks and balances that operate within national systems cannot be replicated at the international level (Bodansky 2012). Nor can they be based purely on notions of "justice." As Buchanan and Keohane (2006) point out, this is in part because questions of what constitutes justice are too disparate and controversial and because it sets the bar too high. They argue that

> even if we all agreed on what justice requires, withholding support from institutions because they fail to meet the demands of justice would be self-defeating from the standpoint of justice itself, because progress toward justice requires effective institutions. To mistake legitimacy for justice is to make the best the enemy of the good (2006, 412).

Instead, these authors suggest, legitimacy judgments should be grounded in the belief that institutions "can be worthy of our support even if they do not maximally serve our interests and even if they do not measure up to our highest moral standards" (Buchanan and Keohane 2006, 410). ICC expert Benjamin Schiff (2010, 6)also takes a middle position on measuring legitimacy, suggesting that "[t]he organization's legitimacy hinges upon relevant constituencies' acceptance of its behavior and at least public embrace (if not private conviction of the virtues) of its value and values."

Where an institution does not completely live up to expectations, in order to maintain legitimacy, it must "possess certain epistemic virtues that facilitate the ongoing critical *revision* of its goals, through interaction with agents and organizations outside the institution" (Buchanan and Keohane 2006, 428, emphasis added). This emphasis on revisability maps neatly onto the concerns of institutionalists, discussed above, about the need to provide opportunities for revision as a principle of good institutional design.

Institutional legitimacy differs within international and national contexts because of differences in the accountability mechanisms available at each level. The absence of formal checks and balances within the international environment means the primary mechanism for holding an institution to account for its actions must be provided by *external epistemic actors*—NGOs, technical experts, and other interested audiences. It is their role to monitor, interpret, and question institutional decisions and outcomes (Buchanan and Keohane 2006; Struett 2008, 154); or, as Barnett and Finnemore (2004, 171) put it, these organizations keep international institutions accountable by "conducting patrols and pulling fire alarms." In relation to international legal institutions specifically, Brunee and Toope (2010, 53–54) suggest that including social actors not only is important for holding institutions to account but is also considered essential to building legitimacy in the first place. Broad participation in the "construction and maintenance of legal regimes" by those subject to their rules is foundational to institutional legitimacy (Brunee and Toope 2010, 53).

An obvious and critical point about the nature of international epistemic communities is that they contain a diversity of actors, each group of which is likely to adopt different perceptions of institutional legitimacy. Factors that may help to legitimize an institution in the eyes of one set of actors may help to delegitimize it in the eyes of another (Bodansky 2008, 317). This creates problems for global institutions that find it "difficult to be accountable to two constituencies that have different expectations regarding what constitutes proper behavior" (Barnett and Finnemore 2004, 171). It is even more difficult where, as in the case of the ICC, the institution must negotiate between a wide range of constituencies, each one of which has different expectations about its performance and priorities (Schiff 2010). As a result, the legitimacy of the ICC is, according to Ben Schiff, dynamic; it is both "tenuous and potentially reversible" (2010, 1).

The ICC's close engagement with and assessment by a range of constituencies have been features of its creation and evolution. Schiff counts as its constituencies the following: states (members and nonmembers); international organizations, especially the UN; NGOs (humanitarian, human rights); victims; expert observers; and perpetrators (2010, 6). NGOs, including women's rights advocates, were particularly influential in shaping the design of the Rome Statute and kept a close watch on the Court in its formative years (Glasius 2006; Struett 2008). Expanding on Schiff, this book suggests that to capture the different ways in which legitimacy has been perceived and has played out during the ICC's construction and maintenance phases, these constituency categories need to be further refined, and that attention needs to be paid to subcategories within each of Schiff's main groupings. For instance, as actions by the African Union have shown (HRW 2014a), states parties often take distinct positions toward the ICC based on regional lines. Most important to this book are divisions within the NGO community, with different civil society organizations reflecting and representing different interests, maintaining different priorities, and demanding different responses from the ICC. For instance, as the following chapters of this book illustrate, the ICC's gender justice constituency often, but not always, aligns closely with victims' rights organizations but much less frequently with defense rights advocates.

Schiff's dynamic model of ICC legitimacy identifies not only different actors but also different dimensions through which legitimacy contestation occurs. The first dimension relates to the *design* of the statute, the establishment of the rules of the game. The inclusive nature of, and prominent participation of NGOs in, Rome Statute negotiations is thought to have given the ICC's design rules widespread legitimacy (Struett 2008, 154). However, although legitimacy questions around the statute were largely settled at the Rome Conference (Struett 2008, 112–113), there remain ongoing legitimacy skirmishes where questions about the need to revise the Statute emerge or where new aspects of the Statute are triggered, such as the provisions related to the crime of aggression, which was negotiated after the Rome Conference. This links to the point made by institutionalists, outlined above, about being alert to the evolution of institutional design processes over time, not just at its "foundational moment."

Schiff's second legitimacy dimension is ICC *operations*. This involves constituencies evaluating the decisions taken by ICC personnel across all Court activities, including through prosecutorial decisions, judicial interpretations, and administrative efforts. Judging operational legitimacy is an ongoing process, and the assessment arising from this process about the Court's legitimacy dividends or deficits will obviously depend on who is undertaking the assessment. Defense rights advocates will have a different view from gender justice actors, who will have a different view from states parties. The final legitimacy dimension relates to the Court's effects, what Schiff defines as its "*consequential* legitimacy" (2010, 7). These effects are difficult to measure, because they are mostly nonmaterial; because they are difficult to measure, they are also highly contested (see Barnett and Finnemore 2004, 168). They are reflected in signals and interpretations of the standards and "justice" meted out by the Court (Schiff 2010, 18–19).

This book builds on Schiff's dynamic legitimacy model and responds to Bodansky's call for more empirical investigation "to determine what standards of legitimacy actors actually apply and how much difference these beliefs make in practice" (2012). Focusing directly on a specific community of actors—the ICC's gender justice constituency—this book charts how well the Court has, in the eyes of these actors, delivered the gender mandate of the ICC, and how any breaches between the Court's performance and promise have influenced their view about the ICC's legitimacy. The argument presented in the following chapters accepts that different constituencies will measure institutional performance differently, differentiating across and within an institutions mandate. As this book illustrates, in judging the ICC's legitimacy, its gender justice constituency has assessed the Court's performance across each category of its multifaceted gender justice framework—which includes *representation, recognition*, and *redistribution* elements. Further, it has also assessed performance *within* each of these categories (e.g., between sex and gender representation provisions) throughout its different *phases* of development. Variations in the instantiation of the Rome Statute's gender justice representation framework give gender justice advocates reason to take a nuanced and differentiated position on the ICC's legitimacy depending on what aspect of these rules is under review, and whether the judgment is being made about its *design, operations*, or *consequences*. Where obvious (sometimes egregious) gaps have emerged in the implementation of the ICC's gender justice mandate, gender actors have called the Court to account and sought reform and revision to its practice. This book argues that to the extent the ICC has demonstrated a willingness to respond to these calls to revise its practices, it has encouraged its gender justice constituency to maintain an ongoing, albeit fragile and tenuous, sense of legitimacy about the Court and a willingness to publicly support its operation into the future.

PART FOUR: RESEARCHING GENDER JUSTICE AT THE ICC, AND OUTLINE

To understand the implementation of the ICC's gender justice mandate, this book uses a qualitative methodological approach, tracing the Court's evolution from the time when it was first mooted in the mid-1990s through the end of 2014, its twelfth year in operation. In historical institutionalist terms, this is a very short period, but it is a crucial one. It covers the central design moments of the ICC and highlights the critical decisions made early on in the life of the Court that are expected under historical institutional theory to influence its future path.

The primary reference material relating to the ICC is voluminous: it includes official court records across the three organs of the Court, including trial transcripts, as well as a vast collection of civil society and media statements and reports. The secondary literature on the court is also exploding, with extensive analysis now emerging on each and every aspect of the ICC's operations. It would be impossible for a single researcher to access or analyze all of this material; court transcripts alone run to thousands of pages. In conducting research, I have selected documents and literature that appear to be the most directly relevant to the questions that structure this book. That it not to say I have only focused on material related to gender justice: on the contrary, I am just as interested in tracing where gender justice concerns have *not* been included as where they have. However, I have selected what I have considered to be the primary documents related to the ICC's internal operations, trials, complementarity regime, and victim-centered processes, within specified limits (see below). Material from the ICC preparatory committees, the 1998 Rome Conference, and the 2010 Kampala ICC Review Conference has also been valuable in interpreting official ICC positions.

In relation to NGO contributions, I have focused particularly on the organizations that have been most closely concerned with gender justice issues at the ICC, the primary documents of the Women's Caucus for Gender Justice and the Women's Initiatives for Gender Justice; statements from other key organizations, including the Coalition for the ICC (CICC), and some of its key members, including REDRESS, Human Rights Watch, Amnesty International, and the International Bar Association, have also been consulted. Because of the existence of multiple official ICC sources and Women's Caucus and Women's Initiatives documents, these are included in notes rather than as in-text references.

To validate these written sources and to gather further insights, I have also undertaken interviews with key actors involved at the ICC. I have interviewed officials across all the organs of the Court, including the President, Justice Song; the second Registrar, Silvana Arbia; the second Prosecutor, Fatou Bensouda; Judge Elizabeth Odio Benito; as well as other officials in the President's Office, Office of the Prosecutor (OTP), Registry, and the TFV. Valerie Oosterveld, a feminist legal expert, a member of the Canadian Rome Statute negotiating team, and a former Women's Caucus member, has been a generous correspondent. Brigid Inder, the Executive Director of the Women's Initiatives for Gender Justice and current Special Gender Advisor to Prosecutor Bensouda, has also given me a number of interviews and generously answered specific inquiries. Where they have agreed, I have identified these respondents in the text, but where they asked for anonymity, their views have been used as background information only. I have also attended as a participant observer a number of formal ICC meetings, including three annual Assembly of States Parties (ASP) meetings in The Hague as a delegate of the Women's Initiatives. All the material gathered for this book has been analyzed manually and through NVIVO software.

One of the methodological challenges I have confronted in researching this book has been identifying the operation of informal rules at the court. This process necessarily requires tracing both what has occurred and what has *not*. This challenge is something Hilary Charlesworth (1999) has discussed in relation to researching international law more generally: that is, the need to be alert to absences, inaction, and silences as well as positive action and overt statements. These silences are crucial to understanding the way gender operates through the law. It is in these silences where we are likely to find the gender "status quo bias," the "taken-for-grantedness" and operation of gender legacies of international law. To capture the operation of informal rules I have analyzed the language, ideas, and decisions incorporated in official ICC and NGO documents, and interviews. More crucially, I have also taken note of where references to gender and gender justice are missing but where, logically, they should appear. This has involved searching for references to key terms—gender, gender justice, women, men, sexual violence, rape, and detailed statutory provisions—in primary documents, in interview transcripts, as a participant observer, and in the secondary literature.

Surveying the implementation of gender justice across all the aspects of the court makes this an ambitious project, but it is made feasible by a number of factors. First, it limits the number of cases under review. Rather than consider all the cases that came before the ICC in the relevant period (a total of twenty-one up to September 2014), this book focuses on two key trials in *Lubanga* and *Katanga*, the only two individuals to have been convicted by the ICC at the time of writing. Both cases relate to the Democratic Republic of Congo and are particularly interesting for the way in which they address crimes of sexual violence.

Further, the analysis of complementarity is also constrained by providing case studies of two states: Colombia and Guinea. These two cases have been under preliminary examination by the OTP for crimes committed under the Rome Statute, including those related to sexual violence. These cases allow for an assessment of arguments about the Court's attention to crimes of sexual and gender-based violence and the impact of this attention on national legal institutions. In analyzing the implementation of the Rome Statute within states parties, the book relies on an analysis conducted with my Ph.D. student, Rosemary Grey, of a database that details (to the fullest extent possible) the record of states parties in legislating to bring the Rome Statute gender articles into effect in national jurisdictions.

Chapter Outline

The following chapters illuminate through a feminist institutionalist approach the evolution and implementation of the Rome Statute's gender justice mandate. They assess how well the ICC's gender justice promise has matched its performance, and the influence this has had on its perceived legitimacy by its gender justice constituency. Chapter 1 situates the ICC in the temporal and spatial political/legal context in which it is nested. This includes a consideration of the gender legacies of international law that help set the temporal context of the ICC. It discusses the design phase of the Court and the contentious politics that led to the formulation of the Rome Statute. The chapter defines the ICC's gender justice constituency and considers in detail the efforts of the Women's Caucus for Gender Justice during the negotiations. A focus of the discussion is the contestation between Caucus with "counter-actors," in the form of conservative civil society groups and religious states, and the impact this struggle had on the final design of the Rome Statute and Caucus actors' view of the legitimacy of these rules.

Chapter 3 focuses on the representation aspect of gender justice at the ICC. It considers negotiations over the Rome Statute's gender representation provisions—both in relation to women victims and the sex and gender expertise of officials—and assesses the implementation of these provisions in the ICC's early years. It highlights some areas of progress in relation to women victims' voices being heard at the ICC, as well as ongoing problems of access. The chapter discusses the significant advances that have been made in terms of the representation of women in the organs of the Court, especially the election of female judges, and in contrast, the difficulty in embedding gender expertise across the organs of the Court. It seeks to explain why sex representation has been easier to entrench than gender expertise through a consideration of the legacies of international law, and assesses the impact of this variation on the views of the ICC's gender justice constituency.

Chapter 4 focuses on the Rome Statute's gender justice recognition elements. It examines closely the design and application of the innovative sexual and gender-based criminal provisions included in the Statute. Through an overarching analysis of the ICC's investigations and prosecutions, and an examination of some of its early cases, the chapter highlights the emergence of significant gaps between these recognition provisions and their implementation. This chapter suggests that the recognition aspects of the Rome Statute's gender mandate have been harder to implement than any other, highlighting the strength of the gender legacies of international law in influencing the operations of the ICC. These outcomes have resulted in a significant legitimacy deficit in the eyes of gender justice actors, who have called for significant reform of ICC practices in this area.

Chapter 5 explores one of the most novel aspects of the Rome Statute: its provisions for redress and redistribution through its reparations mandate. The chapter shows the influence of gender actors on the design of these aspects of the Rome Statute as well as the challenges these actors have faced in having them implemented in practice. While the interpretation of the ICC's reparations mandate has at the time of writing been limited to one case, the case highlights some important lessons for future application of the Court's reparations mandate from a gender justice perspective. This chapter also considers the actions of the Trust Fund for Victims (TFV) in implementing its assistance mandate; work that has resulted in a range of positive redistributive measures for women and girls and for victims of sexual and gender-based violence in ICC situation countries. The divergent outcomes across the ICC's redistributive framework have raised important questions in the mind of gender justice actors about how best to pursue future redistributive claims through the Court, and the value of the Court's reparations processes.

Chapter 6 addresses the complementarity principle, the political compromise at the heart of the Rome Statute that makes the ICC a court of last resort. A core focus of this chapter is the significance of the ICC's "spatial nestedness" in a "post-Westphalian" international relations system for pursuing gender justice through national and international legal venues. It discusses the contestation between gender justice advocates and states over the inclusion of formal gender provisions in the Rome Statute's complementarity framework, and the implications of state resistance to these provisions in terms of gender justice outcomes. Without formal complementarity gender justice rules, advocates have found it difficult to hold Court officials to account for their complementarity decisions, including the failure to address the needs of women and victims of sexual and gender-based violence. Recent efforts by Prosecutor Bensouda to recognize these dimensions through the OTP's Gender Policy may serve to counter this outcome in future and shift the negative views that gender justice actors hold about this aspect of ICC operations.

Chapter 7 brings together the key strands of argument presented throughout the book. It highlights the importance of Fraser's trivalent model of gender justice for understanding the operations of the ICC. It shows the value of a feminist institutionalist approach—including the concepts of formal and informal rules, gender legacies, and nestedness—for explaining the design and evolution of the Court's gender justice mandate. It pays attention to how informal gender rules have combined, contradicted, and sometimes trumped formal rules of the Rome Statute in ways that influence the ICC's gender justice outcomes. To take up Fiona Mackay's point (2014a), in the first decade of ICC operations, officials have too easily "remembered the old" while "forgetting the new," resulting in ongoing gender injustices. The conclusion also notes that incremental changes have occurred, especially in relation to female representation, some court procedures, and victims' assistance, that do offer some potential for transforming the practices of international law. The chapter then demonstrates the significance of the outcomes of the Court's gender justice performance for its ongoing legitimacy, especially in the eyes of the gender justice community. This community has been disappointed by many aspects of ICC operations and has identified a significant legitimacy deficit in particular areas of the Court's design and operations. Nevertheless, this community remains engaged with the Court. The actions of ICC personnel to reform and revise some of its practices have been critical to gender justice advocates' willingness to maintain their efforts to keep the Court accountable and work toward addressing gender injustices through this new arena for international justice. These findings suggest that both institutionalists and legitimacy theorists are right to emphasize the importance of revisability to the actual and perceived outcomes of institutional design and practice.

CHAPTER 2

The International Criminal Court in Time and Space

The ICC is nested in both time and space. This chapter considers the influence of these contextual elements on the ICC's evolution. It examines how its temporal and spatial dimensions affected the development of the gender justice constituency that was established around the Court, and also how these elements shaped the design of the ICC's formal rules, including the gender justice articles that came to be enumerated in the Rome Statute.

This chapter has five parts. Part One provides an outline of the core features of the Statute. Part Two considers the *temporal* context in which the ICC is nested, including the gender legacies of international law. Part Three outlines the ICC's *spatial* nestedness, focusing on the impact of the existing international relations environment on Rome Statute negotiations. Part Four discusses how these spatial and temporal elements influenced negotiations, highlighting the political skirmishes among states, "pro-family" groups, and the gender justice advocates over the definition of gender justice encoded in the Statute. Part Five assesses the view of the ICC's various constituencies about the legitimacy of the Rome Statute at the end of negotiations. In illuminating the contestation and compromises involved in creating the ICC, this chapter reinforces the point made by historical institutionalists about the "messiness" of institutional design processes, and the conflicts arising from multiple institutional designers (Goodin 1996; Lowndes and Roberts 2013, 172), which appear to be especially prominent when it comes to embedding gender justice concerns (Chappell 2006a; Mackay 2014a). It also illustrates the different perspectives of the ICC's multiple, sometimes competing, constituencies, underlining the point that legitimacy is indeed "in the eye of the beholder."

PART ONE: DESIGN FEATURES OF THE ICC

The ICC came into operation in 2002. The Rome Statute that established the Court developed quickly, at least by international standards. In 1993 a proposal to establish the ICC was put on the agenda of the General Assembly of the UN, and in 1994 the International Law Commission put forward a draft statute, one that among other features was noted for its gender insensitivity (Steains 1999). In 1996, PrepCom meetings commenced, and in June and July 1998 the Rome Diplomatic Conference was held to establish the Rome Statute.[1] One hundred forty-eight states attended the conference and took on the complex task of designing the jurisdictional and functional basis of the court, its relationship to states, and other critical provisions, including in relation to gender justice.

At Rome, states established a unique institution. Unlike the UN ad hoc tribunals for the former Yugoslavia (ICTY) and for Rwanda (ICTR), the Rome Statute created a permanent, treaty-based tribunal able to hold *individuals* (not disembodied states) accountable for atrocities under international law. The global reach of the ICC is limited in some significant respects, including its reliance on state cooperation to arrest suspects, and limited resources to pursue all cases. As a result, as feminist legal scholar Katherine Franke notes, the ICC will have to "settle for a minority of cases that can be used to establish important precedent, identify important kingpins or masterminds of the violence, or, in many cases, whomever they can get their hands on" (2006, 821). Nevertheless, its mandate extends farther than any previous international criminal tribunal.

Under the Rome Statute, the ICC has jurisdiction over crimes committed within the territory of a state party, or by a national of a state party operating in other countries, or by non-state party actors through a UN Security Council referral. After much debate among diplomats (see Glasius 2006, Chapter 3), states agreed that the Court's jurisdiction could be triggered through three mechanisms: a state party can refer a situation to the Prosecutor (Article 14);[2] the UN Security Council can refer a situation to the Prosecutor using its powers under Chapter VII of the UN Charter (Article 13(b)); or the Prosecutor can decide to open an investigation in a situation *propio motu* (on his or her own motion), subject to the authorization of the Pre-Trial Chamber (Article 15). The inclusion of this last "trigger" mechanism was highly controversial, providing an avenue for the Prosecutor to initiate proceedings without first obtaining the support of a state party or the UN Security Council (Danner 2003). It was ultimately resolved through an "imaginative" compromise, enumerated under Article 15 (3), which gives the Pre-Trial Chamber responsibility authorizing the Prosecutor's investigation (Glasius 2006, 56). Generally speaking, the ICC's jurisdiction is limited to crimes committed on the territory of a state party or a state that has accepted the jurisdiction of the Court, or crimes committed by a national of a state party or a state that has accepted the jurisdiction of the Court. However, the Court can also exercise jurisdiction in a non-state party where the Security Council refers such a situation to the Prosecutor (Article 13(b)).

At the Rome Conference, states reached a consensus to establish a Court with four organs: the Presidency, the Judicial Chambers, the Registry, and an independent OTP. Negotiators agreed that the ICC's jurisdiction would include four categories of crime: genocide, crimes against humanity, war crimes, and aggression.[3] While some of these crimes have previously been codified under international law, including in the Geneva Conventions and UN Human Rights treaties, the Rome Statute and its two subsidiary sets of rules, the *Elements of Crime Annex* and *Rules of Procedure and Evidence*, extend these rules. The criminal jurisdiction of the ICC reflected important contemporaneous developments in international criminal jurisprudence, especially stemming from the ICTY and ICTR (Lee 1999).

Late in the negotiations, states agreed to include alongside the Rome Statute's "old" retributive justice model a "new" victim-centered restorative justice paradigm (Schiff 2008, 86–88). Given the longstanding retributive focus of international criminal law, the inclusion in the Statute of a restorative approach was a "stunning" development (Schabas 2011, 346). Drawing negative lessons from other international criminal tribunals, where victims' voices had been excluded, the designers incorporated provisions into the ICC's statute allowing victims' "views and concerns to be presented and considered at stages in the proceedings" (Article 68). Together the Rome Statute and the Rules of Procedure and Evidence establish the ICC's victim-centered mandate covering the pretrial, trial, and appeal phases. Victims may appear as witnesses, with their testimony considered as evidence, but there is also scope for victims to give testimony without it being considered as evidence. Victims' statements are a way for the Court to recognize their experiences and to improve its understanding of the context in which atrocities are committed. Further, in a last-minute but groundbreaking move during negotiations, for the first time in an international criminal tribunal victims were given the right to seek reparations in the form of "restitution, compensation and rehabilitation" (Article 75) and other measures, at the completion of a trial following a conviction (McCarthy 2012; see Chapter 5 for details).

A standout feature of the Rome Statute is its novel gender justice mandate that includes *representation, recognition*, and *redistribution* elements, outlined in Box 2.1. In terms of representation, Article 36(8)(a)(iii) of the Rome Statute states that the Court should take into account the need for a "fair representation of female and male judges." Importantly, the Rome Statute pays attention not only to the sex of judges, but their gender expertise as well, noting that in nominating judges, states parties "shall also take into account the need to include judges with legal expertise on specific issues including . . . violence against women or children" (Article 36(8)(b)). Further, Article 42(9) obligates the Prosecutor to appoint advisers with legal expertise on specific issues, including sexual and gender-based violence. The Statute also provides for the appointment of professionals with gender expertise by the Registrar to the Victims and Witnesses Unit (Article 43(6)).

The Rome Statute's gender recognition features are extensive; they provide the most advanced articulation of sexual and gender-based crimes of any international criminal tribunal and set a new standard for the conception of these crimes. For instance, under crimes against humanity the Statute includes "rape, sexual slavery, enforced prostitution, forced pregnancy, enforced sterilization, or any other form of sexual violence of comparable gravity" (Article 7(1)(g)). Similar crimes are enumerated as war crimes (see Article 8(2)(b)(xxii) and 8(2)(e)(vi)). Aside from the recognition of the sexual and gender elements of these crimes, under Article 7(1)(h), gender is also included as a ground for persecution (alongside political, racial, religious, and other such categories). Importantly, Article 21(3) prohibits discrimination based on gender in the application and interpretation of the Statute. This provision places a positive obligation on the ICC's prosecutors and judges to "ensure that in applying and interpreting the law, factors historically utilised to discriminate against groups and identities of people, such as gender, age, race, colour, sexual orientation and social origin, are dismantled in favour of inclusive justice" (Bedont and Hall-Martinez 1999, 69; also see Chappell and Inder 2014).

The Statute's gender recognition features also extend to its procedural rules. It contains innovative provisions to protect witnesses and victims of gender-based violence when giving testimony (Article 68), while the Rules of Procedure and Evidence proscribe the Chamber from admitting any evidence of the rape victim's previous sexual history and remove the need for corroboration (Rule 71 and 63(4)).[4] Under Article 54(1)(b), the Prosecutor is charged with investigating and prosecuting crimes in a way that "respect[s] the interests and personal circumstances of victims and witnesses, including . . . gender" and is also required to "take into account the nature of the crime, in particular where it involves sexual violence, gender violence or violence against children."

The Rome Statute's restorative measures have both recognition and redistributive elements. Provisions enabling the recognition of victims under Article 68 are outlined above. The main instrument for the redistributive element is the incorporation through Article 75 of reparations measures available to victims after a conviction and under Article 79 through establishment of the unique TFV. The ICC is empowered to make reparations orders against a convicted person. These can take the form of "restitution, compensation and rehabilitation" that are available as *collective* and *individual* measures for a wide range of victims. Although not specified in the Rome Statute, the reparation rules do not exclude the possibility of the ICC issuing orders related to a guarantee of nonrepetition, which, as will be discussed in Chapter 5, are essential to securing a redistributive form of gender justice. The Rome Statute provides that these reparations measures are to be administered through the independent TFV, which has a dual mandate: to make reparations rewards after the ICC has rendered a conviction, and to provide general assistance measures. Such measures involve "using voluntary contributions from donors to provide victims and their families in situations where the Court is active with physical rehabilitation, material support, and/or psychological rehabilitation."[5] As with other aspects of the ICC framework, the TFV has a gender justice focus, working to mainstream such concerns across all its programming and in its assistance programs, "specifically targeting crimes of

---

Box 2.1: **THE FORMAL GENDER JUSTICE RULES OF THE ICC**

Gender Representation	Provisions for the representation of women and of gender experts across the ICC organs of the judiciary, Registry, and OTP
Gender Recognition	Recognition of women and of victims of sexual and gender-based violence through: • Substantive crimes • Procedural rules • Acknowledgment of women victims • Work of the OTP and Registry
Gender Redistribution	Access to reparations as well as the TFV assistance mandate, including a gender justice focus

rape, enslavement, forced pregnancy, and other forms of sexual and/or gender-based violence."[6]

The fact that 120 of the 148 states parties in attendance at the Rome Conference supported the innovative Statute was an extraordinary achievement. As Michael Struett suggests (2008, 129), it is easy to underestimate the magnitude of what was achieved by the delegates in Rome, including agreement about judicial procedures, the exercise of jurisdiction, and the convergence of different legal regimes and cultures. That said, the Rome Statute was a result of significant contestation and compromise and reflects the varied interests of its designers; as Schiff explains, the ICC emerged as "an amalgam of normative commitments, legal understandings, political interests, diplomatic bargains, and organization dynamics" (2008, 3). During negotiations, disagreement and contention raged among states, legal experts, and a large civil society contingent across all elements of the Statute, but particularly in relation to the function and independence of the ICC Prosecutor, the crimes over and manner by which the court would exercise jurisdiction, and its gender justice provisions (Glasius 2006; Struett 2008). Negotiators, both states and civil society actors, including gender justice proponents, made compromises: some core demands were adopted; some were diluted; others were abandoned entirely. As will be illustrated throughout this book, these debates, and the compromises that were struck, have helped establish the path of the ICC's development in its early years. The next section explores the context—both temporal and spatial—in which this contestation occurred and assesses the influence of these contextual elements on the formulation of the Court's blueprint.

PART TWO: THE ICC IN TIME

For the purposes of this book, it is useful to consider the ICC as nested in time in two senses. The first sense concerns the emergence of the Court as a product of the politics of the post–Cold War epoch. Although a permanent international criminal tribunal had been mooted since as far back as 1937, proposals for the conception of the ICC attracted serious attention only in the early 1990s. With the end of the Cold War came a greater consensus within the UN, including its Security Council, enabling it to respond to growing international pressure from a range of NGOs to bring "an end to the immunity accorded by international criminal law to perpetrators of crimes against humanity" (Dieng 2002, 690; also see Struett 2008). The fact that during the 1990s the two ad hoc tribunals had been created and were perceived to be operating well strengthened demands for the development of a permanent international body to uphold international criminal law (Glasius 2006, 12–13). As Schiff notes, "the leading lesson of the tribunals was that, in contrast to Cold War intransigence, Security Council members could agree to create international criminal tribunals, and then agree on the mechanism needed to establish and operate them" (2008, 42).

This post–Cold War temporal dimension helped establish the grounds on which to build the ICC's wide-ranging Statute. The politics of the times enabled a break with the "business as usual" style of international negotiations, including a shift from the usual dominance of a handful of powerful states, including the United States, over negotiation outcomes. Although the United States was considered to have played an important and largely constructive role (Schiff 2008, 71) throughout the preparatory committee meetings leading up to the 1998 Rome Conference, and at the Conference itself, many aspects of the proceedings were driven by the interests of the majority of states rather than the usual practice of the most powerful states dominating proceedings. Especially influential was the unofficial 60-plus-member "Like Minded Group," which included Australia, Canada, New Zealand, and many European states who worked closely with other groupings, including southern African and Latin American blocs, to create a strong Court (Glasius 2006, 24–26; Schiff 2008, 70). These states were in turn influenced by, and had an "immediate connection" with, the strong civil society constituency who took advantage of this historical moment to become involved in international criminal law treaty negotiations to an extent not previously tolerated (Glasius 2006, 22; Schiff 2008, Chapter 5). Working under the umbrella of the 800-member CICC, NGOs "cajoled, lobbied and in myriad ways pushed hard for the birth of the International Criminal Court" (Schiff 2008, 144).

The Women's Caucus for Gender Justice was one of the key civil society groups to emerge at this time to take advantage of the openings for participation in Rome Statute negotiations. Created in 1997, the Caucus was established by a number of New York–based feminist activists to lobby for the inclusion of a gender perspective in the Rome Statute (Facio 2004; Glasius 2006, 80). Very quickly the Caucus expanded to include over three hundred international women's organizations and five hundred individuals from across the world. According to one of its members, it worked at all times to include women from conflict areas alongside legal experts (Bedont in Glasius 2006, 81). It became a vocal and independent member of the CICC; Caucus delegates were prominent actors both at the PrepComs leading up to the Rome Conference and at the Conference itself.

Writing about the development of the Women's Caucus, delegate Pam Spees (2003, 1237) notes that it was formed at "a critical moment in the history of the international women's human rights movement." Operating in this context, it was able to draw on the movement's momentum, including that stemming from the 1995 Beijing Fourth World Conference on Women, as well as the work of feminist advocates and legal experts who had been monitoring the work of the Yugoslav and Rwandan tribunals, and which informed the work of the Women's Caucus throughout the ICC negotiation process (Spees 2003, 1237).

The Women's Caucus was able to build alliances within state delegations, including some from the Like Minded Group (Glasius 2006, 81; Oosterveld 2005). Indeed, one leading member, legal expert Valerie Oosterveld, left the Caucus to work with the Canadian state delegation during negotiations. Oosterveld's dual role helped to cement a gender perspective within this important grouping, alongside other Australian gender experts such as Cate Steains (McLeod et al. 2014; Steains 1999). But reflecting the gender politics of negotiations, Oosterveld's position within the Canadian delegation was also attacked by some delegations as evidence of "bias" (Oosterveld, personal communication).

A second temporal factor influencing the development of the ICC, and especially its gender justice provisions, was the ongoing operation of *gender legacies of international law*. During negotiations the Women's Caucus was instrumental in "surfacing" (Copelon 2000) these dimensions. In doing so, they were drawing on extensive research by feminist legal scholars about the ways in which silences and existing formal and informal rules, norms, and processes have operated through international humanitarian, human rights, and criminal law to situate men and women differently before the law, and to produce different sex and gender (in)justice outcomes. The following chapters outline how these gendered aspects of the law have created specific problems of *misrepresentation, misrecognition*, and *maldistribution* and detail attempts first by the Women's Caucus and later by the Women's Initiatives for Gender Justice to address these injustices through the design and operation of the Rome Statute. It is important here to provide an overview of these legacies as they were so influential in setting the context in which the gender justice provisions of the ICC evolved. The existence of these legacies resonates with the arguments of feminist institutionalists that no institution is ever "new"; each is built on the gendered foundations of past rules, norms, and practices (Chappell and Walyen 2013; Mackay 2014a).

Historically, formal and informal rules of international criminal law have been gendered in two senses. The first way is through "gender capture" (Goetz 2007), which is outright male control of the power positions through which the formal rules are made. Men have been the "rule makers" of international law—the judges, lawyers, diplomats, and officials who have set the agenda. The privileges that come from these positions of power (Goetz and Jenkins 2005, 163) have encouraged the incumbents to hold on tightly to them and consciously and unconsciously resist the entry of women into international criminal justice fora. The corollary of men's traditional dominance of international law has been women's absence, which has resulted in women's voices— as judges and advocates as well as victims and perpetrators of war and conflict—being silenced, sometimes intentionally and sometimes inadvertently (see de Guzman 2012, 38; Luping 2009). Feminist legal scholars contend that "[m]any of the gendered problems in international law have stemmed from the absence of women's voices in the highest echelons of international governance" (Pritchett 2008, 271), not least because those men who have held power have "neglected to enumerate, condemn, and prosecute" crimes committed against women (Askin 2003, 296).

The gendered nature of international law has been reflected not only through the actual persons who have controlled these tribunals, but also the operation of what Nancy Fraser terms "androcentrism" (2007, 26) or what Anne Marie Goetz considers the "gender bias" of the law; that is, the

---

Box 2.2: **GENDER LEGACIES OF INTERNATIONAL LAW**

- Women are identified as mothers and dependents rather than as active subjects of the law.
- Crimes commonly experienced by women—especially sexual violence—are considered less grave than other atrocities; no acknowledgment of men's experiences of this violence.
- Women are excluded from reparative responses because of inadequate recognition of their victimization.
- Crimes of sexual and gender-based violence are considered harder to investigate and prosecute; women are retraumatized through the Court process.
- Women are assumed to fabricate charges and to be unreliable witnesses.
- Gender-based crimes of a nonsexual nature are ignored.

"leakage" of discriminatory gender norms into seemingly impartial law and policy (Goetz and Jenkins 2005, 163). These are outlined in Box 2.2. Gender bias has appeared in the formal rules of international law, such as the Geneva Conventions, where women have been incorporated primarily as victims of armed conflict and as mothers, but not as independent actors (Askin 2003; Gardam and Jarvis 2001). Under existing international criminal law, women have not been entitled to the same protection afforded to men in similar circumstances, nor has the law taken into account their unique and varied experiences of and participation in armed conflict (see Mouthann 2011), including as targeted victims of sexual and gender-based crimes (e.g., being forced to be soldiers or the "wives" or sex slaves of soldiers). While these targeted acts have a long history, the law has often ignored them, leaving the victims almost completely invisible in legal proceedings. As feminist legal scholar Kelly Askin (2003, 294) points out:

> Laws of war regulate everything from the minimum number of cards or letters a prisoner of war can receive each month, to provisions requiring opportunities for internees to participate in outdoor sports, to the maximum number of warships a belligerent may have at any one time in the port of a neutral power. Yet despite the fact that many regulations protecting either combatants or civilians are often described in minute and exhaustive detail, very little mention is made of female combatants or civilians.

Where international law has formally addressed those crimes commonly experienced by women, especially those of a sexually violent or gendered nature, they have historically been treated as lesser crimes to those usually suffered by men. For instance, until recently, international rape laws treated it as a crime of honor, not a grave breach of law: these laws have not been about protecting individual women from acts of violence but about protecting men from insults inflicted on dependent women by other men (see Askin 2003; Gardam and Jarvis 2001; Mouthaan 2011). Feminist legal commentators have noted the pervasive view in international law of acts of sexual violence as nothing more than "incidental by-products of the conflict" (Askin 2003, 297), a form of "collateral damage" (Duggan and Abusharaf 2006, 626) rather than a serious human rights violation. This view has had serious effects, limiting women's access to postconflict redress measures, including reparations (De Brouwer 2007; Duggan and Abusharaf 2006). It is not only violations of women's bodily integrity that have been ignored or downplayed: the literature also draws attention to the historical failure of international legal institutions to pay attention to nonsexual violations, especially the "emotional harms, harms to the home and personal spaces, and harms to children and those to whom women are intimately connected" (Ní Aoláin et al. 2011, 153; also see Charlesworth and Chinkin 2000).

Gender biases have not only resulted in the misrecognition of substantive crimes, but have also influenced legal procedures by interfering with the investigation and conduct of trials and the underenforcement of the law (de Guzman 2012, 14). For instance, at the investigation and charging stage, cases of sexual violence have often been seen as being too hard to investigate, largely because of the difficulty of gathering "reliable" evidence (Gazurek and Saris 2002; MacKinnon 2008). This view is based on a range of gender-biased assumptions, including that the testimony of the victims of these acts—primarily women—is less reliable than others, that these victims are unlikely to want to testify, and that it is difficult to devise investigation techniques adequate for interrogating these sorts of crimes. Debunking these views, Catharine MacKinnon (2008, 106) argues:

> At times it may be harder to determine if someone was raped than if that person was killed but rape often leaves distinctive marks psychological as well as physical. Identifying the rapist is not essentially more difficult—and may, at times, be easier—than the murderer who may leave no witnesses.

When it comes to trial processes, especially for victims of sexual violence, the application of insensitive procedures and the application of a "male standard" have been evident. Traditional doctrines of defense have assumed that "woman should fend off violent attack 'like a man' or be considered unchaste and thus unworthy of legal protection for violation" (Ní Aoláin et al. 2011, 164). The male standard has also been reflected in "the 'fresh complaint' doctrine, the myth that the truly virtuous woman would immediately complain of any sexual violation" (Ní Aoláin et al. 2011, 164–165). For those women who have made it to court to seek justice, gender-biased procedures have often retraumatized these victims and exposed them to further violations (Franke 2006; Mertus 2004; Neisah 2011, 145).

The temporal context in which the Rome Statute was developed had positive and negative aspects for those seeking to bring a gender justice focus to negotiations. The historical moment encouraged and enabled the coordination of what could be defined as a transnational gender justice advocacy network (see Keck and Sikkink 1998). However, these advocates were working in a context permeated with gender legacies of international law. These legacies were reinforced by the spatial context in which the Rome Statute system emerged.

PART THREE: THE ICC IN SPACE

The Rome Statute evolved within a specific spatial context—the contemporary international relations environment—that shaped and limited its design. In this environment, states remain preeminent, but as a result of globalization, institutions of global governance also operate to modify states' behavior. Nancy Fraser defines this context as "post-Westphalian" (2009), one in which sovereignty is more disaggregated than previously, with nation-states working closely with and through international institutions, such as the UN treaty system, the European Union, and most recently, the ICC, to address justice claims (Fraser 2009, 14, 87). Key relationships within this context include those between states; between states and institutions of global governance; and between the institutions of global governance themselves. Especially important to the ICC is the UN, especially the Security Council, which, as noted above, has powers under the Statute to refer cases to the Court.

During negotiations over the Rome Statute, interactions between states (and states and civil society) reflected the reality of this contemporary international relations environment. The key players sought to establish a court where State sovereignty was protected, but where they could come together collectively through a new institution of global governance to strengthen accountability for grave breaches of human rights (Simmons and Danner 2010). The creative compromise that allowed this to happen was the principle of complementarity, a compromise that means the ICC "teeters between values of sovereignty and internationalism" (Schiff 2008, 69).

The general principle of complementarity is that "national prosecution of international crimes takes precedence over international prosecution, as long as the national process is legitimate" (Schiff 2008, 77). This principle is not clearly spelled out in the Statute but is embedded in the Preamble and in Article 17, which stipulates that the ICC can intervene to prosecute an alleged criminal only after it has determined that the alleged crimes are sufficiently grave, and when a state has demonstrated it is not undertaking an investigation or prosecution, or the state is taking action but is proven to be "unwilling or unable genuinely to carry out the investigation or prosecution" (Article 17(1)(a); Batros 2011; Nouwen 2013).[7]

The nestedness of the Court in the broader international relations environment, through its complementarity provisions and its relations with the UN in particular, has been critical to the gender justice provisions of the Rome Statute. For the most part, the ICC's spatial nestedness has created a barrier to the expansion of these objectives. This has been most obvious in states' rejection of specific gender justice provisions in the complementarity rules. As explained in Chapter 6, at the point in negotiations where State sovereignty met concerns for gender justice, sovereignty came up trumps. Negotiations led to a gap in the formal rules that has limited the reach of the ICC into states' responses to sexual and gender-based violations.

This outcome is not extraordinary; rather, it reflects a general, longstanding pattern of misrecognizing and ignoring gender injustices within the international relations system. As feminist international relations and governance scholars have demonstrated, historically and in the contemporary world, neither states nor other institutions of global governance have been sensitive to the gender dimensions of their individual or collective practices (Rai and Waylen 2008). As with the gender legacies of the law, international relations and interactions between institutions of global governance have tended toward "gender capture" by men and a "gender bias," which has operated through taken-for-granted gendered rules of international relations (Enloe 2007; True 2010; Whitworth 2008, 5). These rules have included an emphasis on state rather than human security, the reinforcement of hegemonic masculinities that support militarization, and a general lack of concern to disaggregate the consequences of international affairs—conflict, sanctions, global economic relations, and so forth—on women's and men's lives (Rai and Waylen 2008, 7; Whitworth 2008; also see Enloe 2007; Shepherd 2010).

At the time of the Rome Conference, gender justice actors were operating in an international relations environment where their primary concerns had only just started to feature on the international stage—most obviously through the 1995 Beijing Women's Conference and the push for gender mainstreaming through the UN system (Meyer and Prugl 1999; True 2010). Until that time, and in many venues since, states and other international actors have trivialized, ignored, or resisted efforts to include gender justice concerns in international deliberations (Chappell 2006a). Traces of these attitudes carried over into Rome Statute negotiations, where the onus remained with gender justice advocates to demonstrate the importance and relevance of their objectives. They had to work hard to convince states, global governance representatives, and other NGOs that their concerns were, in the first instance, worth deliberating upon, and in the second, worth protecting. Given both the temporal and spatial context in which these gender justice actors were operating, it was no surprise that their efforts were met with contestation and resistance and which resulted in certain of their objectives being compromised or defeated.

PART FOUR: DESIGNING THE ROME STATUTE: CONTESTATION AND COMPROMISE

The groundbreaking gender justice provisions in the Rome Statute reflected an impressive level of influence of Women's Caucus actors and a willingness by state actors to be open to considering gender justice concerns. But this was far from a straightforward process. In advancing their position, the Caucus faced a range of opponents and had to withstand significant compromises and losses, alongside their achievements. The following discussion introduces the key contenders in the politics of gender justice at the ICC and then focuses on the battle between multiple designers over the definition of gender to be included in the Rome Statute.

The Contenders

During the Rome Statute negotiation phase, gender justice advocates collided with other civil society groups and states. Sometimes this collision happened because their interlocutors held strongly opposing views; other times it was a result of disinterest on the part of state negotiators, or the result of states' being unconvinced by arguments that gender mattered to "core" elements of the debate. Leading Women's Caucus lawyer Rhonda Copelon outlines the nature of its opposition:

> On the one hand, we faced increasingly fierce misogynist opposition from the Vatican, the Islamist-oriented Arab League countries, and North American right wing groups... On the other hand, we also had to start from scratch with many delegates who did not see a need for a specific gender perspective and rued the time that introduction of our issues would take (2000, 233).

Oosterveld suggests one explanation for the latter problem: the fact that "many of the state individuals originally assigned to the ICC negotiations were military or legal, but not human rights, experts" (Oosterveld, personal communication).

During Rome Statute negotiations no single multidenominational organization operated in ICC fora to voice shared antifeminist values. Nevertheless, there was a strong alignment of views between religious actors who worked with certain states as "counter-activists" to advance a conservative position on gender issues (Bedont and Hall-Martinez 1999; Chappell 2006a; Glasius 2006, Chapter 5). A central counter-actor here was the Holy See, whose special status at all UN meetings extended to

ICC negotiations. Ireland and Guatemala were two states working alongside the Holy See to push a conservative religious agenda (Chappell 2006a). More controversially—given the existing tensions at the time over Middle Eastern politics between certain Western countries and a number of Arab and Islamic-led states—the Holy See and these Catholic-oriented states aligned themselves with counterparts from the Middle East and Africa, including Syria, the United Arab Emirates, Qatar, and Nigeria, whose points of view on a range of gender-related issues aligned with those of the Vatican (Bedont and Hall-Martinez 1999, 67). These players were also supported by primarily North American–based, Christian "pro-life" and "pro-family" NGOs, including Focus on the Family, Catholic Family and Human Rights Institute, Campaign Life Coalition, and REAL Women of Canada (Chappell 2006a; Glasius 2006, 83–84; Oosterveld 2005).

The presence of these counterforces was neither new nor surprising: their collective presence had been felt at the major UN human rights conferences throughout the 1990s, including the 1993 Vienna Conference on Human Rights, the 1994 Cairo International Conference on Population and Development, and the 1995 Beijing Women's Conference (Buss and Herman 2003, 80–81; Chappell 2006a; Friedman 2003, 313). Their influence was reflected not so much in instantiating new formal rules or language in the consensus documents emerging from these events, but in their ability to block the inclusion of more progressive language in outcome documents; they exerted a conservative force, seeking, often successfully, to preserve the status quo in an effort to protect "family values" and women's separate social roles as wives and mothers (Chappell 2006a).

These conservative forces used similar strategies throughout the Rome Statute process. As in other venues, religious and conservative groups attempted to discredit the Women's Caucus members by constantly referring them as "radical" feminists and therefore out of touch with "real" women (LifeSite 1998; 2000; Mallon 2000; REAL Women, 1998). They also sought to block more progressive language from being included in the Statute. Recalling this period, Oosterveld notes that at first these counterforces were "quiet and subtle." However, by the final set of negotiations in June and July 1998, their position had radically changed "as Christian Right organizations became very organized, working with the Holy See and conservative Middle Eastern States to create a sustained public opposition to the gender provisions that had been already proposed and included in the draft statute" (in McLeod et al. 2014, 358; also see Glasius 2006, Chapter 5).

Some external feminist academics and activists were also critical of Women's Caucus efforts. In the view of some, Caucus members were adopting a narrowly construed "radical" feminist approach to the law (Halley 2008). Others censured the Caucus for its "liberal" or "conservative" feminist orientation and willingness to work within the system (Nesiah 2011). In reality it seems the Caucus embraced feminists with both "liberal" and "radical" perspectives. These divisions influenced the internal operations of the Caucus, sometimes making it difficult for its members to reach agreement. As Oosterveld recalls: "We got very little sleep during these negotiations because it would take so long to come to a consensus feminist position" (in McLeod et al. 2014, 366). Despite these internal differences, Women's Caucus members shared a number of essential positions, including a recognition of the limitations of the law and the tightrope they needed to walk during the negotiations to achieve their core objectives while accepting the need for compromises (Copelon 2000; Facio 2004; Spees 2003, 1237). These advocates entered the process as what might be called "critical friends," acutely conscious of the risks involved in engaging with the law but also recognizing "the existence of the ICC negotiations as an opportunity to codify the integration of gender in international criminal law" (Copelon 2000, 232). Oosterveld reflected this ambivalence when she stated:

> [W]e came to the conclusion that the train is in the station, the train is leaving the station, if we do not jump on the train right now, what is going to be the outcome? We will not be able to change it afterwards, so let us try and change it now, which I realize has its own inherent flaws (McLeod et al. 2014, 366).

Contesting the Definition of Gender

At the Rome Conference, "the term 'gender' became a flashpoint for polarised debate among States, feminist nongovernmental actors and conservative nongovernmental representatives" (Oosterveld 2014, 563; also see Bedont and Hall-Martinez 1999; Copelon 2000). This disagreement over how and whether gender should be defined was not new; it had been a longstanding area of dispute between progressive and conservative transnational actors at other recent UN conferences (Chappell 2006a;

Oosterveld 2005). At the 1995 Beijing Conference, due to irreconcilable differences on the issue between feminist and conservative proponents, the term had been annexed in the resulting Declaration and Platform for Action document. However, delegates at the Rome Conference could not avoid the issue. As a justiciable document under international law, the Rome Statute had to include a definition of gender.

The Women's Caucus came to the Rome Statute negotiations with a clear definition of "gender," understanding it as

> the socially constructed differences between men and women and the unequal power relationships that result. Gender indicates that the differences between men and women are not essential or inevitable products of biological sex differences.[8]

This definition antagonized conservative delegates. During the PrepComs the Holy See and a group of Arab League countries including Syria, the United Arab Emirates, and Qatar contested the inclusion of the notion of gender-based (rather than sex-based) crimes on the basis that the inclusion of these crimes could provide the grounds for homosexuals to claim rights under the Statute (Bedont and Hall-Martinez 1999, 68; Copelon, 2000, 236; Oosterveld 2014). Later at the Rome Conference, defining gender again became a focus of dispute. According to Alda Facio (2004, 327), Women's Caucus director at the time, hostility to inclusion of gender in the Statute "was gradual and spread throughout a number of working groups, particularly those having to do with definition of crimes, composition and general principles." According to key Women's Caucus members, the opposition of certain Arab States "also served as their justification for obstructing many provisions throughout the statute that promoted women's rights" (Bedont and Hall-Martinez 1999, 68), including adding gender under the nondiscrimination clause, and proactive procedural measures. The issue came to a head when the Guatemalan delegation, representing a Catholic-oriented state, formally proposed that the term "gender" be deleted from the Statute (Facio 2004, 327). This initiative took the Women's Caucus off guard. As Oosterveld recalls:

> [W]e were not adequately prepared with research into various definitions of gender used internally within the UN or outside of the UN. Maybe we could have inundated the table with those definitions to come to a solution. On the other hand, what we were asked to do—come up with a state-drafted definition of the term acceptable to all—was new, so we had to walk the fine line of not alienating states (in McLeod et al. 2014, 366).

After further debate, the Guatemalan position was rejected and the term *gender* was incorporated in the Statute—the first time such a definition was included in a legally binding treaty (Spees 2003, 1243). The definition is included in Article 7(3), which states:

> The term "gender" refers to the two sexes, male and female, within the context of society. The term "gender" does not indicate any meaning different from the above.

Its wording reflects a "delicate compromise" (Steains 1999, 371) between negotiators. As Cate Steains, Australian diplomat and coordinator of the gender negotiations, put it:

> While the Statute's definition of "gender" appears, on its face, to be rather unusual (with the tautological second part of the definition), it represents the culmination of hard-fought negotiations that managed to produce the language acceptable to delegations on both sides of the debate (Steains, 1999, 374).

On one hand, by mentioning the "context of society," the definition underscores a feminist understanding of gender as a social phenomenon. On the other, the inclusion of "two sexes" and the additional clause disallowing other interpretations reflect the arguments of conservative religious and state-based actors who held the view that gender must be understood as a *biological* fact and not as *socially* constructed (Copelon 2000, 236; Steains 1999, 371–372).

At the end of negotiations, the various contenders reflected cautious satisfaction with the result. Religious conservatives expressed relief about their "victory" but also warned supporters about the need for continuing vigilance on the issue (Oosterveld 2014). After the Rome Conference, an editorial on LifeSite (1998), a Canadian pro-Christian and antiabortion website, noted that "the words 'within the context of society' in the definition could be used by western activist judges to undermine the traditional values intent of the entire definition of gender." In other words, beneath these conservative actors' sense of success remained a concern that gender could in future be interpreted to encompass homosexual and transgender identities.

Key Women's Caucus advocates, and certain members of the broader feminist legal community, expressed disappointment with the final Rome Statute gender definition, for the very reasons conservative forces were pleased with the resolution (see Charlesworth and Chinkin 2000, 335;

Copelon, 2000; Moshan 1998, 178). Nevertheless, many involved in the process still saw the value in the definition being included, even in its compromised form (see Bedont and Hall-Martinez 1999; Copelon 2000; Oosterveld 2014). In the view of the Women's Caucus director, Alda Facio (1999, n.p.):

> although this definition may be considered imperfect by some, having the term in a legal or "hard" document like the ICC Statute as opposed to a policy or "soft" document such as the Vienna, Cairo and Beijing Platforms, is a definite stride in the right direction toward real justice for women.

Facio went on to encourage feminists to remain active in their advocacy on gender and to seek to have the term more clearly defined in future UN forums, and through intervention in domestic-level legal cases.

More recently, Valerie Oosterveld (2014) has suggested that the definition, like many diplomatic agreements, was an example of "constructive ambiguity." As she explains, "each side gained vague language that can simultaneously mean different things to different people. They also both lost some certainty, in that the actual interpretation was left to the Prosecutor and, ultimately, the judges of the ICC. Each side hoped that the words chosen would lead future Court officials to construe the term to match their views" (see Oosterveld 2014).[9]

The debate over the definition of gender was just one of many contestations between gender justice advocates and other constituencies during the Rome Statute design phase.[10] As the following chapters illustrate, some of the Caucus' other objectives also ended in compromises, some were accepted without concession, and others were rejected entirely. In seeking to shape the contours of the ICC, these advocates were working in a context where both gender legacies of the law and the existing international relations system were at play. These contextual factors and the multiple actors and demands involved contributed to a "messy design process" and the emergence of an imperfect blueprint that would shape both the future developmental path of the Court and the ongoing views of various ICC constituencies about the Court's legitimacy.

PART FIVE: LEGITIMACY, GENDER JUSTICE, AND THE ICC

Women's Caucus members left the Rome Statute negotiation process with a sense of ambivalence about its outcomes. Reminiscing about the concluding night of negotiations, leading Caucus member Barbara Bedont captured their mixed feelings:

> At two o'clock in the morning on July 18th, [1998] . . . in a bar by the Coliseum, a group of Like Minded delegates celebrated the adoption of the statute. I sat amongst them, not knowing how to react to their jubilation. While I was relieved that a statute had been adopted, I couldn't help but mourn the loss of many provisions which would have made the Court stronger. Finally, when some of the delegates started to sing "We are the Champions," I knew the time had come for me to go (1998, 21).

While recognizing its limitations, gender justice advocates also understood that in the context in which it developed, the Rome Statute was a significant step forward in terms of recognition, representation, and redistribution of women victims and victims of gender-based and sexual violence. As Copelon expressed it, despite its limitations the Statute was nevertheless "revolutionary in its thoroughgoing approach to issues of gender in international law" (2000, 239). In the language of legitimacy theory, this core ICC constituency came to view the Rome Statute as having a degree of normative legitimacy—that is, gender advocates focused on the Court accepted that the ICC's formal "rules of the game" were imperfect, but nevertheless satisfied justice standards enough that they considered the Court to have "the right to rule."

For the constituencies who had opposed these gender provisions—because they either disagreed with their substance, or, more benignly, were perplexed by their relevance—their inclusion was not a "deal breaker." These constituencies too left the negotiations with a view of the Rome Statute as one that did not completely satisfy their interests, but generally, as an institution they were willing to support it. There was at least a "perception of legitimacy" (Buchanan and Keohane 2006, 407) among these various communities about the formal rules of the ICC.

The ICC shifted from its design to its operational phase in 2002, after receiving more than the requisite sixty state ratifications needed for it to commence operations. Gender justice advocates went into this next phase with an increased awareness of the deeply entrenched gender-biased legacies of the law and a sense of the oppositional forces that they were likely to be up against during the ICC's early years. They were equally aware that the success of the Rome Statute's gender provisions rested on their successful execution, but that implementation outcomes were far from guaranteed. Although a strong critic of the international feminist justice project, Janet Halley captured well the challenge confronting the Women's Caucus moving into the ICC's operational phase:

> [B]y themselves, these rules [in the Rome Statute] do nothing to change the meaning of IHL [International Humanitarian Law], ICL [International Criminal Law], their enforcement, or the level and types of violence in which people engage. The degree to which one very specific set of feminists were able to inscribe into the Rome Statute legal language compatible with their very specific ideological commitments is quite remarkable. But whether the ICC will understand these words in a feminist way, and certainly, whether the world will thereby begin looking more like one envisioned by the feminist reformers, are entirely distinct questions (2008, 121).

Exhausted by their efforts during Rome Statute negotiations, and perhaps also daunted by this new task of implementing the Statute, many of the individuals involved in the Women's Caucus did not make the transition from the design to the operational phase. By 2003, the Caucus itself had made way for the Women's Initiatives for Gender Justice, with New Zealander Brigid Inder as its Executive Director.[11] Inder, a long-time international women's rights activist, came to the role from outside the Caucus. She credits the Caucus with having the foresight of starting the process of shifting the focus of ICC gender justice advocacy toward operational issues, and the locus of gender activism from New York to The Hague, from where it would be easier to monitor the Court's evolution. This move, according to Inder, "gave everyone the chance for a new page and a fresh start." Inder explained in an interview that on taking over the mantle from the Caucus, the new organization did not want to be "just be a legal monitoring organization, just paying attention to the Court," as had been the necessary focus during the negotiation phase. Instead, her vision was to ensure that the Women's Initiatives was "connected to women most affected by the conflicts under ICC investigation."

As the following chapters illustrate, throughout the first decade of ICC operations, the Women's Initiatives has played a pivotal role in holding the Court accountable for its implementation of the gender provisions of the Rome Statute, in terms of its internal operations, development of its prosecutorial strategy and jurisprudence, and engagement with victims in situation countries. As the organization with the closest watch on the gender justice mandate of the ICC, the Women's Initiatives' views on its performance provide a litmus test for the Court's legitimacy in this area.

The following chapters examine the contestation surrounding the design and implementation of all the gender justice aspects of the Rome

Statute in the early years of the ICC. As with the politics over the definition of gender, each aspect has been influenced to a greater or lesser extent by the spatial and temporal context in which the Court has evolved. Gender justice actors working through the Caucus and then Women's Initiatives alongside other NGOs have had to work with and against these contextual elements to "lock in" new gender representation, recognition, and redistribution provisions in the Statute and to "lock out" old norms, procedures, and rules that work to undermine these provisions. It has been a constant and challenging process, but one where the actors have sometimes been able to create and instantiate new rules that push the boundaries of international law to advance women's rights.

CHAPTER 3

Representing Gender Justice at the International Criminal Court

The Rome Statute includes "novel and progressive" (Rwelimera 1999, 167) provisions to redress the historical underrepresentation of women professionals and gender experts in international criminal tribunals. The Statute also recognizes the right of victims, including specifically women and victims of sexual and gender-based violence, to be represented in ICC proceedings.

The Rome Statute contains provisions that seeks to address *misrepresentation*, one of Nancy Fraser's three axes of gender (in)justice. It does this through provisions related to the representation of women on the bench, the appointment of ICC personnel with gender expertise, and victim standing before the Court. Historically, international criminal law has followed the trend of most other deliberative bodies: those empowered to interpret the law have been men, and the gendered processes through which such interpretation has been undertaken have resulted in either nonrecognition or misrecognition of the experiences of women. Male dominance of international legal institutions has raised questions in the minds of gender justice actors about the legitimacy of international law because of the signals it sends about who is excluded from and included in making legal decisions, the narrow cast able to bring their life experiences to bear on these decisions, and the processes through which these decisions are made.

This chapter focuses on the efforts of gender justice advocates through the Women's Caucus for Gender Justice and the Women's Initiatives for Gender Justice to rebalance the scales of international criminal justice to allow a more equal representation of the sexes and better representation of gender interests at the ICC. It considers these actors' efforts to shift the sex balance of lawmakers and of victims, to bring gender expertise to bear at the Court, and to introduce processes to improve sex and gender representation for victims. It also assesses the arguments underpinning these efforts. It is not the objective of this chapter to consider whether increased representation in any of these categories has improved gender-just outcomes, in terms of recognition or redistribution, as these developments will be discussed in the following two chapters. Rather, the purpose here is to consider what specific claims were made in support of measures for a better balance in terms of sex and of gender expertise at the ICC, the implementation of these measures, and the effect any shift in the traditional profile of international "lawmakers" and "law takers" has had on the view of gender justice actors' about the legitimacy of the Court.

Part One of this chapter builds upon Fraser's theory of representation, sketching the link between misrepresentation and gender justice in relation to international criminal law. Part Two outlines the contestation surrounding gender justice actors' efforts to embed gender-just representation measures in the Rome Statute, and the results of this process, including groundbreaking developments and the gendered legacies carried forward into the ICC from previous international law practices. Part Three analyzes how well these measures have been interpreted and implemented in practice, identifying what's been "locked in" and "locked out" of the path of representative gender justice in the first decade of ICC operations. Finally, using insights from feminist institutionalism, the chapter explains these outcomes and their impact on actors' views of the ICC's design, operational, and consequential legitimacy.

A key finding of this chapter is that the Rome Statute's provisions to enhance female representation in senior positions—which came about as a result of gender justice advocacy—have largely been successful. This outcome has given gender justice actors reason for a strong sense of legitimacy over this aspect of the design and operation of the Rome Statute. Efforts to embed more gender-sensitive processes by appointing gender experts across the Court, and the representation of female victims, have been less effective. The ICC's limited resources have contributed to these problems, but legacies of misrepresentation in international criminal law arising from the temporal nestedness of the Court have also influenced the ICC's practices, "locking out" potential advances in gender-just representation at the Court.

PART ONE: REPRESENTATION: DEFINING THE "WHO" AND "HOW" OF GENDER JUSTICE

Representation is the third strand of Nancy Fraser's trivalent model of gender justice. Having defended for many years a bivalent approach—focused on the distributive and recognition outcomes of justice—Fraser increasingly became aware of the need to make, in her terms, a "major revision" to the model to add a specific political dimension to address misrepresentation (2009, 145). In focusing on representation, Fraser is concerned to delineate between the "who" and the "how" of justice, in distinction to the question of "what" its substance is, understood in terms of distribution and recognition. Clearly, though, as Fraser suggests, these three elements are linked: *who* is empowered to deliberate on justice, and the *processes* through which this is realized, can have an impact on its *substance* (Fraser 2009).

Misrepresentation occurs "when political boundaries and/or decision rules function wrongly to deny some people the possibility of participating on a par with others in social interaction" (Fraser 2009, 18). Fraser's interest in representation raises questions of whether all people, including women and racial and other minorities, "who are included in principle in a given political community really have equal voice" and "can all participate fully, as peers, in political life" (2009, 145). Fraser also explores who is included in, or excluded from, any "symbolic frame" in which justice deliberations are made. In her view, "[w]hen political space is unjustly framed, the result is the denial of political voice to those are cast outside the universe of those who 'count'" (2009, 147). For Fraser, gender justice requires that women have an equal voice with men within all political spheres and are included in the frame through which politics is understood in the first place (2007, 27–29). Such a move may, as legal scholar Susan Williams (2012, 4) notes, require "creating new rules of inclusion and procedure, or whole new structures of democratic decision-making."

Long before Fraser's intervention, feminist legal and political scholars had considered the problem of exclusion of women as a group from, and their lack of equal voice within, all deliberative and democratic institutional boundaries (for a summary of this work in relation to political institutions, see Mackay 2008 and Childs and Lovenduski 2013; on international law see Charlesworth and Chinkin 2000, 81–82). Some of this theorizing assists in giving further substance to the representation aspect of Fraser's model. Political philosopher Anne Phillips is particularly instructive here. In her groundbreaking work on the "politics of presence," Phillips critiques the overemphasis on the representation of *ideas* in deliberative institutional arenas and advances a strong case for the representation of a diversity of *actors*, especially in terms of race and sex representation. In Phillips' view, unequal sex representation suggests that some obstacle stands in the way—either deliberate discrimination or structural power relations (1995, 53). The effect of this exclusion is to keep women in the position of political minors (1995, 39). For Phillips, the presence of women in institutions matters

> even if it proves to have no discernible consequences for the policies that may be adopted. Part of the purpose, that is, is simply to achieve the necessary inclusion: to reverse the previous histories of exclusion and the way these constituted certain kinds of people as less suited to govern than the rest (Phillips 1995, 40).

Building on Phillips' work and focusing on the Westminster Parliament, British sociologist Nirmal Puwar draws attention to how women and other excluded groups, such as ethnic minorities, operate as "space invaders" in institutions that have been for centuries overwhelming male and white (2004, 67). For Phillips the presence of previously excluded actors can in itself be transformative (1995, 45)—it provides a signal that the obstacles over who can exercise political (or judicial power) have been confronted, if not overcome. Puwar agrees that the entry of different bodies into institutional spaces can make a difference, though in her view presence must also come with an alteration in the terms of inclusion to address women's different views, needs, and interests (2004, 77).

Another way of thinking about these issues is through the concept of "gender capture" (Goetz 2007), or outright male control, of political and legal institutions. Gender and judging scholar Sally Kenney emphasizes the importance of female presence to address this capture (2012). In Kenney's view, having women in the judiciary "indicates the belief that women are capable of judging and considering their experiences and perspective is important to democratic deliberation. Moreover it signals that judging, like politics in general, is not an exclusively male preserve" (Kenney 2012, 132). As such, "[w]omen exercising judgment breaks a powerful taboo in our society" (Kenney 2012, 177). Their presence "disrupts the normal assumption that heterosexual white men are the only citizens capable of rendering objective judgment, that only privileged men are naturally suited to assume authority on the part of the state"

(Kenney 2012, 176) or, in the case of the ICC, in institutions of global governance.

None of these scholars argues for the inclusion of more women in deliberative forums on essentialist "difference" grounds; they depart from those who suggest that more women should be included because women will *necessarily* come to different conclusions to male decision makers (for a discussion see Kenney 2012, Chapter 8). Focusing on female judges, Kenney rejects argument that they are more likely to adjudicate cases differently from men or will be more likely to find in favor of women's rights (2012, 41–42): "[f]eminist men judges can advance an equality agenda just as anti-feminist women judges can impede it" (2012, 131). Rosalind Dixon's detailed study of U.S. judicial appointments supports Kenney's thesis, demonstrating that existing evidence fails to support a "female-feminist jurisprudential correlation" (2010, 34). Both Kenney and Dixon suggest that more differences can be found among each sex—between women and between men—in terms of their judging records, and that factors aside from sex, such as ideology and experience, are more important in explaining differences in judicial outcomes.

While discounting an inherent link between sex and judging, these authors remain supportive of the recruitment of more women to the bench and other senior legal positions for legitimacy reasons. They suggest that standards of justice will improve if both women and men who have different gendered life experiences bring these to bear in their adjudication. As Kenney argues:

> [A] jury or judiciary drawn from the full range of citizen identities and experiences is more conducive to the production of justice, will yield better deliberations, and will command more support than a judiciary drawn from a narrow cross-section of the public. (2012, 163)

Nienke Grossman's (2011; 2012) work on judging in international courts further supports this view. She makes the case that representation of women in the judiciary is important for what she terms "sociological legitimacy." As discussed in Chapter 1, sociological legitimacy relates to *perceptions* held by the constituents of these tribunals—states, defendants, and victims—that the composition of the bench reflects a court's *impartiality, fairness*, and *legitimacy*. As Colleen Duggan and Adila Abusharaf suggest: "[u]nderrepresentation of women in the legal profession, both nationally and internationally, sends a clear message that women's input is not recognized as important or valid" (2006, 638). The legitimacy of legal institutions in part rests on the inclusion of previously excluded groups. As Grossman explains:

> Continued exclusion from the bench, as well as from traditional lawmaking bodies, perpetuates perceptions of unfairness and partiality in adjudication. On the other hand, inclusion of previously excluded groups can change perceptions of bias, as well as help to eliminate actual bias in the judicial system (2012, 664).

Given the historical exclusion of women from international courts, a more even sex composition appears to be a signal that they are capable of rendering impartial justice both to women and men (Grossman 2012, 652).

Rejecting the view that women will necessarily judge, prosecute, or vote in favor of women, a range of scholars nevertheless argue that including *feminist-inspired* judicial officers can make a difference to the achievement of gender justice in terms of both recognition and redistribution. In other words, it is not the inclusion of women per se that alters lawmaking—though having them there is an important sign of legitimacy—but the inclusion of women and men who have a gender-just worldview. In Kenney's view:

> We need more feminist judges who understand women's experiences and take seriously harm to women and girls, who ask the gender questions: How might this law, statute, or holding affect men and women differently? . . . [W]ho value women's lives and women's work, who do not believe women to be liars, whores deserving of violence by nature; who question their own stereotypes and predilections and listen to evidence, and who simply put, believe in equal justice for all. It matters who judges are and what their values are. We are not simply looking for the smartest and the most able lawyers for the job. We want the wisest—those who value women and understand gender (2012, 15–16).

These arguments resonate with feminist scholars of international law who have highlighted the importance of including advocates of gender justice—both male and female—as judges, prosecutors, and other senior legal personnel in international tribunals because of their ability to "make visible" or "surface" the different experiences of men and women during war and conflict (for a discussion see Chinkin et al. 2005, 20; Copelon 1994; SáCouto 2012, 392). These scholars have pointed to the difference individuals can make to amplifying gender justice concerns. Patricia Viseur Sellers is one notable case in point. In her role as

Prosecutor at the 2000 Women's International War Crimes Tribunal on Japan's Military Sexual Slavery and as a legal advisor on gender-related crimes for the OTP at the ICTY, Viseur Sellers worked to secure charges of sexual violence (Viseur Sellers 2009, 302–303). Feminist judicial interventions at these tribunals have also been crucial, such as that of Justice Navi Pillay in the Rwandan tribunal's *Akayesu* case[1] (see Luping 2009, 445; SáCouto 2012) and Judge Elizabeth Odio Benito and Judge Gabrielle Kirk McDonald in the *Celebici* case at the ICTY[2] (Sharratt 1999; Velez 2009; Viseur Sellers 2009, 306) (Odio Benito's dissent in the ICC's first trial is discussed in detail below and in following chapters). Judge Pillay herself has observed the importance of having women on the bench:

> Who interprets the law is at least as important as who makes the law, if not more so. . . . I cannot stress how critical I consider it to be that women are represented and a gender perspective integrated at all levels of the investigation, prosecution, defense, witness protection and judiciary (quoted in Bedont and Hall-Martinez 1999, 76).

These senior women legal actors have also identified the importance of the presence of gender-sensitive *men* to establishing new rules and practices to support the representation and recognition of women and of sexual and gender-based violence crimes—citing Theo van Boven, Graham Blewett, and Richard Goldstone at the ICTY and David Crane at the Special Court for Sierra Leone as examples of gender justice change agents (Luping 2009; Viseur Sellers 2009, 306).

The inclusion of legal officers sensitive to gender justice in these international tribunals has not come without contestation. Asking new and different questions and drawing attention to constituencies that have long been ignored have, unsurprisingly, provoked controversy. This point of contestation, where representation meets recognition, is considered in detail in the following chapter.

The turn toward restorative justice measures, alongside the traditional retributive approach within international criminal law, has brought victims into greater focus as a category of "law takers" needing representation. As Kendall and Nouwen put it: "Recognized as 'actors' in international criminal proceedings, victims became participants with interests to be represented" (2014, 238; also see McCarthy 2012). Feminist scholars and activists have been particularly alert to this development and have indeed contributed to it, having documented the many failings of initial attempts to bring more women victims, especially those who had experienced sexual and gender-based violence, into proceedings at the UN ad hoc tribunals (Mertus 2004; Nesiah 2011, 145–146; SáCouto 2012).

With the expansion of the boundaries of international criminal law to give victims representation has come a simultaneous concern to design procedures for victim representation. Conceiving procedures and processes to enable the specific representation of women victims without forcing them to suffer a "revictimization" has been a preoccupation of recent feminist legal scholarship and activism (Ní Aoláin et al. 2011, Chapter 7; SáCouto 2012). These commentators suggest that critical to advancing accountability for sex-based violations is "the detail of the rules and procedures and evidence that underpin and structure the manner in which substantive violations are processed in court" (Ní Aoláin et al. 2011, 168). Designing these procedures has also been a focus of feminist advocacy, such as through the Women's Caucus at the ICC, as detailed below. These actors have argued strongly for the need for international criminal justice procedures to include advocates, investigators, and prosecutors skilled in gender-sensitive techniques as well as gender-sensitive procedures and support services, during and after participation at all stages of proceedings, especially courtroom appearances.

In sum, the arguments for addressing women's misrepresentation—both in terms of their exclusion from the boundaries of the law and the absence of their voice once inside—have focused on the need to increase the number of female personnel and victims, and for gender-sensitive procedures. Scholars calling for an improvement in women's representation in international legal venues have not tended to base their argument on the expectation that women will necessarily adjudicate or otherwise act differently to men. Rather, they build their case on the grounds that including women in senior legal positions is important for its own sake—for the message it sends about women's rights and capacity as citizens and because "a more representative bench commands more legitimacy and is seen to be fairer" (Kenney 2012, 179). Scholars and legal practitioners also suggest that to achieve gender justice objectives *all* legal officers, both men and women, should have a greater understanding of, and sensitivity to, gender justice concerns. These concerns should be reflected in not only decisions about *who* interprets the law, but also the procedures through which it takes place. In advancing these claims, gender justice actors have provoked contestation and controversy, as the story of Rome Statute negotiations and implementation clearly demonstrates.

PART TWO: DESIGNING SEX AND GENDER REPRESENTATION RULES FOR THE ICC

The Women's Caucus for Gender Justice came to the Rome Statute negotiations with a view that the Court "should be equipped and enabled to eliminate common assumptions about and prejudices against women and their experiences."[3] In its view, embedding representative gender justice provisions in the statute was one strategy for achieving this objective (Sadat 2011, 659). In making their case, Women's Caucus advocates drew attention to the historical and contemporary exclusion of women from international law venues, and their lack of equal voice from within (Bedont and Hall-Martinez 1999, 75; Copelon 2000). Demonstrating the poor representation of women in senior legal posts was not difficult: the Caucus was able to point to the International Court of Justice, which between 1946 and 1998 had just one female justice, Dame Roslyn Higgins (Schabas 2011, 375). Closer analogies were the two UN ad hoc tribunals of the ICTY and ICTR, which shared a reputation for low levels of representation of women across all their senior positions, especially in the Chambers (Viseur Sellers 2009). For instance, while two of the four Chief Prosecutors at the ICTY were female, of the fifty-two permanent judges, only nine have been women (17 percent), and no more than three have served on a bench at any one time (see ICTY 2014).

Drawing on the ICTY and ICTR experiences, Women's Caucus members were determined to address the dual problems of the lack of female representation and the absence of gender expertise[4] (SáCouto 2012, 300; Steains 1999, 380). According to leading Women's Caucus advocate Rhonda Copelon:

> We insisted upon a dual standard, one based on gender expertise and one on biology. The judges and other personnel should include gender experts at the same time as they should . . . represent a balance of men and women (2000, 238).

The Caucus identified the presence of women on the bench as benefitting victims, who would be "encouraged to participate by seeing an integrated judiciary."[5] Valerie Oosterveld, explains: "The Caucus members [also] felt strongly that equality in representation would help—when joined with the addition of individuals with gender-sensitivity, which was a separate principle—to increase overall gender knowledge within the ICC (and remedy the problems in this regard extant in 1998 within the ICTY and ICTR)" (Oosterveld, personal communication). According to

Oosterveld, Women's Caucus members believed that "ensuring a gender balance from the beginning meant that there would be no need to 'gender mainstream' the ICC as it would begin in a gender balanced manner" (personal communication). In other words, Caucus members were attempting to avert the problem evident in other international tribunals, such as at the ICTY and ICTR, of attempting to add a concern for sex and gender representation after the fact.

The Women's Caucus had four priorities for advancing representation at the ICC, all of which reflected feminist theorizing in this area. It proposed: "[T]hrough appropriate nomination and election/selection procedures, that, in all organs of the Court and from its inception, there will be (1) a balance between women and men; and (2) persons with demonstrated expertise in gender analysis and crimes of gender and sexual violence."[6,7] In its lobbying efforts to secure its second priority, the Women's Caucus called for the Statute to include provisions for equality on the bench as well as for the appointment of a legal advisor for gender and gender-related crimes in the OTP with the "power and responsibility to oversee the full, fair and respectful integration of gender concerns throughout its operations."[8]

Its third priority was to embed victim participation and representation provisions at all "appropriate stages of the proceedings,"[9] including witness protection measures, and the creation of a Victims and Witnesses Unit (VWU) charged with the "responsibility for ensuring the safety, integrity, and confidentiality of witnesses and those at risk on account of their testimony."[10] Finally, the Caucus supported provisions enabling *amicus curiae* (friend of the court) submissions. These submissions provide the court with additional contextual information about the case before it, and, as the ICTY and ICTR experience showed, can prove critical to the representation and recognition of the interests of gender and sexual violence victims (Bedont and Hall-Martinez 1999, 71; Copelon 2000, 225).

The first two priority areas provoked extensive contestation and strong opposition during the design phase of the Rome Statute. The Women's Caucus initially called for a "balance" of male and female judges—by which it meant no more than 60 percent of either sex in all Court staffing (Oosterveld, personal communication)—and for statutory recognition of women's representation across all the arms of the Court (Bedont and Hall-Martinez 1999, 76; Törnquist-Chesnier 2007, 458). State delegates—including the United States, Scandinavian states, as well as Malawi and New Zealand took up this call for a judicial gender balance at the PrepCom meetings. Other states, notably China and a number of Middle Eastern countries[11] (Rwelamira 1999, 166), "vehemently opposed" the measure, expressing "serious reservations" about the proposal (Copelon 2000, 238; Steains 1999, 376–377). Describing the negotiations, Cate Steains, an Australian delegate, suggests that the basis of this opposition was twofold. Some objections were "based on fundamental philosophical or political objections to promoting the participation of women in this way; others were based on a concern that the reference to 'balance' implied a 50/50 quota system" (1999, 377). Opponents considered quotas unreasonable because they were thought to interfere with the merit-based appointments (Rwelamira 1999, 166).

The view that quotas interfere with merit selection was predictable: in both political and legal spheres, merit is often used as an argument against any sex- or gender-affirmative action proposals. The Women's Caucus appeared to be acutely aware of the contestation the language of quotas would provoke: its use of the term "gender balance" was an attempt to circumvent this debate and at the same time give the notion of balance some legitimacy by drawing on the *Convention on the Elimination of All Forms of Discrimination against Women* and the *Beijing Platform for Action* (Copelon 2000, 238; Oosterveld, personal communication). According to Oosterveld, "[t]he Caucus members were well aware that the term 'quota' had negative connotations associated with it (at least in the eyes of some States) and therefore followed the careful UN language of 'balance'" (personal communication).

At the same time as the "gender balance" debate was taking place, the architects of the ICC were involved in negotiations for the recognition of regional and legal expertise in judicial selection procedures. Interestingly, these did not ignite opposition against non–merit-based selection criteria. This was also predictable: as Kenney explains, such a contradiction is "emblematic of a larger phenomenon" in deliberative institutions where calls for representativeness based on gender or race are "denounced as particularly antithetical to merit selection" but where regional or other forms of representation is not (Kenney 2013, 128). The resistance to gender balance in the negotiations of the Rome Statute demonstrated the point made by feminist scholars about the challenge the mere presence of women presented to existing power relations (Phillips 1999; Puwar 2004, 77), specifically the longstanding privilege men have enjoyed in international legal institutions over time (Askin 2003).

The contestation over female judicial representation at the PrepCom meetings was carried over to the Rome Conference and was "replayed, only this time more passionately" (Steains 1999, 378). Negotiations became deadlocked over the terms "gender" and "balance" until Canada proposed an acceptable compromise replacing both contentious terms with text referring to a "*fair representation* of female and male judges" (Steains 1999; 378, emphasis added). Determining how the vague term "fair representation" was to be achieved in terms of the voting rules was left by the Conference to the first session of the ASP, held in 2002 (see discussion later).

It was not only the presence of women on the bench that created controversy during the negotiations, but also the proposition advanced by the Women's Caucus that staff in all divisions of the ICC—including the bench, OTP, and Registry—be required to have legal expertise "on gender and sexual violence and the protection of children"[12] (Oosterveld, personal communication; Steains 1999). As with the debate on judicial representation, a range of delegates, this time from Egypt, Oman, Syria, and the United Arab Emirates, strongly objected to the reference to specific gender expertise (Bedont and Hall-Martinez 1999, 77; Steains 1999, 381); such expertise were seen by the delegates as "inappropriate and unnecessary" and as not the only issue requiring specialist attention (Steains 1999, 380). Interestingly, Steains notes that the proposal for judicial gender expertise "received considerable attention, while the provision on the Prosecutor's legal adviser on gender received relatively little" (1999, 381). The latter issue was decided early in proceedings, with the inclusion of the term "gender" attracting no substantial opposition, somewhat surprisingly given the negotiating history on other gender terms (Steains 1999, 381).

Relatively uncontentious during the negotiations both at the PrepComs and the Rome Conference were the provisions to support the representation of victims, one of the core priorities of the Women's Caucus. The creation of the VWU, including the need for staff with expertise in trauma related to crimes of sexual violence, "was not seriously challenged" (Steains 1999, 383). Also uncontested were other special protective measures advanced by the Women's Caucus, including specific investigative, procedural, and evidentiary mechanisms required to support victims and witnesses coming forward to report and give evidence in cases of crimes of sexual and gender-based violence (Steains 1999, fn 94). The advocacy efforts of the Women's Caucus and general recognition of the negative experiences of victims at the ICTR were both noted for influencing this outcome (Steains 1999, fn 94).

The ICC's Gender Representation Rules

The agreed provisions emerging from the Rome Conference on *who* would be represented at the ICC "were not as strong as the [Women's] [C]aucus would have liked" (Copelon 2000, 238), lacking the language of gender "balance" and "expertise" in some critical places. Nevertheless, the Rome Statute (and its associated rules) met many of the demands of the Women's Caucus and, as one international law commentator put it, "shines in this respect when compared with its competition" (Schabas 2011, 375). The Statute stipulates that in selecting judges, the states parties must take into account the need for a "[a] fair representation of female and male judges" (Article 36(8)(a)(iii)). Article 44(2) further states that the Prosecutor and the Registrar must "have regard to" the need for a fair representation of male and female staff. The Statute does not require judges to have specific gender expertise, as advocated by the Women's Caucus, but Article 36(8)(b) does require states parties to take into account the need to nominate judges with legal expertise on violence against women and children. Ironically, as Bedont and Hall-Martinez point out, by removing the specific language of "gender expertise" as proposed by the Women's Caucus, these provisions ignore the experiences of male victims of sexual violence (1999, 77). Article 42(9) also requires the Prosecutor to appoint advisers who have expertise on various issues, including, importantly, sexual and gender-based violence.

The rules on *how* representation is to be performed are also included in the Rome Statute and associated documents. Under Article 54(1)(b), the Prosecutor is charged with investigating and prosecuting crimes in a way that "respect[s] the interests and personal circumstances of victims and witnesses, including ... gender." In authorizing the ICC to protect victims and witnesses, the Statute specifies the need to give due attention to victims of sexual violence, which may include the use of *in camera* evidence to shield victims from confronting their aggressors in the courtroom (Article 68(1) and (2); Rules of Procedure and Evidence 72), a measure proposed by the Women's Caucus. The Statute also allows victims to make representations to the Court, including through legal representatives, "where their personal interests" are affected (Article 68(3)), a rule that has the potential to extend access to justice to women who are victims of human rights violations. Rule 103 also allows the Chambers to grant persons or organizations leave to submit *amicus curiae* observations, along the lines proposed by the Women's Caucus. An obvious but often overlooked aspect of the representation aspect of the Court is its provision for interpretation and translation services, which are provided for under Rule 42 of the Rules of Procedure and Evidence (see Koomen 2014). These services literally give "voice" to those victims, witnesses, and accused who do not speak one of the primary languages of the Court, and convey their views to all participants in ICC court proceedings.

The Rome Statute rules relating to victim participation are undoubtedly an advance on preceding international criminal tribunals; nevertheless, many of the specific aspects of victim participation were not elucidated in the formal rules, "thus leaving wide discretion to the judges to actually shape the victims participation scheme" (Smith-van Lin 2013, 182). Ambiguities in the Statute include who can be recognized as a victim and the modalities through which victims can be represented. As will be discussed below, this ambiguity has created some opportunities but also some specific challenges for the representation and participation of women and of victims of sexual and gender-based violence in the first years of the ICC's operation.

In regards to the selection of the eighteen-member judiciary and the Chief and Deputy Prosecutor positions, the Rome Conference delegates agreed to an election through a secret ballot of ASP members.[13] In doing so, the architects were deliberately seeking to circumvent the UN ad hoc tribunal's judicial appointment process, which had been widely criticized for "the unseemly practice of vote trading, where States exchanged their votes with each other for posts in various UN bodies or even unrelated international institutions" (Frey 2004, 12), and "political gamesmanship," which had raised questions of judicial competence by commentators of the UN ad hoc tribunals (Chappell 2010b). The Women's Caucus, other NGOs, and many states believed the ICC's more transparent election process would be more beneficial for women, who had for so long missed out in the backroom deals to appoint judges to the ICTY and ICTR and to international posts more generally (see Chappell 2010b).

After much debate, the ASP agreed in September 2002 to give substance to the commitment to "fair representation" on the bench through a process of minimum candidate voting criteria. States parties were directed to vote for a minimum of: six male and six female candidates; for three candidates from each UN defined region; and for nine candidates with a criminal law background (List A) and five candidates with an international law background (List B) (minus, in all cases, the number of judges of that category remaining in office or elected at previous ballots).[14] Under the voting rules, states parties are also directed to "take account of the need to include judges with legal expertise on specific issues, including, but not limited to violence against women and children."[15] To be successful, candidates require a double majority: they must "obtain the highest number of votes and a two-thirds majority of the States Parties present and voting."[16]

The Rome Statute gave gender justice advocates at the ICC much to celebrate in terms of the representation of women and gender experts, especially those concentrating on sexual and gender-based violence. In the face of strong opposition, the Women's Caucus had secured majority state support for new formal rules that would challenge a range of long-standing legacies of international law concerning both the *who* and *how* of representation: the lack of female presence, the absence of gender expertise, and, inappropriate procedures for dealing with some of the most marginalized victims of war-torn communities, including women and children and victims of sexual and gender-based violence. Some of the language on representation included in the Rome Statute—such as what constituted "fair representation" and "gender expertise" and the nature and modes of participation for victims—was unclear, but this did not overly perturb gender justice actors, who saw these as examples of "constructive ambiguities," possibly able to be exploited to further extend gender justice claims in the ICC's operations phase (Bedont and Hall-Martinez 1999, 77; Steains 1999, 378). At the same time this constituency was under no illusion that provisions related to fair representation would be self-executing. As Rhonda Copelon put it: "political action will be necessary . . . to ensure that 'fair representation' is a balance of women and men and to secure the proper representation of gender experts" (2000, 238).

PART THREE: TIPPING THE SCALES TOWARD A SEX- AND GENDER-BALANCED COURT

In its first decade in operation, the ICC has produced some outstanding results in the implementation of aspects of the Rome Statute's sex, gender expertise, and victim representation provisions. Especially in relation to the Chambers, initially there has been a high degree of convergence between the rules and implementation relating to sex representation and to gender expertise. These outcomes suggest that during the Court's operational phase, gender justice actors, especially the successor to the Women's Caucus, the Women's Initiatives for Gender Justice, have succeeded in exploiting the constructive ambiguities in the Statute to forge a new path for women's representation. However, a close analysis of recent developments also shows that significant gaps still exist in the coverage of representation of sex, gender expertise, and gender-sensitive participation processes across all ICC organs. Coupled with a dramatic, emerging counter-trend in the number of women standing for and being elected to judicial positions, these gaps suggest that the legacies of gender *mis*representation lie close to the surface at the ICC and gender justice actors must continue their efforts to maintain the rules lest these advances of the first decade of ICC practice wither away.

Judicial Sex Representation

After just over a decade in operation, the ICC has become an international trailblazer in terms of judicial sex representation. States parties have nominated female candidates and have been willing to vote, through the ASP, for the elevation of women to the bench. As illustrated in Figure 3.1, the percentage of women standing for election has varied between a high of 42 percent in the 2009 election, where nine of the twenty-one candidates were women, to a low of zero in 2013, at an election to fill one vacancy. An interesting and discouraging trend, highlighted in the table, is that while initially there was a relatively strong interest from states in standing female candidates, recent figures show a consistent decline in this support, with only five female candidates out of seventeen in the 2014 election.

Although making up a smaller percentage of the candidates, women have nevertheless been elected to the bench in greater numbers than men. Indeed, at each election until the eighth election in 2014, the ASP has interpreted the voting rules broadly and met or exceeded the provision to elect the minimum number of female judges to the bench.[17] From the first

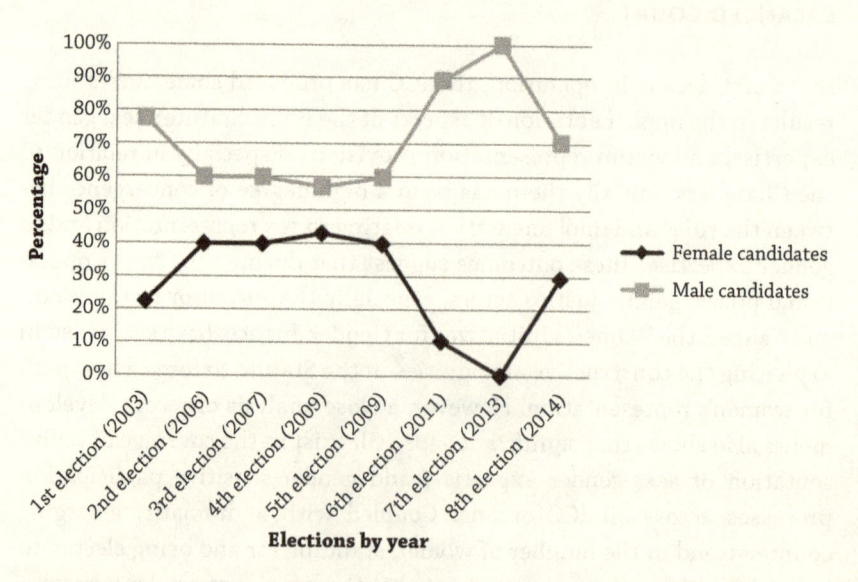

Figure 3.1:
Percentage of candidates for judicial positions.

election in 2003 to 2012, there was an upward trend in female representation on the bench at each election. This trend started to slow at the sixth election, when there was small decline, coinciding with a steep drop in the percentage of female candidates, and a dramatic result in 2014, when no women were elected to the bench. As Figure 3.2 illustrates,[18] the ICC's first bench comprised 38 percent women. By 2007 the percentage of female judges had increased to 44 percent (eight out of eighteen), and by 2009 to 52 percent. After the 2011 election, 54 percent of the bench was female, a figure that increased to 57 percent after the 2013 elections. This placed delegates at the 2014 Twelfth Session of the ASP in the remarkable position—given the history of poor female representation in other international criminal tribunals—of needing to elect at least one *male* candidate to reach the minimum requirements for the representation of men in the ICC judiciary (CICC 2014). The Twelfth Session of the ASP responded with resounding support for male candidates, electing six men to the six vacancies.[19] In an important move, in March 2015 the ICC's bench elected its first female President of the Court, Judge Silvia Fernández de Gurmendi of Argentina. Judge Fernández de Gurmendi is supported in her three-year term by two female Vice Presidents, Judge Joyce Aluoch (Kenya) and Judge Kuniko Ozaki (Japan), to create the ICC's first all-woman Presidency.[20] Respected gender justice advocate Kelly Askin (2015, n.p.) noted these developments as "a significant step forward for the proper representation of women in the top ranks of international justice."

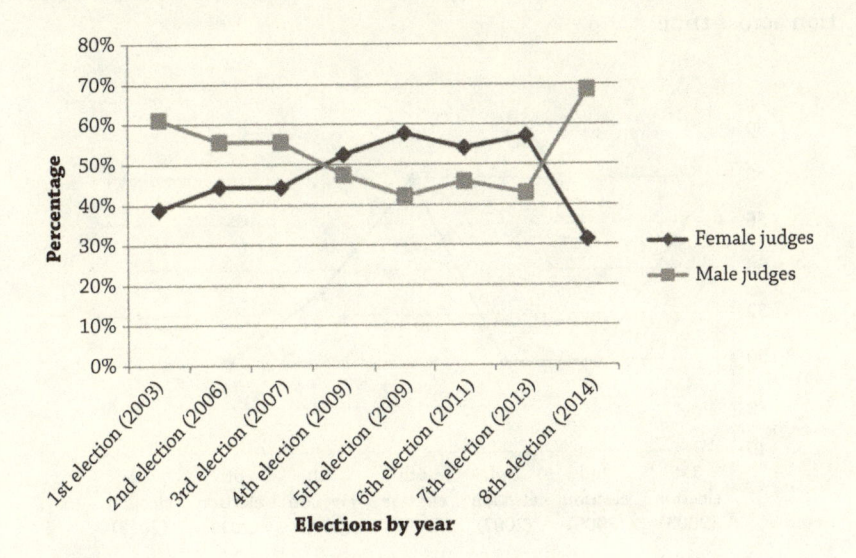

Figure 3.2:
Percentage of judicial positions held by male and female judges: 2003–2014.

An interesting (and seemingly largely unintended) consequence of the ICC's rule requiring the ASP to uphold minimum sex and regional representation criteria is that it provides for a degree of intersectionality on the bench. Unlike other international tribunals, which have been dominated by European, U.S., and other "Western" judges, the Rome Statute's rules on regional representation, combined with minimum sex voting requirements, have resulted in a diverse ICC Chamber. After the 2013 elections, four of the five African judges on the Court were women; overall, fourteen of the twenty-four judges on the bench were from outside Europe, nine of whom were female (see the Appendix). Such diversity far exceeds anything seen in previous international criminal tribunals and suggests that formal rules can make significant difference to overcoming legacies of *under-* and *mis*representation.

Judicial Gender Expertise

The priority of the Women's Caucus to include judges with legal expertise on violence against women or children within the ICC judiciary, pursuant to Article 36(8)(b), also seems to have been enforced. Based on an analysis of official ASP biographies of judicial candidates, many of the present and former members of the bench appear to have some expertise in this area. Indeed, as Figure 3.3 illustrates, since the Court's inception, 50 percent or more of the bench has consistently held such expertise, with some variation across time.

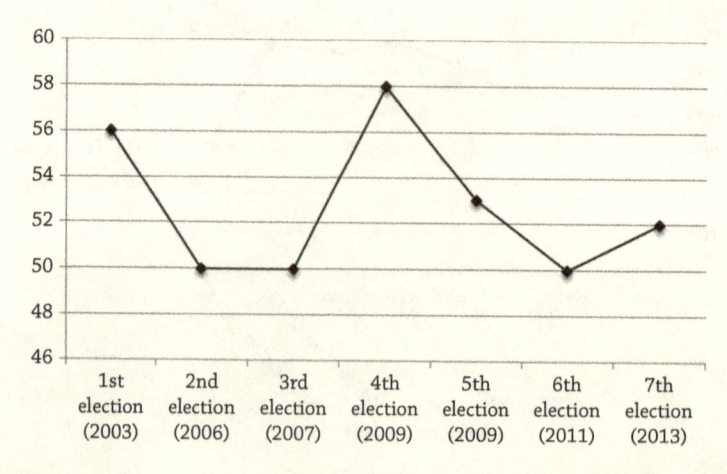

Figure 3.3:
Percentage of judges with gender expertise: 2003–2013.

We must treat these figures with some caution given the low-threshold definition of "expertise" that has been applied to the data. The definition used here includes those judges who have displayed high-level gender proficiency, such as writing multiple scholarly publications on gender and the law and issuing groundbreaking decisions regarding sexual violence in international criminal law tribunals (e.g., Judges Pillay, Odio Benito, Kuenyehia, and Eboe Osuji), as well as those who have emphasized their experience in previously prosecuting or adjudicating sexual violence crimes, but without any dedicated focus on these crimes throughout their career or in any of their scholarship, for example (e.g., Judges Slade and Henderson) (for further details of judicial expertise, see the Appendix). Regardless of the limitations of the tool for measuring expertise, the results are nonetheless impressive; the very fact that judges are keen to identify their work in this area and states are willing to nominate candidates with any level of gender experience is a breakthrough, given the lack of attention to such expertise in previous international tribunals (see Chinkin et al. 2005, 20). The difference this expertise has made to the *recognition* of gender justice issues is considered in the following chapter.

External Gender Expertise in the Courtroom

In an effort to bolster the representation of gender justice issues before the ICC chambers, the Women's Initiatives has been active in using the formal provisions, under Rule 103, to seek *amicus curiae* status, and with some success. Drawing on experience from the UN ad hoc tribunals, where women's rights organizations had demonstrated the value of this avenue for drawing judges' attention to otherwise ignored crimes of sexual violence (Copelon 2000), the Women's Initiatives was the first NGO to apply for leave to file a submission—in 2006 in the *Lubanga* case. It used its submission argue that the Prosecutor expand the charges against the accused to include sexual violence (see further discussion Chapter 4). Though unsuccessful on this occasion, the Women's Initiatives has continued to seek *amicus* status before the Court, submitting six briefs between 2006 and 2013. It was granted leave to present submissions in the *Bemba* case and later in the *Lubanga* hearings. In *Bemba*, it sought, unsuccessfully, to encourage the Court to apply cumulative charges against the accused of rape and outrages upon personal dignity and to demonstrate that this was "consistent with the rights of the accused."[21] In 2012, it was the only women's rights organization to submit observations in the *Lubanga* reparations proceedings.[22] As discussed in Chapter 5, many of the Women's Initiatives' recommendations were incorporated in the reparations judgment.

As with other aspects of the Rome Statute's gender justice mandate, these record improvements in the representation of women and gender experts did not come about of their own accord. In the early years of the Court's development, civil society groups pursuing gender justice goals have followed Copelon's suggestion to use political action to ensure that these elements of the Statute were broadly interpreted and widely enforced. The Women's Initiatives initially led this effort, publishing a detailed dossier on all the judges that includes information about their experience in addressing gender equality issues, including any publications or related rulings.[23] The umbrella organization CICC has also contributed to this effort by hosting panels of judicial candidates at each ASP and by conducting regular election surveys where judicial candidates are asked to detail their expertise, including their experience in addressing sexual and gender-based violence (CICC 2014). Having witnessed the CICC panel for candidates seeking judicial election at the Seventh ASP, it was apparent that even though not every candidate appeared to comprehend fully the nature of the gender expertise provisions, most made an effort to draw attention to their experience in addressing sexual violence, while ASP delegates were forthcoming with questions for the prospective judges related to these matters.

Gender justice advocates' efforts to improve the representation of women and gender experts on the bench have resulted in some significant developments, especially given the strong opposition to these issues in negotiations. However, there are two counter-trends to the initial success. The first trend, indicated above, is the decline in the number of female candidates in judicial elections, and the failure to elect any female judges to fill the six vacant positions in 2014. This suggests that despite early advances, states' support for sex equality on the bench is far from institutionalized at the ICC. The second trend, which is likely linked to the first, is that the legacy of vote trading over international judicial appointments appears to be reasserting itself at the ICC. In the lead-up to the 2014 election, the CICC expressed concern that governments are not determining elections "strictly on merit and qualifications of candidates as proscribed in the Rome Statute" and that "it is clear that the practice of 'reciprocal agreements,' a euphemism for the practice of crude vote-trading, is still predominant" (CICC 2014). Gender justice advocates are well aware of the negative impact such backroom vote trading can have on the election of female judges and those with gender expertise (Askin 2015). The reemergence of these practices—despite the new voting rules—illustrates the tenacity of gender legacies in the practice of the ICC. It also reinforces the point made by feminist institutionalists about the need for ongoing vigilance by gender justice actors to maintain "new rules" lest they be replaced by "old" gender-biased practices (Chappell and Waylen 2013; Mackay 2014a).

Nonjudicial Sex Representation

In line with the priorities of the Women's Caucus, women and gender experts have also been appointed in significant numbers across the ICC organs, as outlined in Figure 3.4. Since the Court's inception, the Women's Initiatives has taken on the task of tracking these figures and calling the ICC to account on the sex balance and gender expertise of its workforce, with good effect. According to the Women's Initiatives' last available survey based on 2012 data, women appear to have been appointed in almost equal numbers to men in the OTP and the Registry (at 46 percent and 51 percent respectively). The Presidency stands out as an exception, with 33 percent of women across all positions—a figure that has remained static since 2005.[24] Impressively, given the poor representation of women professionals in other analogous bodies, in 2011, women held 49 percent of the 362 professional posts across the ICC, excluding the judiciary.[25]

Under the direction of Registrar Silvana Arbia, and after earlier calls from the Women's Initiatives,[26] the ICC has also made an effort to increase the number of female lawyers, especially from Africa, listed to practice at the Court. In 2010, in collaboration with the International Bar Association, the Registry launched the "Call for African Women Lawyers" campaign.

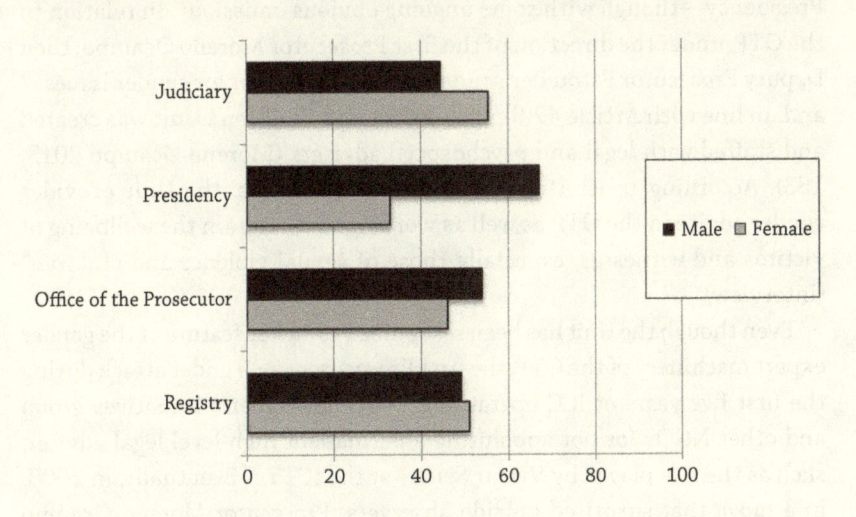

Figure 3.4:
Percentage of male and female staff in ICC organs: 2012.

The campaign was extended again in 2011. Explaining the initiative in a 2012 interview, Registrar Arbia noted:

> It was very important to have in our list of lawyers of Counsel more female lawyers and preferably African female lawyers because our people, our individuals are African . . . So, in order to better represent their interests, I thought that this was very important and with the, in collaboration with the [International Bar Association], which has been very helpful, we launched this campaign . . . I think it will be good because, especially for sexual crimes or sensitive crimes that women are a victim of, it's more easy for them to have a very good relationship with the Counsel who wants to present their case before the judge.

The campaign met with some success. Whereas in 2010 the ICC had only twelve female lawyers on its list eligible to practice at the ICC, by the end of the first year of the campaign thirty-two women lawyers from Africa were registered, and due to its success the campaign was extended into 2011 (Arbia, interview). As with the appointment rules for the bench, this campaign has helped contribute a degree of intersectional representation at the ICC.

Nonjudicial Gender Expertise

Again with ongoing external pressure from the Women's Initiatives, there has been an internal effort to increase the representation of staff with gender expertise across the Court—in the OTP, the Registry, and the Presidency—though with some ongoing obvious omissions. In relation to the OTP, under the direction of the first Prosecutor Moreno Ocampo, then Deputy Prosecutor Fatou Bensouda was the focal point for gender issues,[27] and, in line with Article 42(9), the Gender and Children's Unit was created and staffed with legal and psychosocial advisers (Moreno Ocampo 2013, 153). According to its Director, Gloria Atiba-Davies, the Unit provides gender advice in the OTP as well as working to "maintain the wellbeing of victims and witnesses, especially those of sexual violence and children" (interview).

Even though the Unit has been recognized as an key feature of the gender expert machinery of the OTP, the first Prosecutor came under attack during the first five years of ICC operations from the Women's Initiatives group and other NGOs for not appointing a permanent high-level legal adviser, such as the role played by Viseur Sellers at the ICTY.[28] Eventually, in 2008, in a move that surprised outside observers, Prosecutor Moreno Ocampo partially satisfied this call by appointing well-known U.S. feminist legal scholar Catharine MacKinnon to the position of the Prosecutor's Special Adviser on Gender Crimes.[29] This was not the permanent position envisaged by gender justice advocates but a part-time appointment through which the Prosecutor could consult the adviser as needed. According to the Prosecutor's press release, the new adviser's "immediate priority will be to further develop the approach to gender crimes in the Office's cases. Professor MacKinnon will also be working on Office-wide strategic approaches to gender issues."[30] Commentators read MacKinnon's appointment not only as a sign of Prosecutor Moreno Campo "catching up" with rules of the Rome Statute, but as a response to criticism leveled at the office for not including sexual violence charges in *Lubanga*, the first ICC case to come to trial (Senier 2008; for a full discussion see Chapter 4).

The Women's Initiatives welcomed MacKinnon's appointment but was critical of the terms of the post:

> [A]s it is a part-time position based outside The Hague, the ability of the post to influence and advise on the day-to-day decisions regarding investigation priorities, the selection of incidents and the construction of an overarching gender strategy will be extremely limited.[31]

The Women's Initiatives went on to press for the appointment of a full-time Gender Legal Adviser, a position that it pointed out had been advertised in December 2005 but never filled.[32]

Reflecting on his time as Prosecutor, Moreno Ocampo recognized the work of MacKinnon in providing him with strategic advice (2013, 153). In 2012, when Fatou Bensouda was elected as the ICC's second Chief Prosecutor, she came to the post espousing strong views about the need to better secure gender justice through the work of the OTP. She committed to revisiting "our policies and practices regarding sexual and gender crimes, making sure they are effective and improving them if needed" (Bensouda 2012b). To support her efforts, Bensouda appointed a new part-time gender advisor, Brigid Inder, the long-time Executive Director of the Women's Initiatives. Not surprisingly given the Women's Initiatives' earlier criticism of the part-time nature of the position and Inder's decision to maintain her role as Director of Women's Initiatives alongside her new appointment, her selection provoked some consternation (Limebach 2012). Ultimately, however, Inder's extensive experience in the area and her priority "to further strengthen the institutional approach to a range of gender issues and support office-wide strategic responses to gender-based crimes"[33] demonstrated her commitment and compatibility with Bensouda's agenda and resulted in widespread approval for Inder's appointment by other NGOs and ICC commentators (Amann 2012; Limebach 2012; UIA 2012).

Since taking up her position in mid-2012, Prosecutor Bensouda, working with Inder and others in the OTP, has upheld her strong commitment to gender justice concerns. Her critical reflection on the failures and problems of the OTP's early years of operations—especially inadequacies in properly recognizing, investigating, and prosecuting sexual and gender-based violence—and her willingness to respond to these problems have been critical to ongoing support of gender advocates for the ICC. Bensouda's key contribution to date has been to develop the OTP's first gender policy paper. Many aspects of the wide-ranging paper are directed toward improving the OTP's recognition of women and victims of sexual and gender-based violence (discussed in Chapters 4 and 6). The document also identifies certain representative issues that need addressing, including strengthening sex and gender expertise within the OTP by enhancing gender analysis skills, including "sound knowledge of the statutory provisions regarding sexual and gender-based crimes, and well-developed skills regarding the possible effects of trauma in relation to these crimes."[34]

Outside the OTP, some effort has been made to embed gender expertise in the Court operations, especially in relation to victims, but these have failed to reach the comprehensive coverage envisioned by the Women's Caucus at the negotiation stage. For instance, by 2012 the Registry's VWU, which supports victims and witnesses in preparing to give testimony and provides protection after court appearances, had employed one sexual violence trauma expert. Moreover, this appointment has been made on a temporary basis, which, given the number of victims and witnesses of sexual violence currently and potentially to come before the court, falls significantly short of meeting the demand for such expertise.[35] The Victims' Participation and Reparation Section (VPRS), which processes victims' and witnesses' claims for participation in proceedings and liaises with them throughout the trial, has not appointed dedicated gender staff. Instead, as the Director of the Unit Fiona McKay explained, the VPRS does make an effort to pay attention to the specific challenges facing victims of sexual and gender-based violence. But, as McKay notes, attempting to cover this specialized gender work is a challenge, both because of the skeleton staff of the office—as of June 2012, the section had a total of fifteen staffers to deal with seven situation countries—and because of the magnitude of the work, leading to a backlog in 2011 alone of six thousand claims for victim status[36] (McKay interview).

A similar situation exists within the Outreach Unit. This Unit, which aims to give the communities in ICC situation countries knowledge about the court at all stages of proceedings, manages expectations, and counters misunderstandings and misrepresentations of the Court's role,[37] lacks a gender expert. Nevertheless, its Director, Claudia Perdomo, explained in an interview that the Unit is alert to gender discrimination within situation countries and tries to tailor their programs to ensure women are included in them (Perdomo interview, June 26, 2012). The OPCV, another element of the Rome Statute victim representation framework, is administered by, but independent of, the Registry. It has been established to provide "legal advice and research, and, where deemed appropriate by Chambers, representing victims, as well as appearing before the Chambers in respect of specific issues."[38,39] However, official documents from this Office, including its 2010 handbook on its structure and objectives, are silent on this issue of gender expertise.[40]

The gaps in the coverage of gender expertise across the ICC are not the result of lack of pressure. Each year through its *Gender Report Card*, which forensically assesses all Court operations, the Women's Initiatives has monitored appointments and attempted to hold the ICC accountable for all appointments, including gender experts. It has also sought to encourage women and gender experts to apply for roles at the ICC. As Brigid Inder said in a 2012 interview:

> I think our work from the very first week that we set up Women's Initiatives and my very first week in office, we launched a recruitment campaign to promote positions we thought were critical or strategic, or important, to a very wide range of women's groups of, of legal groups, of associations, of judges, so that more women knew about the opportunities existing at the Court and therefore more women would consider applying.

Inder's further reflections suggest that she believes these efforts in promoting the appointment of women have some efficacy:

> [One well-known feminist activist] tells the story that, when she's been in the hallways at the Court and people are recruiting, they say, "Oh my God, if we don't appoint a woman to this position, Women's Initiatives is going to be on our tail!" So, whatever the motivation is, we don't mind. What we believed we were doing was advocating for implementation of the statute—not beyond that and not more than that.

Implementing measures to achieve a better balance of sex and of gender expertise across the ICC has been one element of its representation strategy in its first decade. Another has been to include victims' voices in proceedings, including women and those experiencing sexual and gender-based violence, and to develop the appropriate processes and procedures through which this inclusion occurs.

Victim Representation: Who

The representation of victims before the ICC is considered a "stunning" development (Schabas 2011, 346), given the longstanding retributive focus of international criminal law. Both male and female victims have availed themselves of the opportunity to register through the VPRS as victims, though with some variation across cases. Figures from 2010 suggested that women are significantly underrepresented as applicants in every situation before the ICC. The figures were worst for the Sudan/Darfur situation, with a male/female differential at 72 percent (14 percent of the victims are female and 86 percent are male), and best in relation to the situation in the Central African Republic (where 42 percent of the recognized victims are female and 58 percent are male).[41] However, the most recent figures available, outlined in Figure 3.5, show a more even sex

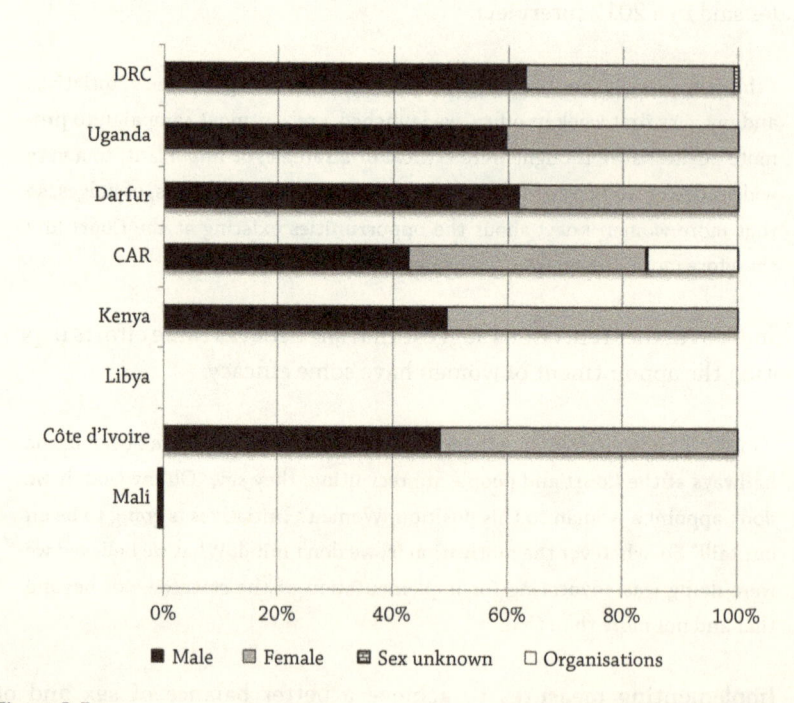

Figure 3.5:
Victims formally accepted to participate in proceedings (situations and cases) up to June 30, 2013.

balance emerging in victim representation, with male victims tending to be better represented in the Democratic Republic of Congo, Uganda, and Darfur situations, but an equal balance in the others. This shift suggests that the VPRS's plans to reach out to international, national, and local women's groups working in situation countries to encourage more female participation at the ICC has had some effect (see De Brouwer 2007, 223).

In the ICC's first decade, outside the VPRS registration processes, the sex balance of victim representation has been much more skewed toward men. For instance, in 2011 women made up only 26 percent of the total participants in the Outreach Unit's interactive sessions. These figures varied between cases, with only 7 percent of women participating in Uganda and 17 percent in Sudan.[42] Further, the OPCV's client base is overwhelming male: in 2011, almost 65 percent of the total victims represented or assisted by the OPCV were men.[43]

Victim Representation: How

As Fraser points out, it is not just *who* has voice that matters to gender justice, but also *how* the representation arena in which this voice is expressed is drawn and operates. Efforts to achieve an element of gender justice in representation procedures and processes at the ICC have produced inconsistent outcomes. While there is some sign that new formal rules advanced by the Women's Caucus during negotiations and embedded in the Rome Statute have taken hold to challenge certain gender legacies, critical gaps remain, and it is in these gaps where legacies of *mis*representation continue to flourish.

OTP staff members have made some effort to recast the processes through which women and girls are represented in the initial investigation and evidence-gathering stages of proceedings. For instance, the Gender and Children's Unit has developed gender-sensitive processes including, according to Director Atiba-Davies, a "procedure which we refer to as 'psycho-social pre-interview assessments' which are conducted in order to ensure that the potential witnesses are fit, physically and psychologically, to go through the interview process, which can be quite traumatic" (interview). The Unit also seeks to coordinate its efforts to avoid retraumatizing victims by working closely with the VWU, to which they refer victims and witnesses requiring protection (Atiba-Davies interview). Despite such efforts, the OTP has faced criticism throughout its initial period in operation for its failure to develop appropriate processes at all stages for the representation of women and victims of sexual and gender-based violence.[44] The

OTP's 2014 gender policy can be seen as a part of its response to these critiques. In line with Article 54(1)(b), the draft details how victims' issues will be dealt with in future investigations and proceedings. It states that the OTP will "be sensitive to the interests and circumstances of victims and witnesses and tak[e] a mainstreamed approach to dealing with sexual and gender-based crimes."[45] The policy indicates that the OTP intends to use different and more innovative evidence-gathering techniques, including forensic and technological tools, to be more sensitive to the challenges of gathering evidence for crimes of a sexual nature, and to allow for more open-ended investigations, to give victims time to come forward to have their experiences included in investigations.[46]

The VWU has also worked to promote gender-just representation procedures for victims. It has assisted in orienting victims and witnesses to courtroom proceedings and has offered "guidance to judges on how to question vulnerable witnesses in a sensitive manner."[47] The VWU's sexual violence trauma expert works with the judiciary to ensure that victims and witnesses of these crimes are given specific protection.[48] In a number of cases, victims of sexual violence have been granted voice and image distortion to protect their identities.[49] In the long-running *Bemba* case, in which the accused is charged with a range of sexual violence crimes, VWU staff members, including a psychologist, have assisted victims of sexual violence during their testimony.[50] These measures go some way to challenging the legacy of international criminal law, which has been evident in the operations of other international tribunals and extensively critiqued by feminist legal scholars (Mertus 2004; Mouthaan 2011, 775), about the gender-biased attitudes toward, and lack of procedural safeguards for, victims of sexual violence in the courtroom; these attitudes and practices result in their retraumatization.

However, the work of the VWU has also been beset by a number of problems. Despite its best efforts, and the provisions of the Rome Statute and the Rules of Procedure and Evidence, the VWU has been unable to completely protect victims of sexual violence from facing the same hostile questioning experienced by their counterparts in other international tribunals. There are signs that at the ICC some victims face constant interruption during their testimony and are asked inappropriate questions and individual female victims of sexual violence have often found it difficult to narrate their own stories in their own terms (SáCouto 2012, 345).

Similarly, the Outreach Unit has struggled in its attempt to implement targeted, gender-just representation processes. Its Director, Claudia Perdomo, explained that the Unit recognized that women face particular challenges in accessing public information due to illiteracy, social isolation, and powerlessness; this makes it difficult for them to participate in outreach activities (interview). She noted that in many countries where the ICC operates, women require permission from their husbands or other male figures to participate in outreach forums. They also have difficulty accessing the usual means of communication, including household radios, which is a major tool of communication used by the Unit.[51] In attempting to address these gender biases, the Unit has introduced sex-segregated outreach activities and sought to engage local women's organizations; it has also created women-only radio clubs to improve their access to ICC broadcasts.[52] Where this has occurred there are signs that this partnership has helped "women and girls break through the social, physical, and psychological barriers that often hinder their access to the ICC."[53]

Despite these efforts, the Outreach Unit still has much work to do. At the 2010 ICC Review Conference, a stocktaking report found that victims in general, but women and children in particular, still lacked sufficient information about the Court.[54] Like other agencies in the Registry, the Outreach Unit is hampered by resource constraints. According to the ICC's 2012 review of its victims' strategy, the Outreach Unit was working in seven situations with the same human resources it had when the Court was engaged in three.[55] These shortcomings have led the Women's Initiatives group to regularly call in its *Gender Report Card* for an increase in Registry staff to "ensure effective programs are developed to reach women and diverse sectors of communities in each of the . . . conflict situations" and to provide safe, alternative forums, especially for the discussion of gender-based crimes.[56]

In its first six years in operation, the OPCV has contributed to contesting and challenging the gender bias underlying international law. For instance, in the *Lubanga* trial, the OPCV sought to ensure that the experiences of girl soldier victims, many of whom had experienced sexual violence, were included in the proceedings despite the Prosecutor not including sexual violence in the charges (Chappell 2014; SáCouto 2012). While these interventions were ultimately rejected both by Lubanga's defense counsel and the majority of judges (SáCouto 2012, 345–346), they were taken up at the verdict and sentencing stage by feminist Judge Elizabeth Odio Benito. As discussed in detail in Chapter 4, in her dissenting opinion, Judge Odio Benito expressed similar views to the arguments advanced by the OPCV (and by the Women's Initiatives in its failed *amicus curiae* submission), which strongly asserted the right to recognition of girl soldier victims of sexual violence.[57]

However, as with other victim-representation agencies, the OPCV faces a number of challenges. These include managing lengthy trials that have hundreds if not thousands of victims who are based in distant, remote locations, as well as language barriers.[58] As with the VPRS and the Outreach Unit, it too confronts a growing workload and inadequate resources. From 2005 to 2010, the OPCV assisted two thousand victims and submitted approximately three hundred submissions in the various proceedings before the court.[59] By 2011, it had 10 permanent staff, working with over 2,100 victim applicants,[60] a figure that is expected to escalate with the caseload of the court. The ICC's 2012 report into its victim framework also noted the problem of inadequate OPCV staffing levels.[61]

One final, but often invisible, aspect of the ICC's procedures relating to victim representation is its translation and interpretation services, provided through the Court Interpretation and Translation Section (Koomen 2014). Interpreters play a critical role in representing victims, serving as facilitators and cultural bridges during face-to-face encounters between witnesses and court personnel. Quoting Viseur Sellers, Koomen explains (2014, 586): "when booth interpreters relay witness testimony to international courtrooms, they literally serve as 'the voice of the witness'." The work of ICC interpreters is complex and challenging: "The demands of language work in international courtrooms are unique. While domestic courts may use consecutive translation between two languages on an as-need basis, international court proceedings negotiate multiple (usually more than two) languages through simultaneous interpretation as a matter of routine" (Koomen 2014, 586). These demands are further extended in cases involving sexual violence, given the stigma attached to these crimes and the difficulties in victims and witnesses relaying accounts of their experiences. Alexandra Tomic, the Director of the ICC's Interpretation Section, is aware of these challenges. Although, as with some other elements of the Registry, the Section does not employ specific gender or sexual violence experts, Tomic is alert to the need for, and challenges of, interpreting the testimony of victims and witnesses of these crimes: "in relation to translating/interpreting sexual crimes it is important to be aware of euphemisms. Accurate translation is important in conjunction with cultural sensitivity and this applies to the professionals who interview victims or witnesses" (interview). To address these challenges the Section undertakes training and workshops to better understand and prepare for cases specifically addressing these crimes.

The design and implementation of new and more gender-sensitive victim-representation procedures has gone some way to meet the demands of gender justice advocates. However, striking gaps remain at each step of the ICC's victim-representation process. These gaps not only create specific problems for the representation of women and victims of sexual and gender-based violence at each stage of proceedings, but they have a compounding effect. By not being engaged in outreach activities, women are less likely to register as victims through the VPRS. This means women lose the opportunity to express their "views and concerns" in proceedings, and ultimately, they miss the chance to assist the judges and the international community more broadly in understanding the extent and nature of crimes committed against them.[62]

Sparked by strong criticisms at the 2010 ICC Review Conference of its treatment of victims, the Court undertook a review of all its victim programs. It paid specific attention to the need to better take into account gender concerns within all its victim activities. The review, delivered to the ASP in 2012, recognized that "[g]ender is a cross-cutting issue with significant impact on victims and on the work of the ICC system with victims and affected communities" and it called for greater coordination across victim-focused agencies.[63] Importantly, the report drew attention to the need for all aspects of the ICC's victims' framework to engage men and boys, both to encourage them to support women's participation and to better understand the impact of gender on men and women within community contexts and to better represent their interests through the Court.[64]

As this review and the emergence of the OTP's gender policy suggest (summarized in Table 3.1), ICC personnel are responding to the Rome Statute's gender justice representation mandate and implementing the formal rules in practice. However, it is also clear that in doing so they are working against deeply embedded gender legacies that sometimes interfere with these efforts, serving to distort and displace representation objectives in favor of the gender status quo.

Table 3.1. GENDER JUSTICE REPRESENTATION: PRIORITIES, RULES, AND ENFORCEMENT

Gender Justice Priorities	Formal Rules	Enforced
A balance between women and men in all organs of the court	✔	✔
Procedures for persons with demonstrated expertise in gender analysis and crimes of gender and sexual violence in all organs of the Court	✔	Partial and incomplete
Victim participation at all stages of proceedings	✔	Partial and incomplete
Victim representation through legal representatives	✔	✔
Creation of VWU	✔	✔
Provision for *amicus curiae* submissions	✔	✔
Trained translators and interpreters	✔	✔

PART FOUR: LEGACIES, LEGITIMACY, AND REPRESENTATIVE GENDER JUSTICE AT THE ICC

The Women's Caucus was a key force behind the design of the Rome Statute's gender representation mandate, while its successor—the Women's Initiatives—has helped drive its implementation. Working with this mandate, gender justice advocates have secured some important achievements in expanding gender representation, but some key measures have languished or have been only partially enforced. Different outcomes can be identified within and between two axes: first, concerning new rules relating to *sex* and to *gender expert* personnel; and second, relating to victims, concerning *who* is represented and *how* this representation occurs. Distinctions across these divisions have arisen as a result of resource constraints, but also because of the operation and effect of gender legacies at the ICC. These outcomes are important to shaping gender advocates' sense of the ICC's past, present, and future legitimacy.

Representation of Sex and of Gender Expertise at the ICC

The greatest point of convergence between the Rome Statute's representation rules and their instantiation relates to achievements in sex representation in ICC appointments. Despite strong opposition to the idea of a sex-balanced Court by some state delegates during negotiations, in practice states have responded to advocates' pressure to nominate female candidates for the judiciary and have regularly elected more than 50 percent women to the bench, exceeding the minimum voting requirement. Further aligning with the priorities of the Statute's gender justice architects has been the election by the ASP of Fatou Bensouda as the second Chief Prosecutor, the election by the Chamber of Silvana Arbia as the Court's second Registrar (2008–2012), the appointment in 2015 of Judge Fernández de Gurmendi as the Court's first female President; and the appointment by senior ICC personnel of a relatively sex-balanced professional workforce. The increased intersection between sex and race representation arising from the ICC's formal voting rules may not have been a conscious goal of the designers, but nevertheless the Court has produced the most diverse bench yet seen under international criminal law.

These outcomes are impressive, especially given women's historical exclusion from international criminal law bodies. However, two trends have emerged that may threaten these gains. The first trend is a reduction in the number of female judicial candidates, which, if it continues over time, is likely to reduce the number of women judges. The second is a reassertion of old-style, informal vote-trading practices that have been shown in other tribunals to interfere with "fair" representation for women. Gender justice actors must work to convince states to reverse the drift back toward these "old" practices to ensure that the hard-won improvements in sex representation are remembered and reinforced.

In comparison to balanced sex representation—which has largely been implemented though not yet institutionalized—the representation of gender expertise has been more difficult to enforce. In contrast to the strong resistance expressed during the negotiation stage, senior ICC personnel appear to have been willing to recognize the call by gender advocates for the need for such expertise in all organs of the Court. However, early rhetorical support has not translated into the appointment of personnel with such expertise, leading to some significant gender knowledge gaps across the ICC.

Victims: Who and How

During the negotiation stage, the Women's Caucus and other advocates successfully pushed for the Rome Statute's innovative victim-representation regime to include women and victims of sexual and gender-based violence and appropriate procedures. Efforts to hold the ICC accountable for these efforts through the Women's Initiatives group, REDRESS, and the Victims' Rights Working Group, have resulted in a gradual improvement in the number of women seeking recognition as victims and being incorporated in ICC proceedings. Equally, ICC personnel have begun to pay greater attention to operationalizing those procedures and processes that are embedded in the Court's Statute and rules aimed at supporting victims of sexual and gender-based violence; where provisions are evidently not working, they have sought to revise them. Two cases in point are the ASP's review of victims' participation procedures and the Prosecutor's 2014 *Policy Paper on Sexual and Gender-based Crimes*. Nevertheless, some substantial gender justice gaps remain across the ICC's victims' framework, leaving those women and sexual violence victims who do come forward exposed to the possibility of being revictimized through Court processes.

Resources and Legacies

How can we explain these mixed developments in the implementation of the Rome Statute's gender-just representation rules? Resource constraints are part of the answer. It costs nothing to put in place rules to elect a female judge, but resources are required to employ additional staff with gender expertise or to incorporate new procedures to better protect vulnerable victims. The Court has been under considerable financial pressure in the past decade; the imposition by the ASP of a "zero-growth" budget position in the years immediately following the global financial crisis came at the same time the ICC experienced a significant growth in its caseload (CICC 2011). In the view of former Registrar Silvana Arbia, who managed the budget (and echoed in interviews by her Registry colleagues Fiona McKay and Claudia Perdomo), the ASP's imposition "almost paralysed the operations of the court" (interview). Financial strain has been acute in the agencies of the Registry who, as noted above, have experienced exponential growth in the number of claimants but with fixed, or in some cases diminishing, resources.[65]

But the point about budgets, no matter how stringent, is that they are also about priorities. Clearly, senior court actors are not deliberately working to thwart gender justice; indeed, there is plenty of evidence to suggest the contrary. However, it may be that in deciding how their budgets are spent, ICC insiders are simply reflecting the longstanding gender logic of appropriateness of international law—demonstrated in Rome Conference debates—that gender justice expertise has never been considered a priority and that there are other interests and issues that are equally if not more important on which to expend scarce ICC resources.

Resources undoubtedly matter, but this chapter argues that rules—both formal and informal—matter more. Dramatic improvements in sex representation demonstrate that new rules can make a difference: they can shift old patterns and bring about change in the gender order. However, emerging counter-trends in sex representation and gaps across the gender representation framework also show that underlying informal gender norms and practices can slip back in to subvert and distort formal rules (Chappell and Waylen 2013; Kenny 2013; Lowndes and Roberts 2013). Changes to gender norms and practices are always hard to enforce, even when actors have the best intentions: at the ICC the legacy of a deprioritization of gender expertise remains "sticky."

Legitimacy and Representative Gender Justice

The success of the Women's Caucus in embedding a range of new provisions of sex representation and gender expertise at the design stage of the ICC was remarkable, given the extent and nature of the opposition it faced. These actors were able to successfully challenge firmly entrenched practices and attitudes within international criminal law that had tolerated an almost complete exclusion of women from deliberative processes, both as "rule makers" and "rule takers." Further, in line with Fraser's conception of representation, they succeeded in helping to embed new rules that expanded the boundaries of the law to incorporate a previously excluded group—victims—and provide new, appropriate procedures through which they could engage with international law. Leaving the Rome Conference with these unequivocal "wins," Women's Caucus members were realistic about the challenges of instantiating these rules, and the need to work with their "constructive ambiguities," but nevertheless walked away with a strong sense of the legitimacy of the *design* of the ICC's sex representation and gender expertise mandate. The Women's Initiatives group then took up the challenge of pushing for the implementation of these rules.

The implementation of the Rome Statute's sex representation provisions has largely been successful. Entering in large numbers, and across a diverse range of races and cultures, women professionals at the ICC are examples of Puwar's "space invaders" (2004), exposing the uniformity and privilege of the previously male bastion of international criminal law. With significant numbers of women professionals in its ranks, the ICC has emerged as a new type of international body, more legitimate in the eyes of the gender justice actors because its personnel better reflect the constituencies with which it engages (Grossman 2011; Kenney 2013). Regardless of the decisions made by these women, the fact that they hold more than half of the positions on the bench, and an equal share of other senior ICC posts, is in itself transformative, sending a message that women have a rightful place as adjudicators and decision makers within core institutions of international criminal justice.

In the Court's operational phase, efforts by gender justice outsiders and supportive ICC personnel to implement other aspects of the Rome Statute's representation mandate have found it difficult to "lock in" many of these new rules. The significant gaps in gender expertise across the Court, weaknesses in the implementation of procedures aimed at protecting many vulnerable female victims, and emerging counter-trends in judicial elections all provide grounds to test gender advocates' view of the legitimacy of these aspects of the Court's work. Nevertheless, these actors remain highly engaged with the Court on these issues: they are actively working to maintain and protect those gains that have been made and avoid slippage back into old norms, practices, and rules (Kenny 2013, 42; Mackay 2014a). The willingness of ICC officials and the ASP to take up suggestions from civil society groups, including the Women's Initiatives, to review and revise aspects of its representation rules and practices—as seen, for example, through reviews of the ASP and the

OTP—has contributed to this ongoing support. The position of ICC-focused gender advocates reinforces the point made by institutionalist and legitimacy theorists, discussed in Chapter 1, about the importance of the revisability of institutions, and constituents' engagement in these review processes, for maintaining legitimacy (see Buchanan and Keohane 2006, 410; Lowndes and Roberts 2013, 198). Because of the ICC's willingness to continue to "fine-tune" its gender justice design features and processes, its gender justice constituents have been prepared to continue to act as "critical friends" of the Court, viewing legitimacy in many areas of its representation mandate as emergent rather than yet fully realized.

Gender justice actors already have some sense of the *consequential* legitimacy of the ICC, at least in terms of sex representation. The implementation of new rules that have enabled women to take an equal place on the bench and in other senior positions sets a new benchmark for other international justice tribunals, and international organizations and national courts more broadly. These actors are able to point to the ICC and demonstrate that shifting the sex composition of international bodies is possible and significant to their legitimacy. As for the outcomes of other aspects of the representative regime, and their impact on these actors' sense of legitimacy, time will tell. There are two likely tests: the first is the ICC's long-term responsiveness to internal, state-based, and external reviews of and recommendations for achieving its representation mandate. The second test is what difference, if any, new female voices and gender expertise and representation procedures will make to the ICC's substantive gender justice outcomes. In other words, does sex and gender *representation* make a difference to the *recognition* of gender injustices in Court decisions and processes? This key question is considered in the following chapter.

CHAPTER 4

Recognizing Gender Justice at the International Criminal Court

The Rome Statute includes provisions to *recognize* gender justice, particularly through the enumeration of crimes. The literature on gender justice at the ICC is largely focused on this criminalization aspect of recognition, and for good reason; as Bedont and Hall-Martinez suggest, "the central pillar of the Statute is the section on the definition of crimes—for the punishment of these crimes is the main purpose of the Statute" (1999, 69). This focus is also understandable given the poor historical record of prosecutions of sexual and gender-based violations under international criminal law, and the hard-fought campaign in Rome to have these violations incorporated in the Statute. The Statute also includes other significant gender justice recognition elements that have received less attention: measures to recognize women victims of the enumerated crimes and to recognize the authority and "voice" of those women and gender experts whose positions have been enabled by the Statute's *representation* provisions (as outlined in the Chapter 3).

In accord with Nancy Fraser's (2007, 26) emphasis on *misrecognition* as one of the three injustices (alongside misrepresentation and maldistribution) that must be addressed to achieve gender justice, this chapter highlights the extensive efforts made by gender justice actors to have sexual and gender violations included in negotiations at Rome; to have them formally recognized in the Statute; and, since 2002, to have the ICC enforce these provisions in practice. It also focuses on the less frequently addressed issue of when and how the voices of women and those employed as gender experts have been recognized in the early operational phase of the Court.[1]

Part One of this chapter outlines Nancy Fraser's conception of recognition and the specific problem identified by feminist legal theorists of the lack of recognition of sex and gender issues in and through international criminal law. Part Two considers the recognition of gender justice actors' demands during the Rome Statute negotiation phase. The implementation and interpretation of sexual and gender-based crimes are addressed in Part Three, along with an account of how well women's experiences and gender expertise have been recognized through Court practices. Part Four analyzes what has been "locked in" and "locked out" in terms of the recognition of crimes and of voices, and considers how these recognition outcomes have influenced gender justice actors' views of the ICC's legitimacy in relation to its design, operation, and consequences.

The chapter argues that the inclusion of gender recognition rules in the Rome Statute was a significant accomplishment for gender advocates, but suggests that securing these pioneering provisions in practice has been a difficult challenge. In the Court's early years, both the OTP and the Chambers have consistently failed to apply these recognition elements of the Statute. Consequently, the ICC has a poor initial record of sexual and gender-based prosecutions; the interpretation of the Rome Statute has tended toward misrecognition of the experiences of women and victims of sexual and gender-based violence, reinforcing the problem of gender bias and gender status subordination under international criminal law. Gender legacies have been a significant influence on these developments, working to "lock out" new provisions in favor of the old. Signs are emerging that Court personnel are learning lessons from these early years and are responding through review and revision of existing practice. The release in June 2014 of the OTP's gender policy paper[2] is an important development in this regard. However, unless members of the judiciary are also willing to take steps to review and reassess their interpretation of the Rome Statute to bring to life its significant gender recognition provisions, gender justice actors will be given good reason to question the Court's ongoing legitimacy.

PART ONE: RECOGNITION AS A PATH TO GENDER JUSTICE

For Nancy Fraser, equal *representation* and a fair *distribution* of resources are necessary but not sufficient conditions for achieving gender justice. A third element—cultural or equal status *recognition*—is also required to address gender injustice that stems from status or cultural *misrecognition*. In Fraser's view, this form of injustice results from androcentrism, which is an "institutionalized pattern of cultural value that privileges traits associated with masculinity, while devaluing everything coded as 'feminine'" (Fraser 2003, 21). Fraser suggests that "not just women but all low-status groups risk feminization and thus depreciation" (2003, 20). Androcentrism is coded in law, policy, and popular culture and leads to "gender-specific forms of *status subordination*" (Fraser 2003, 21; emphasis in original). The harms of gender status misrecognition are numerous. They include "trivializing, objectifying and demeaning stereotypical depictions in the media, harassment . . . in everyday life, exclusion or marginalization in public spheres and deliberative bodies; and denial of the full rights and equal protections of citizenship" (Fraser 2003, 21). Fraser also draws particular attention to sexual assault and domestic violence as consequences of gender status subordination (2003, 21).

Addressing gender misrecognition requires "changing the gender status order, deinstitutionalizing sexist value patterns and replacing them with patterns that express equal respect for women," (Fraser 2003, 21) and, one presumes, respect for those men suffering as a result of their association with femininity. Ultimately, "the aim is to dismantle androcentrism by reconstructing the relations of recognition" (Fraser 2003, 21). For Fraser, not all claims for recognition can, or indeed should, be accepted; recognition is not a matter of self-realization but one of justice (2003, 47). By this Fraser means that claimants for recognition "must show that current arrangements prevent them from participating on par with others in social life" (2003, 38).

As outlined in earlier chapters, feminist legal scholars have long been aware of the androcentric nature of international criminal law and of the way it is "intertwined with a sexed and gendered subjectivity, and reinforces a system of male power" (Chinkin et al. 2005, 44), leaving women and other low-status groups without equal access to the law. As feminist international law scholar Doris Buss encapsulates it, international criminal law was built on a foundation that failed to recognize "the gendered and sexualised forms of harm experienced by women and men in armed conflict" and "the fact that women experience wartime violence in ways particular to them as women" (2011, 413). Fionnuala Ní Aoláin and her coauthors agree, suggesting that "the laws of war were generally constructed from the vista of a soldier's need for ordered rules within which to wage war on behalf of the state. Consequently, women's interests fared notoriously badly when accountability was sought for the behavior of combatants" (2011, 154). In other words, women are often targeted in ways that relate to their position in the "androcentric" gender order—such as through bodily injury and stigmatization resulting from rape or forced pregnancy, through attacks on children to whom they are deeply emotionally bonded, and the destruction of their means of livelihood. As feminist legal scholars have amply demonstrated, international criminal law has largely failed to address impunity for the gendered crimes committed against women during conflict or in situations where widespread or systematic violence occurs: where it has been acknowledged, these experiences have often been trivialized or marginalized (Buss 2011, 413; Chinkin et al. 2005). As a result, women and other groups identified as feminine have suffered what Fraser terms "status subordination," unable to enjoy the protection of international law on a par with others.

Misrecognition under international criminal law has also kept hidden from view certain other groups of women and men who interrupt gender stereotypes. The institutions and practices of international law have struggled to identify and address women as agents of war and conflict—those who have been willing to take up arms and who have themselves been the perpetrators of atrocities. A growing academic interest in these women has revealed the way in which international law and politics has defined them as aberrations, categorizing them as either "whores" or "monsters," without any understanding of the extent or range of women involved in these activities or the conditions leading to their participation in conflict (Mackenzie 2012; Sjoberg and Gentry 2008). Similarly overlooked have been male victims of sexual violence. This is in part a problem of the law not yet developing a gender lens with which to see the complex gender relations that lead to such atrocities—including the motivation of armed groups to "demasculinise" (Sivakumaran 2013, 81) or "feminise" (Leatherman 2011, 9), and thereby demean, these victims There is also a problem of underreporting of these crimes, which is a result of the "shame, confusion, guilt, fear, and stigma that flow from imputing a homosexual and/or feminine identity onto a man in combat" coupled with "a tendency for men to associate their victimization as incompatible with their masculinity, and a lack of vocabulary to describe their sexual violence" (Lewis 2010, 9). The common conflation in international law and politics between "'gender' and 'women,' or between 'victim' and 'woman',", leads to a double misrecognition "such that male victims are marginalized and women's agency is curtailed" (Grey and Shepherd 2013, 117; also see Grey 2014c).

An additionally important element of gender-just recognition, but less frequently discussed than the recognition of crimes, concerns *who is recognized* as having the right to speak and adjudicate in international law proceedings. Like other aspects of recognition, this "female voice" element is linked to representation. Whereas in Fraser's terms gender *representation* relates to who is eligible, and under what conditions individuals gain entry to a deliberative arena (see Chapter 3), gender recognition focuses on the extent to which, once inside these arenas, the contributions of individual women and gender experts are *valued and recognized as legitimate*—as interpreted by their peers, defendants, victims, and the wider community. From this perspective, recognition of the right and ability to adjudicate is separate from gender representation but could be considered as one of its outcomes.

Existing feminist scholarship in this area suggests that women judges and gender experts have suffered from a lack of legitimacy in courts at all levels, including internationally (Grossman 2012; Kenney 2012). Perceived to be disrupting the existing "gendered logic of appropriateness" (Chappell 2006b) or, in Fraser's terms, its androcentrism, such judges and prosecutors often face a backlash, especially where they use a "gender-sensitive" or feminist frame to read the law (Kenney 2012, Chapter 7). This opposition has taken various forms but most commonly is seen in challenges to these judges' and prosecutors' objectivity and through claims of judicial bias and partiality (Kenney 2012, 143). Reflecting on their efforts to bring issues of sexual violence and gender discrimination to the fore at the ICTY, both Patricia Viseur Sellers, Legal Advisor for Gender in the ICTY Prosecutor's Office, and Judge Odio Benito have spoken of a significant personal backlash, including the misrecognition of their efforts as biased and partial (Sharratt 1999; Vélez 2009; Viseur Sellers 2009, 311–312).

In her work on gender representation, feminist political theorist Anne Phillips tackles head on this question of impartiality and judging on gender justice issues. She acknowledges that these issues spark controversy because of the requirement for judges to act, and be seen to act, in ways that are above partial interests (1995, 186). The question posed by Phillips is: how should impartiality be conceived? The problem, in her view, is that impartiality is often interpreted as a "'view from nowhere' untouched by the experiences from which we have come" (1995, 186–187). Instead, she suggests impartiality should reflect "views from everywhere," which makes "securing diversity of the judiciary . . . as important as securing the diversity of the legislative assembly" (1995, 187). Phillips' view of impartiality not only is relevant to questions of *who* is represented on the bench but logically extends to the recognition of the *legitimacy* of the views espoused by those represented on the bench.

To summarize, androcentrism, reflected in a specific "gendered logic of appropriateness" (Chappell 2006b), works to create multiple forms of status misrecognition for women and other "depreciated" groups who lack equal standing, including within the boundaries of international law.

Tackling these forms of misrecognition requires targeted strategies across three areas: the codification of crimes that recognize women's and men's differential, gendered experiences of war and conflict; express measures to give voice to the victims of these crimes; and efforts to promote the legitimacy of women and gender experts, alongside men, in adjudicating these crimes. This next section illustrates gender justice advocacy strategies at the Rome Conference, especially their efforts to secure codification of crimes and to promote the legitimacy of women and gender expertise as key personnel at the Court.

PART TWO: DESIGNING RULES TO RECOGNIZE GENDER JUSTICE

The most detailed and time-consuming advocacy efforts of the Women's Caucus during the Rome Statute negotiations were directed toward the recognition of a range of sexual and gender-based crimes within the ICC's formal rules. These actors also sought other forms of statutory recognition, including protection against gender-based discrimination in the application and interpretation of the law and gender sensitivity in the investigation of crimes. Aligning with the Caucus's advocacy on victims' representation and reparation provisions, it argued for recognition of victims' rights throughout all the operations of the Court (for a full discussion see Chapters 3 and 5). Further, in relation to its priority to achieve representation of women and gender expertise in all ICC organs, the Caucus aimed to give these individuals capacity to "surface" the gender aspects of crimes (Copelon 2000). As with the Women's Caucus's representation and redistribution objectives, many of these recognition aims were met with strong contestation and resistance.

Recognition Negotiations

The Women's Caucus entered the Rome Statute negotiations with the aim of addressing the significant lacunae in international criminal law's coverage of sex and gender-based crimes. As discussed in detail in Chapter 2, existing formal codes either ignored the sexual and gender dimensions of international crimes altogether—such as the conventions on genocide and on torture[3]—or diminished their seriousness by categorizing them as acts related to "honour and dignity" rather than grave breaches of international law, as with the Geneva conventions (Charlesworth and Chinkin 2000; Gardam and Jarvis 2001; Steains 1999, 360).

At the ICTY and ICTR, the formal rules did not codify in any detail crimes of sexual violence. While rape was expressly recognized by the ICTY as a crime against humanity,[4] and by the ICTR as a war crime and as a crime against humanity,[5] both tribunals failed to recognize other forms of sexual violence (Steains 1999, 362). At these tribunals some prosecutors and judges attempted to address these gaps through expansive legal interpretation, resulting in some groundbreaking tribunal decisions recognizing rape as a form of genocide and as a form of torture. Given the nature of the law, these interpretations inevitably attracted controversy for being too radical (see Chappell et al. 2014; Pillay 2010). For instance, Justice Odio Benito's recognition of rape as a form of torture at the ICTY was widely criticized for overreach (Sharratt 1999). The decision of Judge Pillay and her colleagues at the ICTR in *Akayesu*[6]—recognizing rape and other forms of sexual violence as constituting acts of genocide[7]—was viewed by some as an example of "sentimentalism and high-handedness" (Sluiter and Zahar, 2008, xi). Nevertheless, these judgments were a spur to gender advocates in Rome, and alongside the 1993 Vienna World Conference on Human Rights and the 1995 Beijing Fourth World Conference on Women—established the "spatial nest" in which the Rome Statute negotiations were occurring. The concurrence of recent feminist-inspired judgments in these international criminal tribunals and the salience of the international women's rights agenda at this moment in time "gave the Women's Caucus authority for many of its proposals" during the Rome Statute negotiations (Bedont and Hall-Martinez 1999, 67; Spees 2003).

While these contextual factors gave gender justice actors a strong foundation from which to launch their campaign to engender the Rome Statute, it became obvious during the early stages of Statute negotiations that they had a significant struggle ahead. Signs emerged that the legacy of gender misrecognition in international law was being replicated while recent pioneering ad hoc tribunal gender justice jurisprudence developments were being forgotten (Bedont and Hall-Martinez 1999, 74; Steains 1999, 364). Indeed, a primary motivation for the establishment of the Women's Caucus was to respond to this "silencing" and "forgetting"; various feminist legal experts and NGOs aligned because they realized that "the draft statute was evolving into a document which ignored crimes of sexual violence and the lessons of the ICTY and ICTR"[8] (Steains 1999, 365). Coming together under the auspices of the Women's Caucus, and armed with detailed preparatory documents, their aim was to ensure that the core crimes within the jurisdiction of the court—genocide, war crimes, and crimes against humanity[9]—"encompass all possible situations and forms of gross and serious violations committed against women."[10]

Genocide

In relation to the crime of genocide, during the negotiation phase the Women's Caucus argued for two provisions: first, to have sexual violence recognized as a form of genocide[11] and second, for a wider range of groups to be recognized as potential targets for genocidal attack other than the national, ethnic, racial, and religious groups already listed. They called for the Court to also have "jurisdiction over genocide committed against political, gender-based and other social groups including those based on age, health status and disability."[12] In advancing this claim, the Caucus noted that genocidal crimes can be directed toward men and women "based on their perceived or actual gender role in society," such as where young men are targeted for killing to prevent them becoming soldiers, or sexual and reproductive violence against women is conducted to force them to give birth, such as in cases that had come before the ICTY.[13]

War Crimes

The Women's Caucus's interventions during negotiations on war crimes also concentrated on encouraging state delegates to "remember the new." The Caucus drew delegates' attention to the fact that the initial drafts of the Statute still conceived of rape and sexual violence only as an "affront to personal dignity" rather than "more serious crimes of violence,"[14] as had recently been recognized at the ICTY and ICTR. In line with these tribunal developments, it argued that the treatment of sexual violence should be made "consistent with existing customary international law, as violence as the gravest dimension"[15] and sought to have sexual and gender-based crimes included as an element of existing crimes, as well as included separately as freestanding crimes. Leading Caucus member Rhonda Copelon explained the Caucus's dualistic strategy:

> One [aim] was to codify explicitly a range of serious sexual violence crimes in order to ensure that they are always on the checklist and always understood as crimes in themselves. The second [aim] was to incorporate, as a principle, what had developed in the customary law and jurisprudence of the tribunals, that sexual violence must be seen as part of, and encompassed by, other recognized egregious forms of violence, such as torture, enslavement, genocide, and inhumane treatment (2000, 234).[16]

Copelon (2000, 234) went on to explain the rationale behind the approach:

> [D]espite all the public hand-wringing about rape, history teaches that there is an almost inevitable tendency for crimes that are seen ... primarily as crimes against women to be treated as of secondary importance. It makes a difference, to the elements that must be proved, to the penalty imposed, and to the larger cultural understanding of violence against women, to treat rape as torture rather than humiliation. So we need to insist, as a matter of the principle of non-discrimination, that sexual violence be treated as constituting any of the recognized crimes so long as it met their elements, at the same time as it [is] necessary to name the sexual violence crimes specifically.

While most of the central demands of the Women's Caucus to extend war crimes to encompass specific sexual and gender-based crimes were uncontentious, one area of significant opposition arose over the elaboration in the Statute of the crime of enforced pregnancy as a war crime. Caucus calls to include this crime antagonized a number of states and "pro-life" counterforces and, according to many commentators, were among the most difficult and drawn-out debates at the Rome Conference (see Bedont and Hall-Martinez 1999; Copelon 2000, 234; Glasius 2006, 89). The crime of enforced pregnancy typically occurs during armed conflicts between ethnic groups, where the soldiers from one side rape women from the opposing side until they are impregnated. To force them to carry the pregnancy to term, they are confined for the duration to prevent them from having an abortion. The intent of this crime is to produce children whose ethnicity will differ from that of the mother and her community, thereby diluting ethnic ties. By shaming and ostracizing the mother and child, the expectation is that enforced pregnancy will sever their community connection, with the ultimate goal of destroying the rival ethnic group. As witnesses had testified at both the ICTY and the ICTR, enforced pregnancy has become a commonly used weapon of war (see Boon 2001, 656–667). With these testimonies fresh in their mind, Women's Caucus members were determined to see this crime codified in the rules of the ICC.

As with the opposition to the inclusion of gender in the Statute (see Chapter 2), the strongest opposition to these measures came from the Holy See and attracted the support of several Catholic and Arab countries (Steains 1999, 366). The Holy See argued that the term "enforced" was ambiguous and that actions related to the confinement of a woman for the purpose of keeping her pregnant should be prosecuted under existing international law (Holy See 1998, 2). It also asserted that the term could be interpreted to mean denial of pregnancy termination (Holy See 1998, 2).

The Holy See, pro-life NGOs, and some states claimed that recognizing enforced pregnancy in the Statute could establish grounds for prosecuting states who failed to provide abortion on demand (Glasius 2006, 88–89; also see LifeSite 1998; REAL Women of Canada 1998). The Holy See argued that enforced pregnancy raised "the ironic prospect of making the enforcement of legitimate state and conventional law [against abortion] a 'war crime'" (Holy See 1998). Certain Arab States joined the move to obstruct the provision, not because of their opposition to abortion but due to a more general fear that criminalizing these acts could open the door to international intervention in domestic laws more generally, including interference with the applications of Shari'a law (see Organization of Islamic Conference 2000; Tohidi 2003; "Who's Obstructionist?" 1998). The Holy See and other "pro-family" groups were sympathetic to the position of these delegates, arguing that provisions such as enforced pregnancy were the start of a slippery slope toward "the abandonment of national sovereignty, and the establishment of a tyrannical world government" (Campaign Life Coalition 1998, quoted in Glasius 2006, 82).

Women's Caucus activists considered spurious the objections voiced by these religious and state contenders. They dismissed the Holy See's argument that enforced pregnancy was an "ambiguous construction," developed in the jurisprudence of the ICTY and ICTR. As they pointed out, some of the other crimes the Holy See had thought appropriate to prosecute had themselves only recently been developed through the same tribunals. In the view of the Women's Caucus this debate was in part an excuse to introduce the politics of abortion into the ICC agenda. As it noted at the time:

> It is difficult to understand how the debate about the crime of enforced pregnancy has become a debate about abortion. National laws which criminalize the termination of pregnancy are not violations under international law and thus would not come within the ICC's jurisdiction.[17]

Whether or not it was a deliberate tactic on the part of religious and anti-abortion groups, once abortion was on the agenda, the proceedings were considerably delayed. This case also demonstrated the ongoing contentious nature of, and strongly held opposition to, the recognition of certain gender justice elements under international law.

Crimes Against Humanity

The Caucus was equally active seeking recognition of gender and sexual violence in the Statute's crimes-against-humanity provisions. Noting the difficulty in demonstrating that acts of sexual violence meet the threshold of being part of a widespread *and* systematic attack, it argued for the separation of these elements into widespread *or* systematic; it also argued against a nexus between crimes against humanity and war, stating that these crimes "should be punishable when occurring in time of peace and against any population" and, in the case of persecution, "against an identifiable group."[18] It also argued that private as well as state actors should be held responsible for these crimes. This was particularly important because women "are most often the victims of non-state as opposed to state violence in civil society as well as war" (Copelon 2000, 235).

A key objective of the Women's Caucus's advocacy in regard to crimes against humanity was to add a gender dimension to the crime of persecution.[19] In its view, "the addition of 'gender' will ensure full attention to the gravity of gender-based persecution which has all too frequently escaped notice as well as condemnation in the past,"[20] including within the UN's *Convention Relating to the Status of Refugees*[21] (Bedont and Hall-Martinez 1999, 73). In explaining these crimes the Women's Caucus pointed to examples such as "when young boys are either killed to prevent their becoming soldiers" or when "women are coerced into domestic servitude or suffer grave violation of their fundamental rights because they are women, as well as when they are subjected to sexual and gender violence."[22] Recognizing recent developments in human rights law in relation to trafficking, the Caucus also pushed for these acts to be criminalized as an element of enslavement, including trafficking for forced sex, marriage, and labor.[23]

Other Recognition Provisions

Due to the historical exclusion of women and gender issues from international criminal law, the Caucus was alert to the need not only to criminalize specific acts under the Statute, but also to ensure that the ICC would apply and interpret the law in a manner consistent with internationally recognized human rights treaties—including the UN's *Convention on the Elimination of All Forms of Discrimination Against Women* (CEDAW) (1979) and the then recently formulated 1995 Beijing Platform for Action[24]—and be without adverse distinctions on a range of grounds, including gender. It argued that these steps were "particularly indispensable with respect to crimes of sexual and gender-based violence" and were "required by the international mandate to eliminate discrimination against women and end impunity for violence against women."[25]

The lobbying by the Women's Caucus on this provision also sparked resistance and controversy. Again, the Holy See and many of the same states involved in the enforced pregnancy issue resisted including gender in Article 21(3), directing the Court to interpret the Rome Statute in accordance with "internationally recognized human rights" and "without any adverse distinction founded on ground such as gender" among other grounds. Some state delegations were content to retain a human rights interpretation clause but to remove any reference to gender; others sought to remove the clause completely (Steains 1999, 372). Bedont and Hall-Martinez (1999, 69) noted the irony of the latter's position: "in their zeal to marginalize gender issues," this group of Catholic and Islamic delegates was also endangering "a clause that would also protect individuals from religious discrimination." Other states—Australia, Canada, the United States, the Netherlands, and France among them—supported the position of the Women's Caucus, pointing to the well-established recognition in a range of international rights documents of nondiscrimination on gender grounds (Steains 1999, 372). Intervention by these states meant that resistance "dissipated" in relation to this specific clause, but it did not end opposition to gender recognition. Rather, the anti-gender forces merely shifted their efforts toward working for the complete exclusion of a gender definition in the statute—as outlined in Chapter 2, an effort that ultimately resulted in a clarifying statement being added by conservative states about gender referring to "the two sexes," in an attempt to exclude the sociological understanding of the term proposed by gender justice advocates (Oosterveld 2014; Steains 1999, 372).

The Women's Caucus also paid attention to statutory provisions on general criminal law, especially recognizing different modes of liability. It called for the inclusion of a broad conception of liability that: extended to those who aid, abet, and otherwise assist in the commission of a crime; included individuals, especially leaders, who participated in or supported an organization that aims to commit crimes within the Court's jurisdiction; did not shield individuals who held an official position; and, following from the ad hoc tribunals, included command or preferably "superior responsibility."[26]

In its lobbying efforts, the Women's Caucus did not concentrate on linking the gender aspects of crimes to individual criminal responsibility. However, members were no doubt acutely aware from experiences at the ICTY and ICTR of the challenge of proving culpability of senior commanders for acts of sexual violence, especially proving superior knowledge of subordinates committing sexual violence (Jarvis and Salgado 2013, 107–108). As commentators have noted, this challenge arises from two gender legacies: first, a historical lack of understanding and recognition of the conditions under which sexual violence is prevalent or is likely to occur, and second, the absence of gender-sensitive investigation procedures to capture the evidence required to link commanders and other perpetrators to sexual violence (Jarvis and Salgado 2013, 111).

While the Caucus did not make specific arguments in relation to the vexed issue of how to gather the evidence necessary to prove a link between senior commanders and crimes of sexual and gender-based violence, it did advocate strongly during negotiations on other evidence-gathering matters. It argued that the Statute should require the Prosecutor to "implement special measures to ensure the effective investigation and prosecution of crimes, particularly crimes of sexual and gender-based violence and violence against children."[27] In making its case, the Caucus drew attention to gender legacies in this area:

> [t]he utter failure of the ICTR Prosecutor in the *Akayesu* case to effectively seek out and find testimony of sexual violence, which was, in fact, notorious, illustrates why this article is required. The problem [of lack of evidence] was rooted in attitudes about sexual violence, ignorance of legal standards, and disregard of the need to develop special methodologies of investigation.[28]

Alongside the call for these forms of recognition, the Women's Caucus also emphasized the need to further the legitimacy of women and especially gender experts in ICC decision-making (see Chapter 3). In lobbying at Rome, the Caucus's position aligned very closely with Anne Phillips' arguments on the need for inclusion of "views from everywhere" (1995, 187). The Caucus argued:

> The qualifications for the judges of the Court should be designed to produce a balance of diverse experience and expertise and should not include formalistic criteria which might tend to exclude women and other minorities whose career paths have been limited as a result of discrimination.[29]

It also argued for the importance of recognizing the value of gender experts, stating that "gender analysis is essential to the interpretation of international law, evaluation of the sufficiency of the charges or evidence, application of rules of procedure or evidence, and assessment of the credibility of, or protection of, witnesses."[30]

A defining feature of the Women's Caucus's advocacy for gender-just recognition in the Rome Statute was a drive to have state delegates "remember" existing legal standards, human rights norms, and recent ad hoc tribunal jurisprudence that already acknowledged an extensive array of women's rights and gender equality measures. Appeals to these developments appear to have helped their cause. As various first-hand observers noted, in the main, negotiations over most of the Caucus's priorities for the criminal jurisdiction of the ICC "proceeded smoothly, reflecting the widespread acceptance of the fact that the listing of these crimes was merely codifying the current state of international law" (Bedont and Hall-Martinez 1999; Steains 1999, 365). The two obvious exceptions, enforced pregnancy and the inclusion of gender as a grounds of discrimination, were "a sobering reminder of the unrelenting hostility of some States to women's rights," but gender advocates suggest this hostility "must not cloud our recognition of the significant support for criminalizing acts of sexual violence among both governmental and non-governmental participants in the Rome Diplomatic Conference" (Bedont and Hall-Martinez 1999, 74).

The ICC's Gender Recognition Rules

The gender justice recognition rules contained in the Rome Statute were a "major advance" and "significant departure" from anything found in existing international instruments (Steains 1999, 364). The members of the Women's Caucus had good reason to feel pleased with the effectiveness of their lobbying efforts. The draft statute to emerge from the December 1997 Preparatory Commission for the ICC "was substantially more comprehensive" (Glasius 2006, 88) on sexual and gender-based crimes than earlier iterations, with some sections mirroring "almost exactly the wording proposed by the Women's Caucus in their preparatory paper" (Steains 1999, 61). Similarly, the final document to emerge from Rome included many, though not all, of the Caucus's priorities.

Genocide was one area where the Caucus had only limited success. Under the Rome Statute, rape was not explicitly recognized as an act of genocide, nor did the Statute expand the groups against which genocide can occur, as recommended by the Caucus. According to Copelon (2000), as the Statute negotiations occurred immediately prior to the ICTR's *Akayesu* judgment of September 2, 1998—where rape was found to be an act of genocide—the negotiators had considered the definition settled. However, the influence of gender advocacy on genocide became more apparent during post-Rome negotiations over the ICC's Elements of Crimes Annex. Occurring after the pioneering ICTR decision, the Women's Caucus successfully pushed to include sexual violence as an element of genocide in the Annex. The Annex includes a note clarifying that in regard to "genocide by causing serious bodily injury or mental harm" the conduct may include "acts of torture, rape, sexual violence or inhuman or degrading treatment."[31]

Both the category of war crimes and crimes against humanity encoded many of the gender justice elements that were the focus of Caucus lobbying. Under the war crimes provisions, which cover international and noninternational conflict, the Rome Statute includes, under Article 8(2)(b)(xxii): "Rape, sexual slavery, enforced prostitution, forced pregnancy, ... enforced sterilization, and any other form of sexual violence also constituting a grave breach of the Geneva Conventions" (also see Article 8(2)(e)(vi)).

The enumeration of such a broad array of sexual violence crimes takes the Rome Statute much farther than the mandates of either the ICTY or ICTR. The language used in the Rome Statute war crimes provisions makes it clear that the enumerated crimes are crimes of the gravest nature. The clarification "or any other form of sexual violence also constituting a grave breach of the Geneva Conventions" is "a signal that acts of sexual violence can be charged as sexual violence crimes *or* as the other grave breaches crimes ... such as murder, torture, mutilation, enslavement" (Bedont and Hall-Martinez 1999, 72, emphasis added). These qualifications give the ICC capacity to prosecute sexual violence crimes in multiple ways, in line with Women's Caucus's dual-purpose priorities.

The Women's Caucus's further interventions during the negotiations over the Elements of Crimes Annex also saw states codify an expanded definition of the crime of rape, in line with recent ad hoc tribunal jurisprudence.[32] As Pam Spees, one of the Women's Caucus negotiators, explained, after much pressure state delegates agreed to a definition in the Annex that maintains "a focus of the acts of the perpetrator and not on the victim—that is, a victim's lack of consent is not part of the elements, but, rather, the perpetrator's violation of a victim's sexual autonomy is emphasized" (2003, 1241).

The compromise reached over the contentious enforced pregnancy debate was resolved in the Statute through the use of the language of "forced" pregnancy under the war crimes and crimes-against-humanity provisions. Article 7(2)(f) defines the crime as "the unlawful confinement of a women forcibly made pregnant, with the intent of affecting the ethnic composition of any population or carrying out other grave violations of international law." However, it came with a "rather curious" (Steains 1999, 368) caveat: "This definition shall not in any way be interpreted as affecting national laws related to pregnancy," a sentence that "was clearly inserted to protect the anti-abortion laws of the objecting countries" (Glasius

2006, 89; also see Steains 1999). The Caucus members could claim qualified success with these provisions—they had achieved their main goal of codifying the violation for the first time under international law—but they were obliged to compromise and accept the inclusion of the interpretive clause (Facio 1999).

Aside from the recognition of the sexual and gender elements of these crimes, the crimes-against-humanity provisions include gender alongside political, racial, religious, and other such categories as a ground for persecution (Article 7(1)(h)). This was a first under international law. Other crimes-against-humanity articles also reflect the Women's Caucus's preferred position. Copelon summarizes it: "As an overarching matter, the *chapeau* [opening explanatory statement] to crimes against humanity provisions recognizes that crimes of this dimension can be perpetrated against any civilian population, in time of peace as well as war, and by private as well as state actors" (2000, 235) and, in line with Caucus priorities, need to be part of a widespread *or* systematic attack.[33]

Importantly, after facing such strong resistance, Article 21(3) prohibits discrimination based on gender in the application and interpretation of the Statute. This provision places a positive obligation on prosecutors and judges to "ensure that in applying and interpreting the law, factors historically utilised to discriminate against groups and identities of people, such as gender, age, race, colour, sexual orientation and social origin, are dismantled in favour of inclusive justice" (Bedont and Hall-Martinez 1999, 69; also see Chappell and Inder 2014, 662).

The Women's Caucus's priority for the recognition of wide-ranging modes of liability is covered in Part III of the Statute. Under Article 25, the Statute recognizes that individuals are responsible individually or jointly for committing a crime if they order or solicit or induce the commission (or attempted commission) of a crime, or aid, abet or otherwise assist in the commission of a crime or attempted crime. The Caucus's efforts to ensure that the Prosecutor undertakes gender-sensitive investigations are reflected in Article 54(1)(b). Under this provision the Prosecutor is charged with investigating and prosecuting crimes in a way that "respect[s] the interests and personal circumstances of victims and witnesses, including . . . gender" and is also required to "take into account the nature of the crime, in particular where it involves sexual violence, gender violence or violence against children."

As noted in the previous chapter, the Statute also came with provisions for the representation of women and of gender experts under Article 36, relating to the appointment of judges, and Articles 42 and 43, in terms of the appointment of personnel with gender expertise in the OTP and

Registry. The Caucus's aim to ensure that the views of these experts were accepted and reflected in ICC decisions was to be a matter of implementation. The formal rules were in place; the recognition of the legitimacy of the actors to use these rules was yet to be tested.

At the end of the Rome Statute negotiation process the members of the Women's Caucus had good reason to be pleased with their influence on its gender justice recognition elements. It had helped to encourage state delegations to "forget the old" and "remember the new" in the design of the ICC by inserting provisions into the Statute that reflected the most recent jurisprudence stemming from the UN ad hoc tribunals and from developments in women's rights internationally, including outcomes of the Beijing Women's Rights agenda. Skirmishes over the recognition of the crimes of gender persecution and over enforced pregnancy during negotiations reminded these actors of the ongoing contention of their claims and the long road ahead in gaining universal acceptance of gender equality under the law. However, Caucus members' persistence in demonstrating to states the need for and the legitimacy of gender justice measures meant that the foundational rules of the ICC were the most advanced ever under international law in terms of their recognition of gender justice principles. As with all legal instruments, these recognition provisions incorporated a degree of "constructive ambiguity"; whether the gender justice principles were "locked in" in practice now depended on whether prosecutors, judges, and other court personnel displayed sensitivity to these principles when interpreting the Rome Statute.

PART THREE: REMEMBERING AND FORGETTING TO RECOGNIZE GENDER JUSTICE AT THE ICC

The real value of the Rome Statute's encoded recognition elements can only be realized through their implementation. As this section illustrates, it has been a major struggle to have these provisions enacted via investigation, prosecution, and interpretation. Despite having strong rules in place, and constant vigilance on the part of external gender justice advocates and some key internal personnel, there is much evidence that ICC personnel in the OTP and on the bench have forgotten the new rules and reverted to old, informal rules and practices. As a result, the predominant path of the ICC's early years has been toward gender *mis*recognition and ongoing gender status subordination.

This section commences with an overview of the ICC's implementation of the Rome Statute's expansive gender justice criminal base. It first identifies the overarching trends in the prosecution and charging strategy of the OTP and judicial decisions in the ICC's early years, which have been marred by serious instances of *misrecognition*. It then puts these trends into context by considering key developments in four of the Court's early cases—*Prosecutor v. Thomas Lubanga Dyilo (Lubanga), Prosecutor v. Jean-Pierre Bemba Gombo (Bemba), Prosecutor v. Germain Katanga (Katanga)*, and *Prosecutor v. Callixte Mbarushimana (Mbarushimana)*; each highlights different recognition issues. As the first completed trial, *Lubanga* is given the most detailed treatment, highlighting missteps by the OTP and Judiciary, as well as the lack of recognition of the legitimacy of feminist-inspired voices at the ICC. The discussion on *Bemba* highlights problems with the bench in recognizing gender justice principles, while the *Katanga* and *Mbarushimana* discussion shows the ongoing weaknesses in the OTP's approach to addressing sexual and gender crimes. Finally, this section discusses recognition of the treatment of sexual violence against men and the issuing of the first arrest warrant for an alleged female perpetrator.

Prosecuting Gender and Sexual Crimes at the ICC: A Story of Misrecognition?

In the ICC's early years there have been some small signs that issues of gender justice have been better recognized under international law, but as shown in Figure 4.1, the period has primarily been marked by gender status misrecognition being carried over into ICC prosecutions. This misrecognition—which reflects the temporal nestedness of the ICC and the influence of gender legacies of international law—has, as the following discussion illustrates, been reflected in the decisions of different ICC actors at each stage of proceedings: from investigations and charging, which are the core responsibility of the OTP, through to the Pre-Trial, Trial, and Appeals Chamber decisions, involving judicial interpretation of the Statute and evidence.

Reflecting concerns of the Women's Initiatives on the vulnerability of charges of sexual and gender-based violence at the ICC,[34] Rosemary Grey (2015) has undertaken detailed analysis of prosecutorial discretion. Her work has illuminated some distinct patterns in the ICC's sexual and gender-based crime prosecution history. The first pattern (see Fig. 4.1) concerns the falloff of charges during the course of proceedings. Between 2002 and July 2014, the OTP brought fifty-seven charges of sexual and gender-based violence in the twenty cases in which it had applied for an arrest warrant or summons to appear. The Pre-Trial Chamber included

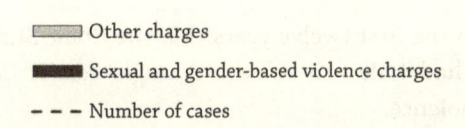

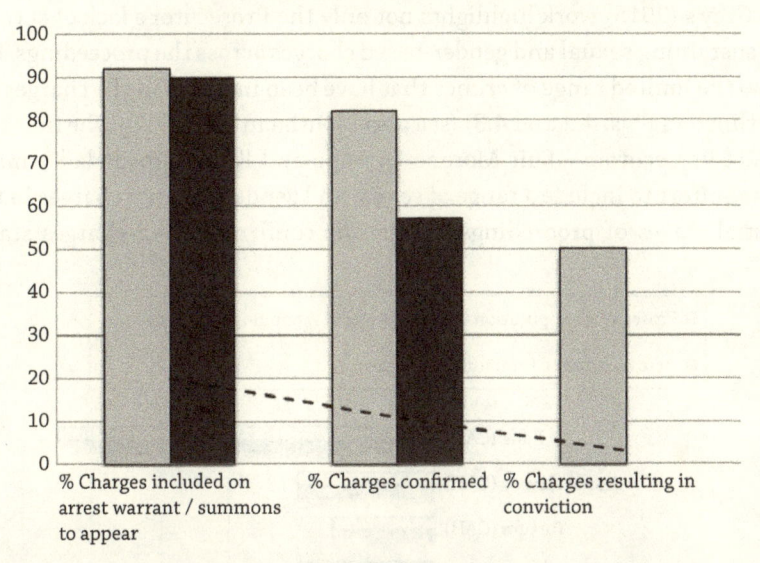

Figure 4.1:
Percentage of successful sexual and gender-based violence charges and other charges at different stages of proceedings, as of July 1, 2014.

fifty-one of these fifty-seven charges of sexual and gender-based violence on the arrest warrant or summons to appear. Of the eleven cases where the Pre-Trial Chamber has issued a decision on the confirmation of charges, the Prosecutor had applied for the confirmation of thirty-five sexual and gender-based crimes, with the Pre-Trial Chamber confirming twenty of these.[35] By early 2014 the Trial Chamber had issued a judgment in three cases, each concerning the situation in the Democratic Republic of Congo, where conflict-related sexual violence is known to be endemic[36] (HRW 2014b). Two of these cases (which were initially joined but were severed in the latter stages of the trial), *Prosecutor v. Mathieu Ngudjolo Chui (Ngudjolo) and Katanga*, included charges, *inter alia*, of rape and of sexual slavery as crimes against humanity and as war crimes.[37] In December 2012, Ngudjolo was acquitted of all charges.[38] In March 2014, Katanga was found guilty of committing a range of crimes but, as detailed below, was acquitted in relation to charges of rape, sexual slavery, and using children to participate actively in hostilities.[39] In the ICC's first case against Lubanga, the accused was convicted on child soldier charges, but no charges of sexual and gender crimes were brought (see details below). To put it starkly, in the first twelve years that the Rome Statute had been in force, the ICC had failed to achieve a single conviction for sexual or gender-based violence.

Grey's (2015) work highlights not only the Prosecutor's lack of success in sustaining sexual and gender-based charges across the proceedings, but also the limited range of crimes that have been included in the charges (as outlined in Figs. 4.2 and 4.3) (see also Mouthaan 2011, 793). The first two Chief Prosecutors—Luis Moreno Ocampo and Fatou Bensouda[40]—made some effort to include a range of sexual and gender violence charges in the initial stages of proceedings, but by the confirmation-of-charges stage,

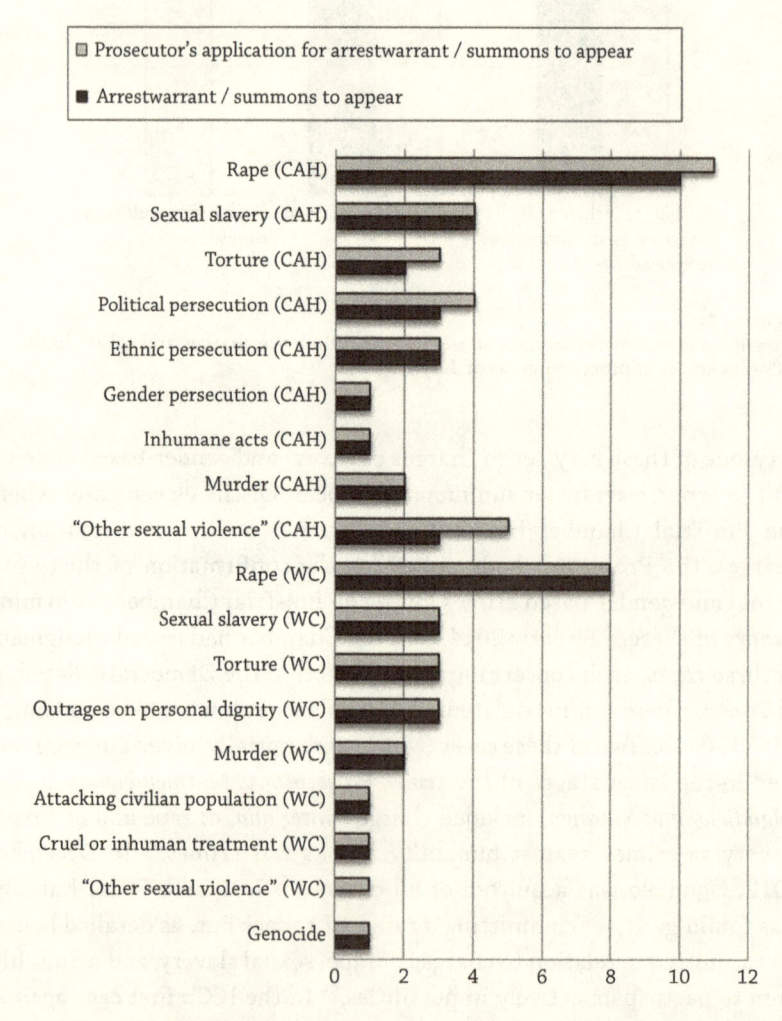

Figure 4.2:
Number of sexual and gender-based violence charges at "arrest warrant/summons to appear" stage as of July 1, 2014.

[106] *The Politics of Gender Justice at the ICC*

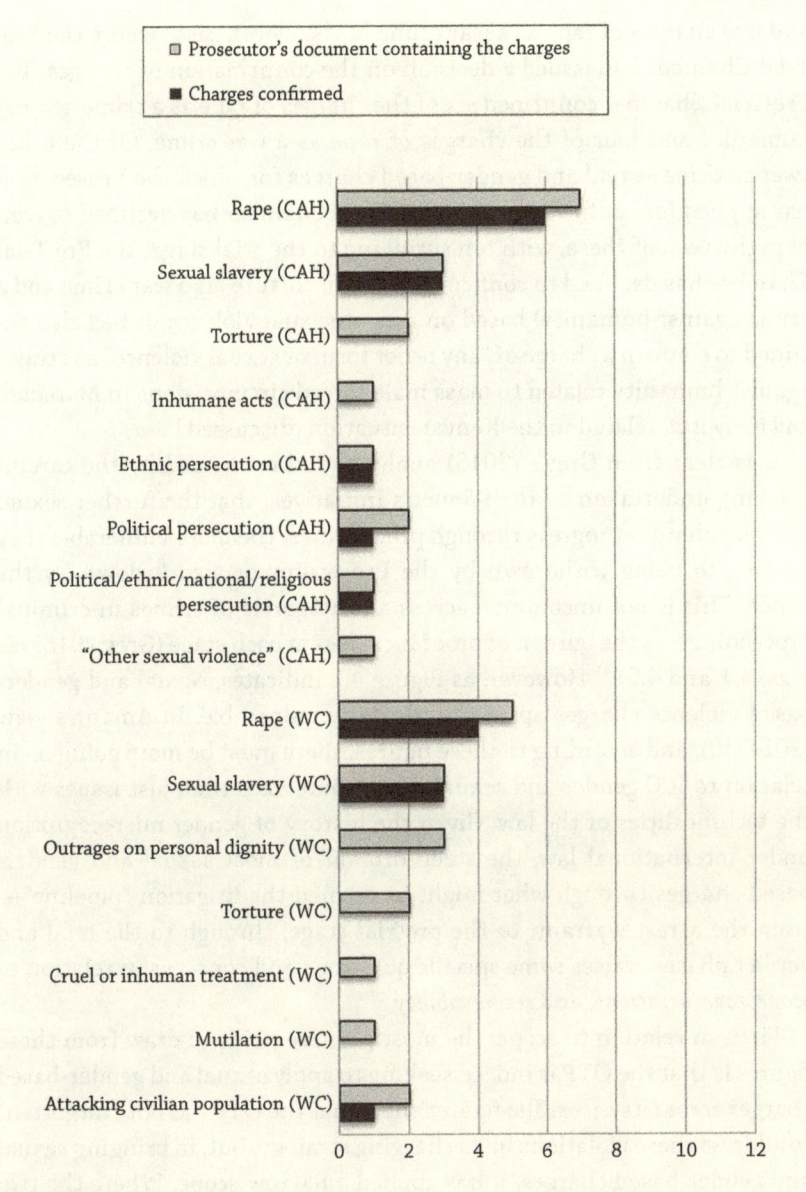

Figure 4.3:
Number of sexual and gender-based violence charges at "confirmation of charges" stage as of July 1, 2014.

many of these have fallen away. As of December, 2014, neither Prosecutor had applied for confirmation of a charge of persecution on gender grounds. Rape—both as a war crime and as a crime against humanity—has been the most common sexual violence charge brought by the OTP at the confirmation stage, with seven charges of rape as a crime against humanity and five charges of rape as a war crime in the eleven cases where the Pre-Trial Chamber had issued a decision on the confirmation of charges. The Pre-Trial Chamber confirmed six of the charges of rape as a crime against humanity and four of the charges of rape as a war crime. Of the other twenty-three sexual and gender-based charges for which the Prosecution has applied for confirmation, the Pre-Trial Chamber has declined to confirm thirteen of these, with ten surviving to the trial stage. The Pre-Trial Chamber has declined to confirm charges of torture (as a war crime and a crime against humanity) based on acts of sexual violence. It has also declined to confirm a charge of "any other form of sexual violence" as crimes against humanity related to mass male forced circumcisions in *Muthaura and Kenyatta*, related to the Kenyan situation (discussed later).

It is clear from Grey's (2015) analysis, and confirmed by the careful tracking undertaken by the Women's Initiatives, that the further sexual violence charges progress through proceedings, the more vulnerable they become to being withdrawn by the Prosecutor or struck down by the bench. This is not uncommon across all categories of crimes in criminal proceedings, as the burden of proof increases at each stage (Grey 2015; see Figs. 4.1 and 4.2).[41] However, as Figure 4.1 indicates, sexual and gender-based violence charges appear particularly vulnerable. In Amann's view (2014, 10), and according to these figures, there must be more going on in relation to ICC gender and sexual crimes outcomes than just issues with the technicalities of the law. Given the history of gender misrecognition under international law, the steep dropoff of most sexual and gender-based charges through what might be termed the litigation "pipeline"—from the arrest warrant, to the pretrial stage, through to the trial and verdict phase—raises some specific questions and concerns in relation to *scope, reverberations*, and *responsibility*.[42]

First, in relation to scope: the most positive point to draw from these figures is that the OTP is indeed seeking to apply sexual and gender-based charges across its cases. The figures show that the OTP has not "forgotten" to address these violations in its charging strategy. But, in bringing sexual and gender-based charges, it has applied a narrow scope. Where the two Prosecutors have paid attention to sexual and gender-based crimes, they have focused on violations that have become more commonly prosecuted in other international criminal tribunals, primarily the crime of rape, with few attempts, and little success, in pursuing the full array of sexual and gender-based crimes available under the Rome Statute. This includes the newly established crimes of gender persecution, where charges have not progressed past the arrest warrant approval stage (see Grey 2015, Chapter 7). Further, while the OTP has attempted to "mainstream" sexual and gender-based violence by prosecuting such violence as genocide, torture, inhumane acts, and so forth, these attempts have been largely unsuccessful (Grey 2015, Chapter 7). Nor has there been a concerted effort to undertake focused, thematic sexual and gender-based violence prosecutions that, as some have suggested, would be useful to highlight the specific nature of these crimes.[43] The dual-pronged approach envisaged by the Women's Caucus, and provided for under the Statute, of the Prosecutor bringing sexual and gender-based violence charges *both* as freestanding crimes and as a feature of other crimes has, in the early years at least, largely failed to eventuate.

The absence of a successful ICC prosecution of any sexual or gender-based violations has reverberated in a range of ways. Importantly, it has left untouched problems of ongoing impunity and lack of accountability for sexual violence and gender-based violations that have been an ongoing feature of international law (Amann 2014, 10); women and victims of sexual violence are still suffering status subordination, despite the new formal rules of the Rome Statute (Chappell 2014). Materially, prosecution failures potentially interfere with the victims of these crimes gaining access to the ICC's reparations regime. As discussed in Chapter 5, a failure to sustain sexual violence and gender-based violence charges through to the verdict stage may pose serious limitations for the recognition of the victims of these crimes at the reparations stage of proceedings, further reinforcing or even worsening their subordinate status in postconflict settings.

Much of the analysis of the ICC's poor record in regard to the prosecution of sexual and gender-based violence has been laid at the door of the Prosecutor, especially of the first Prosecutor, Luis Moreno Ocampo. Reviews of Ocampo's tenure have been withering, including claims he "abused his discretion" in *Lubanga* (see Smith 2011, 500; also see Pritchett 2008). Niamh Hayes' (2013, 9) comment encapsulates a common view:

> Unfortunately, in the decade since [the Rome Statute came into force] the rock which had been painstakingly hauled up the hill by prosecutors and practitioners in the other international criminal tribunals was permitted to tumble back to square one, as the International Criminal Court under (first Prosecutor) Luis Moreno Ocampo regressed in both strategy and practice and competent, focused prosecutions of sexual violence became depressingly scarce once again.

Using more measured tones, Solange Mouthann (2011) argues that under Ocampo the OTP had not learned lessons from other tribunals, resulting in the carryover to the ICC of past prejudices, inadequate investigation and evidence-gathering processes, and weak case strategies.

Two specific legacies appear to have been particularly influential. The first is what could be called the "mode of liability challenge," linking senior officers, who are the central targets of ICC prosecutions, to crimes of sexual violence[44] (Grey 2015). The second relates to a more general problem, outlined in detail below, of the quality of the evidence provided by the OTP to the Chambers.

Despite strong criticism of the Prosecutor from both within and without the Court, it would be unfair to cast all criticism for the ICC's poor sexual violence prosecution in that direction. As the following detailed case studies illustrate, the bench must also take some responsibility. It seems that judges, especially at the pretrial phase, either have "forgotten" existing international law developments or are unaccustomed or uncomfortable with applying the expansive gender recognition rules. Notably, judges have been reluctant to apply Article 21(3) relating to "no adverse distinction founded on gender" in their adjudication. Combined, these limitations have contributed to the obstruction of successful sexual and gender-based violence prosecutions at the ICC.[45]

Misrecognition in *Lubanga*

Lubanga is an archetypal example of the problem of "forgetting the new" and "remembering the old" by a number of key ICC actors, leading to a reinforcement of gender *mis*recognition under international law.[46] A sketch of the details of the case is followed by a brief discussion of the main gender justice misrecognition developments of the trial.

In March 2006, Lubanga was arrested, having been identified as commander in chief of the Forces Patriotiques pour La Libération du Congo (UPC/FPLC) involved in the conflict in the Ituri region of the Democratic Republic of Congo. He was charged with the crimes of the enlistment and conscription of children under the age of fifteen years and using children to participate actively in hostilities. It took the Court six years from the time of Lubanga's arrest to hand down a verdict, finding the accused guilty on all counts. On July 10, 2012, Lubanga received a fourteen-year sentence, including time he had already spent in detention. A month later, the bench handed down its decision on the principles and procedures to be applied to reparations in the case (discussed in Chapter 5). Both the defense and prosecution appealed aspects of the trial chamber's decisions. On December 1, 2014, the Appeals Chamber upheld the verdict and sentencing decisions but left aside the reparations appeal, which was eventually handed down in March 2015.[47]

Prosecutor Ocampo was responsible for the first instance of gender misrecognition in this case when, having initially publically committed to "investigate *all* crimes related to the situation [in the Democratic Republic of Congo] in an impartial way,"[48] he decided to charge Lubanga with only a narrow range of charges. Lubanga was indicted for child soldier war crimes but not sexual violence violations, which were known by the Prosecutor to be pervasive in this conflict (Chappell 2014). When first questioned about the lack of attention to sexual crimes the Prosecutor initially stated that he lacked the time and the evidence to link Lubanga to other crimes (Yates 2009); as time progressed, Ocampo also suggested that the crimes did not meet the crimes-against-humanity threshold test of being "systematic."[49] At the time of Lubanga's arrest, the Prosecutor committed to continuing the investigation into other crimes as allowed under Article 61.[50] Later, in June 2006, the Prosecutor withdrew this commitment, stating he had "temporarily suspended" further investigation into additional charges and had no intention of amending the charges during the proceedings.[51] This was despite the fact that, under Article 61(9), the Prosecutor had from the time of the confirmation of charges in January 2007 to the commencement of the trial in January 2009 to investigate crimes of sexual and gender-based violence and seek permission from the Pre-Trial Chamber to amend the charges, but he declined to do so.

Gender justice actors, including those from Amnesty International, REDRESS, and especially the Women's Initiatives, continued to press the Prosecutor before and during proceedings to remember the expansive gender justice mandate in the Rome Statute and consider applying it in this case. The Women's Initiatives sought to support the Prosecutor's investigations, including undertaking interviews with thirty-one eyewitnesses. According to Women's Initiatives Director Brigid Inder, these interviews showed "that sexual violence appeared to be an integral component of the attacks against the civilian population." The interviews gave the Women's Initiatives "material suggesting a pattern of rape, abduction, sexual slavery and torture by Lubanga's militia, and confirmed that women victims/survivors were willing to be interviewed by the ICC" (Inder 2011, n.p.). On the basis of this information, the Women's Initiatives prepared a dossier for the OTP demonstrating the systematic nature of these crimes. In a 2012 interview, Inder recollected a 2006 meeting with the Prosecutor's office to discuss the charges:

> They [the prosecutor's office] didn't believe there was a pattern or a policy [of sexual violence] . . . Yes, they conceded those crimes were being committed or appeared to be being committed by individual units of the UPC but it wasn't a

policy, it wasn't systemic. And we said, "Well, how many errant militia units do you need before it is systemic? . . . You still have time to open investigations into this, in your ongoing investigations you could be prioritising this." But they didn't intend to and said no, they would not be amending their arrest warrant.

After this initial rejection by the OTP, the Women's Initiatives sought to intervene via another route. During the pretrial confirmation-of-charges proceedings, it attempted to use the Statute's *amicus curiae* provisions (for which the Women's Caucus advocated during negotiations, outlined in Chapter 3). The Women's Initiatives made a request that the Pre-Trial Chamber review the Prosecutor's exercise of discretion in relation to the selection of charges and determine whether broader charges could be considered as provided under Article 61(7).[52] In a case of the bench "forgetting" the broad provisions under the Statute enabling the grounds for such intervention, including Article 21's clause of no adverse distinction based on gender, the Pre-Trial Chamber rejected the Women's Initiatives's submission on technical grounds, preventing the organization from presenting its case.[53]

During the trial, various parties attempted to address the original misrecognition of sexual and gender-based violence. In May 2009, the victims' legal representatives filed an application to have the facts recharacterized under Regulation 55 to include charges of sexual slavery and cruel and inhuman treatment. This application was accepted by Trial Chamber judges Odio Benito and Blattmann in the majority but overturned on appeal.[54] The appeal created "a legal impediment to the consideration of the evidence of sexual violence in the *Lubanga* case which in the event tied the hands of the Trial Chamber at both the judgment and the sentencing stage" (Jørgensen 2012, 665). A consequence of this decision was the erasure of "the distinctively female face of the devastating war in the DRC" (Merope 2011, 32).

These setbacks did not deter the Women's Initiatives and other gender activists from advocating on the issue throughout the trial, including in their annual *Gender Report Card* publications, press releases, and interventions with ICC personnel.[55] Judge Odio Benito also played a role from the bench. Through her questioning of prosecution and Court witnesses, including expert witness Radhika Coomaraswamy, UN Special Representative for Children and Armed Conflict,[56] Judge Odio Benito was able to draw out evidence about the different treatment of boy and girl soldiers in the Democratic Republic of Congo conflict and the explicit sexual and gender-based nature of these experience. This questioning was persistent and detailed: of Judge Odio Benito's 133 questions to prosecution witnesses, 107 related to sexual violence and the presence of women and girls in the armed forces.[57]

In line with, or perhaps in response to, this advocacy during the trial, the Prosecution also changed tack and sought to bring to the fore the sexual and gender-based dimensions of the child soldier crimes. In his opening statement, the Prosecutor drew attention to the fact that young girls were daily victims of rape by their commanders[58] and sexual violence was a feature of their experiences as girl soldiers[59] (Jørgensen 2012, 665). The Prosecutor's closing brief called on the Chamber to interpret "active participation" of child soldiers broadly so as to include the recruitment of girls for sexual purposes and forced marriage. Prosecutor Ocampo encouraged the judges to be mindful of this characterization in making decisions at the sentencing and reparations stages.[60]

The Prosecutor's effort to address the initial misrecognition was a case of "too little, too late." The Trial Chamber expressed frustration with the Prosecutor's strategy of not having included sexual violence charges but seeking to incorporate evidence during the trial of these crimes in relation to child soldiers.[61] Kai Ambos was one of many academic commentators who agreed with the majority, criticizing the Prosecutor for trying to "squeeze the sex crimes" into the crime of using child soldiers "instead of requesting an amendment of the charges" before the commencement of the trial (2012, fn 156, 138).

The Trial Chamber's frustration with the Prosecution's strategy on sexual violence was reflected in its verdict and sentencing decisions. In March 2012, the three-member bench was unanimous in finding the accused guilty on all three counts—conscripting, enlisting, and using child soldiers in the Ituri conflict,[62] with Judge Odio Benito submitting a dissenting opinion (discussed below). The majority verdict decision by Judges Fulford and Blattmann found "that children, mainly girls, were used by UPC/FPLC commanders to carry out domestic work" and that "girl soldiers were subjected to sexual violence and rape." However, the majority determined that because "[s]exual violence does not form part of the charges against the accused and the Chamber has not made any findings of fact on the issue, particularly as to whether responsibility is to be attributed to the accused" it could not include consideration of these acts in the verdict.[63]

In the *Lubanga* sentencing decision handed down on July 10, 2012, the Chamber was again forthright in its criticism of the Prosecutor's treatment of sexual violence. It stated it "strongly deprecates the attitude of the former Prosecutor [Ocampo] in relation to the issue of sexual violence," criticizing him for failing to include charges of sexual violence at any stage of the proceedings while still attempting to suggest "that sexual violence ought to be considered for the purposes of sentencing."[64] After assessing the prosecution and defense arguments, Judges Fulford and Blattmann in the majority argued that the Prosecution had not demonstrated that sexual violence against girl soldiers was "sufficiently widespread" or that Lubanga had "ordered or encouraged sexual violence, that he was aware of it or that it could otherwise be attributed to him in a way that reflects his culpability."[65] The majority ruled that as a result of insufficient evidence linking Lubanga to sexual violence beyond a reasonable doubt, it could not reflect on these crimes in its sentencing decision.[66] It did however leave the door open for considering these crimes in the reparations ruling. As discussed in Chapter 5, the full bench adopted an inclusive approach to victims of sexual and gender-based crimes in its reparations principles, only to have these overturned on appeal.

(Mis)recognition of the Legitimacy of Gender Expertise

Gender justice advocates monitoring *Lubanga* were clearly disappointed that the Chamber did not take the opportunity to use the evidence on sexual violence that emerged at the trial to advance jurisprudence on the issue.[67] The majority decisions on the verdict and sentencing served to compound the misrecognition of the Prosecutor from the start of the case. However, these actors were given an element of satisfaction with Judge Odio Benito's dissenting judgment and sentencing decisions. In her dissent, Judge Odio Benito argued that the Prosecutor was right to see sexual violence as "embedded in the crimes of which Mr. Lubanga is accused"[68] and that it is as "an intrinsic element of the criminal conduct of 'use to participate actively in the hostilities'."[69] Relying on Article 21(3), the no adverse distinction based on gender clause, as the foundation for her interpretation of the Statute (Grey 2014a),[70] the Judge argued: "it is discriminatory to exclude sexual violence which shows a clear gender differential impact from being a bodyguard or porter which is mainly a task given to young boys. The use of young girls and boys bodies by combatants within or outside the group is a war crime and as such encoded in the charges against the accused."[71] Nevertheless, Judge Odio Benito did reproach the Prosecutor, arguing that crimes of sexual violence could have been evaluated separately had the Prosecution included them in the charges.[72] In her sentencing judgment, Judge Odio Benito again "strongly disagree[d] with the Majority of the Chamber that disregards the damage caused to the victims and their families, particularly as a result of the harsh punishments and sexual violence suffered by the victims."[73] In her view, even though Lubanga might not have deliberately discriminated against women, his crimes nevertheless resulted in this effect and should therefore have been taken into account in sentencing.[74]

Throughout the trial and in these judgments, Judge Odio Benito demonstrated a concern to make visible aspects of the crimes experienced by girls that were not otherwise acknowledged.[75] In doing so, this judge was undertaking the role envisioned by gender justice negotiators at Rome: she was applying the broad anti–gender discrimination clause of the Statute to "surface" the gender dimensions of crimes that were otherwise ignored. Judge Odio Benito (Chappell et al. 2014, 650) has been forthright about her responsibility in this regard:

> The Rome Statute created, at least in writing, an inclusive gender-sensitive system whose goals, among others, are to put an end to impunity for the most serious crimes (which sexual violence crimes are), to recognize the rights of victims to participate and to receive reparations. It is impossible to do so without a precise gender perspective. A careful reading of the Preamble spells out these principles and, as a judge, I followed them and also upheld Article 21 of the Statute.

In line with the expectations of gender justice advocates and with existing feminist theory on gender recognition, Odio Benito's gender justice interventions have been contentious. The judge has been the subject of backlash and contestation, which has, predictably, come in the form of attacks on her judicial capacity and impartiality. This was first evident in early 2010 when, referring specifically to her line of questioning of witnesses on sexual violence, the defense called for a determination from the bench about the appropriateness of her interventions. The defense viewed her questions as straying "outside the scope of the charges," seriously affecting her "appearance of impartiality"[76] because they were "demonstrating the Judge's own opinion."[77] Judge Odio Benito, along with Judge Blattmann, also received criticism from ICC commentators in relation to their decision on the recharacterization of the charges to incorporate sexual slavery as an attempt to bring sexual violence "in through the back door" (Jacobs 2012).[78] According to the Women's Initiatives members who were closely monitoring the trial, the litigation, which arose from Judge Odio Benito's questions about sexual violence and on the recharacterization of the charges, had a "chilling" effect on the trial. In its view, after this litigation "Trial Chamber I subsequently appeared to take a more restrictive approach to hearing questions on gender-based crimes posed by the Prosecution."[79]

Clearly these critiques did not deter Judge Odio Benito from continuing to apply a gender lens to the proceedings, including in her dissenting opinions at the verdict and sentencing stage. Here again her position attracted negative commentary. While supportive of an inclusive approach to crimes of sexual violence, Kai Ambos criticized her for overstepping the mark in this case. In his view, the dissent "appears rather as a policy speech for certain constituencies in the NGO community than a strict judicial analysis" (Ambos 2012, fn 156, 138) and also contravened Article 22, which stipulates that definitions of crimes need to be "strictly construed." In a similar vein, Jacobs argued that Judge Odio Benito's dissenting opinions reflected "the latest trend of international decisions [which] is to have a strong dissent from a Latin American Judge trying to push a human rights agenda" (Jacobs 2012).

These challenges to the legitimacy of Judge Odio Benito's position highlight the ongoing contested nature of gender justice claims at the ICC. However, her position and the broader efforts of gender justice advocates also leave a positive gender justice legacy. As a result of *Lubanga*, Prosecutor Bensouda has stated that the OTP took note "of the reactions of civil society and their preference for these [sexual and gender-based violence] aspects to be explicitly charged" (Bensouda 2014, 540). Immediately after the *Lubanga* sentencing decision was handed down in July 2012, Prosecutor Moreno Ocampo sought a second warrant of arrest for an alleged collaborator of Lubanga, Bosco Ntaganda,[80] which included sexual violence charges as war crimes and crimes against humanity. Prosecutor Bensouda added further sexual violence charges against Ntaganda in January 2014, including sexual violence against child soldiers. These latter charges reflected the position of Judge Odio Benito in *Lubanga* to the extent that they challenged the longstanding view of international humanitarian law that war crimes can only be committed against opponents in a conflict and not against members of the "same side," including the sexual exploitation of child soldiers by their commanders (see Grey 2014a; Grey 2014b). The Pre-Trial Chamber confirmed these charges in *Ntaganda* in June 2014.[81]

Lubanga highlights the influence of gender legacies of international law—a failure to recognize gender and sexual violence as grievous acts, and inadequate investigation and evidence-gathering procedures (Chappell 2014). Both of these legacies operated to frustrate the implementation of the Rome Statute's gender justice recognition provisions. This case has also demonstrated the efforts of gender justice actors to correct ongoing misrecognition and the results of these efforts—they produced backlash, but also some important lesson drawing and revision. *Lubanga* is not the only case where new formal rules have collided with old gender norms to produce mixed outcomes. The following discussion briefly sketches instances of gender justice misrecognition in three other ICC cases: the long-running trial against Jean Pierre Bemba, the verdict against Germain Katanga, and the collapse of charges against Callixte Mbarushimana.

Prosecutor v. Jean-Pierre Bemba Gombo

The protracted case against Bemba relates to the Central African Republic situation. Arrested in May 2008, the charges against Bemba—an alleged president and commander in chief of the Mouvement de Libération du Congo—were confirmed in June 2009, and his trial began in November 2010. It remains ongoing at the time of writing. Unlike *Lubanga*, a broad range of sexual crimes were included in the warrant for Bemba's arrest,[82] including his alleged criminal responsibility as a commander for rape as a crime against humanity and a war crime; rape as torture, as a crime against humanity and a war crime; outrages upon personal dignity as a war crime; and other forms of sexual violence as a crime against humanity and a war crime. However, in line with the trend across sexual and gender-based violence cases at the ICC, many of these charges fell away at the confirmation-of-charges stage. Compared to the arrest warrant, Bemba stands trial on the narrow charges of rape as a war crime and as a crime against humanity, among other nonsexual crimes.[83] The reason for the collapse of the broader sexual and gender-based violence charges is twofold: poor evidence presented by the OTP at the confirmation stage and the unwillingness of the Pre-Trial Chamber to recognize existing developments of international law. It is this second point that is the focus of this discussion. *Bemba* provides two clear illustrations of the bench at the pre-trial stage "forgetting the new."

The first example relates to the Pre-Trial Chamber's decision at the arrest warrant stage to decline charges of "other forms of sexual violence" as a crime against humanity and a war crime. While the Chamber accepted there were substantial grounds to believe that women had been forced to undress in order to publicly humiliate them, it reasoned that these acts were not sufficiently *grave*, as compared to other sexual and gender-based crimes set out in the Statute as crimes against humanity (under Article 7(1)(g);[84] for a discussion see Grey 2014c). In making this decision, the

Pre-Trial Chamber "forgot" the existing jurisprudence on forced nudity. In 1998, the ICTR Chamber in *Akayesu* held that sexual violence, including rape and forced nudity, could constitute crimes of genocide, crimes against humanity, and war crimes under the ICTR Statute. This suggests that forced nudity is comparably grave to the other kinds of sexual violence that are explicitly listed as war crimes and crimes against humanity in the Rome Statute (Grey 2014c).

The second example of the bench "forgetting" in *Bemba* concerns the Pre-Trial Chamber's rejection of the Prosecution's efforts to secure cumulative charges based on the conduct of rape. Here was an example of the Prosecution attempting to employ the "dual-track" approach provided for under the Rome Statute as a result of Women's Caucus efforts. The Prosecutor charged Bemba with the crime against humanity and war crime of rape, the crime against humanity and war crime of torture, and rape and other acts as the war crime of outrages upon personal dignity (Oosterveld 2013, 74). The charges of torture and of outrages upon personal dignity were included to take account of the full extent of the harm of the rape, including recognizing those victimized by the crimes by being forced to witness them. In what Oosterveld calls a "confusingly reasoned decision" (2013, 73) the Pre-Trial Chamber rejected the cumulative charging approach, viewing it as placing an unfair burden on the defense and suggesting the "essence of the violation" of the victims of rape could be "fully subsumed under one charge" of rape (Green 2011, 533; Grey 2014c; Oosterveld 2013, 73).[85]

The Prosecutor appealed this decision, and in support of these efforts Women's Initiatives submitted *amicus curiae* observations to the Pre-Trial Chamber. In its submission, written by former gender advisor to the ICTY Prosecutor Patricia Viseur Sellers, Women's Initiatives drew attention to the fact that cumulative charging was an established practice in other international tribunals, including in relation to sexual violence charges, and did not necessarily trample defense rights (see also Green 2011, 535; Oosterveld 2013). It further supported its case by arguing that the ICC's existing legal architecture reinforced such an approach. It pointed to the Elements of Crimes Annex that recognized the possibility that a "particular conduct may constitute one or more crimes."[86] It also suggested that the gender nondiscrimination principles enumerated in Article 21 supported cumulative charging in this case. The *amicus* brief noted that a cumulative approach was necessary to fully "capture the extent of the harm suffered by victims and the multiple purposes of this type of violence in armed conflicts"[87] (see also Green 2011). The Women's Initiatives also contended that cumulative charging was needed in *Bemba* to incorporate not only those who were raped but also those who had suffered as a result of witnessing rape, including "a ten-year-old child, the brother of a rape victim who was beaten while his sister was raped, and the persons who watched the sexual assault of their relatives."[88]

The Appeals Chamber rejected the charges on the same basis as the Pre-Trial Chamber: that is, that the additional charges of torture and outrages of personal dignity that stemmed from the acts of rape were fully subsumed by the count of rape (Oosterveld 2013, 75). As Oosterveld (2013, 76) summarizes it, the Appeal and Pre-Trial Chamber decisions missed the fact that sexual and gender-based crimes may have multilayered functions, and, by doing so, failed to recognize that this "reduced the proper contextualization and breadth of gender-based crimes."

Alongside these two instances of "forgetting," *Bemba* also includes an important instance of a challenge to the recognition of gender expertise. During the trial, the prosecution sought to bring in as a witness sexual violence expert Dr. Nowrojee, who had previously given testimony on sexual violence as a tool of war at the UN ad hoc tribunals. Bemba's defense did not dispute Dr. Nowrojee's expertise in this area but suggested that her evidence would be of a "speculative nature" and that she would not be an impartial witness.[89] The defense cited several remarks attributed to Dr. Nowrojee in which she advocated for a more stringent approach to the prosecution of sexual violence. Impugning her impartiality, the defense concluded that "Dr. Binaifar Nowrojee has a particular agenda and is unsuitable for the task of assisting the Chamber in a neutral and impartial manner."[90] Although the Trial Chamber rejected these arguments, it nevertheless had a negative impact on the provision of gender expertise in this case, with Dr. Nowrojee ultimately declining an invitation to give evidence in *Bemba*.[91]

Prosecutor v. Germain Katanga

The ICC handed down its third judgment in the case against Germain Katanga[92] on March 7, 2014.[93] The trial centered on Katanga's involvement in orchestrating an attack on the village of Bogoro in the region of Ituri of the Democratic Republic of Congo on February 24, 2003. This case (which was initially linked to *Ngudjolo*) was the first in which crimes of sexual violence, including rape and sexual slavery, had been brought. However, Katanga was acquitted of these charges, as well as charges relating to child soldiers. Instead, he was found guilty and given a twelve-year sentence as an accessory for the war crimes of directing an attack against a civilian population, pillaging, and destruction of property, as well as for murder as a war crime and a crime against humanity.[94]

In interpreting sexual and gender-based crimes under the Rome Statute, the Trial Chamber found that elements of the conduct of rape and sexual slavery as war crimes and crimes against humanity had been established in the Bogoro village attack. It concluded that the evidence established beyond reasonable doubt that during the attack combatants intentionally committed rape as a war crime and as a crime against humanity under the Rome Statute. International criminal law expert Carsten Stahn praised the Trial Chamber for its development of substantive law in relation to sexual violence in this case by confirming that that absence of consent does not need to be positively demonstrated in the cases of rape (2014, 820). Stahn also drew attention to the fact that

> [t]he judgment further clarifies the elements of sexual slavery, which is based on the exercise of "powers attaching to the right of ownership." The majority associates ownership with the creation of a "situation of dependence" that deprives the victim of all autonomy... The majority expressly includes situations in which women and girls are forced to "share" their life with a person with whom they must perform acts of a sexual nature (2014, 820).

However, despite these advances the Trial Chamber was not convinced that Katanga was an accessory to these crimes, leading to his acquittal on all sexual and gender-based crimes charges. This case is an example of the problem highlighted by feminist scholars and the Women's Initiatives discussed above of the difficulty of holding accountable the senior military figures who direct troops on the ground to perpetrate acts of sexual and gender-based violence. It also raises questions about whether judges expect a higher standard of evidence of sexual violence crimes as opposed to others. As Stahn (2014, 821) pointed out in relation to this case, the judges' reasoning

> implies that physical destruction (e.g. pillaging) carried greater weight in the purpose than the destruction of community structures through acts of sexual or gender-based violence. This distinction raises doubts whether sexual or gender-based crimes were held to a separate and unjustifiably higher standard.

The primary act of misrecognition in this case came not from the Chamber's acquittal of Katanga on the grounds of sexual and gender-based violence, but weaknesses in the prosecution's evidence presented at trial about his liability for sexual violence and other crimes. Since 2006, Women's Initiatives had "raised concerns with the OTP ... regarding its crucial decision to limit the witness pool on sexual violence, and ultimately to proceed to trial with only three primary witnesses for these crimes."[95] Further, as the Women's Initiatives pointed out from the outset, judges in the Pre-Trial and Trial Chambers have sent strong messages to the Prosecutor about the need to strengthen the evidence to "refine and reinforce" the link between the accused and these particular crimes,[96] a point also emphasized in the academic literature on this case (see Stahn 2014, 821). In her dissenting opinion on the verdict, Judge Christine Van Den Wyngaert was scathing in her criticism of the Prosecution for its "extremely weak" case, its lack of "due diligence," and "credibility problems" throughout the case, including in relation to charges of sexual violence.[97] According to the Women's Initiatives: "certainly it is clear that the Prosecution was not ready in this case to address the additional judicial scrutiny uniquely, but predictably, applied to acts of sexual violence."[98]

Soon after the *Katanga* verdict was handed down, both the defense and the prosecution provided notice that they would appeal. The Prosecutor's notice suggested that the Chamber's adjudication on sexual violence crimes, including the "legal, procedural and factual findings that led to those acquittals," would form the basis of the appeal.[99] In the event, the Prosecutor never released her reasoning for these grounds. In a shock move, in June 2014, following the defense's decision to accept the verdict and sentence, the Prosecutor also withdrew notice to appeal, even though grounds for the two appeals were distinct and unconnected. Her decision not to take up the opportunity to test the Trial Chamber's judgment on sexual and gender-based violence charges provoked widespread condemnation, especially from victims' groups (see Easterday 2014). Lawyers for victims expressed their clients' "astonishment, confusion, disappointment and most profound disagreement with the decision of the Prosecutor" not to pursue an appeal on the judgment (Easterday 2014). The Women's Initiatives, whose Executive Director Brigid Inder simultaneously held the position of the Prosecutor's Special Gender Advisor, came forward with one of the strongest objections to this decision. While acknowledging the weakness in the prosecution's case, the Women's Initiatives believed there were manifest grounds for appeal, including "errors of fact and law regarding the adjudication of rape and sexual slavery in this case."[100] By not pursuing the appeal, the prosecution was contributing to "a step backwards in the body of jurisprudence on sexual violence."[101]

Prosecutor v. Callixte Mbarushimana

Problems with the prosecution's evidence base, including in proving liability, was also made apparent in the collapse of *Mbarushimana*, relating to the Democratic Republic of Congo situation.[102] In 2010 the ICC issued an arrest warrant for Callixte Mbarushimana that included its broadest-ever range of sexual and gender-based crimes—containing rape and sexual violence as forms of torture, mutilation, cruel treatment, other inhumane acts, and gender persecution. In December 2011, a majority of the Pre-Trial Chamber found that there were substantial grounds to believe some of these crimes had been committed by the militia with which the accused was allegedly involved but were not convinced that there were substantial grounds to believe that Mbarushimana was individually criminally responsible for contributing to the crimes as the prosecution alleged.[103] He was immediately released. In handing down its decision, the Chamber strongly criticized the prosecution for its poor presentation of the evidence, with the judges stating that "the charges and these statements of facts in the [document containing the charges] have been articulated in such vague terms that the Chamber had serious difficulties in determining, or could not determine at all, the factual ambit of a number of the charges."[104]

Other Acts of Misrecognition

Lubanga, *Bemba*, *Katanga*, and *Mbarushimana* all highlight to varying degrees significant problems in the recognition of the extensive sexual and gender-based provisions of the Rome Statute. Some of these and other cases also highlight recognition issues concerning those less-well-identified subjects of international law: male victims of sexual violence and female perpetrators of crimes.

The matter of sexual violence against men has so far come before the ICC in *Bemba*, *Lubanga*, and *Prosecutor v. Francis Kirimi Muthaura and Uhuru Muigai Kenyatta* (*Muthaura and Kenyatta*)[105] related to the Kenyan situation. In *Bemba*, the charges included acts of rape upon civilian men as well as women and children. In presenting its case in *Bemba*, the Prosecutor demonstrated some sensitivity to gendered understandings of these crimes, noting that "[m]en were also raped as a deliberate tactic to humiliate civilian men, and demonstrate their powerlessness to protect their families" (Grey and Shepherd 2013, 128). During the trial witnesses of the crimes as well as experts testified about the impact of these acts on masculinity and on broader gender relations within the community in which the crimes took place (Grey and Shepherd 2013, 128). But as Grey and Shepherd (2013, 128) note, such sensitivity has not been reflected across all cases. In *Lubanga*, where sexual violence was incorporated in the Prosecutor's evidence, the focus was on sexual violence against girls, without a detailed exploration of the experience of boy soldiers, especially the harm they suffer as a result of being trained to rape, which Prosecutor Ocampo claimed had occurred in this situation.

Arguably, the most egregious misrecognition of male sexual violence at the ICC came during a 2011 pretrial hearing in *Muthaura and Kenyatta*,[106] related to 2007 postelection violence in Kenya. Here the prosecution attempted to characterize male forced circumcisions and penile amputations as sexual violence (see Grey 2014c, 280). It argued that "these weren't just attacks on men's sexual organs as such but were intended as attacks on men's identities as men within their society and were designed to destroy their masculinity."[107] The judges on the Pre-Trial bench included Ekaterina Trendafilova and Hans-Peter Kaul, who had previously ruled in *Bemba* that forced nudity did not meet the gravity test for crimes against humanity. In this instance, in their view, because "the acts were motivated by ethnic prejudice and intended to demonstrate cultural superiority of one tribe over the other,"[108] they should not be considered crimes of sexual violence. Instead the bench characterized them as acts causing severe physical injuries.[109] In addressing the misrecognition of this decision, Brigid Inder noted that

> what makes these acts a form of sexual violence is the force and the coercive environment, as well as the intention and purpose of the acts . . . The forced circumcision of Luo men has both political and ethnic significance in Kenya and therefore has a specific meaning. In this instance, it was intended as an expression of political and ethnic domination by one group over the other and was intended to diminish the cultural identity of Luo men.[110]

In the view of the Women's Initiatives, the judges were not the only ones to misstep in this case; the organization also blamed the prosecutor for failing to stress the broader gendered context in its application and called on the OTP to improve its presentation of such cases in future[111] (also see Grey 2014c, 280–282).

The ICC has taken its first steps in recognizing the often-ignored female perpetrators of international crimes. In 2012, the Court unsealed an arrest warrant for Simone Gbagbo, former first lady of Côte d'Ivoire, for individual criminal responsibility for four counts of crimes against humanity including rape and other sexual violence, related to postelection violence in the country in 2010 and 2011.[112] Gbagbo had been held in detention by Côte d'Ivoire authorities, who challenged the admissibility of the case to the ICC. They lost their challenge in December 2014, when the ICC demanded that Gbagbo be handed over to the ICC so the charges against her could be tested through a confirmation-of-charges hearing.[113] The arrest warrant and call for Gbagbo to appear before the ICC were important because, as Rosemary Grey and I argue, "it disrupts the 'normal' gender archetypes in international criminal law, thereby making those archetypes suddenly visible." We suggest that

> Charging a woman with international crimes sparks questions about gender that we seldom ask when the subject of the proceedings is a man. It illuminates long-held assumptions embedded in law and in society about who the "normal" suspects/accused in international crimes are. It undermines the usual view of men as the agents and women as the victims of crime. It challenges the dichotomy that sets up men, masculinity and violence on one side and women, femininity and passivity on the other. It upsets the archetype of women as vulnerable, "rapeable," and incapable of wielding power (Grey and Chappell 2012).

These initial outcomes at the ICC concerning male victims of sexual and gender-based violence and female perpetrators of this violence demonstrate that, as with other international criminal law tribunals, there is still a long way to go to adequately recognize the complexities of gendered positions within the law and to undo existing stereotypes about the subjects and agents of sexual and gender-based violations.

Recognition and "Revisability"

As the previous discussion illustrates, both the judiciary and the prosecution carry some responsibility for instances of misrecognition of gender justice in the ICC's early years, contributing to ongoing status submission of many female and particular male victims. Under Prosecutor Bensouda's leadership, there appears to be a concerted effort to learn lessons from these experiences and to recommit the OTP to better reflecting the gender justice provisions of the Rome Statute in practice. Evidenced in her own comments (Bensouda 2014), and more especially in the release in June 2014 of the OTP's *Policy Paper on Sexual and Gender-Based Crimes*, Prosecutor Bensouda has indicated a willingness to tackle many of the problems that have plagued the prosecution from the outset. The policy paper emphasizes the adoption of new approaches to collect stronger evidence using innovative methods to support claims of these crimes and to pay more attention to early evidence gathering. It also highlights the need to pursue charges that reflect the "dual-track" approach favored by the Women's Caucus by bringing "charges for sexual and gender-based crimes explicitly as crimes per se, in addition to charging such acts as forms of other violence within the competence of the Court where the material elements are met, e.g., charging rape as torture."[114] The paper commits the OTP to applying gender persecution charges, which have not yet been successfully prosecuted, and to demonstrating at trial that acts of sexual violence may not include physical conduct, referring specifically to instances of forced nudity.[115] It also emphasizes the need to bring cumulative charges that were so controversial in *Bemba*, "in order to reflect the severity and multifaceted character of these crimes fairly, and to enunciate their range, supported by the evidence in each case."[116] The policy paper considers the longstanding problem of addressing modes of liability in cases of sexual and gender-based violence and explores the potential of bringing charges under Article 28, where military commanders or nonmilitary superiors

> may be held accountable not only where they intended the specific conduct or consequence of sexual and gender-based crimes, but also where they knew, or should have known about, or consciously disregarded information regarding, the commission of such crimes, and failed to take all necessary and reasonable measures within their power to prevent or repress such commission, or to submit the matter to the competent authorities for investigation and prosecution.[117]

The policy paper also makes a point about making better use of Article 21(3), particularly the need for "the application and interpretation of the Statute to be without 'any adverse distinction founded, inter alia, on gender or, other status'," and commits the OTP in future to take into account the evolution of internationally recognized human rights in its prosecution strategy.[118]

The policy paper reflects the temporal and spatial bounds in which the OTP operates: it obviously cannot redress the series of failures in the prosecution of sexual and gender-based violence that have already taken place in the Court's early years. Nor can it address problems in the adjudication of the evidence and interpretation of the Statute by the Chambers. But this attempt at revision does indicate that this crucial organ of the ICC is

Table 4.1. GENDER JUSTICE RECOGNITION: PRIORITIES, RULES, AND ENFORCEMENT

Gender Justice Priorities	Formal Rules	Enforced
Prosecution of sexual violence and gender-based crimes as *standalone crimes*	✔	Partially
Sexual and gender-based violence expressly enumerated as an act of genocide, and as war crimes and crimes against humanity	✘ Genocide^ ✔ War crimes ✔ Crimes against humanity	Partially*
Expanding the list of protected groups under genocide to include gender-based groups	✘	✘
No adverse distinction/anti–gender-discrimination clause	✔	✘
Gender-sensitive investigations	✔	Partially
Recognition of gender expertise	✔	Partially

^Though in ICC. 2000. Elements of Crime Annex.
*Applicable across all categories of crime.

open to learning from its initial missteps and that it is making some effort to redirect its future path.

PART FOUR: LEGACIES OF MISRECOGNITION AND LEGITIMACY AT THE ICC

Remarkable strides were made by gender justice advocates during the Rome Statute negotiations to secure the recognition of a wide range of sexual and gender-based violations through their criminalization, many of which were encoded for the first time under international law. These actors also helped put in place the architecture to have victims recognized, as well as to have the voices of gender justice experts heard across the various organs of the ICC. Some of these provisions provoked strong contestation. Gender justice recognition, which aims to disrupt the androcentrism of international law, upset the gender status quo that a range of religious and state forces fought to uphold. Ultimately, and no doubt in part because of the favorable broader context in which these negotiations were spatially "nested," gender justice actors were able to gain the support of most state delegates, albeit with some compromises.

These strides toward gender-just recognition in ICC practice have not been nearly as successful as gender justice negotiators would have hoped, even given their realistic political perspective. Compared with the representation and redistributive gender justice features of the ICC, these recognition aspects have been by far and away the least well supported in practice (Table 4.1). Indeed, it could be argued these aspects have been upheld more in the breach than in the rule. The poor implementation of these gender justice recognition elements of the Rome Statute is especially concerning given that the ICC's primary objective is to bring to account those most responsible for the crimes enumerated under the Statute's provisions and to end impunity for these crimes.

It is no accident, nor a strike of bad luck, that the ICC ended its first decade without a single prosecution for sexual or gender-based violence. As the above discussion illustrates, this unimpressive record is the result of numerous examples on the part of both the prosecution and the bench of "remembering the old" and "forgetting the new"—which together reinforce what Fraser defines as gender status misrecognition (2007). In selecting charges, gathering evidence, identifying witnesses, and interpreting the evidence and the Statute, ICC officials have often failed to employ the wide-ranging formal rules supporting the recognition of gender justice encoded in the Rome Statute. The view that the first Prosecutor also demonstrated an "obstinate failure to learn from the accumulated practice of previously established international criminal tribunals" (Hayes 2013, 9) can be equally charged against many members of the bench. Moreover, in the few attempts by the Prosecutor, judges, or other experts to apply a broad reading of the gender provisions to ensure that the ICC does not discriminate on the basis of gender, these efforts have met with strong opposition and personal attack, with most of these deliberations ultimately reinforcing the existing gender status quo.

In "remembering the old," ICC actors have enabled gender legacies to seep into Court practices and, if not direct, then heavily influence the early prosecutions at the ICC. Such legacies include an ongoing blindness to the extent, harm, and deliberate use of conflict-related sexual and gender-based violence; a view that such violations are harder to prosecute; a failure to gather evidence early and to believe victims and witness testimony of the experiences of sexual violence; inability to demonstrate the link between senior officers and the actual perpetration of crimes; a limited understanding of the nature and harm of nonpenetrative forms of sexual violence; and a misrecognition of how men and women experience (and perpetrate) these atrocities differently and how these violations link to the gendered *and* ethnic contexts in which many conflicts occur. As a result of the operation of these legacies, the initial path of ICC recognition has been to "lock out" rather than "lock in" the new gender justice recognition rules.

Legitimacy and (Mis)recognition

As with all the Rome Statute gender justice elements, gender misrecognition has influenced actors' views about the legitimacy of the ICC. Having secured so many of their recognition demands, gender justice advocates had good reason at the design stage to view the Rome Statute as having a high degree of legitimacy. Of course there was the expected debate and concession, but the latter was of a degree these actors found acceptable. Although some provisions, such as those concerning genocide, were not included, and another in relation to forced pregnancy came with an interpretive clause, the overarching objectives of the Women's Caucus were not unduly compromised.

By contrast, throughout the ICC's initial operations phase, gender justice actors' sense of the Court's legitimacy has been relentlessly tested. The misrecognition of the new rules of the Rome Statute, leading to the collapse and withdrawal of sexual and gender-based charges, and the withdrawal of appeals to test these decisions seriously undermine the view of gender justice actors that ICC is capable of fulfilling its gender justice recognition mandate. The Women's Initiatives statement that it was "extremely concerned and disappointed" about the Prosecutor's withdrawal of its *Katanga* appeal and concluding that this would have negative "ramifications for the ICC in its future cases"[119] was significant in this regard. Such a strong criticism was especially notable given that Executive Director Brigid Inder of the Women's Initiatives holds the dual position as the Prosecutor's Special Gender Adviser.

However, as with the other gender justice dimensions of the ICC, there may be some signs of change emerging that may (re)commit these actors to the Court in the longer term. The first relates to the willingness of experts to "surface" the gender justice dimensions of prosecutions within the OTP and the Judiciary. Judge Odio Benito is the obvious example here. Despite the backlash she suffered in her efforts to use the gender recognition elements of the Rome Statute, her dissent in *Lubanga* was critically important. In effect, she made a similar contribution to the ICC as she had done at the ICTY (Chappell et al 2014; Sharratt 1999): she placed a spotlight on the limitations and inadequacies of the prosecution's charging strategy and by doing so reminded these key players of the need to refocus and pay attention to these issues in future cases. Her dissenting opinions already appear to be having an influence on the way in which the ICC understands the use of child soldier charges, which is much more sensitive to different experiences of boys and girls. Judge Odio Benito's role in this first case may encourage other judges to take a similar position, thereby strengthening the view of the *consequential* legitimacy of the ICC in the eyes of gender justice advocates.

Prosecutor Bensouda's efforts to revise the practices of the OTP, notably by introducing the first gender policy paper, offer a glimmer of hope to those seeking gender justice recognition at the ICC. As with the Rome Statute, the policy paper has many aspirations in relation to sexual and gender-based persecution. And, as with the designers of the Rome Statute who were drawing on negative experiences from the UN ad hoc tribunals, the Prosecutor and her gender advising team are learning lessons more from the failures of the early years—lessons about what *not* to do—than examples of "best practice."

The successful implementation of this policy paper also has the potential to strengthen the consequential legitimacy of the ICC from the perspective of gender justice advocates. Obviously, this will rely on the ongoing commitment and leadership of Prosecutor Bensouda, but it must extend farther than the OTP. As this chapter has illustrated, in the ICC's early years, even where the Prosecutor has advanced a strong case, the bench has not always been willing to interpret the gender justice recognition elements of the Rome Statute as the gender justice designers intended. To avert a legitimacy crisis it seems necessary in the next phase of the Court's development for ICC judges to engage in a "stock-taking" exercise similar to that undertaken by OTP. Collectively, the Chambers need to more fully comprehend international jurisprudence on these matters and the gender provisions embedded in the Rome Statute's gender justice provisions, and make better use of both this jurisprudence and mandate in their interpretation. Unless or until this occurs, the objectives and implementation of the Rome Statute's gender justice recognition framework will continue to be frustrated, and the gender justice constituency of the ICC will have good reason to call into question the legitimacy of the Court as a mechanism for ending impunity for sexual and gender-based crimes.

The ICC's legitimacy in the eyes of the gender justice community has also rested on efforts of the Court to use its innovative redress provisions to provide a measure of redistribution through reparations, including for those suffering gender injustices. It is to these attempts to address gender *maldistribution* that the following chapter turns.

CHAPTER 5

Redistributing Gender Justice at the International Criminal Court

The ICC is a hybrid tribunal in the sense that it combines a retributive justice regime, aimed at punishing individual perpetrators, and a victims' rights framework, founded on ideas of restorative justice.[1] The victims' framework has variously been described as "novel," "groundbreaking," "a milestone," and "a significant achievement," especially given "there was no true precedent in international criminal tribunals to draw upon" (Ferstman 2002, 670). The Rome Statute gives victims a "double status" (Dwertmann 2010, 1), enabling them to be represented and participate in proceedings, as discussed in Chapter 3, and giving victims an avenue to seek redress through reparations from those individuals found guilty of perpetrating atrocities recognized under the Statute. These trial-based reparations orders are complemented by the creation of the statutorily independent TFV, which has the dual role of implementing ICC reparations orders and providing separate assistance programs to victims within those countries under investigation by the Court.

Court-ordered reparations and the TFV programs are the mechanisms through which the ICC has some capacity to address misrecognition (as discussed in detail in Chapter 4) but also, unusually for an international criminal tribunal, *maldistribution*, including distributive gender injustices in those postconflict states where the Court is active. This chapter outlines the contribution of gender justice actors to the design of the ICC's reparations and assistance rules and traces their interpretation and implementation in the first decade of the Court's operation. It recognizes that in this distinct area of the Court's operation, these actors' efforts have been directed toward both recognition and redistribution. Whereas the recognition aspects have been addressed in the previous chapter, the primary focus here is on the redistribution element, though the two are often closely intertwined and can be difficult to separate for analytical purposes. Part One of this chapter offers a brief discussion of the significance of redistributive mechanisms for gender justice, including the need to tackle structural maldistribution that contributes to conflict-related sexual violence, as well as other gender dimensions of reparative processes. Part Two outlines gender justice actors' demands during the Rome Statute negotiation phase for gender-just restorative justice and identifies the imprint these actors had on the ICC's redress framework. Part Three considers the implementation and interpretation of these formal rules and traces some of the opportunities and challenges gender justice actors have faced in "locking in" these gender justice aspects of the framework in the Court's early years. Part Four analyzes the reasons for these outcomes, and their residual effects, especially concerning gender justice actors' views of the ICC's legitimacy.

The argument advanced in this chapter is that the success of gender justice actors in having some of their *redistributive* demands incorporated into the Statute, alongside other gender *recognition* and *representation* claims, contributed to their initial sense of the ICC's normative legitimacy. By contrast, in the initial period of ICC operations, their view of the Court's *operational* and *consequential* legitimacy (Schiff 2010), at least in relation to its redistributive functions, has been tested. There have been some positive steps toward gender justice, including in the initial interpretation of the relatively ambiguous reparations rules in the ICC's first trial and especially in the implementation of the TFV's assistance mandate. However, the ongoing influence of gender norms, especially the cascade effect of ongoing failures to investigate, charge, and prosecute sexual and gender-based crimes on reparations, has acted as an impediment to achieving redistributive gender justice outcomes in the Court's first decade in operation.

PART ONE: REDISTRIBUTIVE GENDER JUSTICE AND SEXUAL VIOLENCE

Redistribution of resources is one of the three pillars of Nancy Fraser's gender justice model. For Fraser, resource *maldistribution*—along with misrecognition and misrepresentation—is a structural obstacle preventing some people from participating as full partners in social interaction, one that requires correction through processes of redistribution (Fraser

2009, 16). Distributive injustice results from unequal economic structures that deny "people the resources they need in order to interact with others as peers" (Fraser 2009, 16). Maldistribution has a gendered face, affecting men and women differently; it is driven by both "the gender division between paid and unpaid labour and the gender division within paid labor" (Fraser 1997, 21). Addressing it involves eliminating "gender-specific exploitation, marginalization and deprivation" (Fraser 2009, 16) through a transformative redistributive approach. This involves developing "remedies aimed at correcting inequitable outcomes precisely by restructuring the underlying generative framework" (Fraser 1997, 23); the objective of such remedies must be a "deep restructuring of relations of production" (Fraser 1997, 27).

Feminist political economist Jacqui True (2012) has powerfully demonstrated how maldistribution links to the problem of violence against women, including in conflict settings. True argues that

> [A]ll forms of violence against women have a *material* basis that may, over time, become embedded in cultural practices. That is, they are rooted in and heightened by unequal social relations often in impoverished or destabilizing economic and political contexts characterized by stress, displacement, and struggles to obtain and distribute resources for survival or basic needs (2012, 121, emphasis added).

Structural economic problems can work in myriad ways to fuel sexual violence in conflict and postconflict settings. For instance, impoverishment can lead male soldiers to have "a sense of entitlement" to treat the women with whom they interact as they wish (True 2012, 122). Where men are excluded from the economic spoils of war, resentment can further fuel such attitudes and be expressed through violence (True 2012, 122). Research has also demonstrated how poverty can lead to women's involvement in militia and conflict-related trafficking and prostitution (Leatherman 2011, 110). Equally, women's disproportionate economic disempowerment resulting from lack of access to land, limited employment opportunities, increased family responsibilities, and unequal pay, for example, can make them targets of conflict-related sexual violence without the resources to escape or protect themselves from such violence (Cockburn 2004; Duggan and Abusharaf 2006, 628; True 2012, 122).

Historically, restorative justice approaches in general and reparative responses[2] in particular have tended to ignore the position of women who experience conflict-related violence, and the economic deprivation that contributes to its manifestation (De Brouwer 2007; Duggan and Abusharaf

2006). As De Brouwer demonstrates in a study of postgenocide Rwanda, although the UN and other international bodies recognized that women had suffered some of the greatest economic and social hardships as a result of conflict-related sexual violence, reparations efforts were not adequately enforced and failed to redistribute resources to address women's specific needs. The results in the Rwandan context, De Brouwer notes, have been nothing less than devastating: "victims of sexual violence have . . . largely been left uncompensated, while many have already died" (2007, 214). Other research on sexual violence and reparations aimed at redistribution suggests that the Rwandan situation is the rule rather than the exception (Manjoo and McRaith 2011; Rubio-Marín 2009).

There have been three sets of cross-cutting gender legacies that have prevented women and victims of sexual and gender-based violence from accessing reparations processes. The first relates to recognition/definitional issues: crimes committed against women—especially sexual violence—have been seen as the "collateral damage" of warfare but not serious or grave enough to warrant repair; these crimes have generally been left outside the ambit of reparation processes (De Brouwer 2007; Ferstman 2010, 6). Second, women have largely been unrepresented in reparations fora: women have failed to gain access to reparations adjudication bodies due to a lack of information about their rights, as well as social constraints and stigma limiting their opportunities to be involved (De Brouwer 2007; Ferstman 2010, 6). Third, cases related to women's experiences of conflict have been inadequately prosecuted: as outlined in earlier chapters, where cases of crimes against women have made it to the Court, they often collapse before any reparative process is invoked because of inadequate investigatory, evidence-gathering, and charging strategies (Ferstman 2010, 6; Mouthaan 2011; Ní Aoláin et al. 2011). In other words, misrecognition and misrepresentation have helped to reinforce maldistribution by blocking women victims' access to reparative justice. As the following discussion illustrates, it is this third factor in particular that has been influential in shaping gender redistribution efforts during the early years at the ICC.

If and when women are able to access reparations processes, redistributive redress measures can have different gendered effects. A range of reparations measures exist and are now codified in the 2005 *UN Basic Principles and Guidelines on the Right to a Remedy and Reparation for Victims of Gross Violations of International Human Rights Law and Serious Violations of International Humanitarian Law* ("the Basic Principles"[3]). Gender scholars note that most reparations processes apply the principles of *restitution*, *compensation*, and *rehabilitation*. These particular measures, they argue, do little to undermine the structural problems contributing to the types of crimes committed against women in conflict settings, and indeed they can result in a return to the gendered status quo that provided the conditions for sexual violence in the first place (Rubio-Marín 2009). As Ferstman states: "as violence against women is often a manifestation of historically unequal power relations between men and women, restoring the victims to the position before the violation (restitution), when this is what gave rise to the violation, is a feeble end goal" (2010, 6).

In response, these scholars along with many gender justice advocates have called for "transformative" reparations measures that undermine the structural conditions—including political, social, cultural, and economic—leading to the common forms of violence against women (Manjoo and McCraith 2011; Rubio-Marín 2009). As Ní Aoláin, Haynes, and Cahn explain:

> Unless we embed into reparations a means to unsettle preexisting gender hierarchies and undo the structural harms that may, in many cases, be causal to the actual violence and harm experienced during a conflict, we do little to repair for women (2011, 187).

To dismantle these structures, some scholars suggest drawing upon one of the less commonly applied Basic Principles—that of *guarantees of nonrepetition*—which include, *inter alia*, the introduction of measures to reform military and security forces, the independence of the judiciary, human rights law reform, education and training, and the introduction of mechanisms to prevent and monitor social conflict (see Durbach and Chappell 2014). According to Mégret, a guarantee of nonrepetition is "a commitment made by the state (for what it is worth) to never engage again in the practices that led to violations, backed by a number of reform and restructuring initiatives to make good on that promise" (2009, 5). Rashida Manjoo, UN Special Rapporteur on violence against women, its causes, and consequences, argues that

> Guarantees of non-repetition offer the greatest potential for transforming gender relations. In promising to ensure non-recurrence, such guarantees trigger a discussion about the underlying structural causes of the violence and their gendered manifestations and a discussion about the broader institutional or legal reforms that might be called for to ensure non-repetition (2010, 26).

Nonrepetition in this sense has preventive, and therefore potentially transformative, qualities (Durbach and Chappell 2014).

The influence of this line of thinking about nonrepetition can be seen in recent UN Security Council resolutions on women and peace and security, particularly Resolution 2122 (2013) and the civil society–led 2007 *Nairobi Declaration on Women's and Girls' Right to a Remedy and Reparation* (for a discussion on the development of this Declaration see Couillard 2007). The Declaration puts preventive, structural redistributive reparations squarely on the agenda of transnational gender justice advocacy, stating at Article 3(H):

> Reparation must go above and beyond the immediate reasons and consequences of the crimes and violations; they must aim to address the political and *structural inequalities* that negatively shape women's and girls' lives [emphasis added].

PART TWO: DESIGNING A GENDER-JUST REPARATIONS FRAMEWORK FOR THE ICC

Debates about appropriate forms of reparations to address gender injustices have informed the position of ICC gender justice advocates. In return, through their efforts to design and instantiate the Rome Statute reparations framework, these advocates have themselves made an important contribution to better understanding the gender dimensions of reparations. During Rome Statute negotiations, the Women's Caucus was a key player, along with other civil society organizations, such as the Victims Working Group and REDRESS, in influencing states parties to endorse the victims' redistribution provisions, including reparations (McCarthy 2012, 52–53; Schiff 2008, 151). In making their claims, these actors were responding in part to the failure of ICTR and ICTY to adequately respond to victims' experiences (Ferstman 2002, 671; McCarthy 2012, 46; REDRESS 2011, 21–22). They were also influenced by more general trends throughout the 1990s at national, regional, and international levels to use reparations to protect individuals who experience human rights abuses (Falk 2006, 485), to reassert the victim as "a central figure in the criminal justice process" (McCarthy 2009, 252), and to shift the emphasis in international criminal proceedings "to healing the wounded as well as punishing the guilty, and, in practical terms, to enabling victim participation and access to reparations" (Wiersing 2012, 24).

With the Rome Statute negotiations occurring prior to the formulation of the Nairobi Principles, it is unsurprising to find that the Women's

Caucus efforts to influence the Statute did not use the language of transformation, and nor did they emphasize the principle of nonrepetition. However, their lobbying documents do draw on the work of Theo van Boven's draft UN Principles as well as the *Convention on the Elimination of all Forms of Discrimination against Women* in developing its position.[4] The Caucus lobbying documents focused on restitution, compensation, and rehabilitation, emphasizing the latter for addressing the harms of victims of sexual violence.[5] The Women's Caucus documents did include language about the possible use of "other" forms of reparations included under the emerging UN principles[6] but did not specify broader, transformative measures.

The Women's Caucus advanced four core priorities for the Rome Statute's reparations framework: (1) establishing principles relating to reparations in every case where there is a conviction; (2) making provision for collective and social as well as individual redress, ensuring a broad definition of victims to include family members and others, whether or not recognized by the law; (3) enabling victims and other interested persons and entities other than the parties to the case to trigger the Court's authority to make rulings with respect to reparations and to appeal its rulings[7]; and (4) allowing the Court under certain conditions to "order" or to "recommend" that states contribute to reparations.[8]

The rationale behind the Women's Caucus's objective to broaden the category of victims to include those who were not party to the case, but who were nevertheless affected by the conflict, was an acknowledgement of women's historic marginalization in reparations proceedings and an attempt to increase the chances of incorporating victims of sexual violence whose crimes have rarely been successfully prosecuted. Equally, the Women's Caucus's call for collective, as well as individual, reparations orders was aimed at extending redistributive responses to women who, as noted above, have historically been poorly recognized and represented in reparative proceedings.

In seeking to invest the ICC with authority to *order* a state to contribute to any reparations measures where it was implicated in the crimes,[9] the Caucus aimed to embed human rights standards of state responsibility in the Statute.[10] Further, their effort to integrate a provision allowing the ICC to "recommend" that states contribute costs associated with the provision of redistributive measures was a signal that the Caucus understood that the scale and cost of reparations—especially collective reparations in the form of schools and health facilities[11]—were likely to be much greater than the resources at the disposal of any individual defendant.[12] Writing well after the negotiation period,

Mégret's statement nevertheless neatly encapsulates the view of the Women's Caucus at that time:

> Reparations may amount to very little if, time and time again, impecunious convicted individuals are ordered to pay considerable amounts of reparation for which they lack the resources. There is a reason why traditionally reparations strategies have been targeted at the state's relatively deep pockets rather than the state's agents (2012, n.p.).

In sum, through their advocacy at the Rome Conference the members of the Women's Caucus were asking state delegates to support an expansive reparations regime: one that involved direct state commitment, was capable of addressing the legacy of misrecognition and misrepresentation of women in reparations processes, and could produce gender redistributive outcomes in postconflict sites.

Many of the demands of the Women's Caucus and other civil society groups significantly influenced the design of the Rome Statute's reparations regime. As ICC reparations expert Conor McCarthy states: "the decision to establish a regime of victim redress within the framework of the ICC in truth owes much to the lobbying efforts of these organisations" (2012, 53). While the mandate to establish the reparations arm of the Court was widely heralded by lobbying organizations (Dannenbaum 2010, 240), their position was not universally accepted. Many state delegations opposed these provisions because of their potential to distract the Court from what they considered was its "core business": individual prosecutions (McCarthy 2009, 250; Muttukumaru 1999, 262; War Crimes Research Office [WCRO] 2010, 16). Not surprisingly, then, as with many aspects of the Rome Statute, and in line with most institutional design processes (Lowndes and Roberts 2013, Chapter 7), the result of these victims' redress negotiations was "pragmatic compromise rather than a carefully planned over-arching framework" (McCarthy 2012, 53).

THE FORMAL RULES OF THE ICC'S REPARATIONS REGIME

The negotiations on reparations were reflected in Rome Statute Articles 75 and 79 and in Rules 94 to 99 of the Rules of Procedure and Evidence, as well as in the regulations of the TFV.[13] This section outlines these formal rules and highlights those points of alignment and discord between the position of core gender justice actors—the Women's Caucus—and states parties involved in the Rome Statute negotiations.

REPARATIONS PRINCIPLES AND ORDERS

ICC's core reparations provisions are included in Article 75 of the Rome Statute. It provides the ICC with the capacity to develop "principles" (Article 75(1)) and make "orders" (Article 75(2)–(4)) for reparations, but only after an accused has been convicted (Article 75(2)). The Court has the capacity to develop principles "relating to reparations to, or in respect of, victims, *including* restitution, compensation and rehabilitation" (emphasis added; Article 75(1)). The use of the word "including" indicates that the Court is not limited to these modes of redress (Wiersing 2012, 27). Indeed, as McCarthy notes:

> [T]he absence of express limitations on the kind of principles that shall be established pursuant to Article 75(1) indicates that the Statute has been designed to confer a significant degree of discretion upon the Court, enabling it to tailor a body of principles appropriately suited to the specific context in which it operates (2009, 255).

This includes, according to some commentators, awards based on 'transformative' measures, such as those aimed at "guarantees of nonrepetition"[14] (see, e.g., Mégret 2009). Statute drafting history suggests that this language was used deliberately to end a lengthy debate during negotiations over redress terminology (Dwertmann 2010, 48, note 198). In accord with the Women's Caucus position, it was expected that these principles would reflect emerging international standards; since the ICC has become operational, these standards have been further outlined in the UN Basic Principles (De Brouwer 2007) and the gender-sensitive Nairobi Declaration.

The ICC defines "victims" in broad terms, as advocated by the Women's Caucus.[15] Under Rule 85 of the Rules of Procedure and Evidence, victims "mean natural persons who have suffered harm as a result of the commission of any crime within the jurisdiction of the Court" and also may include certain "organisations or institutions that have sustained direct harm" (see De Brouwer 2007, 221). The Rules also allow "family members and other persons that are not direct victims of the crime to be entitled to reparations" (Dwertmann 2010, 89), signaling that these indirect victims may also claim reparations on their own behalf.

For victims to be eligible for reparations through the Rome Statute system, Rule 85 stipulates that there must be a causal link between the harm (understood as damage, loss, or injury) and the crime (see Dwertmann 2010, 78). For reparations to be awarded, "a person must be the victim of a crime that was under prosecution before the Court and that has resulted in a conviction" (Dwertmann 2010, 91). Maintaining the link between the harm and the justice process is seen to be "the *raison d'être* of reparations" (REDRESS 2012, 4).

The reparations orders made by the ICC are discretionary—there is no obligation on the Court to award them in every case. This was a conscious decision of the drafters; their concern was to provide the Chambers some flexibility so as not to jeopardize and delay trials under way at the Court (Dwertmann 2010, 68). This does not meet the standard requested by the Women's Caucus to have them automatically applied in every case of a conviction. However, given the significant external victims' rights advocacy movement surrounding the Court, it is likely the ICC will be under considerable pressure to ensure that this becomes its common practice (within the ICC's resource constraints). Importantly, the Rome Statute was silent on whether the Court should develop guiding reparations principles; as discussed below, it has decided not to. Instead, principles are developed on case-by-case basis.

Despite the advocacy of Women's Caucus and other NGO delegates during the Rome Conference, official delegates declined to give the Court capacity to order states to pay reparations, or to allow the ICC to recommend that states implement those reparations ordered against an individual (Dwertmann 2010, 55; Muttukumaru 1999, 267–268). In 2011 states reiterated this position through an ASP resolution.[16] The Resolution states:

> [A]s liability for reparations is exclusively based on the individual criminal responsibility of a convicted person, under no circumstances shall States be ordered to utilise their properties and assets, including the assessed contributions of States Parties, for funding reparations awards, including in situations where an individual holds, or has held, any official position.[17]

The inability to direct states to implement reparations under the Rome Statute is different from some other systems, such as the Inter-American Court of Human Rights, where states are most often the defendants and in certain circumstances courts have the authority to make orders against states (WCRO 2010, 27).

States are nevertheless involved in reparations proceedings at the ICC. As Ferstman suggests, "their co-operation is essential for the execution of searches and seizures and the identification, tracing and freezing or seizure of proceeds, property and assets and instrumentalities of crimes, for the purposes of facilitation of forfeiture proceedings" (2002, 32). States appear to have accepted this responsibility, noting in the 2011 ASP reparations resolution that they are committed to providing the ICC with "timely and effective assistance" for these efforts.[18] Luke Moffett (2013) has also argued this should be a feature of the ICC's complementarity system (see Chapter 6).

According to the Rome Statute and the Rules of Procedure and Evidence, awards for reparations can be made on an individual or collective basis, or both, taking into account the scope and extent of any damage, loss, and injury (Rule 97). The Women's Caucus emphasized the need for individual and collective reparations during Statute negotiations.[19] Collective reparations are essential to ICC efforts to achieve a measure of reparative justice, especially given "the limited amount of funds that will be available for reparations awards when compared with the rights and needs of victims" (Ferstman 2002, 675). The TFV is expected to manage the implementation of the reparation award, unless it is made directly by the convicted person to an individual (Rule 98). Funds for reparations are to be drawn from the forfeiture of the proceeds of crime and may be complemented by TFV resources (Rule 98; McCarthy 2009).

THE TFV

The ICC's victims' redress architecture also includes the independent TFV, which is established under Article 79 and regulated through Rule 98 and under its own regulations, which were set by the ASP (Dwertmann 2010, 265–266).[20] At the time of the negotiations, the Women's Caucus appeared not to have paid detailed attention to the TFV's mandate.[21] Indeed, it has been argued that, distracted by other aspects of Court design, the TFV was "largely ignored" by all players in the early years of the Court's development and operations (Dannenbaum 2010, 234). Nevertheless, its provisions are in accord with the Caucus's redistributive aims. Commencing operations in 2007, the TFV has been created for the benefit of victims and of their families (Article 79(1)). It acts as a depository for any assets seized from a suspect for the eventual purposes of reparation; once a reparations order is made, the TFV is responsible for administering and implementing it according to Court directions. It also has an important second mandate, which is its "assistance" mandate: this involves "using voluntary contributions from donors to provide victims and their families in situations where the Court is active with physical rehabilitation, material support, and/or psychological rehabilitation."[22] Under the TFV's own regulations, programs are expected to be implemented through intermediaries to avoid victims being stigmatized or endangered by being seen to have contact with the ICC (Ferstman 2002, 227).

The TFV is much less constrained in applying its assistance mandate than its reparations mandate.[23] When applying its assistance mandate, the TFV must work in a situation country of the ICC and must be assisting victims of a crime within the jurisdiction of the Court (Dwertmann 2010, 92). However, there is no requirement that proceedings need to be initiated in respect of that crime for the TFV to render assistance (McCarthy 2009, 268–269). This gives the TFV a significant degree of flexibility compared to the Chambers: it can consult more widely with victims without prejudicing a particular case, can take a broad approach to victimization, and can better decide on appropriate local responses to victims' needs (Weirda and de Grief 2004, 10).[24]

Importantly for this analysis, the TFV has elaborated a gender-sensitive approach to assistance, informed by the Nairobi Declaration, which includes "mainstreaming a gender-based perspective across all programming; and specifically targeting crimes of rape, enslavement, forced pregnancy, and other forms of sexual and/or gender-based violence."[25] This approach carries forward the gender justice redistributive goals of the Women's Caucus. As De Brouwer notes:

> By enabling collective projects, the Trust Fund can reach many more victims of sexual violence than the Court, in particular because the ICC Prosecutor will primarily be concerned with prosecuting the main perpetrators, focusing on certain crimes, thus leaving aside victims of sexual violence not affected by the Prosecutorial Strategy. Furthermore, the Trust Fund may be able to reach unidentified victims of sexual violence who, for instance, due to stigmatisation, shame, or trauma, have not been able to apply for reparation at the Court themselves (2007, 236; also see Durbach and Chappell 2014).

In implementing its assistance mandate the TFV is confronted with two core challenges. The first is to ensure that its efforts remain focused on issues of redress and redistribution, yet distinct from general development activities. This requires that the beneficiaries of any general assistance provided by the TFV must be victims of crimes within the jurisdiction of the ICC, even if these crimes have not been prosecuted. As McCarthy notes, "[a]ny support provided by the Fund must seek to redress the harm victims have suffered as a result of the crime to which they or their loved ones were subjected;" otherwise, its role will "become conflated with that of a charitable organisation providing general assistance to victims of crimes" (2009, 269). The second challenge is addressing large-scale assistance needs within a tightly constrained budget. As TFV commentators have noted, "not all victims of crimes within the jurisdiction of the Court, including victims of sexual violence as well as their families, will be fully assisted in their needs" (De Brouwer 2007, 237) as these will always outstrip resources (McCarthy 2012; Mégret 2012; Moffett 2013; SáCouto and Cleary 2014, 155).

As this brief outline indicates, the design of the reparations and assistance regime of the ICC came to reflect many of the priorities of the Women's Caucus. The formal rules allow for an expansive interpretation of modes of reparation and assistance, as well as a broad definition of victims, opening the possibility for encompassing those suffering harm from sexual and gender-based violence who have traditionally been excluded from reparations processes. The TFV's assistance mandate further expands the redistributive capacity of the ICC system, and its distinctive gender justice focus creates potential for addressing the maldistribution that helps fuel conflict-related sexual violence.

It is also the case, however, as with the Women's Caucus's efforts to embed recognition and representation principles and procedures in the Rome Statute system, that a number of the Caucus's core reparative claims were omitted. While victims are able to apply for recognition as victims and appeal reparations orders (Dwertmann 2010, 261), they cannot trigger them. As a result of the system of state sovereignty in which the ICC is nested, the Women's Caucus's calls for state involvement were rejected: states were unwilling to shackle themselves to a treaty that could imply their complicity in international criminal acts or would expect them to fund redistributive measures for crimes arguably not of their making (see Chapter 6 for a further discussion of the effects of this "nestedness"). These losses were not fatal for gender justice actors' view of the legitimacy of the Rome Statute reparations provisions, but they did send a signal to the incoming Women's Initiatives advocates who took up the challenge of monitoring the ICC's operations. The final rules potentially limited the Court's ability to deliver gender-just reparative measures and meant that gender justice actors would need to stay vigilant to pursuing gender-sensitive redistributive claims in the Court's early implementation and interpretation phase.

PART THREE: FORGING A PATH OF GENDER REDISTRIBUTION AT THE ICC

When the ICC commenced operation in 2002, it had a Statute that included reparative measures that were a novel and largely untested area of international criminal law. Many of the formal principles and procedures of the Court's reparative the mandate were left vague and opaque[26] (Dwertmann 2010, 45). As ICC Judge Christine Van den Wyngaert explains:

> While the Rome Statute is quite vague on victim's participatory rights, it is even vaguer on reparations. Indeed, the drafters could not agree on this subject, and left it to the Court to further decide what it means. This is another example of a "constructive ambiguity" in the Statute, which places a high burden on the shoulders of the judge (2012, 486).[27]

This degree of "constructive ambiguity" (Oosterveld 2014) provided Women's Initiatives actors with an opportunity to take up from where their Women's Caucus counterparts had left off in negotiations and push for further redistribution through these reparations and assistance provisions in the Court's operational phase. It also presented them with a challenge to ensure that the ICC's reparations decisions took gender justice considerations into account.

The following discussion assesses how the initial interpretation and implementation of the Rome Statute and TFV rules directed toward redistribution have helped "lock in" or "lock out" the goals of gender justice actors. It highlights developments in the general interpretation of the reparation rules and considers how the formal rules interacted with gender legacies in the ICC's first (and, at the time of writing, only) reparations ruling in *Lubanga*. It also assesses the implementation of the TFV reparations and assistance mandate aimed at securing gender-just redistributive outcomes.

INTERPRETING THE REPARATIONS RULES

One of the most notable aspects of ICC operations in its first decade is how little time the Court has given to interpreting its reparations rules. This is unsurprising from one perspective; under the Rome Statute, reparations can only come after a conviction. The first conviction, against Thomas Lubanga Dyilo, did not occur until 2012, a decade after the Court commenced operation (see below).

The Court's limited interpretation of the reparations rules has also come about because of its early decision to develop principles under Article 75(1) on a case-by-case basis, through its jurisprudence, rather than to establish a set of standing rules (Van Den Wyngaert 2012, 483). In the early years of Court operations, litigation has clarified a few core reparations-related issues, including the criteria for determining the status of victims; the nature of harm, which can be physical, psychological, or material; and a recognition that harm can be *direct* (suffered by the victims themselves) or *indirect* (experienced by third persons who may have a close relationship with the victim) (Schabas 2011, 352; Wiersing 2012). Importantly for this discussion, given that women have been less well represented than men as victims before the ICC (see Chapter 3), it has also been determined that claims for reparations are not conditional on participation in the criminal proceedings.[28]

The Appeals Chamber's reparations decision in *Lubanga* in March 2015 added further clarity to the principles underlying the ICC's reparations framework. In response to the matters under appear in the *Lubanga* reparations judgment it articulated five key principles: (1) a reparations order must be directed against the convicted person; (2) an order must establish and inform the convicted person of his or her liability; (3) the order must specify the type of reparations ordered, either collective, individual, or both; (4) the order must define the harm caused to direct and indirect victims as a result of the crimes for which the person was convicted, as well as identify the modalities of reparations based on the circumstances of the case; and (5) the order must identify the victims eligible to benefit from reparations or set out the criteria of eligibility[29] (Vignoli 2015).

Despite this latter decision giving some greater precision to the ICC's reparations regime, the Court has resisted developing a general set of overarching reparations principles. Arguably, this move has placed the ICC in a reactive position: according to REDRESS, the Court has been left without "certainty and consistency as a general principle of law" or an inability for "internal preparation, intra-organ coordination and the preparation of external stakeholders" in reparations matters (2011, 24). The Washington-based War Crimes Research Office (WCRO) agrees. It suggests that the lack of a set of established principles "leaves open the possibility for wide discrepancies in the approach to reparations across cases" (WCRO 2010, 29) and notes that

> the significant ambiguity that currently exists as to both procedural and substantive aspects of the Court's reparations scheme is likely to breed frustration on the part of victims and intermediaries seeking to conduct outreach with respect to the scheme (WCRO 2010, 28).

The absence of a core set of reparations principles under the Rome Statute has had a particular impact on the pursuit of redistributive gender justice at the ICC. This is primarily because this absence has been filled by informal rules—specifically the gender legacies of the law—that have worked to dampen efforts to further gender-just distribution through the law. As illustrated in detail in Chapter 4, the historic gendered pattern of prosecutions under international criminal law is again emerging at the ICC: the further a case progresses through the Court's prosecution stages, the fewer sexual and gender-based criminal charges survive (see Chapter 4; Grey 2014a).[30] After almost a dozen years in operation, the ICC has not convicted a single individual for sexual or gender-based violence crimes, leaving the bench little opportunity to develop reparations principles for victims of such crimes (Grey 2014a). But even if such a conviction is made in future, resulting in the award of reparations for sexual and gender-based crimes, the principles established in that trial may not be applied in future cases because these decisions are not precedent setting (SáCouto and Cleary 2014, 153). A decision may have persuasive value in subsequent cases, but there is no guarantee that a different trial chamber would apply the same gender-sensitive standards.

Given that the ICC has at the time of writing handed down only one reparations decision, it is difficult to assess the extent to which the Court will be able and willing to address gender maldistribution through reparations decisions. However, *Lubanga* does help to illustrate the influence of gender legacies and the challenges these create for the achievement of redistributive gender justice at the ICC where crimes of sexual and gender-based violence are poorly prosecuted in the first instance.

GENDER JUSTICE AND REPARATIONS IN *LUBANGA*

On August 7, 2012, Trial Chamber I handed down a decision outlining principles for reparations in *Lubanga*. Earlier that year, Thomas Lubanga Dyilo had been found guilty and sentenced to fourteen years' imprisonment for the war crimes of enlisting, conscripting, and using child soldiers in the Democratic Republic of Congo[31] (see Chapter 4 for a detailed discussion of these decisions). As has been detailed elsewhere, one of the most contentious issues throughout this case was the lack of sexual violence charges in the document containing the charges, which reverberated throughout the trial and into the reparations phase.[32]

This reparations decision was an important moment for the Court, triggering for the first time the Rome Statute's Article 75 provisions.[33] In developing the principles for reparations in *Lubanga*, the Trial Chamber called for submissions from interested parties. It accepted filings from the key organs of the Court, the TFV, as well as five NGOs, including the Women's Initiatives group. As the majority of Trial Chamber declined to consider the evidence of sexual violence against female child soldiers when convicting and sentencing Lubanga, most of these submissions stressed the need for gender sensitivity in the design and implementation of the reparations principles, and the inclusion of girl soldiers and victims of sexual violence as beneficiaries.[34] The Women's Initiatives group provided the most comprehensive gender overview, calling on the Chamber to include a gender perspective in the reparations principles and orders, to recognize the harm caused by sexual violence, and to consult with the victims.[35]

Reflecting the gender justice principles in the Nairobi Declaration and recent developments in gender and reparations scholarship and advocacy, the Women's Initiatives group also encouraged the ICC to institute both collective and individual "transformative reparations" that "address existing gender inequalities within communities" and "contribute to advancing gender equality through the types of programmes funded and the type of support provided to victim communities."[36] The TFV expressed similar sentiments, submitting "that the transformative quality of reparations be explicitly addressed in the Court's principles with a view to eliminating the pre-existing structural inequalities that have led to or encouraged the [sexual and gender-based] violence."[37]

The Trial Chamber took heed of these submissions, adopting a broad approach to reparations in its decision. It noted that "[r]eparations in the present case must—to the extent achievable—relieve the suffering caused by these offences; afford justice to the victims by alleviating the consequences of the wrongful acts; deter future violations; and contribute to the effective reintegration of former child soldiers."[38]

Judges Fulford and Blattmann, who had declined to take into account the evidence of sexual violence at the verdict and sentencing stage (outlined in Chapters 3 and 4), joined their colleague Judge Odio Benito in factoring this evidence into their reparations decision. The full bench applied a "proximate cause" standard to establish the nexus between the harm and the crimes, which was lower than that used in the verdict and sentencing stages[39] in order to cover a wider range of victims than that recognized in the earlier stages. The Chamber agreed that reparations could be granted to direct and indirect victims, the latter including "family members of direct victims; anyone who attempted to prevent the commission of one or more of the crimes under consideration; and those who suffered personal harm as a result of these offences, regardless of whether they participated in the trial proceedings."[40]

In developing reparation principles in *Lubanga*, the judges echoed the Women's Initiatives' submissions, and the earlier priorities of the Women's

Caucus, that the modalities of reparations under Article 75 could extend further than restitution, compensation, and rehabilitation. The Chamber held that reparations could also be symbolic, preventive, and transformative, and should be gender sensitive.[41] It noted that

> The Court must reflect the fact that the consequences of these [sexual and gender violence] crimes are complicated and they operate on a number of levels; their impact can extend over a long period of time; they affect women and girls, men and boys, together with their families and communities; and they require a specialist, integrated and multidisciplinary approach.[42]

The principles developed in this case included the application of individual and collective awards that "are to be applied in a broad and flexible manner."[43] Citing the UN Principles, the Nairobi Declaration, and other treaties, the Chamber stated that "[i]n all matters relating to reparations, the Court shall take into account the needs of all the victims, and particularly children, the elderly, those with disabilities and the victims of sexual or gender violence."[44] In recommending steps for the development of reparations initiatives in the Democratic Republic of Congo, to be delivered through the TFV, the Chamber stressed the need to bring together a team of experts, including specialists in child and gender issues.[45] As the Court had found Lubanga indigent, it directed that the reparations be "supported by the Trust Fund's own resources."[46]

Despite these developments and general language throughout the document about the need to include victims of sexual violence, the Chamber specified that "the 'damage, loss and injury,' which form the basis of a reparations claim, *must have resulted from the crimes of enlisting and conscripting children under the age of 15 and using them to participate actively in the hostilities*" (emphasis added).[47] Consequently, as Pena (2012 n.p.) notes, in the *Lubanga* decision

> while there is a recognition of the specificity and gravity of the harm brought about by sexual violence and the need to integrate this aspect in reparations programmes, it seems that only those victims who are also victims of the charges (i.e. mainly child soldiers) can be compensated for the suffering in relation to rape and other crimes of sexual nature. The extent to which other indirect victims, who suffered personal harm as a result of the offences, can access reparations is unclear.

Further, in line with the case-based reparations regime at the ICC, there is only the potential but no guarantee that the gender-sensitive approach reflected in this reparations decision will carry over into other cases[48]—a point the *Lubanga* judges were keen to emphasize. The bench stated in its decision that the principles were "limited to the circumstances of the present case" and "not intended to affect the rights of victims to reparations in other cases, whether before the ICC or national, regional or other international bodies."[49]

The Trial Chamber's decision was not the last word on reparation principles in *Lubanga*. Victims' legal representatives appealed the reparations decision, including on the grounds that the Trial Chamber erred in deciding to dismiss individual applications for reparation without entertaining them.[50] The Defense also appealed, with two of the four grounds of its appeal relating to, in its view, the Trial Chamber's wrongful recognition of sexual violence crimes. The defense argued that by including victims of sexual and gender-based crimes for reparations purposes, the Trial Chamber "contravened the principle that the convicted person shall only be ordered to make reparation for damage resulting from crimes of which he was found guilty."[51] In its submission, the defense argued:

> Accordingly, not having been prosecuted, established or held against Mr Lubanga, acts of sexual violence cannot, contrary to the Chamber's decision, found an award for reparations against Mr Lubanga for the harm they caused.[52]

It also rejected the Chamber's application of the "proximate cause" standard on the basis that it interferes with fair trial rights.[53]

Almost three years after the Trial Chamber released its reparations decision, the Appeals Chamber handed down its determination on March 3, 2015. It sided with the defense on a number of matters, most important here on the inability of the Court to expand reparations to include victims of sexual and gender-based violence. The Appeals Chamber found that the crimes for which Lubanga was found guilty did not include sexual or gender-based violence, and nor did the Trial Chamber include these crimes as part of the gravity of the crime, or as an aggravating factor.[54] In the view of the Appeals Chamber the Trial Chamber's finding that the acts of sexual violence could not be attributed to Lubanga "amounts to concluding that the Trial Chamber did not establish the harm from sexual and gender-based violence resulted from the crimes for which Mr Lubanga was committed . . . [and] therefore considers that Mr Lubanga cannot be held liable for reparations in respect of such harm."[55] However, the Appeals Chamber did note that the TFV should use its assistance mandate to support any victims of these crimes from the conflict, and reminded the Court and the TFV that any reparations orders should be developed with a gender-sensitive approach.[56]

Many commentators were disappointed by the news of the Appeals Chamber's decision not to recognize the harm of victims of sexual violence in the Ituri conflict (Redress 2015; WIGJ 2015). At the same time they reiterated the need for the Prosecutor in future to pay attention to the charging strategy at the outset to avoid this cascade of gender injustice through the case and into the reparations process. As Carla Ferstman, quoted in a REDRESS press release (2015, 2), noted:

> The overly narrow charging policy in this case has meant that sexual and gender-based violence were never fully part of the prosecution. While the Trial Chamber had nonetheless tried to include these victims within the scope of the beneficiaries of reparations, the Appeals Chamber today made clear than reparations must follow the conviction, and must relate only to those harms provide in the prosecution's case. This is an important lesson for the Prosecutor and the Court as a whole: charges must reflect the full range of harms suffered by victims, or else these victims will be excluded from the reparations process.

The appeal also illuminated the implications—including extensive, drawn-out, and expensive litigation—of the Court's early decision not to formalize guiding reparations principles. It took almost three years for the Appeals Chamber to respond to the Trial Chamber's judgment,[57] leaving victims in the Democratic Republic of Congo frustrated (FIDH 2013). The Appeals Chamber gave the TFV a further six months to draft an implementation plan; that then must go back to a reconstituted Trial Chamber for approval. This process has, according to one commentator, done little to meet the expectations of victims in the Ituri region and leaves open a question of whether the deep divide between "the judicial truth established in the Hague and the reality on the ground" can ever be bridged (Vignoli 2015, 4).

In the medium term, the likelihood of the ICC being able to send a more positive message to victims of sexual and gender-based crimes is not promising. The Court is taking time to commence reparations hearings in *Katanga*: while the ICC's second conviction was confirmed in March 2014, by May 2015 observations from interested parties had been received but reparations hearings had not commenced. When hearings do start, the bench will be confronted with a similar situation as in *Lubanga* because no charges were upheld in relation to sexual or gender-based violence, making it difficult for the judges to apply reparations to these victims. As discussed in the previous chapter, while the majority found that crimes of sexual violence were committed during the attack in which Katanga was involved, they were not convinced that the accused was guilty of committing these acts.[58] Further, in its submission in relation to the Katanga case, the TFV itself identified other limitations the ICC may face in applying a gender inclusive approach in this case.

> The Fund notes that a gender-inclusive approach "ensuring that principles and procedures are accessible to *all* victims in their implementation" [emphasis added] is a laudable as well as challenging principle. This is even more so when a reparation order is rendered many years after the crimes were committed and when victims may be widely scattered. The available time and resources may limit possibilities of reaching out to *all* victims in this specific case.[59]

Once again, the gender legacies of the law in the form of inadequate evidence, mode of liability issues, poor prosecution strategy, and failure of recognition are being carried forward into the redistributive mandate of the ICC. As in *Lubanga*, judges may try to "shoehorn" the interests of victims of sexual and gender-based violence into any reparations principles, but without a conviction based on these crimes, they are restricted in how far they can address this specific victimization through reparations.

REDISTRIBUTING JUSTICE THROUGH THE TFV I: REPARATIONS

Since commencing operations in 2008, the TFV has made little progress on its first mandate: to implement Court-ordered reparations. In the *Lubanga* reparations decision, the Trial Chamber directed the TFV to implement its proposed five-step implementation plan: carrying out assessments to identify localities, consulting with victims and communities, assessing the harm, soliciting victim and community expectations, and collecting requests and proposals for reparations.[60] Only since March 2015 when the Appeals Chamber handed down its decisions on the verdict and reparations in *Lubanga*, has the TFV been able to seriously plan for the application of reparations in the Democratic Republic of Congo.

The sequence of decision making and the extensive delay in the implementation of reparations in *Lubanga* have led some commentators to be highly critical of the ICC's reparations process. As SáCouto and Cleary (2014, 154) point out, the ICC's system that allows for reparations principles or orders to be handed down before any appeal against the judgment has been finalized is highly problematic. Because reparations can only be awarded in cases where an accused is convicted, an acquittal on appeal will overturn any reparations decision, thereby "wasting the resources of the [TFV], . . . the judges, the parties and the participating victims" (SáCouto and Cleary 2014, 154).

It is not just the ICC's processes that are complicating the implementation of the TFV's reparations mandate: resources are also an issue. Even if conviction and reparations decisions are upheld, the TFV has only limited resources to redistribute among the affected population, particularly in cases where an accused is found indigent and cannot pay for the reparations measures themselves. The ICC and by implication the TFV face a significant "reparations gap." In 2014 the TFV had a reserve of €1.8 million for reparations to be used across all ICC cases[61]—a paltry sum given the extent of reparations needed in each of the conflict sites under review.

There is also a risk that the current process will undermine the TFV's core principles, especially the "do no harm" approach that is foundational to its reparative mandate. The TFV outlined this approach in its *Lubanga* submission, arguing that

> [I]n post-conflict situations, reparations have the risk of becoming part of the dynamics of a conflict and may even fuel tensions. Therefore, the Court must strive to "do no harm" or to minimize the harm that may inadvertently result simply from providing reparations to victims.[62]

The delay in proceedings can be seen to be contributing to this problem by exacerbating tensions arising from unmet expectations of victims and a fear that reparations "may not ultimately be forthcoming" (SáCouto and Cleary 2014, 154–155).

Open Society Foundations, an international NGO that is closely tracking ICC-related developments in the Democratic Republic of Congo, suggests that tensions are indeed beginning to surface in the Ituri region. It notes the frustration of victims: not only have they had to wait many years for a decision, but because of the Court's delays and the TFV's inability to implement its reparations plan while the appeal was ongoing, the population remain uncertain about who will receive reparations and what form those reparations will take, and they have found it difficult to insert their concerns into a "very technical legal debate" (Bueno 2012). Locals wonder whether reparations measures will extend to the girls forced into sexual slavery, who were raped and became mothers or were infected with HIV by members of Lubanga's UPC militia and who remain vulnerable to reprisals because of the violations committed against them (Bueno 2012).

REDISTRIBUTING JUSTICE THROUGH THE TFV II: ASSISTANCE

The TFV's reparations mandate may have been curtailed in the ICC's first decade, but the Fund has taken some significant steps in implementing its assistance mandate in a number of states where the Court has opened investigations. To date, its assistance programs have focused on the Democratic Republic of Congo, Uganda, and the Central African Republic.[63] In delivering on its assistance mandate, the TFV has focused specifically on victims experiencing sexual and gender-based violence, widows/widowers, former child solders/abducted youth, orphans and vulnerable children, and families suffering physical and/or mental trauma. As with its reparations mandate, the level of demand for TFV assistance far outweighs its resources. However, in recent years, the TFV has had a surge in financial support. After some lean years resulting from the global economic downturn, at the Twelfth ASP meeting in November 2013 and in the early months of 2014, the TFV received additional financial commitments from a handful of states, significantly boosting its existing income to €19.2 million (as of July 2014).[64] Most of these newly committed funds are for the TFV's assistance programs, which are run through intermediaries, both local and international partners.

The TFV has committed to mainstreaming a gender-based perspective across all programming.[65] This includes requiring its partners to demonstrate in their operations *"accessibility* for applicants that have traditionally lacked access to funding, addressing the *special vulnerability of girls and women"* (McCleary-Sills and Mukasa 2013, 12, emphasis in original) and "taking care to promote women and girls' empowerment and address the specific needs of male and female victim survivors in different age groups"[66] across all its initiatives.

The second strategy of the TFV's gender justice approach is to prioritize the development of programs for victims experiencing gender and sexual violence crimes. This includes initiatives for girls abducted and/or conscripted and enslaved by armed groups and children and women victimized and displaced from their communities by campaigns of mass rape. To support these programs, the TFV has established an earmarked fund, and its personnel have been successful in encouraging ICC states parties to contribute to it. Former UK Foreign Secretary William Hague has been a particular champion of these fundraising efforts. In 2013 Hague spearheaded the G8 Ministers' *Declaration on Preventing Sexual Violence in Conflict*, which included a call for the international community "to increase their efforts to mobilise [sexual violence] funding, including to programs such as the ICC Trust Fund for Victims and its implementing partners" (see US Department of State 2013). During the 2014 London Summit to End Sexual Violence in Conflict, hosted by Hague and Angelina Jolie in her role as Special Envoy of the UN High Commissioner for Refugees, the UK committed a further €1.1 million to the TFV's earmarked fund and encouraged other states to similarly support its work.[67] As of July 2014, the earmarked fund had reached €5 million, almost one quarter of all TFV reserves.[68]

Five years after commencing operations, the TFV had 28 active projects, addressing physical, psychological, and material needs across Uganda and the Democratic Republic of Congo, which it estimates directly and indirectly support over 110,000 victims of crimes under the jurisdiction of the Court (McCleary-Sills and Mukasa 2013, 15). Eight of these projects specifically target victims of sexual and gender-based violence,[69] with many seeking to assist girls and younger women, including those with children from conflict-related rape. Health services funded by the TFV include fistula repair, plastic surgery, orthopedic fitting, and treatment for HIV, AIDS, and other sexually transmitted infections.[70]

Many assistance programs supported by the TFV also have a direct redistributive focus aimed at addressing the conflict-related destruction of property and "the consequences of displacement and loss of income-earning family members, which diminished the sources of livelihood and subsistence" (McCleary-Sills and Mukasa 2013, 31), as well as improving "the economic status of the victims through education, economic development and rebuilding of community infrastructure, and creation of employment opportunities" (McCleary-Sills and Mukasa 2013, 31). Specific material assistance programs include vocational education and training and literacy projects, savings and loan schemes, and agricultural development initiatives, all aimed at facilitating victims' economic activity (McCleary-Sills and Mukasa 2013, 31–35). The TFV has ensured that both women and men are able to access these schemes, with some being primarily targeted toward or led by women, such as a new chili-growing association in Uganda and microcredit schemes in the Democratic Republic of Congo (McCleary-Sills and Mukasa 2013, 8). According to a recent comprehensive independent evaluation of TFV assistance programs by the International Center for Research on Women (McCleary-Sills and Mukasa 2013, 33):

> At the individual and family level, testimonies revealed that apart from the restoration of livelihoods the ability to save, borrow and invest was empowering for group members as evidenced in their strong sense of pride, dignity and self-worth. Among the most significant changes, victim participants indicated

the ability to pay school fees, afford more than one meal a day, improved housing and newfound ability to purchase parcels of land and/or make capital investments for small businesses.

The International Center for Research on Women's evaluation also reports that "across all contexts, victim members and their families reported a positive impact on gender relations at household levels for spouses/partners that jointly participated in the [savings and loan] groups." However, it was noted in the Democratic Republic of Congo context that men generally led these groups (McCleary-Sills and Mukasa 2013, 34).

The evaluation report indicated that the TFV has attempted to integrate gender concerns across all activities but recommended more be done to monitor and enforce this aspect of its framework, including challenging assumptions about "the types of crimes experienced by male and female victims, and, thus, the types of assistance they require" (McCleary-Sills and Mukasa 2013, 40). It also recommended that the TFV provide additional follow-up support to young women victims returning from captivity with children born of rape, who are often not allowed to return to their family homes and find it difficult to be fully integrated as members of the family (McCleary-Sills and Mukasa 2013, 37).

In the ICC's early years, efforts by gender justice actors to use the formal rules to promote gender redistribution—which were embedded in the Rome Statute in part because of the Women's Caucus's efforts—have produced a mixed picture (Table 5.1). The slow pace of trial deliberations has provided gender justice advocates little opportunity to intervene in reparations deliberations. In *Lubanga*, the one case that has completed the reparations phase, gender justice voices were prominent, and the Trial Chamber appeared to pay attention to these claims and make an effort to "fill in the gaps" of the prosecution phase to include victims of sexual and gender-based violence. However, both *Lubanga* and *Katanga* also illustrated the problem of the carryover of gender legacies—especially the impact of inadequate charging and prosecution of sexual and gender-based violence—into the redistributive operations of the Court. The absence of a set of defined principles that embed gender justice concerns in the heart of reparations deliberations has enabled these legacies to move in and fill in the gaps. The TFV's efforts to direct its assistance mandate toward women, girls, and victims of sexual and gender-based violence have demonstrated the value of the ICC's broader redistributive mandate. While the Court was caught up in litigation over its first convicted perpetrator, which ultimately lead to its first reparations decision being overturned on appeal,

Table 5.1. WOMEN'S CAUCUS PRIORITIES FOR THE ICC REPARATIONS PROGRAM

Gender Justice Priorities	Formal Rules	Enforced
Broad modes of reparations, including restitution, compensation, and rehabilitation	✔	✘
Establish principles relating to reparations in every case	✘	N/A
Collective and individual redress	✔	✘
A broad definition of victims to include family members	✔	✔
Enable victims and other interested persons to trigger the Court's authority to make rulings with respect to reparations	✘	N/A
Enable victims and other interested persons to appeal Court rulings with respect to reparations	✔	✔
Allow the Court under certain conditions to "order" or to "recommend" that states contribute to reparations	✘	N/A
Establish TFV with gender justice mandate	✔	✘: *Reparations* ✔: *Assistance*

the TFV has been able to activate its assistance mandate in situation countries, including in the Democratic Republic of Congo, where Lubanga's militia was operating. Working within a constrained resource setting, in its first five years in operation the TFV has offered a wide range of tangible, gender-sensitive redistributive programs to an expansive cohort of victims. If the ICC can claim any advances in addressing gender maldistribution in its first decade, it has been through the work of the TFV that such advances have been achieved.

PART FOUR: LEGACIES, LEGITIMACY, AND REDISTRIBUTIVE GENDER JUSTICE OUTCOMES

These early developments of Court-ordered reparations and the TFV's assistance mandate are helping to forge the path for redistributive gender justice at the ICC. To date, as *Lubanga* and *Katanga* demonstrate, it has been difficult to secure redistributive outcomes through the Rome Statute's reparation rules. The process is inordinately slow, and where adjudication has been possible, though certain judges and gender advocates have worked to exploit the constructive ambiguities of the rules to address gender maldistribution at the reparations phase, this has been a case of "too little, too late." In the main, during the ICC's early years, gender legacies of the law have had a powerful cascade effect through all stages of the trial, including the reparations phase, which has been difficult to turn around. By contrast, the TFV has been able to make some significant strides in addressing gender maldistribution through its assistance mandate.

These developments have seen a dual path emerge at the ICC in relation to redistributive gender justice: the court-ordered reparations path, where gender justice claims have largely been "locked out," and the TFV assistance path, where these claims have been "locked in." The problem of "lockout" will only be addressed when and if the Court challenges the gender legacies in which its operations are temporally nested. The OTP's gender policy (discussed in detail in previous chapters)—aimed at addressing these legacies and improving the ICC's prosecution record of crimes of sexual and gender-based violence—has the potential to have a significant impact throughout the trial phases, and resonate through to the reparations phase. But as with recognition, not all the revision efforts rest on the shoulders of the OTP. Without a set of core principles to guide them, members of the bench also need to "remember" the efforts made by the Trial Chamber judges in the first reparations decision in *Lubanga* to identify the gender justice elements of reparations decisions, and to continue to identify these elements in future judgments.

Gender justice actors' sense of the legitimacy of the ICC's reparations mandate has been influenced by the success of the Women's Caucus in embedding reparations rules in the Rome Statute, the dual-track development of these rules in practice, and recent reform efforts to bring gender justice concerns more to the fore at the ICC.

The Women's Caucus and other NGOs sensitive to gender justice issues left the negotiations phase with a strong sense of legitimacy about the design of the ICC's reparations mandate. Through their lobbying efforts, these actors influenced the integration of redistributive features into the ICC's formal reparations rules and helped embed an expanded view of victims, features that would be able to help redress the harms of those historically excluded from reparations processes. The fact that restorative justice approaches were a novel addition to international criminal justice law no doubt assisted their cause, giving them fewer and less-entrenched rules and practices to unravel during negotiations.

Throughout the operations phase, gender justice advocates' sense of legitimacy about this aspect of the Court's mandate has been tested. The lack of an overarching reparations framework has enabled old gender norms to infiltrate the ICC's work on reparations. The failure to adequately prosecute crimes of sexual and gender-based violence in its first two cases has made the Court's reparations regime appear selective and unfair to victims of these crimes, and could possibly do more harm than good in the fragile postconflict contexts in which it will be implemented[71] (REDRESS 2011, 33). In Frédéric Mégret's view (2012, n.p.), the ICC's reparations program is at risk of creating

> two types of victims, "super victims" who, as a result of having suffered at the hands of someone convicted by the Court, benefit from a quite strong victim reparations regime; and "ordinary victims" who, as a result of having suffered at the hands of someone not convicted (or not apprehended) by the Court will have to make do with whatever alternative system of reparation exists, if at all.

There is an obvious gender justice dimension to this disparity, given the poor record of the ICC in its first decade in investigating and successfully prosecuting the perpetrators of sexual and gender-based violence (as detailed in Chapter 4).

Early adjudication of the ICC's reparations mandate has also influenced gender justice actors' sense of the operational legitimacy of the Court. From a positive perspective, the Trial Chamber incorporation of a gender-inclusive approach in *Lubanga*, calling for processes, principles, and future measures to involve women and men and to address crimes of sexual violence, was noted and welcomed by the Women's Initiatives group and others. The Women's Initiatives group referred to the *Lubanga* Trial Chamber reparations decision as "highly significant" and as addressing "some of the underlying injustices and inequalities and may contribute, even if in some small way, to transforming communal and gender relations."[72] REDRESS (2012) also welcomed the decision, especially the willingness of the Court to embrace international norms and provide "that reparations are implemented without any discrimination regarding age, ethnicity or gender and that reparation measures are devised to take into account the age of victims and the sexual violence they may have suffered." REDRESS (2012) also favorably noted the Chamber's determination that "reparations should not be limited to the relatively small group of victims that participated in the trial and those who applied for reparations."

At the same time, these actors have recognized that because of the poor prosecution of sexual and gender-based violence during the *Lubanga* case, the Trial Chamber had very little discretion in extending the cohort of beneficiaries.[73] Only a narrow range of victims of sexual and gender-based violence was included in the decision, a decision that was overturned by the Appeals Chamber, given the prosecution's limited charging strategy and the Trial Chamber judges' unwillingness to recognize crimes of sexual violence in the sentencing, or as an aggravating factor. Further, as noted above, NGOs on the ground have recognized the serious problems in conflict-affected communities stemming from the drawn-out appeal process, significantly threatening the TFV's application of the "do no harm" principle.

The least ambiguous reason for continued gender justice support for the redistributive functions of the ICC is the TFV's gender-sensitive assistance program. More than any other aspect of the ICC system, the independent TFV has demonstrated a commitment to mainstreaming a gender-just approach and to ensuring that this is operationalized in its programs in situation countries. Unimpeded by strict criminal legal rules and processes, the TFV has used its capacity to redistribute resources to those who have historically been disadvantaged in the conflict-ridden societies in which the Court is operating. Women, girls, and victims of sexual violence have all been beneficiaries of the TFV's programs. This includes empowering these victims economically, through material redistributive programs. Alert to the resource restrictions on TFV programs, gender justice advocates can nevertheless see significant progress in this area of ICC operations; compared with the Court-ordered reparations system, it offers a more hopeful prospect for attaining redistributive gender justice in the future (see Durbach and Chappell 2014).

As with other aspects of Court operations, it is too early to fully assess the grounds upon which gender justice actors might evaluate the consequential legitimacy of the ICC's redistributive gender justice mandate. As the above discussion shows, the Women's Caucus, its heir, Women's Initiatives, and other gender-sensitive NGOs, such as REDRESS, have made a significant contribution to all aspects of the Court's restorative justice system. In particular, they have influenced the design of the reparations framework and the interpretation of this framework in *Lubanga* and stand ready to do the same in *Katanga*. They have also demonstrated strong support for the work of the TFV.[74] Such involvement suggests they remain committed to furthering all aspects of the Court's reparative work and consider that despite its limitations, there remain opportunities to direct the ICC's future redistributive path in ways that can produce better gender justice outcomes.

The ICC's formal rules and informal gendered norms have combined with resource constraints to influence the path of gender-just redistribution at the Court. But it is important to remember that the Court is spatially nested in a broader environment, an international system in which the norm of state sovereignty remains preeminent. Not unless or until states undertake action to complement the reparative functions of the ICC will there be adequate redress for all victims of all crimes, including redistributive measures for women, girls, and victims of sexual and gender-based crimes (see Moffett 2013, 14). It is this notion of complementarity—which links the Court to states parties—that is the focus of the next chapter.

CHAPTER 6

Complementing Gender Justice at the International Criminal Court

The Rome Statute's complementarity provisions are recognized as a cornerstone of the ICC system and are one of its key innovations.[1] The complementarity principle is designed to leave states with primary responsibility for prosecuting crimes encoded in the Rome Statute and to make the ICC a court of last resort. Yet under the Statute there is no formal link between these complementarity innovations and its key gender justice principles. This places an onus on actors within and outside the ICC to make a conscious, concerted effort to bring a gender justice perspective to bear on complementarity deliberations. The task of linking these elements rests primarily with the OTP in its preliminary examinations where jurisdictional issues are assessed, and the Pre-Trial Chamber in its admissibility deliberations. When either the OTP or the Chamber fails to link complementarity to gender justice concerns, the Court misses the opportunity to address gender injustices through ICC prosecutions. It may also miss the chance to extend the expressive power of the Rome Statute through "positive" complementarity measures, such as encouraging states parties to address domestic-level impunity for sexual and gender-based violations.

Complementarity is at the heart of ICC/state relations and as such is connected to the primary norm of international relations—state sovereignty. Sovereignty helps set the context in which the ICC is "nested." As this chapter will demonstrate, it is significant for the ICC's gender justice deliberations and outcomes that at precisely the point where the Rome Statute meets questions of state sovereignty—through its complementarity provisions—there are no formal gender justice rules.

Although not articulated in the Rome Statute's complementarity provisions, and largely ignored in the generalist literature in the area,[2] the complementarity principle has important gender justice dimensions, as well as the capacity to influence gender justice outcomes (see Chappell et al. 2013; Kapur 2012; Ní Aoláin 2014). Gender justice is relevant to assessing the existence and genuineness of domestic proceedings. It is also linked to complementarity in its "positive" guise, notably the ICC's capacity to use pressure or encouragement to trigger state-based responses to sexual and gender-based violations.

Part One of this chapter discusses the link between state sovereignty and complementarity. It engages with Nancy Fraser's argument about the emergence of a "post-Westphalian frame" (2009) through which sovereignty operates in the contemporary world and considers the relevance of this frame for understanding the broader context in which the Rome Statute is "nested." Part Two outlines the gender justice dimensions of complementarity and the largely unsuccessful efforts of the Women's Caucus to have these recognized in the Rome Statute. Part Three focuses on the implementation of complementarity in the ICC's early years. It provides a general overview, then draws on the OTP's preliminary examinations in the cases of Colombia and Guinea to highlight the "gender justice complementarity shadow" (Chappell et al. 2013) created by the Court in its first decade. Part Four engages more directly with the "positive" aspects of complementarity, providing a gender analysis of data on the implementation of Rome Statute in states parties, demonstrating their very uneven response to the adoption of gender justice provisions in domestic law. Part Five considers the key factors influencing the ICC's performance in relation to gender justice and complementarity and discusses the influence of this performance on the Court's gender justice constituency, particularly its assessment of the ICC's design and operational legitimacy.

This chapter amplifies the point made in earlier chapters about the importance of the Court's "nestedness" (Mackay 2014a)—both *temporally*, through gender legacies, and *spatially*, through the broader international relations system through which states parties operate—for understanding the codification and implementation of the Rome Statute's representation, recognition, and redistribution gender rules. In this chapter "nestedness" applies in both senses but the spatial element is particularly salient; the ICC's place in the broader international relations environment has influenced the design and operation of the Court's complementarity framework and its links—or lack thereof—to gender justice issues. The chapter also highlights the point made by feminist legal scholars and institutionalists of the critical role that formal rules play in enforcing accountability, and the problems that arise for securing gender justice when significant gaps and silences exist in these codified rules. The chapter argues that failure to incorporate an explicit gender focus in the Rome Statute's complementarity rules and the general disregard for such concerns in the implementation of complementarity principles in the Court's first decade present an ongoing challenge to the legitimacy of the Court in the eyes of its gender justice constituency.

PART ONE: THE ICC AND GENDER JUSTICE THROUGH A "POST-WESTPHALIAN" FRAME

In the view of Nancy Fraser, the international relations system is undergoing a transformation away from the long-held Westphalian model, where exclusive power rested with nation-states, to a "post-Westphalian" one, which reflects a new "multi-level structure of governmentality in which the national State is but one level among others" (Fraser 2009, 126; also see Barnett and Finnemore 2004, 164–165). In Fraser's view, this new model has arisen due to processes of globalization and the resulting "spillover" across borders of justice concerns—including environmental, economic equality, and human rights issues (Fraser 2009, 24). As Fraser notes:

> Under current conditions, one's chances to live a good life do not depend wholly on the international political constitution of the territorial states in which one resides. Although the latter remains undeniably relevant, its effects are meditated by other structures, both extra-and non-territorial (2009, 24).

In this new environment, sovereignty has far from disappeared, but it no longer operates in the same way; sovereignty is more disaggregated, as nation-states work closely with, and through, international institutions, such as the UN treaty system, the European Union and other regional entities, and the ICC, to address justice claims (Fraser 2009, 14, 87).

Fraser draws attention to how the shift toward a post-Westphalian model of international relations can support, and is also in part driven by, gender injustices of misrepresentation, misrecognition, and maldistribution within nation-states. Given "women's vulnerability to transnational forces" (Fraser 2009, 112)—such as multinational corporations, interstate and intrastate military forces, and the like—the transnational women's rights movement has come to believe that "women's chances for living good lives depend at least as much on processes that trespass the borders of territorial states as on those contained within them" (Fraser 2009, 113).

The ICC is considered by some as an exemplar of this shift in the international relations system toward a post-Westphalian model (Fraser 2009, 126; Simmons and Danner 2010); it indicates a process of criminal law being "unbundled" from the state and "rebundled and rescaled" upward to the international level (Fraser 2009, 126), enabling victims and others justice seekers to escape the state-level criminal justice system and seek global accountability. The ICC's second Prosecutor, Fatou Bensouda's, view of the ICC also accords with this position:

> With the adoption of the Rome Statute model, states parties shifted the paradigm from the Westphalian model of national self-regulation to the model of international scrutiny under the United Nations Security Council supervision and now to the Rome Statute model of the rule of law (2012b).

According to ICC scholars Beth Simmons and Allison Danner, the design features of the ICC, including the Prosecutor's ability to investigate crimes on his or her own motion (*proprio motu*) and the potential for UN Security Council referrals of non–states parties, mean that the Court is "far less protective of state sovereignty than was originally contemplated or has ever existed in modern history" (2011, 229).

The existence of the ICC can indeed be seen to accord with Fraser's view of the shift toward a post-Westphalian model with its capacity to prosecute individuals at the international level for a range of atrocities committed within and across state borders. At the same time, it is important to note that state sovereignty, albeit in an attenuated form, remains central to the design of the Rome Statute and to the environment in which it is nested.

The link between the Rome Statute system and state sovereignty is provided through the principle of complementarity. This principle is a political and legal compromise built into the heart of the ICC system, intended to strike a balance between the jurisdiction of the Court and states. In deliberations over the creation of the ICC, states decided to reverse the practice used in ICTY and ICTR that gave primacy to these international tribunals over national courts (Kleffner 2008, 95), a model that reflects more closely Fraser's post-Westphalian frame. Under the complementarity provisions outlined in the Preamble and Article 17 of the Rome Statute, the ICC's designers inverted the tribunal model, leaving states with the primary responsibility for prosecuting crimes included in the Rome Statute. The ICC's complementarity provisions, as Kleffner argues, "bear witness to the fact that States were much more concerned about safeguarding their sovereign prerogative to punish . . . perpetrators than they were in the context of the ad hoc tribunals" (2008, 96). Their aim was to ensure that the ICC would "supplement—rather than supplant—domestic criminal law prosecutions" (Simmons and Danner 2011, 230). As Prosecutor Bensouda (2012b) explains it, "as opposed to the ad hoc tribunals . . . ICC does not have primacy over the crimes. We are a backup system. We are a system that complements the national efforts."

Establishing a court of last resort, ICC designers sought to create an institution whose primary influence came not through prosecutions in The Hague but through the ratification, implementation, and enforcement of the Rome Statute at the national level (Drumbl 2011). This view was reflected in a statement of the ICC's first Prosecutor, Luis Moreno Ocampo:

> The effectiveness of the International Criminal Court should not be measured only by the number of cases that reach the Court. On the contrary, the absence of trials by the ICC, as a consequence of the effective functioning of national systems, would be a major success.[3]

Underlying the Prosecutor's statement reflects the *positive*, catalytic role complementarity can play, one that is aimed at "enriching the jurisprudence of national courts and challenging [national] prosecutors and judges to display greater zeal in the serious violations of human rights" (Schabas 2011, 58). Nouwen refers to this approach as "complementarity as big idea" (2013, 11). Together, the narrow technical admissibility rules that determine whether the state or the ICC will investigate and prosecute the case, and this more informal "big idea" view of complementarity that has emerged in practice, combine to create the ICC's complementarity "system."

The ICC's complementarity system is one where accountability is "rebundled" upward from the national level to the international level, but only when a case meets certain legal criteria. It is also a system where new norms of accountability are meant to disseminate downward, with the ICC encouraging (and, where necessary, threatening) states to undertake their own investigations and prosecutions and to get their own legal regimes in order. A fundamental gap in this system is that complementarity does not address specific gender injustice dimensions of state criminal codes and practices, either in its technical admissibility rules or in its "positive" guise. As a result, and as illustrated in the following discussion, this has diminished the potential value of the ICC as a post-Westphalian institution for addressing inter-, intra- and trans-national gender injustices.

PART TWO: NEGOTIATING COMPLEMENTARITY

In contrast to the success of the Women's Caucus in embedding gender justice recognition, representation, and redistribution principles in many of the aspects of the Rome Statute, it had little success in securing these principles in the ICC's overarching complementarity regime. This was not for want of trying.

In their lobbying, Women's Caucus members argued that the complementarity rules were fundamental to the ICC's capacity to address impunity for sexual and gender-based violence crimes, and if designed correctly, could improve accountability for the crimes committed against all victims, including in national jurisdictions (Spees 2003, 1246). According to its lobbying documents, Caucus members petitioned states through the PrepCom meetings and at the Rome Conference to recognize the gender dimensions of two core elements of the complementarity admissibility criteria: that is, whether a state was *unable* or *unwilling* to investigate and prosecute alleged crimes under the Statute.

In considering the state's *ability*, Caucus members argued that the ICC should be able to take on, and indeed retry, national cases where the definition of the crime in the domestic criminal code was inconsistent with the Rome Statute.[4] They argued that the inability test should specifically include situations "where procedural or evidentiary requirements particular to sexual violence preclude or unreasonably obstruct a proper conviction."[5] This would include situations where a state's penal codes treat rape as a crime of honor rather than a violent crime equal to other forms of assault, or where evidentiary rules treat women's testimony as less than that of men (UN Women 2011). The Caucus also suggested that a failure to secure the trust of victims—that is, where victims are unwilling to come forward to press charges due to distrust of national legal processes—should be treated as a sign of "inability."[6]

The Caucus also sought to give ICC judges the power to interpret a state's *unwillingness* to prosecute to include national "proceedings . . . where charges of sexual and gender violence are not considered along with other offenses or where discriminatory substantive or procedural rules or the discriminating application of law or rules, preclude impartial proceedings."[7] Moreover, in its view, "the Court should find a case of rape admissible where a State prosecution required showing the victim's 'honesty' (i.e. chastity) or the corroboration of her and his testimony, or permitted the introduction of irrelevant, inflammatory evidence or the punishment was trivial."[8] Further, on unwillingness, the Women's Caucus' argued that

> complementarity is particularly significant for victims of sexual and gender-based violence in situations where local authorities seek to shield the perpetrators from responsibility or local law fails to reflect the seriousness of these crimes or where the legal criteria, procedures, and evidentiary rules for adjudicating guilt are tainted by sexual discrimination and prejudice and guarantee an impartial trial.[9]

In making these arguments the Caucus was asking the designers to create a complementarity system in which, in its admissibility deliberations, the Court would subject states to the standards of gender justice provided under the Rome Statute. Where these standards were not met, the Caucus sought to have the ICC investigate and prosecute the case. Essentially, Caucus members were adopting a post-Westphalian frame; in their view well-documented weaknesses in the codification of sexual and gender-based violence in domestic jurisdictions should be grounds for a complementarity challenge, potentially shifting cases from the national to the international level, thereby opening a new avenue for accountability for victims of such violence outside their state jurisdiction.

The Women's Caucus's position on extending the complementarity provisions to take into account gender justice considerations failed to attract the support of state negotiators at the Rome Conference. In the end the Caucus retreated from advocating on the issue, stating it was "reluctant to urge that stronger standard under Article 15 [later Article 17] be negotiated at this time given the difficulty of the issue and the degree of consensus agreed at the August 1997 PrepCom."[10] The political realism of the Caucus members did not diminish their disappointment or concerns: in their view the absence of specific gender justice complementarity provisions "could result in impunity for crimes of sexual and gender violence" in the ongoing work of the ICC.[11]

Gender biases at the Rome Conference interfered with the Women's Caucus's ability to gain traction on gender justice complementarity provisions. As Valerie Oosterveld, explained in a personal communication, because complementarity was framed as a jurisdictional issue, it was a considered a matter outside the remit of the Caucus and an area over which it was not considered to have any expertise. In Oosterveld's view (personal communication):

> It became obvious in corridor discussions during the Rome Conference that many States considered matters related to the complex jurisdiction provisions to be "gender-neutral" and therefore felt either confused or hostile to the fact that the Caucus even had an opinion on the jurisdictional provisions.

There was also a broader dimension to states' resistance to Women's Caucus recommendations, related to the ongoing salience of state sovereignty norms. The failure to embed gender justice principles in the Rome Statute's complementarity provisions in some respects mirrored the reparations debate, where states used sovereignty arguments to refuse to take responsibility for the redistributive provisions contained in the Rome Statute (see Chapter 5). Agreeing to complementarity as a general principle, states demonstrated a willingness to give the ICC jurisdiction over specific crimes committed within their territory and under strict criteria. However, negotiations revealed a consensus among official delegates about the boundary of this jurisdiction: they strongly resisted any incursion on their control over national law, including greater scrutiny of the gender justice gaps therein. Clearly, the post-Westphalian frame had its limits.

The Rome Statute's Complementarity Provisions: The Technical View

The ICC's formal complementarity rules agreed to at the Rome Conference are enshrined in Article 1 of the Statute, which confirms that the ICC "shall be complementary to national criminal jurisdictions," and in Article 17, which sets out the criteria for determining the admissibility of cases before the Court.[12] The application of these technical aspects of complementarity occurs at various stages of the ICC's proceedings. The earliest application is at the "preliminary examination" stage, such as those currently under way in Guinea and Colombia (see Part Three of this chapter). During a preliminary examination the ICC Prosecutor collects and analyzes information on potential cases to determine whether to open a formal ICC investigation.[13]

In making this determination, the Prosecutor is required to apply the two-step admissibility test set out in Article 17(1)(a).[14] The first step considers whether the case "is being investigated or prosecuted by a State which had jurisdiction over it." If the state has taken *no* such action, then the case is admissible to the ICC. However, if the state *is* investigating or prosecuting the case, then the Prosecutor must consider a second step, namely whether the state is "unwilling" or "unable" to carry out the proceedings "genuinely"[15] (also see Batros 2011, 569). If the state *is* unwilling or unable, then the case is admissible despite the existence of proceedings at the national level. The Pre-Trial Chamber may apply these same admissibility tests once an arrest warrant or summons to appear has been issued, either on its own motion, at the request by the Prosecutor, or in response to an admissibility challenge by the suspect or the state (Article 19(1)–(3)).

The Statute offers some guidance as to what the terms "unwillingness" and "inability" mean. In assessing "unwillingness," the ICC must consider whether the purpose of the national proceedings is to shield the person from criminal responsibility for crimes within the jurisdiction of the Court, whether there has been an unjustified delay in the proceedings, or whether the proceedings lacked independence or impartiality or were otherwise "inconsistent with the intent to bring the person concerned to justice" (Article 17(2)).[16] In assessing "inability," the Court must consider whether "due to a total or substantial collapse or unavailability of its national judicial system, the State is . . . unable to carry out its proceedings" (Article 17(3)). Importantly, the admissibility provisions allow the ICC to reprosecute a case that has already been prosecuted by the state, if the domestic proceedings were intended to "shield" the person from criminal responsibility for crimes within the jurisdiction of the Court or were not conducted independently, impartially, and with an "intent to bring the person concerned to justice"—in other words, a sham trial (Article 17(2)(c); Article 20(3)).

In clarifying the meaning of unwillingness and inability, the Rome Statute does not expressly recognize the types of gender injustices in domestic law highlighted in Women's Caucus advocacy, including legal obstructions facing victims of sexual and gender-based violence in having their cases investigated and prosecuted domestically.

The ICC's Informal Complementarity Rules: Complementarity as a "Big Idea"

The "big idea" approach to complementarity is not tethered to the formal rules of the Rome Statute but encompasses emerging, informal rules, which conceive of the concept as a way for the ICC to catalyze justice efforts at the national level (Nouwen 2013; Kleffner 2009, 41–53; Schabas 2011, 58). This informal approach is much closer to Fraser's post-Westphalian model of how ICC operations might work to enhance accountability for international crimes.

ICC scholars have identified the Rome Statute's catalyzing effect as operating through a "carrot-and-stick" approach—either through threats of ICC intervention if the state does not respond to pressure to act[17] or through a more "positive" approach that envisions a cooperative relationship between the Court and national actors, including the ICC taking on the "big fish" and leaving the "small fry" to state jurisdictions (Nouwen 2013, Chapter 1), as well as the ICC providing encouragement and some assistance for domestic investigations and prosecutions (Burke-White 2011; Stahn 2008).

Central to the "big idea" notion is that states should introduce legislation to implement the Rome Statute crimes into national penal codes to ensure that perpetrators can be brought to justice at the national level. Although it is sometimes controversially implied that the Statute imposes this "obligation" (Amnesty International 2010; Mégret, 2011), most Rome Statute experts reject this view (Cryer 2010, 75; Nouwen 2011, 214; Stahn 2008, 92). More usually, the obligation to incorporate the Rome Statute crimes into domestic law is framed as a (nonlegal) obligation that arises from a commitment to international criminal justice (Cryer 2010, 75). At its broadest, complementarity as a "big idea" envisions states undertaking reforms to their national justice systems to ensure that the Rome Statute crimes can be investigated and prosecuted domestically (although the Statute does not direct states to do so). In addition to legislative amendments, ICC constituencies have made calls to improve victim protection and participation, stamp out corruption, provide better training and security to judicial personnel, and make the overall justice system more accessible to the public (Mégret 2011, 364–365). These "big idea" aspects potentially offer a way to address the state-level gender injustices noted by the Women's Caucus, including inadequate legislation that fails to encompass a wide range of sexual and gender-based crimes or treats them as less grave, or inadequate investigatory and prosecution procedures.

PART THREE: COMPLEMENTARITY IN PRACTICE

In the Court's early years, the consequences of an absence of clear gender justice principles in the ICC's complementarity framework have been apparent in its implementation. Specific gender justice silences have been reproduced in the Court's interpretation of the technical rules and in its positive approaches to complementarity. As a result of these problems it has been argued that a "gender justice shadow of complementarity" has emerged at the ICC (Chappell et al. 2013). This argument mirrors the work of Kevin Jon Heller (2006), who has proposed that there is a "shadow side" of complementarity in relation to due process rights. Heller argues that while the Rome Statute establishes the highest standards of due process for cases before the ICC, the complementarity provisions do not adequately ensure due process rights in national jurisdictions. Here it is suggested that there is a shadow side to complementarity in relation to gender justice: the Rome Statute provides a more developed articulation of gender justice than any prior instrument of international criminal law, yet the disconnect between these gender provisions and complementarity undermines the Court's ability to extend gender justice measures at the domestic level.

Complementarity Jurisprudence: Reinforcing Silences and Opening New Avenues

The Court's early jurisprudence on admissibility presents a mixed picture in terms of gender justice. Certain silences have been reinforced. This has been obvious in litigation concerning the interpretation of a "case," in order to determine whether the state is investigating or prosecuting the *same* "case" as the one before the ICC. In 2006, in relation to the Democratic Republic of Congo situation, the Pre-Trial Chamber defined a "case" as proceedings against the same person for the same conduct with which the ICC is concerned.[18] The Appeals Chamber later refined this to mean proceedings against the same person and *"substantially* the same conduct."[19] It is relevant that this test does not require the state to characterize the conduct it is investigating or prosecuting according to the language of the Rome Statute: it would suffice that the state was pursuing the violation as an "ordinary crime" under its domestic penal code[20] (Nouwen 2011, 212–216).

The problem with this test is that it potentially reinforces gender misrecognition and misrepresentation. National criminal codes commonly fail to criminalize many acts of sexual violence recognized under the Rome Statute, and where they are criminalized, such crimes often reflect long-standing legacies of the law and are treated as crimes of "honor" and as having lesser gravity than other violations (UN Women 2011). For instance, few jurisdictions recognize sexual slavery or enforced pregnancy as specific crimes. Further, where sexual violence crimes are encoded in domestic law, they are often understood as individual acts perpetrated by one person against another and incidental to conflict[21] rather than as widespread and systematic acts driven by political and policy imperatives,[22] as is the case with crimes against humanity and war crimes (see Copelon 2000; Duggan and Abusahraf 2006, 627; Ní Aoláin et al. 2011, 161).

The application of the Rome Statute admissibility test that requires investigation and prosecution for the "same person for the same conduct" but *not* under the "same rules" also provides little protection for victims of conflict-related sexual and gender-based violence crimes. At the national level, where such victims are able to access the justice system, these crimes are at best only partially encoded and attract weak sanctions; at the same time, because the complementarity rules do not take these weaknesses into account, these victims are unable to access the ICC and its expansive gender justice rules.

The ICC has started laying out some general principles concerning questions of whether a particular state is *able* or *willing* to prosecute a case. It is possible that these will provide some grounds for pursuing gender justice admissibility claims in future. In the ICC's *Gaddafi* case, Libya lodged an admissibility challenge, seeking to maintain jurisdiction over the proceedings. In 2013, the Pre-Trial Chamber found that Libya had not shown that it was investigating the case and had also not shown that it was able to conduct the proceedings genuinely. Specifically, the Pre-Trial Chamber found that the Libyan judicial system was "unavailable" for the purpose of Article 17(3) because Libya was unable to obtain custody of Gaddafi and was unable to gather the relevant testimony, and serious practical impediments prevented Gaddafi from accessing legal representation.[23] As such, the Pre-Trial Chamber found the case admissible before the ICC. In 2014, the Appeals Chamber upheld this decision.[24]

Although *Gaddafi* does not deal with sexual or gender-based violence per se, it does provide some encouragement to those seeking to "upscale" accountability for sexual or gender-based violence to the ICC in future. This is because inadequate evidence-gathering procedures and court processes, such as have been identified in *Gaddafi*, are also common challenges faced by those seeking to prosecute cases of sexual and gender-based violence[25] domestically (SáCouto and Cleary 2009). To take advantage of this jurisprudence would require a relevant case, as well as judges with gender expertise, able to recognize the relevance of ongoing gender injustices to admissibility arguments. Here is an example of the need for Fraser's integrative approach to gender justice: gender recognition and representation must reinforce each other to produce change (see Chapter 1).

Preliminary Examinations: Forgetting and Remembering Gender Justice

In the ICC's early years, gender justice concerns have not featured in ICC complementarity jurisprudence, nor have they been given obvious attention in the OTP's preliminary examinations. These examinations are provided for under the Rome Statute to help ascertain admissibility, but the OTP has also used them in a "big idea" sense as a way to actively encourage states to investigate and prosecute crimes at the domestic level. This "positive" approach to preliminary examinations was outlined by the ICC's first Prosecutor, Luis Moreno Ocampo, when he stated that "the preliminary examination phase offers the most promising, or at a minimum the first opportunity, for the OTP to serve as a catalyst for the initiation of national proceedings" (2011, 25). The forms of persuasion that the Prosecutor mentioned were available included supporting justice efforts at the national level—a form of "positive complementarity"—or threatening the state with ICC intervention if it could not or would not bring the perpetrators to justice (Moreno Ocampo 2011, 18). In a 2012 interview, the second Prosecutor, Fatou Bensouda has indicated that she too views the preliminary examination phase as a catalytic tool: "I think what announcing preliminary examinations can do is trigger national efforts . . . it encourages them to also engage or at least assure that they're investigating and prosecuting" (2012a).

In a study of preliminary examinations in Guinea and Colombia, Chappell, Grey, and Waller (2013) have illuminated how little attention the OTP has paid to gender justice issues at the preliminary examination phase in either a technical or "big idea" sense of complementarity. As the following summary of this study shows, the OTP's assessments of whether these states are meeting the "same person/same conduct" test and whether they are able and willing to undertake investigations and prosecutions genuinely have overlooked glaring gender injustices in domestic evidence-gathering procedures, laws, and court processes that have prevented proper investigation and prosecution of sexual and gender-based violations.

Gender Justice Silences in the Guinea and Colombia Preliminary Examinations

Guinea and Colombia have been under preliminary examination by the OTP since 2009 and 2004, respectively.[26] As of January 2015, in both sites the OTP has determined that crimes within the jurisdiction of the ICC—including sexual and gender-based crimes—appear to have been committed, and it is assessing the potential cases for complementarity and gravity.[27]

The trigger for the Guinea examination, a state party to the Rome Statute since 2003, was the violent intervention in September 2009 by state security forces at a demonstration in the nation's capital, Conakry[28] (Human Rights Watch [HRW] 2009; United Nations Security Council [UNSC] 2009, 18). Investigating the events, a UN Commission of Inquiry concluded that a massacre had occurred and "109 females, including a number of minors, were victims of rape and other forms of sexual violence" (UNSC 2009, 24). This included seventy-seven instances of rape, forty-two of which involved multiple perpetrators ("gang rape"). The Commission also documented five cases of sexual slavery in which female protesters were raped in detention for several days, and six cases of other sexual violence, including the mutilation of sexual organs and the discharging of firearms into the vagina (UNSC 2009, 24–27). The UN report named five senior officials who might be liable for these atrocities under international criminal law, including Captain Moussa Dadis Camara, the Guinean president at the time of the attack (UNSC 2009, 48–55; also see HRW 2009, 55).

Since commencing the preliminary examination, the OTP has demonstrated an ongoing interest in the case. As of November 2013, the OTP had conducted eight missions to Guinea,[29] three of which included Fatou Bensouda, in her role as Deputy Prosecutor and then as Prosecutor.[30] The OTP has determined that crimes against humanity, including rape and other sexual violence, appear to have been committed and has moved on to assessing complementarity.[31]

Colombia is a very different case. A state party to the Rome Statute since 2002,[32] the OTP initiated a preliminary examination in Colombia in 2004, with a wider range of crimes and actors than in Guinea. The investigations are set against a backdrop of a fifty-year internal conflict characterized by extreme violence, drug trafficking, and political corruption.[33] The preliminary examination is concerned with the alleged commission of a range of crimes, including killings; enforced disappearances; forcible transfer of populations; severe deprivation of liberty; torture; conscripting, enlisting, or use of children in hostilities; and, notably, rape and sexual violence.[34] Acts of sexual violence in the Colombian conflict have targeted primarily women and girls and have been used by all sides to humiliate the victims, exploit them as sexual slaves, displace families for the acquisition of land, terrorize communities, and/or effect revenge on adversaries (Amnesty International 2011, 9). Like elsewhere in the world, in Colombia these acts have been underreported and poorly documented.

The previous ICC Prosecutor, citing Inter-Institutional Committee of Justice and Peace research, suggests that "at a minimum, more than 700 women have been victims of rape and sexual violence up to 2009."[35] Other research identifies a significantly higher number of sexual and gender-based violence victims, including one study estimating that between 2001 and 2009, almost half a million women were subjected to sexual violence crimes in the context of the Colombian armed conflict (Campaign Rape and other Violence: Leave my Body Out of War 2011, 14).

In both preliminary examinations under review, the ICC OTP has asked two fundamental questions to assess whether it has jurisdiction over the situations: (1) whether Guinean and Colombian authorities are investigating or prosecuting the same person(s) and same conduct as the ICC would investigate or prosecute and (2) if so, whether they are "willing and able" to do so genuinely. Its tentative answer to both these questions is "yes," therefore leaving the national level with jurisdiction. However, the OTP continues to conduct ongoing preliminary examinations in both sites, leaving open the possibility that the OTP will elevate the status of either or both of these cases to formal investigations under the ICC.[36] Without access to the documentation provided to the OTP—which is unavailable for legal reasons—it is impossible to ascertain the exact extent to which gender justice considerations have been raised as part of the OTP's analysis. Based on available information, it does appear that in both cases the bar has been set very low by the OTP for assessing action, willingness, and ability for sexual violence and gender-based crimes. However, the release of the OTP's gender policy, which includes details on complementarity, suggests, that the treatment of sexual and gender-based violence is becoming more central to the OTP's preliminary examination assessments.

Guinea: Action, Ability, and Willingness

In Guinea, the OTP has tolerated a slow pace of judicial action in relation to the Conakry massacre. In the first year after the violence the government appointed three judges to investigate, but little more was done. In 2011 the OTP reported that action under the new government had been hampered by the "the lack of suitable security and logistical conditions." However, it was satisfied that these conditions had been addressed and that national investigation had started moving at a "fairly slow but steady pace."[37] In the OTP's November 2012 report on preliminary examinations, it suggested "notable progress has been achieved" because Guinean investigating judges had filed charges against two of the individuals named as suspects by the UN Commission. The OTP concluded that "the facts do not support a finding of admissibility at this stage."[38]

Two specific gender justice concerns arise from the OTP's conclusion. First, implicit in this conclusion is a finding that the "same persons" of interest to the ICC have been investigated at the national level.[39] This finding is questionable given that (based on publicly available information) neither the former president (who is in exile) or the former minister of presidential security, both of whom were identified as potential suspects by the UN Commission, has been investigated or charged (HRW 2012). In other words, two of the "same persons" allegedly responsible for the sexual violence and other crimes are not being held to account.

The second problem concerns the lack of transparency about which particular crimes have been charged. While the OTP has found there is a reasonable basis to believe that crimes against humanity were committed in Conakry, including rape and other forms of sexual violence, no publicly available information exists about the exact nature of the charges that have been made.[40] It is therefore impossible to confirm whether acts of sexual violence are being investigated at the national level.[41] It also appears most likely, though impossible to assess due to lack of information, that the "same conduct" test has not been met with respect to crimes of a sexual nature. This is because the Guinean penal code does not cover all the alleged acts of sexual violence committed during the stadium violence. While the penal code does criminalize rape, it does not allow for the prosecution of the "other sexual violence" cited by the OTP—which presumably refers to the sexual slavery and sexual mutilation documented by the UN (HRW 2011, 42).

The OTP also considered the genuineness of the proceedings, including whether Guinea were *unwilling* or *unable* to investigate or prosecute the relevant cases. In Guinea (and in Colombia), the OTP noted the delays in bringing perpetrators to justice but found these delays to be justified and has not suggested that there are any other grounds to establish unwillingness or inability.[42] However, a gender justice analysis challenges this view. Specifically, on the "same conduct" test, the Guinean penal code does not include all the crimes alleged to have occurred at the Conakry massacre. As noted above, cases may be inadmissible before the ICC even if the conduct is charged as "ordinary crimes" rather than "international crimes" under domestic law. However, in Guinea, the gaps in the penal code suggest that these alleged acts of sexual slavery and sexual mutilation could not be charged, even as "ordinary crimes."

The penal code *does* criminalize rape; however, this crime is defined very narrowly, which arguably means that Guinea is "unable" to conduct the proceedings genuinely. In the Guinea penal code, rape is described as an "immoral offence,"[43] a categorization that grossly misrecognizes the physical and psychological effects of the crime and diminishes its gravity. The weak provisions on rape and the complete exclusion of sexual slavery and other sexual violence crimes in the Guinean penal code point to an absence of jurisdiction under domestic law, rendering it unavailable for victims of these crimes. The OTP's 2012 and 2013 reports[44] on the Guinea preliminary examination are silent on whether any attention has been given to these specific gender dimensions of inability in Guinea.

Colombia: Action, Ability, and Willingness

Similar gender justice gaps arise in relation to the OTP's admissibility assessment in the Colombian preliminary examination. In November 2012, eight years after the ICC had commenced its preliminary examination into Colombia, the OTP published an extraordinary interim preliminary examination report on the situation.[45] The report concluded that crimes that may constitute "crimes against humanity and war crimes, including rape, sexual slavery and enforced prostitution and other forms of sexual violence"[46] had been committed, including by the Revolutionary Armed Forces of Colombia (FARC) and the National Liberation Army (ELN), demobilized paramilitary groups, and other armed groups,[47] and therefore it was obliged to assess whether Colombia was investigating or prosecuting these crimes.

Unlike many other countries affected by conflict, Colombia has a relatively well-developed, functioning legal system, albeit "not without its limitations and shortcomings" (Ambos and Huber 2011, 7). It has created several transitional justice mechanisms, including national proceedings against paramilitaries in ordinary courts, proceedings in military courts against army officials, and the adoption of the "Justice and Peace Law." However, as detailed in Chappell et al. (2013), each of these mechanisms has serious limitations in its coverage of sexual and gender-based crimes, as well as the country's track record in holding perpetrators of such violence to account. For instance, while the Colombian penal code includes some of the Rome Statute's classification of crimes against humanity, including rape, sexual slavery, and enforced prostitution,[48] it omits forced pregnancy and enforced sterilization—two crimes that the OTP report noted have been widespread during the Colombian conflict.[49] Further, according to the OTP, despite the widespread commission of conflict-related sexual violence crimes, less than a handful of persons have been tried for these crimes: until May 2012 only four individuals—two paramilitary members and two army officials—had been convicted of these crimes through the ordinary court system.[50] In 2013 the OTP's preliminary examination report noted that Colombian military courts could not try crimes of sexual violence; the Colombian Congress had delineated jurisdiction for these crimes to the civil courts,[51] but as the above evidence suggests, these cases have not been vigorously pursued under civil law.

The third aspect of the Colombian transitional justice system, the 2005 "Justice and Peace Law," which seeks to induce "paramilitaries to demobilize and confess their crimes in exchange for reduced sentences"[52] of up to five to eight years, has paid inadequate attention to sexual and gender-based violence. Further, according to the OTP's 2012 report, only "79 cases of sexual violence had been confessed under Justice and Peace Law proceedings, out of 26,026 total confessions made by former members of paramilitary groups."[53] Even by the OTP's estimate of a minimum of seven hundred cases of sexual and gender-based violence crimes,[54] these confessions correspond to less than 10 percent of potential cases and pale in comparison to other reports of the widespread nature of sexual violence (Campaign Rape and other Violence: Leave my Body Out of War 2011, 14).

Despite these gender justice limitations across the Colombian justice system, as with Guinea, the ICC OTP has tentatively concluded that the Colombian authorities meet the threshold for action on investigation or prosecution.[55] Human rights observers and scholars have challenged the OTP's assessment (Amnesty International 2012; Chappell et al. 2013; Lawyers Without Borders 2012), including on gender justice grounds. It is clear from the prosecution record across all the justice venues that very few persons have been tried for sexual violence crimes.[56] Indeed, the OTP has itself "noted the inadequacy of prosecutorial and judicial activity in relation to [sexual violence] crimes."[57]

However, such acknowledgment has not appeared to influence the OTP's admissibility assessment in Colombia. The OTP has determined that Colombia appears able and willing to investigate and prosecute the same persons for the same conduct. It has found "no reason at this stage to doubt the genuineness of such proceedings" in ordinary courts or the Justice and Peace Law process, and it does not consider delays, especially in the application of this law, as indicating unwillingness.[58] Academics and civil society groups have questioned the OTP's interpretation. They have raised concerns about the voluntary nature of the Justice and Peace

Law and its application to only a small proportion of paramilitary armed groups (Ambos 2010), suggesting that proceedings may be undertaken in a manner "inconsistent with an intent to bring the person concerned to justice" (Meertens 2012, 10). Referring specifically to gender justice concerns, Amnesty International (2012) has pointed to the OTP's failure to explicitly include conflict-related sexual violence in its unwillingness assessment.

As with Guinea, the OTP has suggested that Colombia is able to prosecute genuinely most categories of crimes or persons under examination (although it has noted insufficient prosecutions in some unspecified areas).[59] This is despite the "unavailability" of forced pregnancy, specifically, and enforced sterilization in the penal code. There remain other significant gaps in Colombia's legislative framework that could also preclude the prosecution of conflict-related sexual violence crimes, such as the failure to characterize such crimes as crimes against humanity; maintaining a statute of limitations for sexual crimes; ongoing impunity for these committed under an order of the government or a superior; and ongoing protection for investigating superiors who were aware of such crimes being committed and failed to act (Amnesty International 2012, 39–41; Haupt 2011, 25–27).

In applying the technical complementarity rules in Colombia, the OTP has tentatively found that the potential cases would be inadmissible before the ICC. However, there are signs that under Prosecutor Bensouda the OTP is attempting to use complementarity in a "big idea" sense to encourage greater domestic-level action on conflict-related sexual and gender-based violence. In its 2012 Colombia report, the OTP called on the Colombian Attorney General to respond to a 2008 Colombian Constitutional Court ruling (Auto 092/2008) to investigate 183 specific cases of sexual violence crimes against forcibly displaced women. It recommended the Attorney General "carry out relevant activities to factually verify the occurrence of the crimes and to pursue investigations" into the specified cases[60] (Amnesty International 2011, 7). More positively, in its 2013 report, the OTP noted the Colombian Congress draft legislation on access to justice for victims of sexual violence in the context of the armed conflict and lent its support to the passage of the legislation (ICC OTP 2013, 35). Such encouragement is an example of positive complementarity in practice in support of gender justice.

Although Guinea and Colombia are in many respects different cases, together they highlight a gender justice shadow of complementarity. A lack of integration in the Rome Statute of its gender justice and complementarity rules has meant that the former have been given very little attention in preliminary examinations. States have maintained jurisdiction over crimes even when they have done little or nothing to bring to account the perpetrators of sexual crimes. The appointment of a Prosecutor more attuned to these concerns is starting to be reflected in preliminary examination reports.

New Efforts to "Lock In" a Gender Justice Approach to Complementarity

These gender justice silences and gaps in the ICC's complementarity regime have not gone unnoticed. Feminist legal scholars have argued the need for the ICC Prosecutor to "examine a state's laws, procedures, and policies governing the investigation and prosecution of sexual violence and gender-based crimes, even where the State seems capable and willing to try other crimes" (SáCouto and Cleary 2009, 344; see also Chappell et al. 2013; Kapur 2012). The Women's Initiatives has also continually advocated on the issue, calling on the ICC to pay more attention to the gender elements of this core principle. For instance, at the 2010 Rome Statute Review Conference in Kampala, Women's Initiatives' Executive Director, Brigid Inder, lobbied strongly for the recognition of the gender dimensions of complementarity[61] (Inder 2013, 322). Her view has been reflected in Women's Initiatives statements, including in its Report on the Review Conference:

> The ongoing absence or weakness of domestic laws on sexual and gender-based violence, combined with gender-biased court procedures and personnel, and inadequate police capacity, could conspire to create a state of unwillingness and inability to genuinely prosecute gender-based crimes.[62]

Unfortunately, as with Rome negotiations, at Kampala these arguments appeared to fall on deaf ears. Gender issues were absent in all official discussions of the principle, including in the states parties' position paper on complementarity, the conference panel reviewing the principle, and the final complementarity resolution.[63]

As noted above, especially with the 2012 election of Fatou Bensouda as Prosecutor, there appears to be some evidence of a shift in attention toward the gender justice aspects of complementarity. This has been apparent through "positive" complementarity moves, such as that noted above in relation to Colombia. But this is not an isolated case. In the preliminary examination of Nigeria, which commenced in 2010, the Prosecutor has paid particular attention to the plight of women and girls. In May

2014, in response to the Boko Haram militia's kidnapping of over two hundred schoolgirls (Mark 2014), which sparked the international "Bring Back Our Girls" social media campaign, Prosecutor Bensouda released a statement noting that she was "deeply troubled and alarmed" by these acts and suggesting that these crimes could fall within the jurisdiction of the ICC.[64] In her statement, the Prosecutor reminded officials in the Nigerian government that they have primary responsibility for investigating and prosecuting such acts but that such a case "may become admissible before the ICC if there are no relevant investigations or prosecutions in Nigeria, or if the national authorities are unwilling or unable to carry out genuine investigations or prosecutions."[65]

The OTP's 2014 gender policy paper further reflects a greater recognition of the gender justice elements of complementarity in practice. The policy paper advances a positive gender justice complementarity approach, stating that the OTP

> will seek to encourage genuine national investigations and prosecutions by the State(s) concerned in relation to sexual and gender-based crimes. It will also encourage relevant national authorities and other entities to address barriers to genuine proceedings, and to provide support for the victims of such crimes.[66]

The policy paper also pays attention to the need to include gender justice considerations in OTP preliminary examinations under the technical rules of complementarity. Significantly, the policy paper takes seriously the arguments made by gender justice advocates from the time of the Rome Conference onward of the need to assess the genuineness of national proceedings from a gender perspective. Specifically, the paper notes the need for the OTP to take account of barriers, including

> discriminatory attitudes and gender stereotypes in substantive law, and/or procedural rules that limit access to justice for victims of such crimes, such as inadequate domestic law criminalising conduct proscribed under the Statute; the existence of amnesties or immunity laws and statutes of limitation, and the absence of protective measures for victims of sexual violence. Other indicators of an absence of genuine proceedings may be the lack of political will, including official attitudes of trivialisation and minimisation or denial of these crimes; manifestly insufficient steps in the investigation and prosecution of sexual and gender-based crimes, and the deliberate focus of proceedings on low-level perpetrators, despite evidence against those who may bear greater responsibility.[67]

Table 6.1. GENDER JUSTICE AND COMPLEMENTARITY: PRIORITIES, RULES, AND ENFORCEMENT

Gender Justice Priorities	Formal Rules	Enforcement	Response
Action: Take into account gender deficiencies in national law in assessing state investigation and prosecution.	✘	"Same person, same conduct test": this test does not recognize the political nature of sexual violence crimes, the full range of acts that are gender and sexual crimes, and the gravity of these crimes.	OTP gender policy recognizes gender justice elements of investigation and prosecution.
Unwillingness: Include state failure to bring sexual violence charges.	✘	State failure has not been taken into account to date in preliminary examinations or adjudication.	OTP gender policy recognizes gender justice elements of unwillingness.
Inability: should include weak laws that fail to recognize the gravity of sexual and gender-based violence.	✘	Inadequate state laws have not yet been taken into account.	OTP policy recognizes gender justice elements of ability.

The articulation in the policy paper of these gender dimensions of genuine ability and willingness is a significant step forward for the ICC. This formal recognition of the gender justice dimensions of complementarity in the OTP gender policy partially redresses the statutory silence on the issue and the Court's haphazard approach to gender and complementarity in its first decade, as outlined in Table 6.1. While these new rules are yet to be tested, it is hoped that they will lead to greater attention to and consistency in the treatment of sexual and gender-based crimes in assessing complementarity in future.

PART FOUR: LEGISLATING FOR GENDER JUSTICE

The Rome Statute is directed toward addressing impunity and improving accountability for atrocities internationally. However, its complementarity rules stop short of obliging states parties to implement legislation to "domesticate" its provisions (Mégret 2011, 376). Although the Rome Statute system meets some elements of a post-Westphalian model, such an obligation was a step too far for state negotiators at Rome. Instead, "States are expected to create conditions for the effective investigations and prosecution of crimes at the domestic level" (Stahn 2008, 99). Given that the Rome Statute offers "international best practice" in its recognition of war crimes, crimes against humanity, and genocide, human rights advocates have been hopeful that in creating these conditions states would seek to implement its provisions as far as possible, including encoding the Rome Statute's advanced gender justice rules (Amnesty International 2010). Many states have a great deal of room for improvement in this area, with national penal codes often falling well short of Rome Statute standards (see Chapter 4). As a recent UN Women report has noted in relation to rape:

> While almost all countries criminalize rape, penal codes often define sexual violence very narrowly, with many still framing the problem in terms of indecency or immorality, or as a crime against the family or society, rather than a violation of an individual's bodily integrity (2011, 33).

Although not legally required, the closer states mirror the Rome Statute's gender justice provisions, the greater the chance that impunity for gender injustices can be addressed. This is because states are likely to have a greater capacity than the ICC to undertake prosecutions, with the ICC taking the "big fish" and leaving the others to national jurisdictions (Franke 2006, 821). But for such prosecutions to be successful states need strong gender justice laws, such as those contained in the Rome Statute.

It has been a methodological challenge to gauge how well ICC states parties are responding to the call of NGOs and others to import Rome Statute provisions domestically (see Mégret 2011). As with other international treaties, states can select which crimes contained in the Rome Statute they wish to implement into national penal codes. How states undertake this process differs based on whether they have a "monist" system, where international treaties are automatically incorporated into law, or a "dualist" system, where the national government becomes a signatory and then implements separate legislation to bring the treaty into effect. Tracing implementation has been especially difficult in dualist systems: some have implemented standalone ICC implementing legislation, while others have amended existing penal codes to add genocide, war crimes, and crimes against humanity provisions.

No complete, comprehensive database on ICC implementing legislation exists. Amnesty International attempted to track implementation in the early years, reporting in May 2010 that "less than one third of the States Parties have enacted legislation seeking to implement fully both their co-operation and complementarity obligations into national law." Furthermore, Amnesty reported, much of the legislation that had been enacted was "significantly flawed" (Amnesty International 2010, 3). The ICC ASP has not itself produced a comprehensive implementation database, but it has supported, through its Legal Tools program, a "National Implementing Legislation Database"[68] that tracks the implementation of available legislation in English, largely excluding jurisdictions that have deposited their legislation in French (the ICC's second official language) or other languages.

In 2013, with Rosemary Grey, I undertook a gender analysis of the Legal Tools database and the domestic implementing legislation of individual states parties to the Rome Statute where it was available in English. Through this method we were able to analyze the legislation for 50 of the then 121 states parties to the Rome Statute. The analysis deliberately coincided with the end of the ICC's first decade in operation. The available legislation in English was drawn from across different regions: sixteen states (out of twenty-five) in Western Europe and others; seventeen (out of eighteen) in Eastern Europe; four (out of thirty-three) from Africa; nine (out of eighteen) in Asia; and four (out of twenty-seven) in Latin America.

Our analysis of the available legislation showed significant lacunae across these fifty states parties in the implementation of the gender mandate of the Rome Statute, specifically in relation to the gender and sexual violence provisions included under provisions for the war crimes and crimes against humanity. These gaps are illustrated in Figures 6.1 and 6.2.[69]

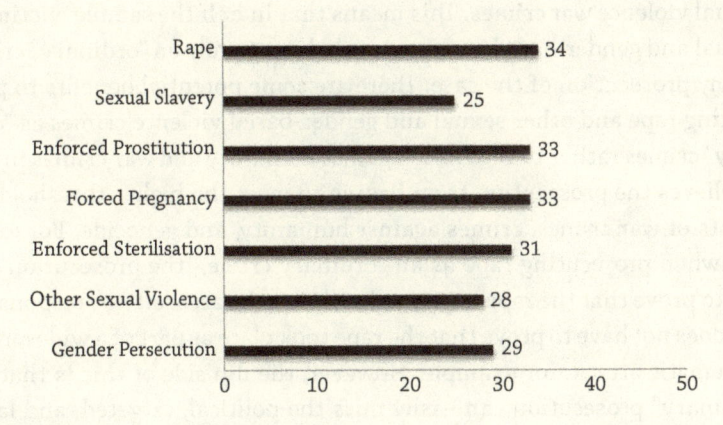

Crime	Number
Rape	34
Sexual Slavery	25
Enforced Prostitution	33
Forced Pregnancy	33
Enforced Sterilisation	31
Other Sexual Violence	28
Gender Persecution	29

Figure 6.1:
Number of states parties with domestic legislation covering sexual and gender-based violence crimes against humanity in the Rome Statute.

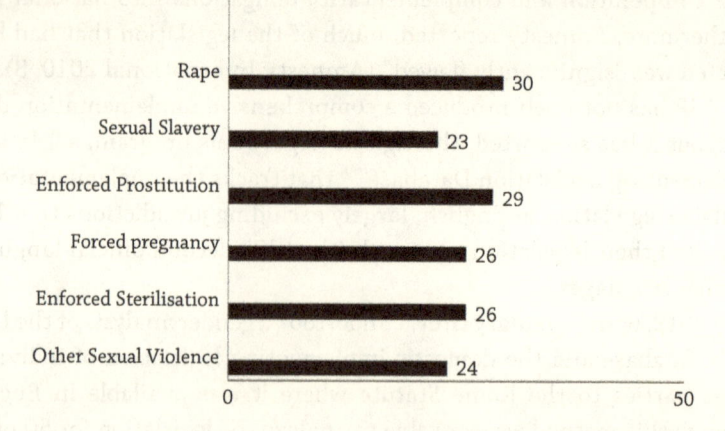

Crime	Number
Rape	30
Sexual Slavery	23
Enforced Prostitution	29
Forced pregnancy	26
Enforced Sterilisation	26
Other Sexual Violence	24

Figure 6.2:
Number of states parties with domestic legislation covering sexual and gender-based violence war crimes in the Rome Statute.

As these figures show, within this available legislation rape is the violation most commonly recognized under both crimes against humanity (34/50) and war crimes (30/50), with sexual slavery the least (25/50 and 23/50 respectively). This is perhaps not surprising given rape has been criminalized at the international level and in most national jurisdictions for many years, whereas sexual slavery has been recognized as a crime under international criminal law arising from case law at the UN ad hoc tribunals in the 1990s. Nevertheless, it is important to reflect on the fact in regard to rape criminalization, 40 percent of these states under review lack legislation covering rape as either a war crime or a crime against humanity. Moreover, of these fifty states, only half recognize most of the other sexual violence war crimes. This means that in half the sample, victims of sexual and gender-based violence would have to rely on "ordinary" crimes in any prosecution of the case. There are some potential benefits to prosecuting rape and other sexual and gender-based violence crimes as "ordinary" crimes rather than crimes against humanity and war crimes in that it relieves the prosecution from having to meet the higher threshold elements of war crimes, crimes against humanity, and genocide. For example, when prosecuting rape as an "ordinary crime," the prosecution only has to prove that the rape happened and that the accused was responsible, but does not have to prove that the rape took place as part of a widespread/systematic attack, for example. However, the flip side of this is that any "ordinary" prosecution can easily miss the political, targeted, and large-scale nature of these crimes, misrepresenting their significance to the broader conflict.

Delving deeper into the actual provisions of the available implementing legislation, it is clear that the broad-based definitions used in the Rome Statute are also often not reflected in domestic war crimes or crimes against humanity. Limitations in rape crimes are the most obvious and easiest to track. The definition of rape used in domestic penal codes is often much narrower than that provided in the Rome Statute and ICC Elements of Crime document. For a start, whereas the Rome Statute Elements of Crime document provides a sex-neutral definition of rape, many penal codes retain sex-specific definitions, excluding men from being recognized as victims of such crimes. This is obvious, for instance, in the cases of Switzerland, Latvia, Hungary, Fiji, and Tanzania (database held with author). In these last four states, as well as others, rape is still understood as a moral crime, a crime of honor, rather than a grave breach of international law as is the case under the Rome Statute (see Chapter 4 for a full discussion). The Afghanistan legislation refers to acts of violation against the chastity of another and imposes particularly harsh penalties for "deflowering a maiden"—entirely misrepresenting the seriousness of the crime. In the penal codes of both Fiji and Tanzania, rape is categorized under "crimes against morality." In many cases, domestic legislation forgoes the Rome Statute's broad-based definition of rape as a form of bodily invasion and contains a narrower understanding as rape as sexual intercourse, thereby misrecognizing many acts of sexual violence that are a feature of conflict-related sexual violence—such as where weapons are used to penetrate sexual organs (Lake 2014, 7)—and that are able to be charged as rape in the ICC. Finally, much state legislation retains a consent-based approach to rape rather than embracing the shift toward greater recognition of the coercive environment within which rape occurs, which has been reflected in recent international jurisprudence and included in the ICC's Elements of Crimes Annex.

States were unwilling to cede to the ICC their right to determine the nature and form of national criminal law. Upholding sovereignty norms, which enabled states to "pick and choose" what aspect of the Statute to incorporate domestically, secured state party ratification of the Rome Statute but has resulted in significant gaps in the coverage of the Statute crimes at the national level. This gap is especially apparent in relation to state coverage of Rome Statute-standard sexual and gender-based provisions. Many states have chosen not to strengthen the gender justice provisions of national penal codes, or where they have, the provisions fall short of the high standard encoded in the ICC's formal rules. The issue here is that the Rome Statute's complementarity regime positions the ICC as a court of last resort, meaning that in a tussle between international and national law, the latter will most likely prevail unless a state party is not actively investigating or prosecuting the case, or is unable or unwilling to do so genuinely. Where national laws fail to adopt Rome Statute standards and maintain gender discriminatory provisions, impunity for and misrepresentation of sexual and gender-based violence will remain a significant problem.

PART FIVE: NESTEDNESS, RULES, AND LEGITIMACY

Two of the ICC's innovative features—complementarity and gender justice—are not integrated in its formal rules, despite calls by gender advocates at Rome for ICC designers to do so. The failure to bring together these two features highlights two important points made by feminist institutionalists. First, in explaining institutional *design*, it is necessary to take into account the specific spatial context in which an institution is "nested." Second, it is important not to discount the importance of formal rules in securing gender-just institutional *outcomes*.

The negotiations to establish the ICC in some ways illustrated a shift toward a post-Westphalian model where justice issues previously only dealt with at the level of the nation-state—including prosecuting conflict-related violence—were "upscaled" to a permanent international treaty body. However, there was a limit on the extent to which states were willing to cede sovereignty to the Court, limits that were reflected in the complementarity principle. Unsuccessful efforts by gender justice advocates at the Rome Conference to convince states to embrace a Court with powers to interrogate and intervene to address weak domestic-level gender justice laws signified that these limits had a gendered foundation. The Rome Statute remains nested in an international system in which state sovereignty trumps new international gender justice norms. This context has served to lock in longstanding gender legacies at the national level, make it difficult to "rebundle" and "upscale" prosecutions for sexual and gender-based violence to the international level, and limit the gender justice scope of the Court.

The Rome Statute's spatial nestedness in the international system has influenced its design, including the decision of states parties not to incorporate specific gender complementarity rules. An absence of formal rules that would have required the Court to link and to assess the gender justice dimensions of complementarity has in turn influenced ICC outcomes in this area. It has meant that the Court is unable to direct states parties to legislate to bring domestic law into line with its gender provisions, reinforcing gender misrecognition in national legislation. It has also served to marginalize gender justice concerns in the complementarity work of the ICC, including its early complementarity jurisprudence and preliminary examination investigations.

The lesson to draw from developments at the ICC in relation to complementarity is, as Charlesworth has noted (1999), that silences and gaps in formal institutional rules matter to gender justice outcomes. Without formal rules, ICC officials have no obligation to incorporate a gender justice approach in their complementarity deliberations, and it is hard for gender justice actors to hold Court personnel to account. Sometimes, senior officials, such as the second Prosecutor, have been willing to apply a gender justice lens. However, relying on individuals to make the link and to "remember" that complementarity has significant gender justice dimensions is a tenuous and unreliable foundation from which to build a gender-sensitive complementarity framework. This is not to suggest that formal rules do all the work on their own—as other chapters in this book have amply demonstrated, informal rules operating as legacies also influence institutional outcomes. Informal rules operate both by undermining and displacing but also sometimes bolstering and extending gender justice objectives. But this case shows that formal rules including codified policies do matter; the implementation by the OTP of "positive complementarity" policies may yet yield important developments in gender justice within states parties, such as through encouraging states to address gender discriminatory behavior. Formal provisions including OTP policies will not on their own resolve gender injustices of misrepresentation, misrecognition, and maldistribution, but they provide a critical starting point for achieving change. This is not least because formal rules lay the foundation for holding officials accountable for their action or lack thereof.

Unlike its efforts with other aspects of the Rome Statute, the Women's Caucus had little success during the design phase to influence its core complementarity provisions. Although the Caucus made an effort to draw states' attention to the gender dimensions of this core principle, states were unwilling to compromise their sovereignty in order to be more accountable for national gender justice laws. By withdrawing from Rome Statute negotiations on the issue, Women's Caucus members indicated that their case for engendering complementarity could not compete with states' determination to control their own laws. Their failure to influence the design of this critical aspect of the Statute understandably diminished the Women's Caucus's view of the legitimacy of the ICC's design, leading its members to warn that silences in the Statute would cement impunity for crimes of sexual and gender-based violence. However, this view did not discourage future gender justice advocates from attempting to bring a gender perspective to bear on ICC complementarity deliberations.

During the first decade of ICC operations, Women's Initiatives advocates have adopted a view on complementarity similar to that of the Women's Caucus. The Women's Initiatives has continually pointed out the gender justice gap in this framework and, at Kampala and elsewhere, pushed for Court personnel to take steps to recognize gender injustices at the national level in its admissibility deliberations and preliminary examinations. Decisions by ICC personnel concerning preliminary examinations and early complementarity jurisprudence appear not to have reflected this call, confirming the earlier prediction by Women's Caucus actors that the absence of formal gender complementarity rules would lead to ongoing impunity for sexual and gender-based violations both at national and international levels. The gender justice gaps in the complementarity system have led gender actors to express concerns about the legitimacy of the complementarity regime. Commenting on the early years of ICC practice, Patricia Viseur Sellers, a leading feminist international gender justice law practitioner and scholar, suggested that

> If cases are inadmissible [before the ICC], yet women do not receive legal redress, substantively or procedurally, in their national jurisdictions, and thus cannot reasonably exhaust their local remedies, or are subjected to gender "sham" trials, then it should be deem[ed] that the ICC complementarity does not function as envisioned (2009, 323).

What are the signs for a more gender-just complementarity regime at the ICC into the future? Although not related to crimes of sexual or gender-based violence, recognition by judges in *Gaddafi* of the limitations of Libya's judicial processes holds out some promise for the ICC's gender justice constituency. It opens a potential window of opportunity for gender advocates to press for greater recognition of the gaps in national criminal codes for prosecuting sexual and gender-based violence and the "unavailability" of unjust national justice systems for victims of these crimes. More directly, moves to address gender justice have arisen through the development of the OTP's gender policy. Identification in the policy of the gender justice dimensions of states' ability and willingness to investigate and prosecute international crimes as well as its push for consideration of gender injustices in the application of complementarity in its "big idea" guise are encouraging. Taking up issues long advocated by gender justice actors, Prosecutor Bensouda's policy initiatives give these actors a growing sense of legitimacy of the ICC's complementarity regime, and good reason to keep pressure on all organs of the Court to bridge the divide between this core aspect of the Rome Statute and its gender mandate.

As with other areas, the strength with which the gender justice constituency will view the Court's future, consequential legitimacy will depend on ICC practice going forward. The fact that the OTP has now clearly identified gender justice principles as important to preliminary examinations is an important first step, but this must be implemented in practice. Further, judges need to demonstrate in their deliberations greater concern for national-level gender justice gaps that make states unable to genuinely investigate and prosecute sexual and gender-based crimes. Without formal rules to fall back on, members of the gender justice constituency will need to work harder in this area than any other to ensure that Court officials recognize the gender justice dimensions of complementarity, and that the Women's Caucus's prediction about ongoing impunity for sexual and gender-based violence does not become a reality.

The ICC fits within Fraser's post-Westphalian frame—up to a point. While gender justice issues spill over national boundaries and require transnational and international responses, states still hold strongly to their sovereignty claims over these issues and seek to limit international intervention to address these concerns. The absence of formal gender justice complementarity rules in the Rome Statute is evidence of the strength of sovereignty claims. The consequence of gender justice silences in regard to this core principle has been ongoing impunity for sexual and gender-based crimes—precisely as predicted by the Women's Caucus at the Rome Conference. Incremental shifts toward greater recognition of the gender justice dimensions, especially by the second ICC Prosecutor, highlight the significance of gender expertise for gender justice outcomes. However, relying on individuals, rather than codified rules, to recognize and respond to gender injustices is precarious. Formalizing gender justice principles in the OTP policy is a positive step forward, but ensuring their implementation will remain an ongoing challenge. Gender advocates will need to continue to force ICC officials to remember the "new" and forget the "old" and to contest assertions that state sovereignty should trump accountability for gender injustices.

CHAPTER 7

Legacies and Legitimacy of International Gender Justice

Now that the international criminal justice project genie is out of the bottle, it cannot easily be put back in. For the foreseeable future, the ICC will sometimes struggle and sometimes even fail. But it will not go away and it will not become irrelevant. In the end, it will persist and succeed because of what it stands for (Alex Whiting 2015).

Attempts to advance the gender justice mandate of Rome Statute through the ICC have resulted in mixed outcomes: some of the objectives of the mandate's designers have been "locked in" while others have been "locked out" of the Court's initial developmental path. This concluding chapter explains these uneven results by bringing together the key arguments of this book about the opportunities and obstacles to gender change. In doing so, this chapter engages with the two central questions driving this study: (1) Why has it been so difficult to implement some of the Rome Statute's substantive gender justice rules and not others? (2) What are the consequences of the gender justice outcomes produced by the ICC in its initial phase for the future of the Court and for international gender justice actors?

Part One discusses the value of Nancy Fraser's trivalent justice framework for understanding the different dimensions of gender justice and for envisioning a transformational approach to advancing such justice through the ICC. While there is much to lament in terms of lost opportunities for advancing gender justice in the Court's early years, this discussion emphasizes the small wins and changes that have been made possible as a result of the engagement of a gender justice constituency with the ICC. It suggests that any transformative gender justice outcomes arising from the Court are most likely to arise from the minor victories, the fragile and incremental shifts in the way in which actors within and outside the ICC use the formal rules and challenge existing legacies to recognize, represent, and redistribute justice to women and to victims of sexual and gender-based violence. While Fraser draws attention to the essential elements of a transformative gender justice, her framework does not explain why it is so difficult to implement and institutionalize gender change. Part Two draws on feminist institutionalism to investigate this puzzle and sketches out a conceptual scaffold for understanding the challenges to, and opportunities for, gender-just institutional change. Three pillars support this scaffold: formal rules and institutional contextual and spatial "nestedness." Part Three addresses the link between gender justice outcomes at the ICC and the Court's ongoing legitimacy. Building on Benjamin Schiff's (2010) dynamic model of the ICC's legitimacy, this discussion suggests that to understand the link between gender justice and the ICC's legitimacy it is necessary to differentiate between and among constituencies, institutional developmental phases, and aspects of the Rome Statute's gender justice mandate. It also highlights the significance of institutional *revisability* to the maintenance of the ICC's legitimacy in the eyes of its gender justice epistemic community.

PART ONE: TOWARD A TRANSFORMATIONAL ACCOUNT OF GENDER JUSTICE

Nancy Fraser's trivalent model of gender justice has provided a valuable framework for assessing the operation of gender justice at the ICC. The three categories of representation, recognition, and redistribution included in Fraser's model map neatly on to the gender mandate embedded in the Rome Statute and have helped to structure and give logic to the investigation of this mandate throughout this book. Identifying and dissecting the different aspects of gender justice and injustice is an important task, as each is analytically distinct, stems from unique causes, and requires different remedies (Fraser 2007). However, as Fraser also reminds us, it is necessary to pay attention to the way each aspect is intertwined with and interconnects and reinforces the others (2009, 165). In Fraser's view, there can be "no redistribution or recognition without representation" and equally no recognition or redistribution without either of the other dimensions (2009, 165).

The interaction between the different elements of gender injustice links to a key objective of Fraser's approach: to find *transformative* as opposed to ameliorative or affirmative remedies to promote gender justice.[1] Transformative remedies are those that restructure the "the underlying generative framework" (1997, 23) and destabilize the gender status quo. To be transformative, strategies need to tackle each of the three dimensions of gender injustice—misrepresentation, misrecognition, and maldistribution—individually. However, because these three dimensions are also "thoroughly imbricated with one another" (Fraser 2007, 26), gender justice responses must simultaneously address the intersections between each dimension.

As this book has demonstrated, at the Rome Conference and throughout the ICC's early years, separate rules and policies have been designed and adopted to address each dimension of gender injustice that have arisen from historical international relations practices and international law. These practices and laws have ignored, patronized, or blatantly discriminated against women and victims of sexual violence. As detailed in previous chapters, built into the design of the ICC are formal rules that have potentially transformative elements to bring about greater representation, recognition, and redistribution; such rules have the capacity to reposition women and victims of sexual and gender-based violence as autonomous, active subjects under international criminal law to an extent not previously possible. The key to tapping the potential of these remedies lies in their implementation, and, as this book illustrates, it has been at this point that the ICC has often been found wanting. The implementation of many of the formal gender justice rules at the ICC has fallen well short of the objectives of their designers, with significant gaps and inconsistencies emerging within and across each of the three dimensions of gender justice.

To summarize the arguments presented in this book, ICC actors have made the most progress in advancing the Court's representative mandate, especially in relation to securing gender-just representation within the judiciary. However, it is important to qualify this by restating the point made in Chapter 3 that it has been *sex* rather than *gender representation* that has been best implemented, leaving obvious gaps in gender justice expertise available across all the organs of the Court. As detailed in Chapter 4, actors' efforts to bring about greater recognition of gender justice concerns in prosecutions have been least successful, especially in cases concerning victims of conflict-related sexual violence. This is a major disappointment for those who have seen the prosecutorial aspect of the ICC's operations as most central to its overarching mandate to end impunity for gender and sexual violence atrocities. With regard to securing gender-just redistribution, as Chapter 5 explained, as yet little progress has been made; where advances have occurred, they have come primarily through the statutorily independent TFV rather than as a result of determinations of the ICC per se. To date, the application of ICC's complementarity provisions, outlined in Chapter 6, has largely been blind to the needs of victims of sexual and gender-based violence.

Limits to the enactment of the ICC's gender justice rules are further magnified when an integrated lens is applied across the Court's representation, recognition, and redistribution mandates. There appear to have been few attempts to bridge the divide of the Rome Statute's complementarity and gender justice mandates, and no obvious attention has been paid to the cascade effects of early decisions in one area on another. For instance, gaps and deficiencies in the rules, structures, and resources to support the *representation* of victims of sexual violence, detailed in Chapter 3, have significantly reduced the chances of these victims receiving just *recognition* at the ICC. Further, as the discussion of gender and reparations demonstrated, lack of *recognition* of sexual violence crimes in prosecutions has significantly reduced opportunities for *redistribution* through Court-ordered reparations: the decrease in sexual and gender-based crimes from the warrant stage through the pretrial and trial stages has meant that judges have been unable to adjudicate on these matters for the purposes of reparation.

It is not surprising that various elements of the Rome Statute's gender justice mandate have failed to be implemented. As will be discussed further below, gender injustices in international law have become so congealed over time that unsetting them is likely to require a concerted effort over the long term. As with other institutional arenas, such as state-level bureaucracies and legislatures, because of the multilayered and embedded nature of gender injustices, any change, especially that which is transformative in nature, is unlikely to occur quickly. For example, a single breakthrough prosecution will be insufficient on its own to shift the "gender logic of appropriateness" of international criminal law. Rather, change will most likely emerge over time in incremental, fragile steps across all aspects of the ICC's gender mandate, driven by the efforts of vigilant gender justice actors acting as critical friends both inside and outside the Court.

Some signs of incremental change are apparent at the ICC and need to be included in any overarching assessment of the Court's early years. Though modest and easily overlooked, these positive steps toward gender justice are nevertheless potentially transformative to the extent that they can contribute to undermining the underlying generative foundations of international law. There is no doubt that "male capture" of international lawmaking positions has been challenged. The appointment of women to the bench is an important development for its own sake. As argued in Chapter 3, it sends an important signal that women have the right and capacity to adjudicate on the most serious international crimes. The fact that some of these judges bring expertise in gender analysis and crimes of sexual violence provides an opportunity for a more expansive reading of the law, even though the application of such expertise can still provoke backlash and claims of partiality. The election by the ASP of second Prosecutor Fatou Bensouda has been highly significant. Bensouda has made it clear that "as a woman, as a lawyer and as a Prosecutor" she is unwilling to be a bystander in the face of crimes of sexual and gender-based violence. Her commitment to combatting these crimes has been evident in many public statements and put into action via the launch of the OTP's first sexual and gender-based violence crimes policy.[2] Registry staff members have also supported gender change in providing protection measures to victims of sexual and gender crimes who come forward to testify. The efforts of TFV staff members to mainstream gender justice objectives and prioritize programs for sexual violence victims in postconflict settings is another example of shifting the gender biases of the law. Each of these developments signifies important advances in gender representation, recognition, and redistribution compared with earlier (and indeed many extant) international criminal tribunals and provides evidence that some of the intentions of the designers of the Rome Statute's gender justice mandate are gradually being realized.

Nancy Fraser's trivalent transformative model of gender justice not only has been valuable for analyzing ICC developments but also serves as a template for future Court practice. It suggests the need for Court personnel to pay attention to developments within and between each dimension of gender justice, recognize and build on small gains, and provide ongoing support to the gender justice epistemic community who help keep the Court accountable for its commitment to ending impunity for sexual and gender-based violence. While this model is valuable in these two senses, it does not explain resistance to the implementation of gender justice rules. For such an explanation it is necessary to turn to feminist institutionalism.

PART TWO: UNDERSTANDING GENDERED INSTITUTIONAL CHANGE AND RESISTANCE

This study of the ICC has illuminated some important general points for better understanding gendered change and resistance. Through the analysis a conceptual scaffold has emerged for understanding gendered change, supported by three pillars: formal rules and temporal and spatial "nestedness." Combined, these pillars help explain why some aspects of the ICC's gender mandate have been better implemented than others, and they may be useful in explaining gender change in other contexts. These conclusions come with the caveat that any assessment of gender change must take place over time, and as the Rome Statute is a new institution operating through a newly established Court, the assessments made here will require reevaluation over time. Nevertheless, after over a decade of ICC operations, clear indications have emerged about the Court's initial trajectory and the various aspects of the Rome Statute mandate that are being "locked in" and "locked out" of its developmental path.

Formal Rules

The chapters of this book have detailed the efforts of gender justice actors to embed within the Rome Statute a formal, far-reaching gender justice mandate covering each dimension of Fraser's gender justice model. The Women's Caucus and other gender justice actors, operating in conjunction with state delegations, designed these rules. As the previous chapters have detailed, some of these provisions were accepted without question. Some were controversial, sparking significant contestation and debate. The outcome of this contestation meant gender justice actors were ultimately forced to accept a range of compromises, as well as the occasional defeat, in the design of the formal rules. In terms of compromises, the Rome Statute's definition of gender is the most obvious, but there were many others, such as raising the threshold for crimes against humanity, the inclusion of enforced pregnancy provisions, and vague rules covering reparations. Many of these compromises have led to "constructive ambiguities" in the formal rules of the Statute (Oosterveld 2014). Such ambiguities, as Oosterveld (2014) points out, can cut both ways: they can produce gaps through which progressive gender justice interpretations of the formal rules can emerge, or the very opposite.

Many of the ambiguities in the Rome Statute are yet to be tested, including in relation to the definition of gender (Oosterveld 2014). Where some have been interpreted, especially concerning crimes of sexual violence, the outcomes have mostly been negative. Judges have tended to adopt a narrow reading of the Statute and where they have had room for a broader gender-just interpretation, have generally resisted it, including an unwillingness to apply progressive jurisprudence from the UN ad hoc tribunals. As discussed in Chapter 4, the ICC Chambers have refused to accept, in line with rulings from the Rwandan tribunal, that forcing women to undress in public in order to humiliate them met the gravity threshold for a crime against humanity. The Chamber also dismissed the Prosecutor's attempt to link charges of rape and of torture, to allow the Court to recognize not only the harm of the rape to victims themselves but also the harm suffered by their family members who were forced to watch the violation. Such cumulative effects were recognized at the Yugoslav and Rwandan tribunals. In one of the most contentious rulings, in a Kenyan case, the Chamber refused to accept that forced circumcision and penile amputations were sexual crimes, reflecting a very narrow understanding of the gendered nature and varied experiences of sexual violence.

Although gender justice actors' efforts to use the formal rules at the ICC have produced mixed outcomes, the existence of these rules, however vague, has proven to be much more valuable to advancing change than having none at all. Rules give actors a foundation for making claims, holding the Court accountable and for encouraging further negotiation and reinterpretation. For instance, in their annual *Gender Report Cards*, which provide forensic detail on ICC operations, the members of Women's Initiatives have been relentless in their critique of the Chamber's rulings and have continued to pressure the judges to better familiarize themselves with the object and purpose of these gender provisions in the Statute.

By contrast, where formal gender justice rules do not exist, experience at the ICC demonstrates that it is much more difficult for gender justice claims to gain attention. The losses suffered by gender justice advocates during negotiations over the Rome Statute—especially in relation to the complementarity provisions—demonstrate this point well. The unwillingness of state delegates at Rome to link gender justice concerns to complementarity—the key political compromise in the Statute—has resulted in these concerns being marginalized in preliminary examinations and other complementarity processes. Also, without an explicit link between gender justice and complementarity in the Rome Statute, states parties are let off the hook when they fail to include gender justice provisions in their domestic ICC implementing legislation. The absence of formal rules makes it difficult for gender justice actors to hold the Court accountable for its actions in this critical area. This is a case of gender justice concerns being "locked out" in the initial developmental path of the ICC and reinforces Hilary Charlesworth's (1999) important point about the influence of silences and gaps in the law on poor gender justice outcomes. In this case, the prediction of the Women's Caucus[3] has been confirmed: the absence of formal gender justice complementarity rules has helped to reinforce ongoing impunity for sexual and gender-based crimes within national and international tribunals.

Throughout the Court's early years, formal rules have helped provide a foundation for the advancement of gender justice. They have given actors within and outside the Court the basis on which to make their claims, advance progressive interpretations of the law, and to achieve some (albeit limited) successes. As projected, ambiguous rules have proved to be a mixed blessing: mostly interpreted without regard to the objectives of the designers of the gender justice mandate, they nevertheless have the potential in future to bring about a more expansive reading of the law. Where formal rules have been entirely absent, the results have been stark, in a negative sense. New formal rules may not be the complete answer to advancing gender justice, but the experience at the ICC suggests that having them in place is a prerequisite for driving institutional change toward gender justice outcomes.

Temporal Nestedness

Feminist institutionalist research has demonstrated that formal gender justice rules are rarely implemented in full, and so it has been the case with the Rome Statute. This book provides some of the answers as to why this implementation gap arises. As discussed in Chapter 2, and outlined in Box 2.2, informal rules and practices in the form of gender legacies provide the temporal context in which the Court is nested, and they can be seen to have had a significant influence on the interpretation of these rules and on reinforcing existing gaps and silences in the law. The existence of these legacies resonates with the arguments of feminist institutionalists that no institution is ever "new"; each is built on the gendered foundations of past rules, norms, and practices (Chappell and Waylen 2013; Mackay 2014a).

The impact of these legacies has been clearly on display throughout the ICC's early years in operation:

- accusations of bias and lack of impartiality against those judges seeking to apply the gender-just rules of the Rome Statute;
- failure of the bench to apply the full scope of the Statute when relevant or to apply existing progressive gender jurisprudence in cases related to sexual and gender-based crimes;
- inadequate evidence-gathering techniques leading to the collapse of gender-based charges;

- hostile questioning of witnesses and victims in the courtroom;
- insufficient allocation of resources to outreach services targeting women and sexual violence victims;
- lack of attention to sexual and gender-based crimes in complementarity assessments; and
- misrepresentation and misrecognition of the experiences of male victims of sexual and gender-based violence.

In the view of Women's Initiatives Executive Director Brigid Inder, the consequences of these "blind spots" are

> an insufficient assessment of the evidence, unintended invisibility of gender issues in the adjudication and interpretation of the law, and an impunity gap on sexual violence that emboldens perpetrators and betrays victims of these crimes (2014, 1).

Because gender legacies tend to operate as informal rules and practices—working under the surface to shape the attitudes and actions of institutional actors—they are much more difficult to tackle than any limitations in the formal rules (Chappell and Waylen 2013). Gender legacies slip in to the gaps between the formal rules and their interpretation to distort and displace the intentions of designers (Chappell 2014; Thelen and Mahoney 2010). As detailed in Chapter 4, much criticism about failures to implement the gender justice mandate has been leveled at the first Prosecutor Moreno Ocampo, especially the perceived misrecognition in his discretionary judgment in the first case against Democratic Republic of Congo militia leader Lubanga. This book has argued that this was an example *par excellence* of "remembering the old and forgetting the new" when it came to gender justice concerns. However, as also discussed in Chapter 4, in their adjudication ICC judges too have demonstrated a lack of attention to, and understanding of, the formal gender justice rules of the Rome Statute, reinforcing longstanding gender legacies of international law. This is not to say that these actors are themselves inherently gender biased; indeed, the public statements and previous professional histories of many ICC judges suggest otherwise. Rather, it is to argue that many on the bench remain blinkered to the gendered logic of appropriateness of international law and, where they have been aware, have demonstrated an uneasiness, indeed a timidity, in tackling and unsettling the status quo. This is probably not unrelated to the fact that when judges do attempt to provide an expansive reading of the law, as Judge Benito did in *Lubanga*, they can easily become targets for attack for "judicial activism" and "overreach."

Undermining gender legacies is a long-term task, and one that for the time being will likely remain in the hands of gender justice actors. Just as these actors had to fight hard for the inclusion of gender-just rules, they must now remain attentive to the ICC's implementation record. But ultimately it is the Court's key actors—the Prosecutor, Judges, Registrar, and states parties—that have the primary responsibility for enacting the rules. For gender change to occur, these internal actors must respond to the calls of gender justice advocates to "remember" the formal gender remedies that are at their disposal in the Rome Statute and to construe the Statute's ambiguities through a gender justice lens. The Court's key actors must also: continue to support the representation of both sexes and gender justice expertise when electing and appointing key personnel on the bench, OTP, and Registry; recognize the different position and needs of different categories of victims; and, make better strategic choices about which cases and charges to pursue, backed up by appropriate evidence-gathering methods and techniques. The ASP must also demonstrate a willingness to fund the ICC at a level that enables it to carry out all aspects of its mandate, including the resource-intensive gender justice component. Importantly, as noted above, Court personnel must also pay attention to the way different forms of gender injustice interact and devise new policies and approaches that take an integrated approach to addressing these issues.

Spatial Nestedness

The third pillar influencing the gender justice outcomes of the ICC relates to the Court's spatial nestedness. As outlined in Chapter 2, the ICC is nested within an international system where the norm of state sovereignty remains salient—despite some shift toward what Fraser identifies as a post-Wesphalian epoch. The Court is profoundly influenced by its relations with states—both states parties and nonsignatories—and with other international organizations, most importantly the UN and its Security Council, among others. This spatial nestedness can be seen to have had both a positive and negative influence on ICC gender justice outcomes.

On a positive note, the spatial context has been advantageous for advancing gender justice claims at the ICC. During the Rome Statute negotiations, this context could be considered "permissive" to gender justice demands, providing a foundation on which to base claims to women's rights and the protection of victims of sexual and gender-based violence. The negotiating context was shaped by some progressive jurisprudence arising from the UN ad hoc tribunals, ongoing reverberations of the 1995

Beijing Fourth World Conference on Women, as well the growing influence of a transnational movement committed to the international recognition of "women's rights as human rights." A range of international conventions and declarations, including the UN *Convention of the Elimination of All Forms of Discrimination against Women* (1979), and civil society's *Nairobi Declaration on Women's and Girl's Right to Reparation* (2007), also provided an important underpinning for the development of the gender justice framework of the ICC, and in its operational phase in the interpretation of the rules. For instance, as discussed in Chapter 4, the Trial Chamber referenced these external normative frameworks extensively in setting out the reparations principles in *Lubanga*.

Efforts have also been made within the UN and at the ICC to link the Rome Statute's gender mandate to the broader UN women's rights framework and the Security Council's Women's Peace and Security agenda, made explicit in the most recent Security Council Women's Peace and Security resolutions 2106 (2013) and 2122 (2013). Notably, Prosecutor Bensouda has participated in numerous UN women's events and has provided advice in the development of international initiatives in the area of sexual and gender-based violence, including the *International Protocol on the Investigation and Documentation of Rape and Sexual Violence in Conflict* launched at the 2014 Global Summit to End Sexual Violence in Conflict (Adams 2014). Much more can be done to strengthen the coordination and implementation of ICC and UN initiatives. As Prosecutor Bensouda bluntly stated in her December 2014[4] address to the Security Council in relation to the Darfur situation:

> Women and girls continue to bear the brunt of sustained attacks on innocent civilians. But this Council is yet to be spurred into action. Victims of rapes are asking themselves how many more women should be brutally attacked for this Council to appreciate the magnitude of their plight.

The Prosecutor's statement suggests that the spatial context in which the ICC operates can also be a negative influence on the implementation of the Court's gender justice mandate. As discussed in Chapter 6, commentators have argued that the ICC is unique in presenting a challenge to state sovereignty norms, primarily through the principle of complementarity. Nevertheless, these norms continue to play a critical role in influencing the Court's design and operations. State intransigence at the UN Security Council to support ICC investigations is one example. Another case in point is the refusal of states during Statute negotiations to agree to a system that would make states responsible for reparations in those cases where convicted offenders are without the means to pay them. The complementarity provisions that enable states the first option of investigating and prosecuting the accused, and that apply national rather than international law to conflict-related sexual and gender-based violence crimes, are another key example. Given the weak domestic laws on gender and sexual violence outlined in earlier chapters, these provisions reinforce the existing gender justice impunity gap at both national and international levels and frustrate the intentions of the Court's gender mandate.

To understand why the ICC's gender mandate has been only partially implemented, it is necessary to look further than Fraser's trivalent gender justice model and toward feminist institutionalism. Drawing on the feminist institutionalist literature, it has been possible to highlight three elements influencing gender change: the operation and interpretation of the formal rules, which have in turn been influenced by the temporal and spatial nestedness of the Court. As this discussion highlights, gender change has not been completely stymied. Where it has occurred, it has been pushed by outsiders and supported by insiders, who have been willing to recognize and remedy gender legacies, drawing on a permissive external environment.

But obstacles remain. The influence of the external environment has created problems, while ongoing legacies of the law, reflecting the temporal context, have had a strong influence. These legacies have proven to be very "sticky"; hard to see and to tackle, they help to "lock out" new formal rules and reinforce the gender status quo. An important lesson from this study is that to uncover how gender works in a setting such as the ICC, it is as important to account for *actions not undertaken* as it is to analyze those that have. *Not* investigating crimes that have been documented, *not* including gender-based crimes in the charges, and *not* accounting for evidence of these crimes in the verdict each demonstrates and reinforces gender biases in the law. It is what the ICC has *failed to do*, as much as what it has done, that demonstrates the ongoing influence of the temporal and spatial context in which it is nested. Understanding the reasons for the gaps and failures in the implementation of the Court's gender provisions is important for all actors seeking gender change but is especially so for internal Court actors on whose shoulders the legitimacy of the ICC rests.

PART THREE: GENDER JUSTICE AND LEGITIMACY AT THE ICC

The ICC's normative legitimacy, its authority to rule, was largely established through the Rome Statute negotiation process and appears to have been widely accepted, as evidenced by the ratification by 122 states parties of the Rome Statute at the end of the ICC's first twelve years in existence. But legitimacy is never stable; as Schiff suggests, it is always "tenuous and potentially reversible" (2010, 1). As discussed in Chapter 1, the Court's sociological legitimacy—relating to perceptions of its right to rule—must be maintained over time and is determined by continual reassessment by its various constituencies.

Like other international organizations, the ICC is not embedded in a system of checks and balances but is kept accountable primarily through engagement with multiple epistemic audiences. In calling the ICC to account, constituents recognize that the Court cannot meet all of their demands all of the time, but they do expect that it will address some of their demands some of the time, and always be willing to justify its decisions. To maintain legitimacy across its constituencies, the ICC also needs to demonstrate a willingness to revise its rules, policies, and practices when they fall short. Where there is a major discrepancy between what the Court has promised to deliver and its performance, legitimacy gaps arise (Barnett and Finnemore 2004, 168).

Schiff's analysis of the ICC's legitimacy highlights its particular and dynamic nature. Schiff identifies various constituencies engaged with the ICC, each of which perceives the Court's legitimacy differently. These audiences include states (members and nonmembers); international organizations, especially the UN; NGOs (e.g., humanitarian, human rights); victims; expert observers; and perpetrators (Schiff 2010, 6). In assessing legitimacy at the ICC, Schiff also draws attention to its various time dimensions or stages of development. His model identifies three dimensions: the design, operational, and consequential phases. Applied throughout the previous chapters, Schiff's model has been valuable in teasing out the varying position of the ICC's gender justice constituency on the Court's legitimacy across each phase.

However, this book concludes that Schiff's model can be refined to better account for nuances in the dynamics of ICC legitimacy. In relation to identifying constituencies, this study suggests that the constituency classifications need to be further divided to take account of subcategories of actors. For instance, there are obvious differences between states parties, with African Union and European Union states adopting widely differing points of view. As illustrated in Chapter 2 and throughout this book, applying the umbrella term "NGO" is too broad, given the range of views that sit under its awning. For instance, justice and conservative "family values" organizations both fit within the NGO category, but they view the ICC's legitimacy in diametrically opposite terms. To properly scrutinize the dynamics of legitimacy it is therefore important to specify the subcategory of actor that is being analyzed.

The experiences of gender justice advocates at the ICC have also illuminated the need to make distinctions about which aspect of the Rome Statute mandate is being assessed within each timeframe. As discussed throughout this book, at each stage of the ICC's development, gender justice advocates have made legitimacy assessments across each category of the Court's multifaceted gender justice mandate. Variations in the instantiation of the Rome Statute's gender justice framework have given gender justice advocates reason to take a differentiated position on the ICC's legitimacy depending on what aspect of these rules is under review and at what stage the assessment is being made.

Using this dynamic approach to legitimacy, this book has been able to identify a nuanced and differentiated view of the ICC's legitimacy from the perspective of its gender justice audience. During the *design* phase, gender justice advocates accepted that certain compromises were necessary and some losses were inevitable, but they exited the negotiation process with the knowledge that they had had a significant influence on the design of the Rome Statute across the three dimensions of gender justice. To paraphrase Buchanan and Keohane (2006), although the final provisions of the Rome Statute did not maximally serve gender advocates' interests or measure up to their highest moral standards, these actors left the design phase with a strong sense of the Court's right to rule.

Throughout the initial *operational* phase, the ICC's gender justice constituency has taken a differentiated view of the Court's legitimacy across the different aspects of its mandate. It has evaluated the Court as having greater legitimacy in relation to its gender representation mandate compared with its complementarity objectives, with a mixed assessment of its legitimacy in relation to its redistribution goals. Unquestionably, the largest gender justice legitimacy gap has emerged in relation to the ICC's recognition mandate. The Court's failure to secure a single conviction for sexual or gender-based crimes more than a decade after it commenced operation has seriously tested the gender justice constituency's view of the legitimacy of this aspect of the ICC's operations.

Two factors have helped salvage the ongoing relationship between the Court and its gender justice constituency, for the time being at least. First is the knowledge that incremental gender justice gains have been made outside the recognition element of the gender mandate. These gains have signaled to this constituency that it is possible to make inroads on gender injustices, albeit small and fragile advances, and have provided these actors with a platform to extend these gains in future. Second, and critically important, has been a willingness of Court personnel to respond to calls from gender justice actors for revision and reform. The 2012 review of the implementation of the victims' rights strategy is one example of critical reflection and learning. The most important has been the OTP's 2014 *Policy Paper on Sexual and Gender-Based Crimes*. Comprehensive in scope, the policy explicitly draws lessons from earlier practices and weaknesses in the prosecutorial strategy, not only in relation to case selection but also in evidence-gathering methods, engaging with victims and witnesses, and carrying out preliminary examinations. It is aimed directly at integrating a gender perspective into all aspects of the OTP's operations.[5] The key to this is, of course, in its application. As the Prosecutor herself has noted: "I harbor no illusions: the real impact of this policy will be determined by the success of its implementation."[6]

These findings support arguments in the literature, discussed in Chapter 1, that *revisability* is central to the ongoing legitimacy of institutions (Lowndes 2005). The reform efforts of certain ICC personnel indicate that they are not all blind to the gender justice legitimacy gap that has emerged; it illustrates that they are seeking to learn from the missteps of the early years and work to reverse some of gender provisions "locked out" of the initial path of ICC development. The extent to which these and other internal actors are in future willing to reinterpret the Statute in line with gender justice objectives and revise its practices to reflect these goals is key to maintaining the support of its key constituency of gender justice actors.

Considering the question of the sustainability of the ICC's fragile legitimacy into the future, this study concludes that the full weight of the burden should not be placed on the Court's shoulders but should be shared among its various constituencies. The most fundamental support constituents can give the Court in this regard is not to overburden it with expectations—to avoid pushing the ICC toward "mission creep." This builds on Barnett and Finnemore's important point that the constituencies of international organizations (2004, 158–159) often pressure them not just to fulfill but to go beyond their broad, aspirational (and often vague) mandates, even though it is outside the scope of their resources or organizational capacity to do so. To some extent, all the constituencies of the ICC are guilty of this practice, including its gender justice community. An obvious case in point was discussed in Chapter 5, with the demand by some of these actors for the ICC to deliver "transformative reparations" when arguably the Court has neither the statutory powers nor financial resources to do so. As highlighted in that discussion, the internal and external push by the Court to implement transformative reparations leaves it vulnerable to attack for not fulfilling its promises and risks raising expectations and exacerbating conflict on the ground (see Mégret 2012). The ICC's constituencies need to resist demanding more from the Court than it is able to deliver. To do otherwise will have serious implications for the consequential legitimacy of the ICC.

Like all international organizations, the ICC's aspirations are not matched by its capacity, a fact made amply apparent in the Court's first decade. This is not to let the ICC off the hook for the poor implementation of aspects of its gender justice mandate but to ask its constituency to follow the ICC's recent practice of revising policies—to take stock, reevaluate the ICC's capabilities in light of its early developments, and try to better align its objectives with these limitations.

As my colleagues and I have argued elsewhere in relation to the operation of the ICC in the Asia Pacific region (see Waller et al. 2014), a further step the ICC's gender justice constituency and the broader transnational women's rights movement can take to help shore up the ICC's legitimacy is to help catalyze the ICC's mandate, especially through its complementarity provisions, to strengthen gender justice at the national level. This could include gender justice groups operating within national settings to support investigation and evidence-gathering processes. Most productively, these organizations could work to encourage states to ratify the Rome Statute and then, importantly, implement its advanced gender justice rules into the local penal code helping to strengthen state-level accountability mechanisms. Bringing domestic laws up to a standard equivalent to the Rome Statute is not only one way to lift the burden from an overloaded and underresourced ICC but is likely to be a more fruitful avenue for addressing impunity for conflict-related sexual violence crimes than a handful of high-profile prosecutions in The Hague.

CONCLUSION

To return to the beginning, it is clear that the gendered consequences of war, captured so elegantly in Rubens' masterpiece on the cover of this book, still resonate in the practice of international criminal law. The effort to redraw the boundaries of the law to better recognize men's and women's experiences of conflict has been a contested and iterative process. The outcomes of the ICC's first dozen years suggests that there are still many gaps and pockets of resistance and a long way to go to achieve complete gender equality under international law. Old gender biases in international law have been reinforced and new rules that were meant to provide greater access to victims of gender-based crimes have been distorted and displaced. At the same time, some potentially transformative rules are in the process of being implemented, and the longstanding problem of "gender capture" is being addressed through the election and appointment of women to senior positions across the organs of the ICC. What is required now are gender-sensitive investigations, convincing evidence, targeted charges, bold judging, and adequate financing. External pressure from its committed gender justice constituency will be essential to securing these requirements. The closer the alignment between the ICC's gender justice rules and practices, the stronger will be its foundations and the more robust its legitimacy. If past experiences are a window into the future, this alignment will not come easily, and it is likely to arrive in small, contentious steps. But the effort will be worth it if it results in a more complete understanding of, and accountability for, the consequences of war for women and girls and men and boys.

APPENDIX
Election of Judges to the ICC 2003–2013

FIRST ELECTION: FEBRUARY 2003[1]

Male judges	11 out of 18
Female judges	7 out of 18
Judges with gender expertise	10 out of 18

Judge		Place of origin	Sex	Gender expertise
		Judges elected (18)		
1	BLATTMANN, René	Latin American & Caribbean States (Bolivia)	M	✘
2	CLARK, Maureen Harding	Western Europe & Other States (Ireland)	F	✔
3	DIARRA, Fatoumata Dembele	African States (Mali)	F	✔
4	FULFORD, Adrian	Western Europe & Other States (UK)	M	✔
5	HUDSON-PHILLIPS, Karl T.	Latin American & Caribbean States (Trinidad and Tobago)	M	✘
6	JORDA, Claude	Western Europe & Other States (France)	M	✘
7	KAUL, Hans-Peter	Western Europe & Other States (Germany)	M	✘
8	KIRSCH, Philippe	Western Europe & Other States (Canada)	M	✘
9	KOURULA, Erkki	Western Europe & Other States (Finland)	M	✘
10	KUENYEHIA, Akua	African States (Ghana)	F	✔
11	ODIO BENITO, Elizabeth	Latin American & Caribbean States (Costa Rica)	F	✔
12	PIKIS, Gheorghios M.	Asia-Pacific States (Cyprus)	M	✘
13	PILLAY, Navanethem	African States (South Africa)	F	✔
14	POLITI, Mauro	Western Europe & Other States (Italy)	M	✔
15	SLADE, Tuiloma Neroni	Asia-Pacific States (Samoa)	M	✔
16	SONG, Sang-hyun	Asia-Pacific States (Republic of Korea)	M	✘
17	STEINER, Sylvia H. de Figueiredo	Latin American & Caribbean States (Brazil)	F	✔
18	USACKA, Anita	Eastern European States (Latvia)	F	✔

SECOND ELECTION: JANUARY 2006[2]

Male judges	10 out of 18
Female judges	8 out of 18
Judges with gender expertise	9 out of 18

	Judge	Place of origin	Sex	Gender expertise
Judges elected (6)				
1	KAUL, Hans-Peter	Western Europe & Other States (Germany)	M	✘
2	KOURULA, Erkki	Western Europe & Other States (Finland)	M	✘
3	KUENYEHIA, Akua	African States (Ghana)	F	✔
4	SONG, Sang-hyun	Asia-Pacific States (Republic of Korea)	M	✘
5	TRENDAFILOVA, Ekaterina	Eastern European States (Bulgaria)	F	✘
6	USACKA, Anita	Eastern European States (Latvia)	F	✔
Judges remaining in office (12)				
1	BLATTMANN, René	Latin American & Caribbean States (Bolivia)	M	✘
2	CLARK, Maureen Harding	Western Europe & Other States (Ireland)	F	✔
3	DIARRA, Fatoumata Dembele	African States (Mali)	F	✔
4	FULFORD, Adrian	Western Europe & Other States (UK)	M	✔
5	HUDSON-PHILLIPS, Karl T.	Latin American & Caribbean States (Trinidad and Tobago)	M	✘
6	JORDA, Claude	Western Europe & Other States (France)	M	✘
7	KIRSCH, Philippe	Western Europe & Other States (Canada)	M	✘
8	ODIO BENITO, Elizabeth	Latin American & Caribbean States (Costa Rica)	F	✔
9	PIKIS, Gheorghios M.	Asia-Pacific States (Cyprus)	M	✘
10	PILLAY, Navanethem	African States (South Africa)	F	✔
11	POLITI, Mauro	Western Europe & Other States (Italy)	M	✔
12	STEINER, Sylvia H. de Figueiredo	Latin American & Caribbean States (Brazil)	F	✔

Appendix: Election of Judges to the ICC 2003–2013

THIRD ELECTION: DECEMBER 2007[3]

Male judges	10 out of 18
Female judges	8 out of 18
Judges with gender expertise	9 out of 18

Judge		Place of origin	Sex	Gender expertise
Judges elected (3)				
1	COTTE, Bruno	Western Europe & Other States (France)	M	✘
2	SAIGA, Fumiko	Asia-Pacific States (Japan)	F	✔
3	NSEREKO, Daniel David	African States (Uganda)	M	✘
Judges remaining in office (15)				
1	BLATTMANN, René	Latin American & Caribbean States (Bolivia)	M	✘
2	DIARRA, Fatoumata Dembele	African States (Mali)	F	✔
3	FULFORD, Adrian	Western Europe & Other States (UK)	M	✔
4	KAUL, Hans-Peter	Western Europe & Other States (Germany)	M	✘
5	KIRSCH, Philippe	Western Europe & Other States (Canada)	M	✘
6	KOURULA, Erkki	Western Europe & Other States (Finland)	M	✘
7	KUENYEHIA, Akua	African States (Ghana)	F	✔
8	ODIO BENITO, Elizabeth	Latin American & Caribbean States (Costa Rica)	F	✔
9	PIKIS, Gheorghios M.	Asia-Pacific States (Cyprus)	M	✘
10	PILLAY, Navanethem	African States (South Africa)	F	✔
11	POLITI, Mauro	Western Europe & Other States (Italy)	M	✔
12	SONG, Sang-hyun	Asia-Pacific States (Republic of Korea)	M	✘
13	STEINER, Sylvia H. de Figueiredo	Latin American & Caribbean States (Brazil)	F	✔
14	TRENDAFILOVA, Ekaterina	Eastern European States (Bulgaria)	F	✘
15	USACKA, Anita	Eastern European States (Latvia)	F	✔

FOURTH ELECTION: JANUARY 2009[4]

Male judges	9 out of 19
Female judges	10 out of 19
Judges with gender expertise	11 out of 19

Judge		Place of origin	Sex	Gender expertise
Judges elected (6)				
1	ALUOCH, Joyce	African States (Kenya)	F	✔
2	MONAGENG, Sanji Mmasenono	African States (Botswana)	F	✔
3	SAIGA, Fumiko	Asia-Pacific States (Japan)	F	✔
4	SHAHABUDDEEN, Mohamed	Latin American & Caribbean States (Guyana)	M	✔
5	TARFUSSER, Cuno	Western Europe & Other States (Italy)	M	✔
6	VAN DEN WYNGAERT, Christine	Western Europe & Other States (Belgium)	F	✖
Judges remaining in office (13)				
1	*BLATTMANN, René	Latin American & Caribbean States (Bolivia)	M	✖
2	COTTE, Bruno	Western Europe & Other States (France)	M	✖
3	DIARRA, Fatoumata Dembele	African States (Mali)	F	✔
4	FULFORD, Adrian	Western Europe & Other States (UK)	M	✔
5	KAUL, Hans-Peter	Western Europe & Other States (Germany)	M	✖
6	KOURULA, Erkki	Western Europe & Other States (Finland)	M	✖
7	KUENYEHIA, Akua	African States (Ghana)	F	✔
8	ODIO BENITO, Elizabeth	Latin American & Caribbean States (Costa Rica)	F	✔
9	NSEREKO, Daniel David	African States (Uganda)	M	✖
10	SONG, Sang-hyun	Asia-Pacific States (Republic of Korea)	M	✖
11	STEINER, Sylvia H. de Figueiredo	Latin American & Caribbean States (Brazil)	F	✔
12	TRENDAFILOVA, Ekaterina	Eastern European States (Bulgaria)	F	✖
13	USACKA, Anita	Eastern European States (Latvia)	F	✔

*Judge Blattmann's term ended in 2009 but he remained an *id litem* judge in Trial Chamber I.

Appendix: Election of Judges to the ICC 2003–2013

FIFTH ELECTION: NOVEMBER 2009[5]

Male judges	8 out of 19
Female judges	11 out of 19
Judges with gender expertise	10 out of 19

Judge		Place of origin	Sex	Gender expertise
Judges elected (2)				
1	FERNÁNDEZ DE GURMENDI, Silvia	Latin American & Caribbean States (Argentina)	F	✘
2	OZAKI, Kuniko	Asia-Pacific States (Japan)	F	✔
Judges remaining in office (17)				
1	ALUOCH, Joyce	African States (Kenya)	F	✔
2	BLATTMANN, René	Latin American & Caribbean States (Bolivia)	M	✘
3	COTTE, Bruno	Western Europe & Other States (France)	M	✘
4	DIARRA, Fatoumata Dembele	African States (Mali)	F	✔
5	FULFORD, Adrian	Western Europe & Other States (UK)	M	✔
6	KAUL, Hans-Peter	Western Europe & Other States (Germany)	M	✘
7	KOURULA, Erkki	Western Europe & Other States (Finland)	M	✘
8	KUENYEHIA, Akua	African States (Ghana)	F	✔
9	MONAGENG, Sanju Mmasenono	African States (Botswana)	F	✔
10	NSEREKO, Daniel David	African States (Uganda)	M	✘
11	ODIO BENITO, Elizabeth	Latin American & Caribbean States (Costa Rica)	F	✔
12	SONG, Sang-hyun	Asia-Pacific States (Republic of Korea)	M	✘
13	STEINER, Sylvia H. de Figueiredo	Latin American & Caribbean States (Brazil)	F	✔
14	TARFUSSER, Cuno	Western Europe & Other States (Italy)	M	✔
15	TRENDAFILOVA, Ekaterina	Eastern European States (Bulgaria)	F	✘
16	USACKA, Anita	Eastern European States (Latvia)	F	✔
17	VAN DEN WYNGAERT, Christine	Western Europe & Other States (Belgium)	F	✘

SIXTH ELECTION: DECEMBER 2011[6]

Male judges	11 out of 24
Female judges	13 out of 24
Judges with gender expertise	12 out of 24

Judge		Place of origin	Sex	Gender expertise
Judges elected (6)				
1	CARMONA, Anthony Thomas Aquinas	Latin American & Caribbean States (Trinidad and Tobago)	M	✘
2	DEFENSOR-SANTIAGO, Miriam	Asia-Pacific States (Philippines)	F	✘
3	EBOE-OSUJI, Chile	African States (Nigeria)	M	✔
4	FREMR, Robert	Eastern European States (Czech Republic)	M	✔
5	HERRERA CARBUCCIA, Olga Venecia	Latin American & Caribbean States (Dominican Republic)	F	✘
6	MORRISON, Howard	Western Europe & Other States (UK)	M	✘
Judges remaining in office (18)				
1	ALUOCH, Joyce	African States (Kenya)	F	✔
2	BLATTMANN, René	Latin American & Caribbean States (Bolivia)	M	✘
3	*COTTE, Bruno	Western Europe & Other States (France)	M	✘
4	*DIARRA, Fatoumata Dembele	African States (Mali)	F	✔
5	FERNÁNDEZ DE GURMENDI, Silvia	Latin American & Caribbean States (Argentina)	F	✘
6	*FULFORD, Adrian	Western Europe & Other States (UK)	M	✔
7	KAUL, Hans-Peter	Western Europe & Other States (Germany)	M	✘
8	KOURULA, Erkki	Western Europe & Other States (Finland)	M	✘
9	KUENYEHIA, Akua	African States (Ghana)	F	✔
10	MONAGENG, Sanju Mmasenono	African States (Botswana)	F	✔
11	*ODIO BENITO, Elizabeth	Latin American & Caribbean States (Costa Rica)	F	✔
12	OZAKI, Kuniko	Asia-Pacific States (Japan)	F	✔
13	SONG, Sang-hyun	Asia-Pacific States (Republic of Korea)	M	✘
14	*STEINER, Sylvia H. de Figueiredo	Latin American & Caribbean States (Brazil)	F	✔

Appendix: Election of Judges to the ICC 2003–2013

Judge		Place of origin	Sex	Gender expertise
Judges elected (6)				
15	TARFUSSER, Cuno	Western Europe & Other States (Italy)	M	✔
16	TRENDAFILOVA, Ekaterina	Eastern European States (Bulgaria)	F	✘
17	USACKA, Anita	Eastern European States (Latvia)	F	✔
18	VAN DEN WYNGAERT, Christine	Western Europe & Other States (Belgium)	F	✘

*Judges Fulford, Odio Benito, Cotte, Diarra, and Steiner's terms ended in 2012 but they remained in office as *id litem* judges.

SEVENTH ELECTION: NOVEMBER 2013[7]

Male judges	9 out of 21
Female judges	12 out of 21
Judges with gender expertise	11 out of 21

Judge		Place of origin	Sex	Gender expertise
Judges elected (1)				
1	HENDERSON, Geoffrey A.	Latin American & Caribbean States (Trinidad and Tobago)	M	✔
Judges remaining in office (20)				
1	ALUOCH, Joyce	African States (Kenya)	F	✔
2	COTTE, Bruno	Western Europe & Other States (France)	M	✘
3	DEFENSOR-SANTIAGO, Miriam	Asia-Pacific States (Philippines)	F	✘
4	DIARRA, Fatoumata Dembele	African States (Mali)	F	✔
5	EBOE-OSUJI, Chile	African States (Nigeria)	M	✔
6	FERNÁNDEZ DE GURMENDI, Silvia	Latin American & Caribbean States (Argentina)	F	✘
7	FREMR, Robert	Eastern European States (Czech Republic)	M	✔
8	HERRERA CARBUCCIA, Olga Venecia	Latin American & Caribbean States (Dominican Republic)	F	✘
9	KAUL, Hans-Peter	Western Europe & Other States (Germany)	M	✘

Judge		Place of origin	Sex	Gender expertise
		Judges elected (1)		
10	KOURULA, Erkki	Western Europe & Other States (Finland)	M	✘
11	KUENYEHIA, Akua	African States (Ghana)	F	✔
12	MONAGENG, Sanju Mmasenono	African States (Botswana)	F	✔
13	MORRISON, Howard	Western Europe & Other States (UK)	M	✘
14	OZAKI, Kuniko	Asia-Pacific States (Japan)	F	✔
15	SONG, Sang-hyun	Asia-Pacific States (Republic of Korea)	M	✘
16	STEINER, Sylvia H. de Figueiredo	Latin American & Caribbean States (Brazil)	F	✔
17	TARFUSSER, Cuno	Western Europe & Other States (Italy)	M	✔
18	TRENDAFILOVA, Ekaterina	Eastern European States (Bulgaria)	F	✘
19	USACKA, Anita	Eastern European States (Latvia)	F	✔
20	VAN DEN WYNGAERT, Christine	Western Europe & Other States (Belgium)	F	✘

NOTES

CHAPTER 1

1. I am grateful to both Susan Williams (2012) and Fiona Mackay (2008) for redirecting me back to Fraser's framework after presenting their own excellent applications of it.
2. Applying the term "victim" here, rather than the term "victim/survivor" or "survivor," as is common in much of the literature on sexual violence, is not intended in any way to diminish the agency of those who experience such crimes. Rather, it is to acknowledge that in the context of this study, this is the status with which individuals come before the ICC. This status gives them standing in ICC proceedings and, potentially, a route to access reparations and other restorative measures.
3. They also usefully delimit the term by suggesting that when behavior has *"no pattern, or when there is no socially shared understanding of the right behavior* in a given setting", it cannot be described as an institution (Azari and Smith 2012, 39, emphasis added).

CHAPTER 2

1. UN GA. 1998. A/CONF.183/9.
2. A "situation" refers to a site with physical and temporal boundaries. For example, in 2005 the UN Security Council referred "the situation in Darfur since 1 July 2002" to the ICC Prosecutor (UNSC. 2005. S/RES/1593 (2005)).
3. This latter category was the most contentious, with states agreeing to put aside the definition of "aggression" until the seven-year review of the Rome Statute. At the review meeting in Kampala in 2010, states parties agreed to a definition as well as regime for the ICC to exercise jurisdiction. This regime is expected to come into operation in 2017 (see ICC. 2010. RC/Res.6.).
4. WCGJ. 1997. "Recommendations and Commentary . . . "
5. TFV. 2014. "At Global Summit . . . "
6. *Ibid*.
7. Moreover, Article 20 of the Rome Statute upholds the principle of *ne bis in idem*, or double jeopardy, which means that once a national court has prosecuted a case, if the proceedings are deemed legitimate, the ICC cannot reprosecute it.
8. WCGJ. 1997. "Recommendations and Commentary . . . ," 1.
9. At the time of writing, the ICC has not adjudicated on the definition, so it is difficult to know how the Court will apply the concept in practice.

10. As the following chapters illustrate, other major skirmishes took place over reference to the gender balance of the judiciary, the inclusion of the crime of forced pregnancy, and the gender dimensions of complementarity. The Caucus was also involved in minor clashes over the reference to gender in the general nondiscrimination clause and the gender dimension of slavery (Bedont and Hall-Martinez 1999, 69; Glasius 2006, 85; WCGJ. 1998. "Gender Justice and the ICC")—disputes that were eventually resolved to the satisfaction of the Caucus (Glasius 2006, 85).

11. At the time of writing, Inder remains in this position and since 2013 has also been the Special Gender Advisor to the Prosecutor of the ICC, Fatou Bensouda.

CHAPTER 3

1. While at ICTR, Justice Pillay requested the Prosecutor amend the charges to include sexual violence as a form of genocide in the *Akayesu* case after hearing testimony about this violence (Luping 2009, 445).
2. In this case Judge Adolphus Karibi-Whyte (presiding), Judge Elizabeth Odio Benito, and Judge Saad Saood Jan pronounced rape as a form of torture (MacKinnon 2005).
3. WCGJ. 1998. "Submission to the Standing Committee..."
4. *Ibid.*
5. WCGJ. 1998. "Recommendations and Commentary...," 33.
6. *Ibid.*, 1.
7. *Ibid.*
8. WCGJ. 1998. "Don't Miss this Historic Opportunity..."
9. WCGJ. 1998. "Submission to the Standing Committee...," 5–6.
10. WCGJ. 1998. "Recommendations and Commentary...," 1.
11. UN General Assembly. 1996. "Report of the Preparatory Committee..."
12. WCJG. 1998. "Submission to the Standing Committee..."
13. Pursuant to Article 43 (4), the Registrar is elected through a secret ballot of the Chamber.
14. ICC ASP. 2004. ICC-ASP/3/Res. 6, 14(B)(20)(c).
15. *Ibid.*, 14(B)(19).
16. ICC ASP. 2003. ICC-ASP/1/3/Add. 1.
17. The Rome Statute stipulates the Chamber comprise eighteen members. At any time, more than eighteen judges may be on the bench as judges' terms are extended until cases are being completed. The calculations here are on all full sitting Chambers, excluding *ad litem* judges.
18. Note these figures do not include *ad litem* judges (i.e., those appointed only for the duration of a particular case).
19. ICC-CPI-20,150,310-PR1095.
20. ICC-CPI-20,150,311-PR1096.
21. WIGJ. 2012. *Gender Report Card 2012*, 107–108; WIGJ. 2012. "Legal Filings...," 4.
22. WIGJ. 2012. *Gender Report Card 2012*, 208.
23. WIGJ. 2008. "Preliminary Dossier..."
24. WIGJ. 2012. *Gender Report Card 2012.*
25. *Ibid.*, 14.
26. See WIGJ. 2005. *Gender Report Card 2005*; WIGJ. 2006. *Gender Report Card 2006.*
27. ICC OTP. 2008. ICC-OTP-20,081,126-PR377.

28. See WIGJ. 2008. *Gender Report Card 2008*, 12.
29. ICC OTP. 2008. ICC-OTP-20,081,126-PR377.
30. *Ibid.*
31. WIGJ. 2008. *Gender Report Card 2008*, 21.
32. *Ibid.*
33. ICC OTP. 2012. ICC-OTP-20,120,821-PR833.
34. ICC OTP. 2014. "Policy Paper of Sexual and Gender...," 14.
35. As of February 2014 there were twenty-one cases before the Court from seven situation countries. In *Prosecutor v. Jean-Pierre Bemba Gombo*, 4,121 victims alone have been recognized (ICC. 2012. ICC-PIDS-CIS-CAR-01-009/12_ENG).
36. ICC ASP. 2012. ICC-ASP/11/40.
37. ICC ASP. 2006. ICC-ASP/5/12, 5.
38. A statutorily independent Office of Public Counsel for Defence also exists at the ICC.
39. ICC OPCV. 2010. ICC-OPCV-B-001/10_Eng, 3.
40. *Ibid.*; ICC ASP. 2012. ICC-ASP/11/40, 74.
41. In the situation in the Democratic Republic of Congo, 30 percent of victims are female and 70 percent are male; in Uganda, 32 percent of victims are female and 68 percent are male; in Kenya, 36 percent of victims are female and 64 percent are male (WIGJ. 2011. *Gender Report Card 2011*, 83).
42. WIGJ. 2011. *Gender Report Card 2011*, 35.
43. *Ibid.*, 83.
44. See WIGJ. 2011. *Gender Report Card 2011*, 72; WIGJ. 2012. *Gender Report Card 2012*, 48.
45. ICC OTP. 2014. "Policy Paper of Sexual and Gender...," 17.
46. *Ibid.*
47. ICC. 2010. "Review Conference of the Rome Statute...," 5.
48. WIGJ. 2010. *Gender Report Card 2010*.
49. *Ibid.*
50. ICC. 2012. ICC-01/05-01/08-T-220-ENG CT WT 01-05-2012 1-56 NB T.
51. See above interview with Claudia Perdomo, June 26, 2012.
52. *Ibid.*
53. ICC. 2010. RC-2010/RC/11, 95.
54. ICC. 2010. "Review Conference of the Rome Statute...," 80.
55. ICC ASP. 2012. ICC-ASP/11/40, 12.
56. See, for example, WIGJ. 2010. *Gender Report Card 2010*, 61.
57. ICC. 2012. ICC-01/04-01/06-2842.
58. ICC OPCV. 2010. ICC-OPCV-B-001/10_Eng, 3, 9.
59. *Ibid.*, 8.
60. WIGJ. 2011. *Gender Report Card 2011*, 83.
61. ICC ASP. 2012. ICC-ASP/11/40,18.
62. WIGJ. 2011. *Gender Report Card 2011*, 76.
63. ICC ASP. 2012. ICC-ASP/11/40, 1.
64. *Ibid.*, 4.
65. *Ibid.*

CHAPTER 4

1. The Rome Statute also gives recognition to the victims of sexual and gender-based crimes and women. For a discussion of these elements see Chapter 3.
2. ICC OTP. 2014. "Policy Paper of Sexual and Gender..."

3. UN GA. 1948. *Convention on the Prevention and Punishment of the Crime of Genocide*; UN GA. 1984. *Convention against Torture and Other Cruel, Inhuman or Degrading Treatment or Punishment.*
4. UNSC. 1993. *Statute of the International Tribunal for . . . Yugoslavia,* Article 5(g).
5. UNSC. 1994. *Statute of the International Criminal Tribunal for . . . Rwanda,* Article 4(e) and Article 3 (g).
6. In *Akayesu*, rape was recognized as a crime against humanity and as a war crime and defined in a way that removed the consensual element—which places the onus on the victim—and focused on coercion (see MacKinnon 2006).
7. Rape and sexual violence was understood as a form of genocide because it was capable of causing "serious bodily or mental harm to members of the group" (ICTR. 1998. ICTR-96-4-T, para. 706).
8. WCGJ. 1998. "Submission to the Standing Committee . . .," 7.
9. In relation to the crime of aggression, the Caucus agreed that such a crime should be included in the Statute, that the crimes constituting such an act should not be exhaustive and should not be defined by the UN Security Council (WCGJ. 1998. "Gender Justice and the ICC," 4).
10. WCGJ. 1998. "Submission to the Standing Committee," 7, 5.
11. WCGJ. 1998. "Gender Justice and the ICC," ii.
12. *Ibid.,* 11.
13. *Ibid.,* 2.
14. WCGJ. 1997. "Action Alert . . ."
15. WCGJ. 1998. "Gender Justice and the ICC," 11.
16. See also *Ibid.*
17. WCGJ. 1998. "Gender Justice and the ICC."
18. *Ibid.,* 16.
19. *Ibid.*
20. *Ibid.,* 18.
21. *Ibid.,* 18.
22. *Ibid.,* 18.
23. *Ibid.,* 16.
24. *Ibid.,* 25.
25. *Ibid.*
26. *Ibid.,* 27–28.
27. *Ibid.,* 39
28. *Ibid.*
29. *Ibid.,* 32.
30. *Ibid.,* 38.
31. ICC. 2000. PCNICC/2000/1/Add.2 (2000), Article 6, fn 3.
32. *Ibid.,* Article 7(1)(g)-1.
33. As opposed to *and* in previous drafts.
34. WIGJ. 2012. *Gender Report Card 2012,* 106.
35. *Prosecutor v. Thomas Lubanga Dyilo; Prosecutor v. Bosco Ntaganda; Prosecutor v. Germain Katanga; Prosecutor v. Mathieu; Prosecutor v. Callixte Mbarushimana; Prosecutor v. Jean-Pierre Bemba Gombo; Prosecutor v. Bahar Idriss Abu Garda; Prosecutor v. Abdallah Banda Abakaer Nourain; Prosecutor v. William Samoei Ruto and Joshua Arap Sang; Prosecutor v. Uhuru Muigai Kenyatta; Prosecutor v. Laurent Gbagbo.*
36. UNSC. 2014. S/2014/181.

37. ICC case numbers: *Katanga* ICC-01/04-01/07; *Ngudjolo Chui* ICC-01/04-02/12.
38. ICC. 2012. ICC-01/04-02/12-3-tENG.
39. ICC. 2014. ICC-01/04-01/07-3436.
40. Prosecutor Moreno Ocampo held the position from 2003 to 2012 and Prosecutor Bensouda from 2012. Her term will expire in 2021. She was Deputy Prosecutor from 2004 to 2012.
41. At the ICC, for the Pre-Trial Chamber to issue a warrant of arrest or a summons to appear it requires the prosecution to provide "*reasonable grounds* to believe the person has committed a crime within the jurisdiction of the Court" (Article 58(1)(a); emphasis added). At the confirmation of charges there must be "*substantial grounds* to believe that the person committed the crime charged" (Article 61(7)). For an accused to be found guilty by the Trial Chamber, the onus on the prosecution is to demonstrate that it is "*beyond reasonable doubt*" that the accused committed the crimes with which he or she was charged (Article 66(3)).
42. I am indebted to Rosemary Grey for her painstaking research from which I base my analysis. Rosemary's Ph.D. dissertation provides a wide-ranging and detailed analysis of the Prosecutor's discretion in relation to sexual and gender-based crimes at ICC (Grey 2015).
43. For a range of assessments of the value of thematic sexual and gender-based violence prosecutions, see Bergsmo, 2012.
44. WIGJ. 2012. *Gender Report Card 2012*, 112.
45. *Ibid.*, 107.
46. For a more detailed discussion of this case, see Chappell 2014.
47. ICC. 2014. ICC-01/04-01/06-T-364; ICC. 2015. ICC-01/04-01/06-3129 03-03-2015 1/97 NM A A2 A3
48. ICC OTP. 2004. "Statement of the Prosecutor...," emphasis added.
49. WIGJ. 2006. *Gender Report Card 2006*.
50. ICC OTP. 2008. ICC 01/04-01/06-170.
51. *Ibid.*
52. WIGJ. 2011. *Gender Report Card 2011*, 130.
53. *Ibid.*
54. ICC. 2009. ICC-01/04-01/06-1891.
55. See WIGJ's website: http://www.iccwomen.org/.
56. ICC. 2009. ICC-01/04-01/06-T-223-ENG.
57. WIGJ. 2010. *Gender Report Card 2010*, 132.
58. ICC. 2009. ICC-01/04-01/06-T-107-ENG, 11.
59. See for instance *Ibid.*, 10, 11; WIGJ. 2012. *Gender Report Card 2012*, 160; WIGJ. 2009. *Gender Report Card 2009*, 69–71.
60. ICC. 2011. ICC-01/04-01/06-2748-Red, para. 139.
61. See for example the tense exchange on these issues between the Prosecutor and the Bench in closing statements: ICC-01/04-01/06-T-356-ENG, 55.
62. ICC. 2012. ICC-01/04-01/06-T-359-ENG.
63. *Ibid.*, para. 29.
64. ICC. 2012. ICC-01/04-01/06-2901, para. 60.
65. *Ibid.*, para. 74.
66. *Ibid.*, para. 75.
67. WIGJ. 2012. "First Sentencing Judgement..."
68. ICC. 2012. ICC-01/04-01/06-2842, para. 21.

69. *Ibid.*, para. 20.
70. *Ibid.*, para. 6.
71. *Ibid.*, para. 21.
72. *Ibid.*, para. 20.
73. ICC. 2012. ICC-01/04-01/06-2901, para. 2.
74. *Ibid.*, para. 21.
75. ICC. 2012. ICC-01/04-01/06-2842, para. 16.
76. ICC. 2010. ICC-01/04-01/06-2360.
77. WIGJ. 2010. *Gender Report Card 2010*, 132–133.
78. REDRESS Director Carla Ferstman rejects such criticism, arguing that the use of Regulation in *Lubanga* was not "purporting to propose new charges, but [providing] supplementary legal qualifications to the existing charges" (2012, 806).
79. WIGJ. 2010. *Gender Report Card 2010*, 132.
80. ICC. 2012. ICC-01/04-611-Red.
81. ICC. 2014. ICC-01/04-02/06-309.
82. ICC. 2008. ICC-01/05-01/08-15.
83. ICC. 2009. ICC-01/05-01/08-424.
84. ICC. 2008. ICC-01/05-01/08-14-tENG, para. 40.
85. ICC. 2009. ICC/01/05-01/08-424, paras. 204–205, 310–312.
86. ICC. 2000. PCNICC/2000/1/Add.2, para. 9.
87. WIGJ. 2011. "Legal Eye on the ICC."
88. *Ibid.*
89. WIGJ. 2010. *Gender Report Card 2010*, 115; ICC. 2010. ICC-01/05-01/08-706, para. 15.
90. ICC. 2010. ICC-01/05-01/08-706, para. 17.
91. ICC. 2010. ICC-01/05-01/08-896-AnxA.
92. The first was *Lubanga*; the second was the acquittal of Katanga's co-accused Mathieu Ngudjolo Chui in December 2013 (ICC. 2012. ICC-01/04-02/12-3-tENG).
93. ICC. 2014. ICC-01/04-01/07-3436.
94. Judge Christine Van den Wyngaert issued a dissenting opinion against the majority on all charges (ICC. 2014. ICC-01/04-01/07-3436-AnxI).
95. WIGJ. 2014. "Statement of the Women's Initiatives . . ."
96. As the Women's Initiatives group pointed out, at the confirmation-of-charges stage, the sexual violence charges were "the only crimes confirmed by a majority of judges and not by the full bench" (WIGJ. 2014. "Statement of the Women's Initiatives . . .").
97. ICC. 2014. ICC-01/04-01/07-3436-AnxI, especially see Section III. However, Judge Van den Wyngaert also noted that these problems appeared to have improved under Prosecutor Bensouda.
98. WIGJ. 2014. "Statement of the Women's Initiatives . . ."
99. ICC. 2014. ICC-01/04-01/07-3462.
100. WIGJ. 2014. "Statement of the Women's Initiatives . . ."
101. *Ibid.*
102. ICC. 2012. ICC-PIDS-CIS-DRC-04-003/11_Eng.
103. WIGJ. 2012. *Gender Report Card 2012*, 115–117.
104. ICC. 2011. ICC-01/04-01/10-Red, para. 110.
105. Together Muthaura and Kenyatta had their charges confirmed, but the charges against Muthaura were withdrawn in March 2013.
106. ICC. 2014. ICC-01/09-02/11.

107. ICC. 2011. ICC-01/09-02/1 l-T-5-Red-ENG, para. 88.
108. ICC. 2012. ICC-01/ 09-02/11-382-Red, para. 266.
109. *Ibid.*
110. WIGJ. 2014. *Gender Report Card 2013*, 72.
111. *Ibid.*
112. ICC. 2012. ICC-02/11-01/12.
113. ICC. 2014. ICC-CPI-20,141,209-PR1075.
114. ICC OTP. 2014. " Policy Paper of Sexual and Gender . . .," 6.
115. *Ibid.*, 13.
116. *Ibid.*, 6.
117. *Ibid.*, 31.
118. *Ibid.*, 15.
119. WIGJ. 2014. "Statement of the Women's Initiatives . . ."

CHAPTER 5
1. Elements of this chapter draw upon arguments developed in Durbach and Chappell (2014).
2. Restorative justice contrasts with retributive justice. Whereas the latter is focused on perpetrators and punishing them for the violations they commit, restorative justice seeks to repair the harm caused by criminal behavior. Reparations are a form of restorative justice used to redress the harm suffered by victims of crime (for a discussion see Hoyle and Ullrich 2014).
3. These include the right to restitution, compensation, rehabilitation, satisfaction, and guarantees of nonrepetition.
4. See WCGJ. 1998. "Recommendations and Commentary . . ."; WCGJ. 1998. "Gender Justice and the ICC," 50–53.
5. WCGJ. 1998. "Recommendations and Commentary . . ."; WCGJ. 1998. WCGJ. 1998. "Gender Justice and the ICC," 50.
6. WCGJ. 1998. "Recommendations and Commentary . . .," 1.
7. WCGJ. 1998. "Gender Justice and the ICC," 50.
8. *Ibid.*, 52.
9. *Ibid.*, 53.
10. *Ibid.*, 53.
11. *Ibid.*, 53.
12. *Ibid.*
13. ICC ASP. 2005. ICC-ASP/4/Res. 3.
14. ICC. 2012. ICC-01/04-01/06-2904, para. 222.
15. WCGJ. 1998. "Recommendations and Commentary . . .," 1.
16. ICC. 2011. ICC-ASP/10/Res. 3.
17. *Ibid.*, para. 2.
18. *Ibid.*, para. 3.
19. WCGJ. 1998. "Gender and the ICC," 51.
20. ICC ASP. 2005. ICC-ASP/4/Res. 3.
21. Indeed, the Women's Caucus argued in favor of direct payment of reparations to victims by the Court where possible, over the option of channeling reparations through a trust fund (WCGJ. 1998. "Gender and the ICC," 52).
22. TFV. n.d. "The Two Roles . . ."
23. The TFV's "assistance" mandate was formalized only after extensive litigation, having been challenged by the Office of Public Counsel for Defence (see Dannenbaum 2010).

24. TFV. 2010. "Recognizing Victims . . ."
25. TFV. n.d. "The Two Roles . . ."
26. WIGJ. 2012. *Gender Report Card 2012*, 206.
27. And, at least in the *Lubanga* judgments, discussed later in this chapter, Judges have passed this responsibility on to the shoulders of the TFV.
28. ICC. 2012. ICC-01/04-01/06-2904; ICC. 2013. ICC-01/04-02/06-67, para. 13.
29. ICC. 2015. ICC-01/04-01/06 A A 2 A 3.
30. WIGJ. 2012. *Gender Report Card 2012*, 103.
31. ICC. 2012. ICC-01/04-01/06-2842.
32. ICC. 2012. ICC-01/04-01/06-2853.
33. However, this decision failed to include a ruling on any individual awards or any specific reparations orders (SáCouto and Cleary 2014, 152). These tasks were left to the TFV (ICC. 2012. ICC-01/04-01/06-2919-tENG).
34. See: ICC OTP. 2012. "OTP Briefing: Principles . . ."; TFV. 2012. "Mobilising Resources . . ."
35. WIGJ. 2012. *Gender Report Card 2012*, 207.
36. ICC. 2012. ICC-01/04-01/06-2853, para. 35; also see WIGJ 2012. *Gender Report Card 2012*, 207–208.
37. ICC. 2012. ICC-01/04-01/06-2872, para. 77.
38. ICC. 2012. ICC-01/04-01/06-2904, para. 179.
39. *Ibid.*, para. 249.
40. *Ibid.*, para. 194.
41. *Ibid.*, para. 222.
42. *Ibid.*, para. 207.
43. *Ibid.*, para. 180.
44. *Ibid.*, para. 189.
45. *Ibid.*, para. 264.
46. *Ibid.*, paras. 269, 271.
47. *Ibid.*, para. 247.
48. WIGJ 2012. *Gender Report Card 2012*, 205.
49. ICC. 2012. ICC-01/04-01/06-2904, para. 181.
50. ICC. 2012. ICC-01/04-01/06-2914-tENG, paras. 11–15.
51. ICC. 2012. ICC-01/04-01/06-2919-tENG, para. 5.
52. *Ibid.*, para. 40.
53. *Ibid.*, para. 5.
54. ICC-01/04-01/06 A A 2 A 3, para. 197.
55. *Ibid.*, para. 198.
56. *Ibid.*, para. 199
57. ICC. 2012. ICC-01/04-01/06-2948-Conf-tENG; ICC. 2012. ICC-01/04-01/06-2949-tENG; ICC. 2012. ICC-01/04-01/06-2919-tENG.
58. ICC. 2014. ICC-01/04-01/07-3436.
59. ICC. 2015. ICC-01/04-01/07-3548 13-05-2015 1/44, para. 28
60. ICC. 2012. ICC-01/04-01/06-2904, paras. 283–288.
61. TFV. n.d. "The Two Roles . . ."
62. ICC. 2012. ICC-01/04-01/06-2872, para. 65.
63. However, due to a deteriorating security situation, the TFV indefinitely suspended its activities in Central African Republic in March 2013.
64. TFV. 2014. "A Road to Recovery . . . ," 8.

65. *Ibid.*, 12–13.
66. TFV. n.d. "The Two Roles . . ."
67. TFV. 2014. "Trust Fund for Victims receives over €5 million . . ."
68. *Ibid.*; TFV. 2014. "A Road to Recovery . . .," 6.
69. TFV. 2014. "A Road to Recovery . . .," 15–23.
70. TFV. 2012. "Mobilising Resources . . ."; TFV. 2014. "A Road to Recovery . . ."
71. WIGJ. 2012. *Gender Report Card 2012*, 210.
72. WIGJ. 2012. "Statement on the First Reparations . . .," 2.
73. WIGJ. 2014. *Gender Report Card 2013*.
74. See for instance, WIGJ. 2012. *Gender Report Card 2012*, 57–58; WIGJ. 2011. *Gender Report Card 2011*, 80–81.

CHAPTER 6

1. Parts One and Two of this chapter draw upon Chappell, Grey, and Waller (2013).
2. This was made most obvious in Stahn and El Zeidy's (2011) seminal two-volume edited collection on complementarity, which, while addressing multiple and complex aspects of the concept, does not in any one of its forty chapters pay attention to its gender dimensions, while the domestic prosecution of international crimes of sexual and gender-based violence barely rates a mention.
3. ICC OTP. 2003. "Paper on Some Policy Issues . . ."
4. WCGJ. 1998. "Gender Justice and the ICC."
5. *Ibid.*, 25.
6. WCGJ. 1997. "Recommendations and Commentary . . .," 15.
7. *Ibid.*
8. *Ibid.*
9. *Ibid.*, 11.
10. WCGJ. 1998. "Gender Justice and the ICC," 24.
11. *Ibid.*, 24.
12. Article 17(1)(d) also requires the Court to establish that the case is of sufficient gravity, an issue that is not explored here as it does not implicate state sovereignty.
13. Pursuant to Article 53(1)(b) the Prosecutor is also required to consider whether a crime within the Court's jurisdiction appears to have been committed, whether the case would be sufficiently grave to justify further action by the Court, and whether applying the full machinery of the ICC to the case would be in the interests of justice.
14. Article 53(1)(b) states: "In deciding whether to initiate an investigation, the Prosecutor shall consider whether . . . the case is or would be admissible under article 17."
15. ICC. 2009. ICC-01/04-01/07-1497, para. 78.
16. This is not an exhaustive list; in *Katanga*, the Pre-Trial Chamber held that in addition to the types of unwillingness described in Article 17(2), "there is also the case of a State which may not want to protect an individual, but, for a variety of reasons, may not wish to exercise its jurisdiction over him or her. This second form of 'unwillingness,' which is not expressly provided for in article 17 of the Statute, aims to see the person brought to justice, but not before national courts" (ICC. 2009. ICC-01/04-01/07-1213-tENG, para. 77). The Appeals Chamber neither confirmed nor rejected this so-called "second form for

'unwillingness'" (ICC. 2009. ICC-01/04-01/07-1497, para. 73). For a discussion, see Cross and Williams (2010, 340–343) and Chappell et al. (2013, 460).
17. Contrary to expectations, several states parties have actually *invited* the ICC to investigate and prosecute crimes on their territory. This unexpected phenomenon of self-referrals indicates that, *contra* to the "classic" view, states may consider it in their interest to hand cases over to the ICC rather than conduct the proceedings domestically (Schabas 2011, 157).
18. ICC. 2006. ICC-01/04-520-Anx2, para. 31.
19. ICC. 2011. ICC-01/09-02/11-274, para. 1, emphasis added.
20. This was confirmed in a 2013 decision by the Pre-Trial Chamber decision on the admissibility of *Gaddafi* (ICC. 2013. ICC-01/11-01/11-344-Red, paras. 85–88).
21. Although as Jacqui True (2012,Chapter 7) demonstrates, a false dichotomy has been created between conflict-related and non–conflict-related violence. It is important to see gender-based violence as operating on a continuum rather than the former being treated as an extraordinary (and somehow more important) experience.
22. Such policies include using these crimes to destroy not only individuals but also the broader community and, in the case of genocide, the ethnic composition of the group.
23. ICC. 2013. ICC-01/11-01/11-344-Red, paras. 199–215.
24. ICC. 2014. ICC-01/11-01/11-547-Red.
25. WCGJ. 1998. "Gender Justice and the ICC"; WIGJ. 2010. "Report on the 10-year Review . . ."
26. Details of OTP Preliminary Examinations are available at: http://www.icc-cpi.int/en_menus/icc/structure%20of%20the%20court/office%20of%20the%20prosecutor/comm%20and%20ref/Pages/communications%20and%20referrals.
27. ICC OTP. 2012. *Report on Preliminary Examination Activities 2012*, 5–6.
28. *Ibid*., 33.
29. ICC OTP. 2013. *Report on Preliminary Examination Activities 2013*, 45.
30. ICC OTP. 2012. *Report on Preliminary Examination Activities 2012*, 36.
31. *Ibid*., 34–36.
32. When Colombia ratified the Rome Statute in 2002, it made a declaration according to Article 124 of the Rome Statute not accepting the jurisdiction of the ICC with respect to war crimes for a period of seven years. That reservation expired on November 1, 2009. The ICC therefore has jurisdiction over crimes against humanity and genocide since November 1, 2002, and for war crimes from November 1, 2009, onward (see ICC OTP. 2012. *Report on Preliminary Examination Activities 2012*, 23).
33. The conflict centers on the government and several illegal armed groups, specifically the Revolutionary Armed Forces of Colombia (FARC) and the National Liberation Army (ELN). Right-wing paramilitary organizations, such as the United Self-Defense Forces of Colombia and other "criminal bands," have also been implicated, sometimes operating in collusion with government security forces (ICC OTP. 2012. *Report on Preliminary Examination Activities 2012*).
34. ICC OTP. 2012. *Report on Preliminary Examination Activities 2012*.
35. ICC OTP. 2012. *Situation in Colombia Interim Report*, 15–16.
36. See ICC OTP. 2013. *Report on Preliminary Examination Activities 2013*.

37. ICC OTP. 2012. *Report on Preliminary Examination Activities 2012*, 35.
38. *Ibid.*, 36.
39. *Ibid.*, 35–36.
40. *Ibid.*, 34.
41. Chappell et al. (2013) reported in their article that in December 2012, Human Rights Watch could not obtain information on the charges related to the Guinea massacre (see HRW 2012, 3). On February 10, 2012, the UN reported that Thégboro Camara had been charged for mass rape; however, Chappell et al. could find no other source to confirm this information and the UN News Centre did not respond to the author's request for the source of its information on the charges (United Nations News Centre, 2012).
42. ICC OTP. 2012. *Report on Preliminary Examination Activities 2012*, 28, 35.
43. Code Pénal de la Republique de Giunee, Law N ° 98/036, section VII, Article 321.
44. ICC OTP. 2012. *Report on Preliminary Examination Activities 2012*; ICC OTP. 2013. *Report on Preliminary Examination Activities 2013*.
45. ICC OTP. 2012. *Situation in Colombia Interim Report*.
46. *Ibid.*, 49–50.
47. *Ibid.*, 67.
48. Unofficial translation of the Colombian penal code, http://www.wipo.int/wipolex/en/details.jsp?id=7305 (accessed 25 February 2013).
49. ICC OTP. 2012. *Situation in Colombia Interim Report*, 67.
50. *Ibid..*, 67. While there were forty ongoing cases, the OTP did not clarify how many of these involved paramilitary groups.
51. ICC OTP. 2013. *Report on Preliminary Examination Activities 2013*, 32.
52. ICC OTP. 2012. *Report on Preliminary Examination Activities 2012*, 23.
53. ICC OTP. 2012. *Situation in Colombia Interim Report*, 67–68.
54. *Ibid.*, 16.
55. *Ibid.*, 62–69.
56. *Ibid.*, 66–68.
57. ICC OTP. 2012. *Report on Preliminary Examination Activities 2012*, 28.
58. *Ibid.*, 26–27.
59. ICC OTP. 2012. *Situation in Colombia Interim Report*, 62.
60. *Ibid.*, 67.
61. WIGJ. 2010. "Report on the 10-year Review . . .," 40–41.
62. *Ibid.*, 41.
63. WIGJ. 2010. *Gender Report Card 2010*, 78.
64. ICC OTP. 2014. " Statement of the Prosecutor . . . Nigeria."
65. *Ibid.*
66. ICC OTP. 2014. " Policy Paper of Sexual and Gender . . .," 24.
67. *Ibid.*, 23.
68. See: http://www.legal-tools.org/en/what-are-the-icc-legal-tools/.
69. These figures relate to only those fifty states with legislation available in English.

CHAPTER 7
1. Affirmative remedies are those that do not disturb the underlying generative framework (Fraser 1997, 23).
2. ICC OTP. 2014. "Launch of the ICC . . ."

3. WCGJ. 1998. "Gender Justice and the ICC."
4. ICC OTP. 2014. "Statement to the United Nations . . . Darfur."
5. See: ICC OTP. 2014. "Launch of the ICC . . ."
6. ICC OTP. 2014. "Closing Remarks . . ."

APPENDIX

1. Data from ASP. "Election of the judges of the International Criminal Court (continued), Note by the Secretariat, Addendum, Annex 1," December 12, 2002 (ICC-ASP/1/4/Add.1): http://www.iccnow.org/documents/CVDigest-200212Eng.pdf

- BLATTMANN: No gender expertise (3–7).
- CLARK: "Ms. Clark has particular expertise within the meaning of article 36 (8) (b) of the Statute as a trial lawyer and as a government adviser with regard to sexual offences and other violent offences against women and children and with regard to the needs and rights of victims" (44).
- DIARRA: "great champion of the rights of women and children" (53). "Officer of the Commission for the Advancement of Women, October 1993-June 1994" (55). "Chairperson of the National Preparatory Committee for the Fourth World Conference on Women (Beijing, 1995), January-August 1995" (56).
- FULFORD: "legal expertise in . . . Violence against women and children: his extensive courtroom experience includes cases of rape and other serious sexual assault; he is one of a limited number of judges in England and Wales authorized to try rape and serious sex cases" (70).
- HUDSON-PHILLIPS: No gender expertise (86–90).
- JORDA: No gender expertise (91–95).
- KAUL: No gender expertise (120–126).
- KIRSCH: No gender expertise (127–134).
- KOURULA: No gender expertise (135–140).
- KUENYEHIA: "lectured and researched on a range of subjects including . . . gender and the law" (141); "demonstrable expertise in gender and women's affairs. She has just been elected a member of the Committee on the Elimination of Discrimination against Women" (142). Author of multiple scholarly publications on women and the law (143–147).
- ODIO BENITO: "The work of Ms. Odio Benito during her five years on [the ICTY] . . . contributed significantly to the decision, when the Rome Statute of the International Criminal Court was being discussed and adopted, to categorize crimes committed against women in the context of armed conflict as international crimes" (190). "See in particular her role in the ICTY's Ćelebici case . . . She has worked particularly in the area of the human rights of women and the domestic and international access to criminal justice by women who are victims of violence" (193).
- PIKIS: No gender expertise (201–204).
- PILLAY: "participated in the landmark judgement of that Court in the Akayesu case, which deals with rape as a form of genocide . . . she has also written and spoken on the subject of violence against women and children." (205). "Authored 'The Rule of International Humanitarian Jurisprudence in Redressing Crimes of Sexual Violence', in Essays in Memory of Judge Cassese,

edited by Judge Fausto Pocar et al. (forthcoming, 2003); 'Sexual Violence in Times of Conflict: The Jurisprudence of the International Criminal Tribunal for Rwanda,' in Civilians in War, edited by Simon Chesterman (Lynne Reinner, 2001)" (208).

- POLITI: "has been seated in trial chambers that hear criminal cases involving human rights violations and violence and abuse against women and children, a qualification referred to in paragraph 8 (b) of article 36 of the Rome Statute" (210); "legal expertise on specific issues such as violence against women and children (article 36.8 (b)). In particular: As a judge of the Tribunals of Oristano and Milan, he dealt with numerous cases of human rights violations and violence and abuse against women and children" (211).
- SLADE: "With respect to article 36.8 (b), Mr. Slade has legal expertise on a wide range of specific issues relevant to the work of the Court, including . . . violence against women and children. His courtroom experience includes dealing with cases of rape, murder and other serious cases of violence and sexual assaults" (231–232).
- SONG: No gender expertise (244–248).
- STEINER: "legal expertise and experience in . . . violence against women and children" (250). Teaching/lecturing experience includes: "Classes at the Human Rights and Protection of Women's Rights Basic Course Project, organized by the Centre for the Study of State and Society (CEDES), Campinas, Sao Paulo . . . Lecture at the Meeting for Women's Rights Conventions, organized by the Brazilian National Bar Association, Women Lawyer's Commission, Sao Paulo Section" (251–252).

USACKA: "The Government of Latvia believes that Professor Uscaka's courtroom experience, deep knowledge of international human rights and expertise in gender issues make her an outstandingly well-qualified candidate for the position of judge in the International Criminal Court. Her candidature is also highly recommended by the International Association of Women Judges and the Centre for Women's Global Leadership" (261). Participated in training program called "Gender, Justice and the ICC" (263).

2. ASP. "Second election of the judges of the International Criminal Court (continued): Addendum," December 16, 2005 (ICC-ASP/4/33/Add.1): http://www.iccnow.org/documents/ICC-ASP-4-33-_Add1_FINAL_English.pdf

TRENDAFILOVA: No gender expertise (74–84).

3. ASP. "Election of judges to fill three judicial vacancies of the International Criminal Court (continued): Addendum," October 2, 2007 (ICC-ASP/6/15/Add.1): http://www.iccnow.org/documents/ICC-ASP-6-15-Add1_English.pdf

- COTTE: No gender expertise (3–9).
- SAIGA: "Member of the Committee on the Elimination of Discrimination Against Women (CEDAW)" (38); "excellent knowledge and experiences of gender issues including violence against women" (38).

NSEREKO: No gender expertise (22–35).

4. ASP, "Third election of judges of the International Criminal Court: Addendum," December 8, 2008 (ICC-ASP/7/33/Add.1): http://www.iccnow.org/documents/ICC-ASP-7-33-Add.1_English.pdf

- ALUOCH: "Justice Aluoch has been involved in promoting children's and women's rights" (7). "At the national level, Justice Aluoch has played an active role in the reform of laws relating to women . . . She currently chairs the Task Force responsible for operationalizing Kenya's new Sexual Offences Act, 2006" (8).
- MONGAGENG: "Justice Monageng is a strong advocate for women's rights and has been actively involved in various national and regional initiatives, aimed at scaling up women's empowerment and gender mainstreaming on the continent" (86).
- SHAHABUDDEEN: "experience and expertise in relevant areas of international law pertinent to the judicial work of the Court, such as . . . law pertaining to violence against women and children" (115).
- TARFUSSER: "He prosecuted crimes against individuals, child abuse and sexual crimes committed against women and children. . . . judicial expertise on gender issues, including, but not limited to, violence against women" (146).

VAN DEN WYNGAERT: No gender expertise (164–173).

5. Women's Initiatives for Gender Justice. "Profile of Judicial Candidates Election – November 2009," October 22, 2009: http://www.iccnow.org/documents/Profile_of_Judicial_Candidates_Nov2009_FINAL_22Oct.pdf

- OZAKI: "1997: Member of the Japanese delegation to the Queensland, Australia Crime Commission. Contributed to the creation of 'Model Strategies and Practical Measures on the Elimination of Violence against Women in the Field of Crime Prevention and Criminal Justice'; 2000: Led Japanese delegation in UN 23rd Special Session of the General Assembly on 'Women 2000: gender equality, development and peace for the twenty-first century'; Relevant Publications: 'Gender as the mainstream in the United Nations,' in: Toshiya Ueki & Hiroyuki Tosa (ed.), International Law, International Relations and Gender (Tohoku University Press, 2007)" (14).

FERNÁNDEZ DE GURMENDI: No gender expertise (13–15).

6. ASP. "Fourth election of judges of the International Criminal Court: Addendum," November 23, 2011, ICC-ASP/10/18/Add.1: http://www.icc-cpi.int/iccdocs/asp_docs/ASP10/ICC-ASP-10-18-Add.1-ENG.pdf

- DEFENSOR-SANTIAGO: No gender expertise (46–51).
- CARMONA: No gender expertise (21–28).
- EBOE OSUJI: RESEARCH TOPICS: "Definition and analysis of rape in International criminal law; Rape as genocide; Rape and superior responsibility in international law; Forced marriage and international criminal law; Reparation for sexual violence against women during war; Prosecution of sexual violence as part of transitional justice efforts in postconflict societies" (53). Details of expertise in gender/sexual violence (54–55).

- FREMR: "expertise in . . . working with women and child victims of violent crime who require special treatment in court" (63). Judge on ICTR *Nizeyimana* case involving rape. "The presentation of evidence started in January and is to be closed in June. It has involved the questioning of raped women which requires special approach from judges" (66).
- HERRERA CARBUCCIA: "experience in . . . in the prosecution of crimes of a sexual nature" (71). However, no other evidence of expertise in gender/sexual violence.

MORRISON: No gender expertise (97–99).

7. ASP. "Election of a judge to fill a judicial vacancy of the International Criminal Court: Note by the Secretariat," October 21, 2013 (ICC-ASP/12/45): http://www.icc-cpi.int/iccdocs/asp_docs/ASP12/ICC-ASP-12-45-ENG.pdf

HENDERSON: "Justice Henderson has adjudicated over many complex criminal cases involving . . . rape, incest, sexual offences . . . Both in his capacity as a former Prosecutor as well as in his current portfolio as a Judge of the Supreme Court of Trinidad and Tobago, Justice Henderson would have presided over or prosecuted cases involving violence against women and children" (5).

BIBLIOGRAPHY

1998. "Who's Obstructionist? Arabs Ask" [editorial]. *Terraviva: The Conference Daily Newspaper.*
2007. *Nairobi Declaration on Women's and Girls' Right to a Remedy and Reparation.* Declaration from the International Meeting on Women's and Girls' Right to a Remedy and Reparation, Nairobi, March 19–21. Accessed January 16, 2015. http://www.fidh.org/IMG/pdf/NAIROBI_DECLARATIONeng.pdf.
Adams, Cathy. 2014. *Statement by Cathy Adams, Legal Director to the UK Foreign and Commonwealth Office, on Cooperation in relation to Sexual and Gender-Based Crimes to the ICC Assembly of State Parties.* Accessed January 9, 2015. https://www.gov.uk/government/speeches/uk-is-proud-that-155-states-have-now-endorsed-the-declaration-of-commitment-to-end-sexual-violence-in-conflict.
Amann, Diane Marie. 2014. "The Post-Postcolonial Women or Child." *University of Georgia School of Law Research Paper Series.* Paper No. 2014–16, April.
Amann, Diane. 2012. "Brigid Inder named ICC Special Gender Advisor". Accessed December 12, 2014. http://www.intlawgrrls.com/2012/08/brigid-inder-named-icc-special-gender.html.
Ambos, Kai. 2010. *The Colombian Peace Process and the Principle of Complementarity of the International Criminal Court: An Inductive, Situation-based Approach.* Berlin: Springer-Verlag, 63–83.
Ambos, Kai. 2012. "The First Judgment of the International Criminal Court (Prosecutor v. Lubanga): A Comprehensive Analysis of the Legal Issues." *International Criminal Law Review* 12: 115–153.
Ambos, Kai, and Florian Huber. 2011. "The Colombian Peace Process and the Principle of Complementarity of the International Criminal Court: Is there Sufficient Willingness and Ability on the Part of the Colombian Authorities or Should the Prosecutor Open an Investigation Now?" Extended version of the Statement in the *"Thematic session: Colombia," International Criminal Court Office of the Prosecutor—NGO Roundtable, The Hague, 19–20 October 2010.* Göttingen, Germany: Institute for Criminal Law and Justice.
Amnesty International. 2010. *International Criminal Court, Rome Statute Report Card (Part One).* London: Amnesty International.
Amnesty International. 2011. *This is What We Demand. Justice! Impunity for Sexual Violence Against Women in Colombia's Armed Conflict.* London: Amnesty International.

Amnesty International. 2012. *Colombia: Hidden from Justice: Impunity for Conflict-related Sexual Violence, A Follow-up Report*. London: Amnesty International.

Annesley, Claire, and Francesca Gains. 2010. "The Core Executive: Gender, Power and Change." *Political Studies* 58(5): 909–929.

Arbia, Silvana. *Interview with the [former] Registrar, Registry, International Criminal Court*. The Hague: International Criminal Court, June 26.

Askin, Kelly. 2003. "Prosecuting Wartime Rape and Other Gender-Related Crimes under International Law: Extraordinary Advances, Enduring Obstacles." *Berkeley Journal of International Law* 21: 288–349.

Askin, Kelly. 2014. "Katanga Judgment Underlines Need for Stronger ICC Focus on Sexual Violence." *Voices: Open Society*, March 2014. Accessed May 21, 2014. http://www.opensocietyfoundations.org/voices/katanga-judgment-underlines-need-stronger-icc-focus-sexual-violence.

Askin, Kelly. 2015. "For the First Time, a Woman Judge Heads the International Criminal Court." March 11. Accessed March 15, 2015. http://www.opensocietyfoundations.org/voices/first-time-woman-judge-heads-international-criminal-court

Atiba-Davies, Gloria. 2012. *Interview with the Head of the Gender and Children's Unit, Office of the Prosecutor, International Criminal Court*. The Hague: International Criminal Court, June 26.

Azari, Julia R., and Jennifer K. Smith. 2012. "Unwritten Rules: Informal Institutions in Established Democracies." *Perspectives on Politics* 10(1): 37–55.

Banaszak, Lee A., Karen Beckwith, and Dieter Rucht. 2003. *Women's Movements Facing the Reconfigured State*. Cambridge: Cambridge University Press.

Barnett, Michael N., and Martha Finnemore. 1999. "The Politics, Power and Pathologies of International Organizations." *International Organization* 53(4): 699–732.

Barnett, Michael N., and Martha Finnemore. 2004. *Rules for the World: International Organizations in Global Politics*. Ithaca, NY: Cornell University Press.

Batros, Ben. 2011. "The Evolution of the ICC Jurisprudence on Admissibility." In *The International Criminal Court and Complementarity Volume 1*, edited by Carsten Stahn and Mohamed M. El Zeidy, 558–602. New York: Cambridge University Press.

Beckwith, Karen. 2005. "A Common Language of Gender?" *Politics & Gender* 1(1): 128–137.

Bedont, Barbara. 1998. "Negotiating for the International Criminal Court." *Peace Magazine*, Sept.-Oct., 21.

Bedont, Barbara, and Katherine Hall-Martinez. 1999. "Ending Impunity for Gender Crimes under the International Criminal Court." *Brown Journal of World Affairs* 6(1): 65–85.

Bennoune, Karima. 2012. "Productive Tensions: Women's Rights NGOs, the 'Mainstream' Human Rights Movement, and International Law Making." In *Non-State Actors, Soft Law and Protective Regimes: From the Margins*, edited by Cecilia M. Bailliet, 125–150. Cambridge: Cambridge University Press.

Bensouda, Fatou. 2012a. *Interview with the Chief Prosecutor of the International Criminal Court*. The Hague: International Criminal Court, June 26.

Bensouda, Fatou. 2012b. *The International Criminal Court: A New Approach to International Relations*. Council of Foreign Relations, September 21. Accessed August 10, 2014. http://www.cfr.org/courts-and-tribunals/international-criminal-court-new-approach-international-relations/p29351.

Bensouda, Fatou. 2014. "Gender Justice and the ICC: Progress and Reflections." *International Feminist Journal of Politics* 16(4): 538–542.

Bergsmo, Morten, ed. 2012. *Thematic Prosecution of International Sex Crime*. Beijing: Torkel Opsahl Academic EPublisher.

Bodansky, Daniel. 2008. "The Concept of Legitimacy in International Law." In *Legitimacy in International Law*, edited by Rüdiger Wolfrum and Volker Röben, 309–318. Berlin: Springer.

Bodansky, Daniel. 2012. "Legitimacy in International Law and International Relations." *Working paper for the Sandra Day O'Connor College of Law, Arizona State University*. Phoenix: Arizona State University.

Boon, Kristin. 2001. "Rape and Forced Pregnancy under the ICC statute: Human Dignity, Autonomy and Consent." *Columbia Human Rights Law Review* 32: 634–675.

Brown, Sara E. 2014. "Female Perpetrators of the Rwandan Genocide." *International Feminist Journal of Politics* 16(3): 448–469.

Brunnée, Jutta, and Stephen J. Toope. 2010. *Legitimacy and Legality in International Law: An Interactional Account*. Cambridge: Cambridge University Press.

Buchanan, Allen, and Robert O. Keohane. 2006. "The Legitimacy of Global Governance Institutions." *Ethics & International Affairs* 20(4): 405–437.

Bueno, Olivia. 2012. "Local Communities Divided on the Question of Reparations in the Lubanga Case." *International Justice Monitor*, November 7. Accessed May 21, 2014. http://www.ijmonitor.org/2012/11/local-communities-divided-on-the-question-of-reparations-in-the-lubanga-case/.

Burke-White, William. 2011. "Reframing Positive Complementarity." In *The International Criminal Court and Complementarity*, edited by Carsten Stahn and Mohamed M. El Zeidy, Vol. 1, 341–360. New York: Cambridge University Press.

Buss, Doris. 2011. "Performing Legal Order: Some Feminist Thoughts on International Criminal Law." *International Criminal Law Review* 11: 409–423.

Buss, Doris, and Didi Herman. 2003. *Globalizing Family Values: The Christian Right in International Politics*. Minneapolis and London: University of Minnesota Press.

Buss, Doris, and Ambreena S. Manji, eds. 2005. *International Law: Modern Feminist Approaches*. Portland, OR: Hart Publishing.

Caglar, Gulay, Elisabeth Prugl and Susanne Zwingel, eds. 2013. *Feminist Strategies in International Governance*. London: Routledge.

Campaign Rape and other Violence: Leave my Body Out of War. 2011. *First Survey on the Prevalence of Sexual Violence against Women in the Context of the Colombian Armed Conflict, 2001–2009*. Accessed January 16, 2015. http://www.peacewomen.org/assets/file/Resources/NGO/vaw_violenceagainstwomenincolombiaarmedconflict_2011.pdf.

Campbell, John. 2004. *Institutional Change and Globalization*. Princeton, NJ: Princeton University Press.

Campbell, John L. 2009. "Institutional Reproduction and Change." In *Oxford Handbook Comparative Institutional Analysis*, edited by Glenn Morgan, John L. Campbell, Colin Crouch, Ove K. Pedersen, and Richard Whitley, 87–115. Oxford: Oxford University Press.

Chappell, Louise. 2002. *Gendering Government: Feminist Engagement with the State in Australia and Canada*. Vancouver: University of British Columbia Press.

Chappell, Louise. 2003. "Women, Gender and International Institutions: Exploring New Opportunities at the International Criminal Court." *Policy, Organisation and Society* 22: 3–25.

Chappell, Louise. 2006a. "Contesting Women's Rights: Charting the Emergence of a Transnational Conservative Patriarchal Network?" *Global Society* 20(4): 491–519.

Chappell, Louise. 2006b. "Comparing Political Institutions: Revealing the Gendered 'Logic of Appropriateness'." *Politics and Gender* 2(2): 223–234.

Chappell, Louise. 2010a. "Comparative Gender and Institutions: Directions for Research." *Perspectives on Politics* 8(1): 183–189.

Chappell, Louise. 2010b. "Gender and Judging at the International Criminal Court." *Politics and Gender* 6(3): 484–495.

Chappell, Louise. 2014. "Conflicting Institutions and the Search for Gender Justice at the International Criminal Court." *Political Research Quarterly* 67(1): 183–196.

Chappell, Louise, Andrea Durbach, and Elizabeth Odio Benito. 2014. "Judge Odio Benito: A View of Gender Justice from the Bench." *International Feminist Journal of Politics* 16(4): 648–653.

Chappell, Louise, Rosemary Grey, and Emily Waller. 2013. "The Gender Justice Shadow of Complementarity: Lessons from the International Criminal Court's Preliminary Examinations in Guinea and Colombia." *International Journal of Transitional Justice* 7(3): 455–476.

Chappell, Louise, and Brigid Inder. 2014. "Advocating for International Gender Justice." *International Feminist Journal of Politics* 16(4): 655–664.

Chappell, Louise and Fiona Mackay. 2015. "Critical Friendship. Critical Friends and De(con)structive Critics: Dilemmas of Feminist Engagement with Global Governance and Gender Reform Agendas". Paper presented at the European Consortium for Political Research. 4th European Conference on Politics and Gender. June 11–13 Uppsala, Sweden.

Chappell, Louise, and Georgina Waylen. 2013. "Gender and the Hidden Life of Institutions." *Public Administration* 91(3): 599–617.

Charlesworth, Hilary. 1999. "Feminist Methods in International Law." *American Journal of International Law* 93(2): 379–394.

Charlesworth, Hilary. 2012. "Conclusion: Centrality and Marginality in International Law." In *Non-State Actors, Soft Law and Protective Regimes: From the Margins*, edited by Cecilia M. Bailliet, 281–288. Cambridge: Cambridge University Press.

Charlesworth, Hilary. 2013. "International Human Rights Law: A Portmanteau for Feminist Norms?" In *Feminist Strategies in International Governance*, edited by Gulay Caglar, Elisabeth Prugl, and Susanne Zwingel, 21–36. London, Routledge.

Charlesworth, Hilary, and Christine Chinkin. 2000. *The Boundaries of International Law: A Feminist Analysis*. Manchester: Manchester University Press.

Childs, Sarah and Joni Lovenduski. 2013. "Political Representation." In *The Oxford Handbook of Gender and Politics*, edited by Georgina Waylen, Karen Celis, Johanna Kantola, and S. Laurel Weldon. Oxford, Oxford University Press.

Chinkin, Christine, Shelly Wright, and Hilary Charlesworth. 2005. "Feminist Approaches to International Law: Reflections from Another Century." In *International Law: Modern Feminist Approaches*, edited by Doris Buss and Ambreena Manji, 17–46. Oxford: Hart Publishing.

CICC (Coalition for the International Criminal Court). 2014. "States: Nominate the Most Highly Qualified ICC Judicial Candidates. Nominations and elections must be fair, transparent and merit-based." Press release, April 28. Accessed January 15, 2015. http://coalitionfortheicc.org/documents/CICCPR_ ICCELECTONS_APRIL2014.pdf.

Coalition for the International Criminal Court (CICC). Budget and Finance Team. 2011. Comments and Recommendations to the Tenth Session of the Assembly of States Parties. November 29.

Cockburn, Cynthia. 2004. "The Continuum of Violence." In *Sites of Violence: Gender and Conflict Zones*, edited by Wenona Giles and Jennifer Hyndman, 24–45. Berkeley: University of California Press.

Code Pénal de la Republique de Giunee, Law N 98/036, section VII, Article 321.

Connell, Raewyn. 1987. *Gender and Power: Society, the Person, and Sexual Politics*. Cambridge: Polity Press.

Coomaraswarmy, Radhika. 2014. "Women and Children: The Cutting Edge of International Law." *16th Annual Grotius Lecture delivered at the Annual General Meeting of the American Society of International Law*, Washington, DC, April 9.

Copelon, Rhonda. 1994. "Surfacing Gender: Re-engraving Crimes Against Women in Humanitarian Law." *Hastings Women's Law Journal* 5: 243–265.

Copelon, Rhonda. 2000. "Gender Crimes as War Crimes: Integrating Crimes against Women into International Criminal Law." *McGill Law Journal* 46(1): 217–240.

Couillard, Valérie. 2007. "The Nairobi Declaration: Redefining Reparations for Women Victims of Sexual Violence." *International Journal of Transitional Justice* 1(3): 444–453.

Cross, Matthew, and Sarah Williams. 2010. "Recent Developments at the ICC: Prosecutor v Germain Katanga and Mathieu Ngudjolo Chuiç: A Boost for 'Cooperative Complementarity'?" *Human Rights Law Review* 10(2): 340–343.

Cryer, Robert. 2010. *An Introduction to International Criminal Law and Procedure*. New York: Cambridge University Press.

Dannenbaum, Tom. 2010. "The International Criminal Court, Article 79, and Transitional Justice: The Case for an Independent Trust Fund for Victims." *Wisconsin International Law Journal* 28(2): 234–298.

Danner, Allison Marston. 2003. "Enhancing the Legitimacy and Accountability of Prosecutorial Discretion at the International Criminal Court." *American Journal of International Law* 97: 510–552.

De Brouwer, Anne-Marie. 2007. "Reparation to Victims of Sexual Violence: Possibilities at the International Criminal Court and at the Trust Fund for Victims and Their Families." *Leiden Journal of International Law* 20: 207–237.

de Guzman Margaret, M. 2012. "An Expressive Rationale for the Thematic Prosecution of Sex Crimes." In *Thematic Prosecution of International Sex Crime*, edited by Morten Bergsmo, 11–44. Beijing: Torkel Opsahl Academic EPublisher.

Dieng, Adama. 2002. "International Criminal Justice: From Paper to Practice—A Contribution from the International Criminal Tribunal for Rwanda to the Establishment of the International Criminal Court." *Fordham International Law Journal* 25: 688–707.

Dixon, Rosalind. 2010. "Female Justices, Feminism, and the Politics of Judicial Appointment: A Re-Examination." *Yale Journal of Law and Feminism*. 21 (2): 297–338.

Drumbl, Mark. 2011. "Policy Through Complementarity: The Atrocity Trial as Justice in The International Criminal Court and Complementarity: From Theory to Practice." In *The International Criminal Court and Complementarity*, edited by Carsten Stahn and Mohamed M. El Zeidy, Vol. 1, 197–232. New York: Cambridge University Press.

Duggan, Colleen, and Alida Abusharaf. 2006. "Reparation of Sexual Violence in Democratic Transitions: The Search for Gender Justice." In *The Handbook of Reparations*, edited by Pablo de Grieff, 623–649. Oxford: Oxford University Press.

Durbach, Andrea, and Louise Chappell. 2014. "'Leaving Behind the Age of Impunity': Victims of Gender Violence and the Promise of Reparations." *International Feminist Journal of Politics* 16(4): 543–562.

Dwertmann, Eva. 2010. *The Reparations System of the International Criminal Court: Its Implementation, Possibilities and Limitations*. Leiden: Martinus Nijhoff Publishers.

Easterday, Jennifer. 2014. "Lack of Appeal in Katanga is Unjust, Victims Lawyers Say." *International Justice Monitor*, July 14. Accessed July 30, 2014. http://www.ijmonitor.org/2014/07/lack-of-appeal-in-katanga-is-unjust-victims-lawyers-say/.

Engle, Karen. 2005. "Feminism and its (Dis)contents: Criminalizing Wartime Rape in Bosnia and Herzegovina." *American Journal of International Law* 99(4): 778–816.

Enloe, Cynthia. 2007. *Globalization and Militarism: Feminists Make the Link*. Lanham, MD: Rowman and Littlefield.

Facio, Alda. 1999. "Integrating Gender into the World's First Permanent Criminal Court." New York: Women's Caucus for Gender Justice. Accessed November 15, 2014. http://www.iccwomen.org/wigjdraft1/Archives/oldWCGJ/resources/bplus5/part1.htm.

Facio, Alda. 2004. "All Roads Lead to Rome, but Some Are Bumpier Than Others." In *Global Issues, Women and Justice*, edited by Sharon Pickering and Caroline Lambert, 308–334. Sydney: Federation Press.

Falk, Richard. 2006. "Reparations, International Law and Global Justice." In *The Handbook of Reparations*, edited by Pablo de Greiff, 478–503. Oxford: Oxford University Press.

Ferstman, Carla. 2002. "The Reparation Regime of the International Criminal Court: Practical Considerations." *Leiden Journal of International Law* 15(3): 667–686.

Ferstman, Carla. 2010. "Procedural and Substantive Obstacles for Reparations for Women Subjected to Violence through Judicial and Administrative Forums." *Panel Discussion on Reparations for Women Subjected to Violence, Palais Des Nations*, June 8.

Ferstman, Carla. 2012. "Limited Charges and Limited Judgments by the International Criminal Court: Who Bears the Greatest Responsibility?" *International Journal of Human Rights* 16(5): 796–813.

FIDH (Fédération internationale des ligues des droits de l'Homme). 2013. *DRC: Denial of Justice for Victims of Sexual Violence*. Accessed December 19, 2014. https://www.fidh.org/International-Federation-for-Human-Rights/Africa/democratic-republic-of-congo/14338-drc-denial-of-justice-for-the-victims-of-sexual-crimes.

Finnemore, Martha, and Stephen Toope. 2001. "Alternatives to 'Legalization': Richer Views of Law and Politics." *International Organization* 55(3): 743–758.

Fioretos, Orfeo. 2011. "Historical Institutionalism in International Relations." *International Organization* 65(2): 367–399.

Franke, Katherine M. 2006. "Gendered Subjects of Transitional Justice." *Columbia Journal of Gender and Law* 15(3): 813–828.

Fraser, Nancy. 1997. *Justice Interruptus: Critical Reflections on the Postsocialist Condition.* New York: Routledge.

Fraser, Nancy. 2003. "Social Justice in the Age of Identity Politics: Redistribution, Recognition and Participation." In Nancy Fraser and Axel Honneth. *Redistribution or Recognition: A political-philosophical exchange.* London: Verso.

Fraser, Nancy. 2007. "Feminist Politics in the Age of Recognition: A Two-Dimensional Approach to Gender Justice." *Studies in Social Justice* 1(1): 23–35.

Fraser, Nancy. 2009. *Scales of Justice: Reimaging Political Space in a Globalizing World.* New York: Colombia University Press.

Fraser, Nancy, and Axel Honneth. 2003. *Redistribution or Recognition?: A Political-Philosophical Exchange.* London: Verso.

Frey, Barbara. 2004. "A Fair Representation: Advocating for Women's Rights in the International Criminal Court." Center on Women and Public Policy, Humphrey Institute of Public Affairs, University of Minnesota.

Friedman, Elisabeth J. 2003. "Gendering the Agenda: The Impact of the Transnational Women's Rights Movement at the UN Conferences of the 1990s." *Women's Studies International Forum* 26(3): 313–331.

Gardam, Judith G., and Michelle J. Jarvis. 2001. *Women, Armed Conflict and International Law.* The Hague: Kluwer Law International.

Gatens, Moira. 1998. "Institutions, Embodiment and Sexual Difference." In *Gender and Institutions: Welfare, Work and Citizenship,* edited by Moira Gatens and Alison Mackinnon, 1–16. Cambridge: Cambridge University Press.

Gazurek, Eva, and Anne Saris. 2002. *The Protection of Women as Witnesses and the ICTR: Recommendations for Policies and Procedures for Respecting the Rights, Addressing the Needs and Effectively Involving Women in the ICTR Process.* Irchester, UK: Coalition for Women's Human Rights in Conflict Situations.

Glasius, Marlies. 2006. *The International Criminal Court: A Global Civil Society Achievement.* London: Routledge.

Goetz, Anne Marie. 2007. "Gender Justice, Citizenship and Entitlements: Core Concepts, Central Debates and New Directions for Research." In *Gender Justice, Citizenship and Development,* edited by Maitrayee Mukhopadhyay and Navsharan Singh, 15–57. Ottawa: Zubaan, International Development Research Centre.

Goetz, Anne Marie, and Rob Jenkins. 2005. *Reinventing Accountability: Making Democracy Work for Human Development.* Basingstoke, UK: Palgrave Macmillan.

Goodin, Robert E. 1996. *The Theory of Institutional Design.* Cambridge: Cambridge University Press.

Goodman, Ryan, and Derek Jinks. 2004. "How to Influence States: Socialization and International Human Rights Law." *Duke Law Journal* 54(3): 621–703.

Green, Laurie. 2011. "First-Class Crimes, Second-Class Justice: Cumulative Charges for Gender-Based Crimes at the International Criminal Court." *International Criminal Law Review* 11: 529–541.

Grey, Rosemary. 2014a. "Prosecuting Sexual Violence Against Child Soldiers: The *Ntaganda* Case at the International Criminal Court." *International Feminist Journal of Politics* 16(4): 601–621.

Grey, Rosemary. 2014b. "The Ntaganda Confirmation of Charges Decision: A Victory for Gender Justice?" *Beyond The Hague Blog*, June 12. Accessed August 12, 2014. http://beyondthehague.com/2014/06/12/the-ntaganda-confirmation-of-charges-decision-a-victory-for-gender-justice/.

Grey, Rosemary. 2014c. "Conflicting Interpretations of 'Sexual Violence' in the International Criminal Court." *Australian Feminist Studies* 29(81): 273–288.

Grey, Rosemary. 2015. *Prosecuting Sexual and Gender Violence in the International Criminal Court: Something Old, Something New*. Thesis submitted towards a Doctoral Degree at the University of New South Wales. Sydney: The University of New South Wales.

Grey, Rosemary, and Louise Chappell. 2012. "Simone Gbagbo & The International Criminal Court: The Unsettling Spectre of the Female War Criminal." *IntLawGrrls Blog*, November 26. Accessed January 13, 2015. http://www.intlawgrrls.com/2012/11/simone-gbagbo-international-criminal.html.

Grey, Rosemary, and Laura Shepherd. 2013. "'Stop Rape Now?': Masculinity, Responsibility, and Conflict-related Sexual Violence." *Men and Masculinities* 16(1): 115–135.

Grossman, Nienke. 2011. "Sex Representation on the Bench and the Legitimacy of International Criminal Courts Challenges and Opportunities." *International Criminal Law Review* 11(4): 775–802.

Grossman, Nienke. 2012. "Sex on the Bench: Do Women Judges Matter to the Legitimacy of International Courts?" *Chicago Journal of International Law* 12 (2): 647–684.

Group of Eight. 2013. *Declaration on Preventing Sexual Violence in Conflict*. London. Accessed April 15, 2013. http://www.unrol.org/files/G8%20Declaration%20Sexual%20Violence%20in%20Conflict%20-%20April%202013.pdf

Halley, Janet. 2008. "Rape at Rome: Feminist Interventions in the Criminalization of Sex-Related Violence in Positive International Criminal Law." *Michigan Journal of International Law* 30(1): 1–123.

Haupt, Susana Arango. 2011. "The Obligation to Legislate Crimes Against Humanity in the Colombian Criminal Code." *Joaçaba* 12(2): 25–62.

Hawkesworth, Mary. 2006. *Globalization and Feminist Activism*. New York: Rowman and Littlefield.

Hayes, Nimah. 2013. "Sisyphus Wept: Prosecuting Sexual Violence at the International Criminal Court." In *The Ashgate Companion to International Criminal Law: Critical Perspectives*, edited by William Schabas, Yvonne McDermott, and Niamh Hayes, 7–43. Farnham: Ashgate.

Heller, Kevin Jon. 2006. "The Shadow Side of Complementarity: The Effect of Article 17 of the Rome Statute on National Due Process." *Criminal Law Forum* 17(3): 255–280.

Helmke, Gretchen, and Steven Levitsky. 2004. "Informal Institutions and Comparative Politics: A Research Agenda." *Perspectives on Politics* 2(4): 725–740.

Holy See. 1998. "Intervention of the Holy See Diplomatic Conference of Plenipotentiaries on the Establishment of an International Criminal Court." Working Group on War Crimes. Accessed June 14, 2004. http://147.222.27.5/people.dewolf/hs.html.

Hoyle, Carolyn, and Leila Ullrich. 2014. "New Court, New Justice? The Evolution of 'Justice for Victims' at Domestic Courts and at the International Criminal Court." *Journal of International Criminal Justice* 12(4): 681–703.

HRW (Human Rights Watch). 2009. *Guinea: September 28 Massacre Was Premeditated.* New York: Human Rights Watch. Accessed October 20, 2013. http://www.hrw.org/news/2009/10/27/guinea-september-28-massacre-was-premeditated.

HRW (Human Rights Watch). 2011. *Guinea: We Have Lived In Darkness.* New York: Human Rights Watch. Accessed September 20, 2012. http://www.hrw.org/reports/2011/05/24/we-have-lived-darkness-0.

HRW (Human Rights Watch). 2012. *Waiting for Justice: Accountability before Guinea's Courts for the September 28, 2009 Stadium Massacre, Rapes, and Other Abuses.* December. Accessed January 16, 2015. http://www.hrw.org/reports/2012/12/05/waiting-justice-0.

HRW (Human Rights Watch). 2014a. *African States: Reject Immunity for Leaders.* New York: Human Rights Watch. Accessed August 30, 2014. http://www.hrw.org/news/2014/08/24/african-states-reject-immunity-leaders?utm_source=CICC+Newsletters&utm_campaign=9d10b7b188-188_29_14_GlobalJustice_Weekly&utm_medium=email&utm_term=0_68df9c5182-5189d10b7b188-356530197&ct=t%288_29_14_GlobalJustice_Weekly%29.

HRW (Human Rights Watch). 2014b. *Democratic Republic of Congo: Ending Impunity for Sexual Violence: New Judicial Mechanisms Needed to Bring Perpetrator to Justice.* New York: Human Rights Watch. Accessed January 15, 2015. http://www.hrw.org/sites/default/files/related_material/DRC0614_briefingpaper_brochure%20coverJune%209%202014.pdf.

ICC (International Criminal Court). 2006. *Situation in the Democratic Republic of Congo: Decision on the Prosecutor's Application for Warrants of Arrest, Article 58.* Pre-Trial Chamber I, 10 February. ICC Doc. No. ICC-01/04-520-Anx2.

ICC (International Criminal Court). 2006. *Situation in the Democratic Republic of Congo in the case of the Prosecutor v Thomas Lubanga Dyilo: Decision concerning the Pre-Trial I's Decision of 10 February 2006 and the Incorporation of Documents into the Record of the Case against Mr. Thomas Lubang Dyilo.* Pre-Trial Chamber I, 24 February. ICC Doc. No. ICC-01/04-01/06-8.

ICC (International Criminal Court). 2008. *Situation in the Central African Republic in the case of the Prosecutor v Jean-Pierre Bemba Gombo: Warrant of Arrest for Jean-Pierre Bemba Gombo Replacing the Warrant of Arrest Issued on 23 May 2008.* Pre-Trial Chamber III, 10 June. ICC Doc. No. ICC-01/05-01/08-15.

ICC (International Criminal Court). 2008. *Situation in the Central African Republic in the case of the Prosecutor v Jean-Pierre Bemba Gombo: Decision on the Prosecutor's Application for a Warrant of Arrest against Jean Pierre Bemba Gombo.* Pre-Trial Chamber III, 10 June. ICC Doc. No. ICC-01/05-01/08-14-tENG.

ICC (International Criminal Court). 2009. *Situation in the Democratic Republic of Congo: Case ICC-01/04-01/06: Procedural Matters Hearing.* Trial Chamber I, 22 January. ICC Doc. No. ICC-01/04-01/06-T-107-ENG.

ICC (International Criminal Court). 2009. *Situation in the Democratic Republic of Congo in the case of the Prosecutor v Thomas Lubanga Dyilo: Joint Application of the Legal Representatives of the Victims for the Implementation of the Procedure under Regulation 55 of the Regulations of the Court.* Trial Chamber I, 22 May. ICC Doc. No. ICC-01/04-01/06-1891.

ICC (International Criminal Court). 2009. *Situation in the Central African Republic in the case of the Prosecutor v Jean-Pierre Bemba Gombo: Decision Pursuant to Article 61(7)(a) and (b) of the Rome Statute on the Charges of the Prosecutor Against*

Jean-Pierre Bemba Gombo. Pre-Trial Chamber II, 15 June. ICC Doc. No. ICC-01/05-01/08-424.

ICC (International Criminal Court). 2009. *Situation in the Democratic Republic of Congo in the Case of the Prosecutor v. Germain Katanga and Mathieu Ngudjolo Chui: Reasons for the Oral Decision on the Motion Challenging the Admissibility of the Case (Article 19 of the Statute)*. Trial Chamber II, 16 June. ICC Doc. No. ICC-01/04-01/07-1213-tENG.

ICC (International Criminal Court). 2009. *Situation in the Democratic Republic of Congo in the Case of the Prosecutor v. Germain Katanga and Mathieu Ngudjolo Chui: Judgment on the Appeal of Mr. Germain Katanga against the Oral Decision of Trial Chamber II of 12 June 2009 on the Admissibility of the Case*. The Appeals Chamber, 25 September. ICC Doc. No. ICC-01/04-01/07-1497.

ICC (International Criminal Court). 2010. *Situation in the Democratic Republic of Congo in the case of the Prosecutor v Thomas Lubanga Dyilo: Decision on Judicial Questioning*. Trial Chamber I, 18 March. ICC Doc. No. ICC-01/04-01/06-2360.

ICC (International Criminal Court). 2010. *Review Conference of the Rome Statue of the International Criminal Court*. Kampala, 31 May-11 June 2010. Accessed January 14, 2015. http://www.icc-cpi.int/iccdocs/asp_docs/ASP9/OR/RC-11-ENG.pdf.

ICC (International Criminal Court). 2010. *Resolution RC/Res.6: The Crime of Aggression*. Adopted at the 13th plenary meeting, 11 June. ICC Doc. No. RC/Res.6.

ICC (International Criminal Court). 2010. *Situation in the Central African Republic in the case of the Prosecutor v Jean-Pierre Bemba Gombo: Defence Observations on the Experts Proposed by the Prosecution*. Trial Chamber III, 15 June. ICC Doc. No. ICC-01/05-01/08-706.

ICC (International Criminal Court). 2010. *Stocktaking of International Criminal Justice: The Impact of the Rome Statute System on Victims and Affected Communities*. ICC Doc. No. RC-2010/RC/11.

ICC (International Criminal Court). 2010. *Annex A. Withdrawal of Expert Witness in Bemba Trial*. ICC Doc. No. ICC-01/05-01/08-896-AnxA. Registry, 23 September. Accessed January 16, 2015. http://www.icc-cpi.int/iccdocs/doc/doc940517.pdf.

ICC (International Criminal Court). 2011. *Situation in the Democratic Republic of Congo in the case of the Prosecutor v Thomas Lubanga Dyilo: Prosecution's Closing Brief*. Trial Chamber I, 1 June. ICC Doc. No. ICC-01/04-01/06-2748-Red.

ICC (International Criminal Court). 2011. *Situation in the Republic of Kenya: The Prosecutor v. Francis Kirimi Muthaura, Uhuru Muigai Kenyatta and Mohammed Hussein Ali: Decision on Prosecutor's Application for Summonses to Appear for Francis Kirimi Muthaura, Uhuru Muigai Kenyatta and Mohammed Hussein Ali*. Pre-Trial Chamber II, 8 March. ICC Doc. No. ICC-01/09-02/1 l-T-5-Red-ENG.

ICC (International Criminal Court). 2011. *Situation in the Republic of Kenya: The Prosecutor v. Francis Kirimi Muthaura, Uhuru Muigai Kenyatta and Mohammed Hussein Ali: Judgment on Appeal of the Republic of Kenya against the Decision of Pre-Trial Chamber II of 30 May 2011 entitled "Decision on the Application by the Government of Kenya Challenging the Admissibility of the Case Pursuant to Article 19(2)(b) of the Statute."* The Appeals Chamber, 30 August. ICC Doc. No. ICC-01/09-02/11-274.

ICC (International Criminal Court). 2011. *Situation in the Democratic Republic of the Congo in the Case of the Prosecutor v. Callixte Mbarushimana: Decision on the*

Confirmation of Charges. Pre-Trial Chamber I, 16 December. ICC Doc. No. ICC-01/04-01/10-Red.

ICC (International Criminal Court). 2012. *Situation in the Republic of Kenya in the Case of the Prosecutor v. Francis Kirimi Muthaura, Uhuru Muigai Kenyatta and Mohammed Hussein Ali : Decision on the Confirmation of Charges Pursuant to Article 61(7)(a) and (b) of the Rome Statute.* Pre-Trial Chamber II, 23 January. ICC Doc. No. ICC-01/09-02/11-382-Red.

ICC (International Criminal Court). 2012. *Situation in the Republic of Cote D'Ivoire in the Case of the Prosecutor v. Simone Gbagbo Warrant of Arrest for Simone Gbagbo.* Pre-Trial Chamber III, 29 February 2012. ICC Doc. No. ICC-02/11-01/12-1.

ICC (International Criminal Court). 2012. *Situation in the Democratic Republic of Congo in the case of the Prosecutor v Thomas Lubanga Dyilo: Judgment Hearing.* Trial Chamber I, 14 March. ICC Doc. No. ICC-01/04-01/06-T-359-ENG.

ICC (International Criminal Court). 2012. *Situation in the Democratic Republic of Congo in the case of the Prosecutor v Thomas Lubanga Dyilo: Judgment pursuant to Article 74 of the Statue.* Trial Chamber I, 14 March. ICC Doc. No. ICC-01/04-01/06-2842.

ICC (International Criminal Court). 2012. "ICC—President of the Assembly: The Verdict in the Lubanga Case, International Criminal Court." Press release, March 14. ICC Doc. No. ICC-ASP-20120314-PR775.

ICC (International Criminal Court). 2012. *International Criminal Court. 2012. Situation in the Democratic Republic of Congo in the case of the Prosecutor v. Callitxte Mbarushimana, Case No. ICC-01/04-01/10: Information Sheet.* Updated 27 March. ICC Doc. No. ICC-PIDS-CIS-DRC-04-003/11_Eng.

ICC (International Criminal Court). 2012. *Situation in the Democratic Republic of Congo in the case of the Prosecutor v Thomas Lubanga Dyilo: Women's Initiatives for Gender Justice Request for Leave to Participate in Reparations Proceedings.* Trial Chamber I, 28 March. ICC Doc. No. ICC-01/04-01/06-2853.

ICC (International Criminal Court). 2012. *Situation in the Democratic Republic of Congo in the case of the Prosecutor v. Thomas Lubanga Dyilo: Observations on Reparations in Response to the Scheduling Order of 14 March 2012,* Trial Chamber I, 25 April. ICC Doc. No. ICC-01/04-01/06-2872.

ICC (International Criminal Court). 2012. *Situation in the Central African Republic in the Case of the Prosecutor v Jean-Pierre Bemba Gombo: Trial Hearing.* Trial Chamber III, 1 May. ICC Doc. No. ICC-01/05-01/08-T-220-ENG CT WT 01-05-2012 1-56 NB T.

ICC (International Criminal Court). 2012. *Situation in the Democratic Republic of Congo in the case of the Prosecutor v Thomas Lubanga Dyilo: Observations of the Women's Initiatives for Gender Justice on Reparations.* Trial Chamber I, 10 May. ICC Doc. No. ICC-01/04-01/06-2876.

ICC (International Criminal Court). 2012. *Situation in the Democratic Republic of Congo: Prosecutor's Application under Article 58.* Pre-Trial Chamber II, 14 May. ICC Doc. No. ICC-01/04-611-Red.

ICC (International Criminal Court). 2012. *Situation in the Democratic Republic of Congo in the case of the Prosecutor v Thomas Lubanga Dyilo: Decision on Sentence pursuant to Article 76 of the Statute.* Trial Chamber I, 10 July. ICC Doc. No. ICC-01/04-01/06-2901.

ICC (International Criminal Court). 2012. *Situation in the Democratic Republic of Congo in the Case of the Prosecutor v Thomas Lubanga Dyilo: Decision Establishing the Principles and Procedures to be applied to Reparation.* Trial Chamber I, 7 August. ICC Doc. No. ICC-01/04-01/06-2904.

ICC (International Criminal Court). 2012. *Situation in the Democratic Republic of the Congo in the Case of the Prosecutor v. Thomas Lubanga Dyilo. Defence document in support of the appeal against Trial Chamber I's Decision establishing the principles and procedures to be applied to reparation rendered on 7August 2012.* The Appeals Chamber, 6 September. ICC Doc. No. ICC-01/04-01/06-2948-Conf-tENG.

ICC (International Criminal Court). 2012. *Situation in the Democratic Republic of Congo in the case of the Prosecutor v Thomas Lubanga Dyilo: Appeal against Trial Chamber I's Decision Establishing the Principles and Procedures to be Applied to Reparation of 7 August 2012.* The Appeal Chamber, 3 September. ICC Doc. No. ICC-01/04-01/06-2914-tENG.

ICC (International Criminal Court). 2012. *Situation in the Democratic Republic of Congo in the Case of the Prosecutor v Thomas Lubanga Dyilo: Defence Document in Support of the Appeal against Trial Chamber I's Decision Establishing the Principles and Procedures to be Applied to Reparation, Rendered on 7 August 2012.* The Appeals Chamber, 10 September. ICC Doc. No. ICC-01/04-01/06-2919-tENG.

ICC (International Criminal Court). 2012. *Situations in the Democratic Republic of the Congo in the case of the Prosecutor v. Germain Katanga and Mathieu Ngudjolo Chui: Decision on the Implementation of Regulation 55 of the Regulations of the Court and Severing the Charges against the Accused Persons.* Trial Chamber II, 21 November. ICC Doc. No. ICC-01/04-01/07-3319.

ICC (International Criminal Court). 2012. *Situation in the Democratic Republic of Congo in the Case of the Prosecutor v Thomas Lubanga Dyilo: Mr. Thomas Lubanga's Appellate Brief against Trial Chamber I's 10 July 2012 Decision on Sentence Pursuant to Article 76 of the Statute.* The Appeals Chamber, 3 December. ICC Doc. No. ICC-01/04-01/06-2949-tENG.

ICC (International Criminal Court). 2012. *Situation in the Democratic Republic of the Congo in the Case of the Prosecutor v. Mathieu Ngudjolo, Judgment pursuant to article 74 of the Statute.* Trial Chamber II, 18 December. ICC Doc. No. ICC-01/04-02/12-3-tENG.

ICC (International Criminal Court). 2012. *Situation in the Central African Republic in the Case of the Prosecutor v Jean-Pierre Bemba Gombo: Case Information Sheet.* ICC Doc. No. ICC-PIDS-CIS-CAR-01-009/12_ENG.

ICC (International Criminal Court). 2013. *Situation in the Democratic Republic of the Congo in the Case of the Prosecutor v. Bosco Ntaganda: Decision Establishing the Principles on the Victims Application Process.* Pre-Trial Chamber II, 28 May. ICC Doc. No. ICC-01/04-02/06-67.

ICC (International Criminal Court). 2013. *Situation in Libya in the Case of the Prosecutor v. Saif Al-Islam Gaddafi and Abdullah Al-Senussi: Decision on the Admissibility of the Case against Saif Al-Islam Gaddafi.* Pre-Trial Chamber I, 31 May. ICC Doc. No. ICC-01/11-01/11-344-Red.

ICC (International Criminal Court). 2014. "Simone Gbagbo case: ICC Pre-Trial Chamber I rejects Côte d'Ivoire's challenge to the admissibility of the case and reminds the Government of its obligation to surrender Simone Gbagbo." Press Release, 11 December. Accessed 16 January 2015. http://www.icc-cpi.int/en_menus/icc/press%20and%20media/press%20releases/Pages/pr1075.aspx.

ICC (International Criminal Court). 2014. *Situation in the Democratic Republic of the Congo in the Case of the Prosecutor v. Germain Katanga: Jugement rendu en application de l'article 74 du Statut [French version]*. Trial Chamber II, 7 March. ICC Doc. No.ICC-01/04-01/07-3436.

ICC (International Criminal Court). 2014. *Situation in the Democratic Republic of the Congo in the Case of the Prosecutor v. Germain Katanga, Prosecution's Appeal against Trial Chamber II's "Jugement rendu en application de l'article 74 du Statut."* The Appeals Chamber, 9 April. ICC Doc. No. ICC-01/04-01/07-3462.

ICC (International Criminal Court). 2014. *Situation in Libya in the Case of the Prosecutor v. Saif Al-Islam Gaddafi and Abdullah Al-Senussi: Judgment on the Appeal of Libya against the Decision of Pre-Trial Chamber I of 31 May 2013 entitled "Decision on the Admissibility of the Case against Saif Al-Islam Gaddafi."* The Appeals Chamber, 21 May. ICC Doc. No. ICC-01/11-01/11-547-Red.

ICC (International Criminal Court). 2014. *Situation in the Democratic Republic of the Congo in the Case of the Prosecutor v. Germain Katanga: Minority Opinion of Judge Christine Van den Wyngaert*. Trial Chamber II, 7 March. ICC Doc. No. ICC-01/04-01/07-3436-AnxI.

ICC (International Criminal Court). 2014. *Situation in the Democratic Republic of the Congo in the case of the Prosecutor v. Bosco Ntaganda: Decision Pursuant to Article 61(7)(a) and (b) of the Rome Statute on the Charges of the Prosecutor Against Bosco Ntaganda*. Pre-Trial Chamber II, 9 June. ICC Doc. No. ICC-01/04-02/06-309.

ICC (International Criminal Court). 2014. *Situation in the Republic of Kenya in the Case of the Prosecutor v. Uhuru Muigai Kenyatta : Defence Response to "Prosecution notice regarding the Provisional Trial Date" (ICC-01/09-02/11-944) and Request to Terminate the Case against Mr. Kenyatta*. Trial Chamber V(B), 10 September. ICC Doc. No. ICC-01/09-02/11.

ICC (International Criminal Court). 2014. *Appeals Hearing for the Delivery of a Judgment (ICC-01/04-01/06)*, The Appeals Chamber, 1 December. ICC Doc. No. ICC-01/04-01/06-T-364-ENG.

ICC (International Criminal Court). 2014. "Six New Judges Sworn in Today at the Seat of the International Criminal Court." ICC-CPI-20150310-PR1095.

ICC (International Criminal Court). 2015. "Judge Fernández de Gurmendi elected ICC President for 2015–2018; Judges Aluoch and Ozaki elected First and Second Vice-President respectively." ICC-CPI-20150311-PR1096.

ICC ASP (International Criminal Court Assembly of States Parties). 2003. *Assembly of States Parties to the Rome Statute of the International Criminal Court: First session (first and second resumptions)*. New York, 3–7 February and 21–23 April. ICC Doc. No. ICC-ASP/1/3/Add.1.

ICC ASP (International Criminal Court Assembly of States Parties). 2004. *Resolution ICC-ASP/3/Res.6: Procedure for the nomination and election of judges of the International Criminal Court*. Adopted at the 6th Plenary Meeting, 10 September. ICC Doc. No. ICC-ASP/3/Res.6.

ICC ASP (International Criminal Court Assembly of States Parties). 2005. *Regulations of the Trust Fund for Victims, Resolution ICC-ASP/4/Res.3*. ICC Doc. No. ICC-ASP/4/Res.3.

ICC ASP (International Criminal Court Assembly of States Parties). 2006. *Strategic Plan for Outreach of the International Criminal Court*. ICC Doc. No. ICC-ASP/5/12. Accessed February 12, 2014. http://www.icccpi.int/NR/rdonlyres/FB4C75CF-FD15-4B06-B1E3-29E22618FB404%20C/185051/ICCASP512_English1.pdf.

ICC ASP (International Criminal Court Assembly of States Parties). 2011. *Resolution ICC-ASP/10/Res.3: Reparations.* Adopted at the 7th Plenary Meeting, 20 December. ICC Doc. No. ICC-ASP/10/Res.3.

ICC ASP (International Criminal Court Assembly of States Parties). 2012. *Report of the Court on the Revised Strategy in Relation to Victims: Past, Present and Future.* Eleventh session, The Hague, 14–22 November. ICC Doc. No. ICC-ASP/11/40.

ICC OPCV (International Criminal Court Office of Public Counsel for Victims). 2010. *Helping Victims Make their Voice Heard: 5 Years of Activities.* The Hague: International Criminal Court. ICC Doc. No. ICC-OPCV-B-001/10_Eng. Accessed January 14, 2015. http://www.icc-cpi.int/NR/rdonlyres/ 01A26724-F32B-4BE4-8B02-A65D6151E4AD/282846/LRBookletEng.pdf.

ICC OTP (International Criminal Court Office of the Prosecutor). 2003. *Paper on Some Policy Issues before the Office of the Prosecutor.* September. Accessed January 16, 2015. http://www.icc-cpi.int/nr/rdonlyres/1fa7c4c6-de5%20f-42b7-8b25-60aa962ed8b6/143594/030905_policy_paper.pdf.

ICC OTP (International Criminal Court Office of the Prosecutor). 2004. *Statement of the Prosecutor Luis Moreno Ocampo to Diplomatic Corps.* ICC Office of the Prosecutor. The Hague, Netherlands, February 12. Accessed January 13, 2015. http://www.icc-cpi.int/NR/rdonlyres/0F999F00-A609-4516-A91A-80467BC432D3/143670/LOM_20040212_En.pdf.

ICC OTP (International Criminal Court Office of the Prosecutor). 2008. *Statement by Luis Moreno-Ocampo, Chief Prosecutor of the International Criminal Court: Press Conference in relation with the surrender to the Court of Mr Thomas Lubanga Dyilo.* The Hague: International Criminal Court, 18 March. ICC Doc. No. ICC 01/04-01/06-170.

ICC OTP (International Criminal Court Office of the Prosecutor). 2008. "ICC Prosecutor appoints Prof. Catharine A. MacKinnon as Special Adviser on Gender Crimes." Press release, 26 November. ICC Doc. No. ICC-OTP-20081126-PR377.

ICC OTP (International Criminal Court Office of the Prosecutor). 2011. *Statement by Fatou Bensouda, Prosecutor Elect of the International Criminal Court at the Launch of the Gender Report Card of the International Criminal Court 2011.* New York: Women's Initiatives for Gender Justice, December 13. Accessed May 14, 2014. http://www.icc-cpi.int/NR/rdonlyres/BCB9AB3%20F-4684-4684EC3-A677-673E8E443148%20C/284154/111213StatementFB.pdf.

ICC OTP (International Criminal Court Office of the Prosecutor). 2012. "ICC Prosecutor Fatou Bensouda Appoints Brigid Inder, Executive Director of the Women's Initiatives for Gender Justice, as Special Gender Advisor." Press release, August 21. ICC Doc. No. ICC-OTP-20120821-PR833.

ICC OTP (International Criminal Court Office of the Prosecutor). 2012. *Report on Preliminary Examination Activities 2012.* November. The Hague: Office of the Prosecutor, International Criminal Court.

ICC OTP (International Criminal Court Office of the Prosecutor). 2012. *Press Statement by Ms Fatou Bensouda, Deputy Prosecutor of the International Criminal Court* (April 5).

ICC OTP (International Criminal Court Office of the Prosecutor). 2012. *Situation in Colombia Interim Report.* November. The Hague: Office of the Prosecutor, International Criminal Court.

ICC OTP (International Criminal Court Office of the Prosecutor). 2012. *OTP Briefing: Principles and Procedures of Reparation Process Established in Lubanga Case.*

Issue #129, 8–27 August. Accessed January 16, 2014. http://www.icc-cpi.int/NR/rdonlyres/8A4D5456-4DA2-4D24-A338-591995AF727E/284861/OTPBriefing827August2012.pdf.

ICC OTP (International Criminal Court Office of the Prosecutor). 2013. *Report on Preliminary Examination Activities 2013*. November. The Hague: Office of the Prosecutor, International Criminal Court.

ICC OTP (International Criminal Court Office of the Prosecutor). 2014. *Policy Paper of Sexual and Gender-based Crimes* June. The Hague: Office of the Prosecutor, International Criminal Court.

ICC OTP (International Criminal Court Office of the Prosecutor). 2014. *Statement of the Prosecutor of the International Criminal Court, Fatou Bensouda, on the Abduction of Schoolgirls in Nigeria*. May 8.

ICC OTP (International Criminal Court Office of the Prosecutor). 2014. *Launch of the ICC Office of the Prosecutor's Policy Paper on Sexual Violence and Gender-Based Crimes*. ICC Office of the Prosecutor. New York: United Nations, December 7. Accessed January 5, 2015. http://www.icc-cpi.int/iccdocs/otp/Prosecutor%27s%20opening-closing%20remarks-07-11-2014.pdf.

ICC OTP (International Criminal Court Office of the Prosecutor). 2014. *Closing Remarks at the Launch of the ICC Office of the Prosecutor's Policy Paper on Sexual Violence and Gender-Based Crimes*. ICC Office of the Prosecutor. New York: United Nations, December 7. Accessed January 5, 2015. http://www.icc-cpi.int/iccdocs/otp/Prosecutor%27s%20opening-closing%20remarks-07-11-2014.pdf.

ICC OTP (International Criminal Court Office of the Prosecutor). 2014. *Statement to the United Nations Security Council on the Situation in Darfur, pursuant to UNSCR 1593 (2005)*. New York: United Nations Security Council, December 12. Accessed January 11, 2015. http://www.icc-cpi.int/iccdocs/otp/stmt-20threport-darfur.pdf.

ICC (International Criminal Court). 2015. *Situation in the Democratic Republic of the Congo n the Case of the Prosecutor v. Thomas Lubanga Dyilo. Judgment on the appeals against the "Decision establishing the princples and procedures to be applied to reparations" of 7 August 2012 with AMENDED order for reparations (Annex A) and public annexes 1 and 2*. ICC Doc. No. ICC-01/04-01/06-3129 03-03-2015 1/97 NM A A2 A3.

ICC (International Criminal Court). 2015. *Situation in the Democratic Republic of the Congo in the case of the Prosecutor v. Germain Katanga. Trust Fund for Vicitims Observations on Reparations Procedure*. ICC Doc. No. ICC-01/04-01/07-3548 13-05-2015 1/44 NM T.ICTY. 2014. Judges. Accessed 10 January 2015. http://www.icty.org/sid/151.

Inder, Brigid. 2011. "Reflection: Gender Issues and Child Soldiers the case of Prosecutor v Thomas Lubanga Dyilo." Accessed August 31. http://www.lubangatrial.org/2011/08/31/reflection-gender-issues-and-child-soldiers-the-case-of-prosecutor-v-thomas-lubanga-dyilo-2/.

Inder, Brigid. 2012. *Interview with the Director of the Women's Initiatives of Gender Justice*. The Hague: Women's Initiatives of Gender Justice, June 26.

Inder, Brigid. 2013. "Partners for Gender Justice." In *Sexual Violence as an International Crime: Interdisciplinary Approaches*, edited by Anne-Marie de Brouwer, Charlotte Ku, Renne Romkens, and Lariss can den Herik, 315–338. Cambridge: Intersentia.

Inder, Brigid. 2014. "Launch of the Policy on Sexual and Gender-Based Crimes." ICC Office of the Prosecutor. New York: United Nations. December 7. Accessed January 5, 2015. http://www.iccwomen.org/documents/Launch-of-the-ICCs-Policy-on-Sexual-and-Gender-Based-Crimes.pdf.

International Criminal Court. 2000. *Elements of Crimes*. ICC Doc. No. PCNICC/2000/1/Add.2.

International Criminal Tribunal for Rwanda. 1998. *Prosecutor v. Akayesu, Case No. ICTR-96-4, Judgment*. September 2.

Jacobs, Dov. 2012. "Lubanga Decision Roundtable: Lubanga, Sexual Violence and the Legal Re-Characterization of Facts." *Opinio Juris Blog*, March 18. Accessed November 20, 2013 http://opiniojuris.org/2012/03/18/lubanga-decision-roundtable-lubanga-sexual-violenceand-the-legal-re-characterization-of-facts/.

Jarvis, Michelle, and Elena Martin Salgado. 2013. "Future Challenges to Prosecuting Sexual Violence under International Law: Insights from ICTY Practice." In *Sexual Violence as an International Crime: Interdisciplinary Approaches*, edited by Anne-Marie de Brouwer, Charlotte Ku, Renne Romkens, and Lariss can den Herik, 101–122. Cambridge: Intersentia.

Jørgensen, Nina H. B. 2012. "Child Soldiers and the Parameters of International Criminal Law." *Chinese Journal of International Law* 11(4): 657–688.

Kapur, Amrita. 2012. "Complementarity at Work in Unwilling States: Raising the Threshold of Accountability for Gender-Based International Crimes." Conference Paper presented at the "Justice for All? The International Criminal Court—A Conference: 10 year Review of the ICC," The University of New South Wales, Sydney, Australia, February 15.

Katzenstein, Mary Fainsod. 1998. *Faithful and Fearless: Moving Feminist Protest inside the Church and Military*. Princeton, NJ: Princeton University Press.

Keck, Margaret E., and Kathryn Sikkink. 1998. *Activists Beyond Borders: Advocacy Networks in International Politics*. Ithaca, NY: Cornell University Press.

Kenney, Sally. 2012. *Gender & Justice: Why Women in the Judiciary Really Matter*. New York: Routledge.

Kenny, Meryl. 2007. "Gender, Institutions and Power: A Critical Review." *Politics* 27(2): 91–100.

Kenny, Meryl. 2013. *Gender and Political Recruitment: Theorizing Institutional Change*. Basingstoke: Palgrave Macmillan.

Keohane, Robert, and Lisa L. Martin. 2003. "Institutional Theory as a Research Program." In *Progress in International Relations Theory: Appraising the Field*, edited by Colin Elman and Miriam F. Elman, 71–108. Cambridge, MA: MIT Press.

Kleffner, Jann. 2008. *Complementarity in the Rome Statute and National Criminal Jurisdictions*. Oxford: Oxford University Press.

Kleffner, Jann. 2009. "Complementarity and Auto-Referrals." In *The Emerging Practice of the International Criminal Court*, edited by Carsten Stahn and Göran Sluiter, 41–53. Leiden: Koninklijke Brill.

Koomen, Jonneke. 2014. "Language Work at International Criminal Courts." *International Feminist Journal of Politics*. 16 (4): 581–600.

Koremenos, Barbara, Charles Lipson, and Duncan Snidal. 2001. "The Rational Design of Institutions." *International Organization* 55(4): 761–799.

Krook, Mona L. 2009. *Quotas for Women in Politics: Gender and Candidate Selection Reform Worldwide*. Oxford: Oxford University Press.

Krook, Mona Lena, and Fiona Mackay, eds. 2011. *Gender, Politics and Institutions: Towards a Feminist Institutionalism*. Basingstoke: Palgrave.

Krook, Mona L., and Jacqui True. 2012. "Rethinking the Life Cycles of International Norms: The United Nations and the Global Promotion of Equality." *European Journal of International Relations* 18(1): 103–127.

Kuovo, Sari, and Zoe Pearson, eds. 2011. *Feminist Perspectives on Contemporary International Law*. Oxford: Hart Publishing.

Lake, Milli. 2014. "Ending Impunity for Sexual Based Crimes: The International Criminal Court and Complementarity in the Democratic Republic of Congo." *African Conflict and Peacebuilding Review* 4(1): 1–31.

Lauth, Hans-Joachim. 2000. "Informal Institutions and Democracy." *Democratization* 7(4): 21–50.

Lawyers Without Borders. 2012. *The Principle of Complementarity in the Rome Statute and the Colombian Situation: A Case that Demands More than a "Positive" Approach*. Quebec: Lawyers Without Borders Canada. Accessed January 13, 2015. http://www.iccnow.org/documents/asf_rapport-anglais-complementarity_and_colombia.pdf.

Leach, Steve, and Vivien Lowndes. 2007. "Of Roles and Rules: Analysing the Changing Relationship between Political Leaders and Chief Executives in Local Government." *Public Policy and Administration* 22(2): 183–200.

Leatherman, Janie L. 2011. *Sexual Violence and Armed Conflict*. Cambridge, UK: Polity.

Lee, Roy S. 1999. "The Rome Conference and its Contributions to International Law." In *The International Criminal Court: The Making of the Rome Statute*, edited by Roy S. Lee, 1–39. The Hague: Kluwer Law International.

Levitsky, Steven, and Dan Slater. 2011. "Ruling Politics: The Formal and Informal Foundations of Institutional Reform." Paper presented at the Workshop on Informal Institutions, Harvard University.

Lewis, Dustin A. 2010. "'Unrecognized Victims: Sexual Violence Against Men in Conflict Settings Under International Law.'" *Wisconsin International Law Journal* 27: 1–49.

LifeSite. 1998. "International Criminal Court Approved: LifeSite Special Report." *LifeSite News*, July 19.

LifeSite. 2000. "Radical Feminists Laud International Criminal Court." *LifeSite News*, March 9.

Limebach, Dulcie. 2012. "The ICC's New Gender Adviser Knows the Court Well." *PassBlue: Covering the UN*, August 22. Accessed May 15, 2014. http://passblue.com/2012/08/22/the-iccs-new-gender-adviser-knows-the-court-well/.

Lovenduski, Joni. 1998. "Gendering Research in Political Science." *Annual Review of Political Science* 1(1): 333–356.

Lovenduski, Joni. 2005. *Feminizing Politics*. Cambridge: Polity Press.

Lowndes, Vivien. 2005. "Something Old, Something New, Something Borrowed . . . : How Institutions Change (and Stay the Same) in Local Governance." *Policy Studies* 26 (3/4): 291–310.

Lowndes, Vivien, and Mark Roberts. 2013. *Why Institutions Matter: The New Institutionalism in Political Science*. Basingstoke: Palgrave.

Lowndes, Vivien, and David Wilson. 2003. "Balancing Revisability and Robustness?: A New Institutionalist Perspective on Local Government Modernisation." *Public Administration* 81(2): 275–298.

Luping, Dianne. 2009. "Investigation and Prosecution of Sexual and Gender-Based Crimes before the International Criminal Court." *American University Journal of Gender, Social Policy, & the Law* 17(2): 431–496.

MacKinnon, Catharine A. 2008. "The ICTR's Legacy on Sexual Violence." *New England Journal of International and Comparative Law* 14(2): 211–220.

Mackay, Fiona. 2008. "'Thick' Conceptions of Substantive Representation: Women, Gender and Political Institutions." *Representation* 44(2): 125–139.

Mackay, Fiona. 2013. "New rules, old rules and the gender equality architecture of the UN—the creation of UN Women." Conference Paper presented at the American Political Science Association Conference, Chicago, August 30.

Mackay, Fiona. 2014a. "'Nested Newness,' Institutional Innovation, and the Gendered Limits of Change." *Politics & Gender* 10(4): 549–571.

Mackay, Fiona. 2014b. "Global Governance and UN Women: Nested Newness and the Gendered Limits of Institutional Reform." Conference Paper presented at the International Studies Association Conference, Toronto, March 27.

Mackay, Fiona, Meryl Kenny, and Louise Chappell. 2010. "New Institutionalism Through a Gender Lens: Towards a Feminist Institutionalism?" *International Political Science Review* 31(5): 573–588.

Mackay, Fiona, and Georgina Waylen. 2009. "Critical Perspectives on Feminist Institutionalism." *Politics and Gender* 5(2): 237–280.

Mackay, Fiona, and Georgina Waylen, eds. 2014. "Newness, Gender and Institutions" Special Issue. *Politics & Gender* 10(4).

Mackenzie, Megan H. 2012. *Female Soldiers in Sierra Leone: Sex, Security and Post-Conflict Development*. New York: New York University Press.

Mahoney, James, and Kathleen Thelen. 2010. *Explaining Institutional Change*. Cambridge: Cambridge University Press.

Mallon, John. 2000. "Evangelicals, Rabbi support Vatican at UN." *Inside the Vatican*.

Manjoo, Rashida. 2010. *Report of the Special Rapporteur on Violence Against Women, its Causes And Consequences*. New York: Office of the High Commissioner for Human Rights, April 19. A/HRC/14/22.

Manjoo, Rashida, and Calleigh McRaith. 2011. "Gender-Based Violence and Justice in Conflict and Post-Conflict Areas." *Cornell International Law Journal* 44(1): 11–31.

March, James G., and Johan P. Olsen. 1989. *Rediscovering Institutions: The Organizational Basis of Politics*. New York: The Free Press.

Mark, Monica. 2014. "Families of Abducted Girls Fight Boko Haram—and a Supine Government." *The Guardian*, July 24. Accessed August 14, 2014. http://www.theguardian.com/world/2014/jul/24/-sp-families-abducted-girls-fight-boko-haram-supine-government.

McCarthy, Conor. 2009. "Reparations under the Rome Statute of the International Criminal Court and Reparative Justice Theory." *International Journal of Transitional Justice* 3(2): 250–271.

McCarthy, Conor. 2012. *Reparations and Victim Support in the International Criminal Court*. Cambridge: Cambridge University Press.

McCleary-Sills, Jennifer, and Stella Mukasa. 2013. *External Evaluation of the Trust Fund for Victims Programmes in Northern Uganda and the Democratic Republic of Congo: Towards a Perspective for Upcoming Interventions*. Washington: International Center for Research on Women (ICRW).

McKay, Fiona. 2012. *Interview 2012 Director of the Victims Participation and Reparation Section, Victims and Witnesses Unit, Registry, International Criminal Court*. The Hague: International Criminal Court, June 26.

McLeod, Laura, Rachel Johnson, Sheila Meintjes, Alice Brown, and Valerie Oosterveld. 2014. "Gendering Processes of Institutional Design: Activists at the Negotiating Table." *International Feminist Journal of Politics* 16(2): 354–369.

Meertens, Donny. 2012. *Forced Displacement and Gender Justice in Colombia: Between Disproportional Effects of Violence and Historical Injustice*. New York: International Center for Transitional Justice and Brookings-LSW Project on Internal Displacement.

Mégret, Frédéric. 2009. "The International Criminal Court and the Failure to Mention Symbolic Reparations." *International Review of Victimology* 16(2): 127–147.

Mégret, Frédéric. 2011. "Too Much of a Good Thing? Implementation and the Uses of Complementarity." In *The International Criminal Court and Complementarity*, edited by Carsten Stahn and Mohamed M. El Zeidy, Vol. 1, 361–390. New York: Cambridge University Press.

Mégret, Frédéric. 2012. "Reparations before the ICC: the Need for Pragmatism and Creativity." *ICC Forum*, February–June. Accessed June 10, 2013. http://iccforum.com/reparations#Megret.

Merope, Sienna. 2011. "Recharacterizing the Lubanga Case: Regulation 55 and the Consequences for Gender Justice at the ICC." *Criminal Law Forum* 22(3): 311–346.

Mertus, Julie. 2004. "Shouting From the Bottom of the Well." *International Feminist Journal of Politics* 6(1): 110–128.

Meyer, Mary K., and Elisabeth Prügl, eds. 1999. *Gender Politics in Global Governance*. Lanham, MD: Rowman & Littlefield.

Moffett, Luke. 2013. "Reparative Complementarity: Ensuring an Effective Remedy for Victims in the Reparation Regime of the International Criminal Court." *International Journal of Human Rights* 17(3): 368–390.

Moghadam, Valentine M. 2005. *Globalizing Women: Transnational Feminist Networks*. Baltimore: John Hopkins University Press.

Molyneaux, Maxine. 2007. "Refiguring Citizenship Research Perspectives on Gender Justice in the Latin American and Caribbean Region." In *Gender Justice, Citizenship and Development*, edited by Maitrayee Mukhopadhyay and Navsharan Singh, 58–115. Ottawa: Zubaan, International Development Research Centre.

Moreno Ocampo, Luis. 2011. "A Positive Approach to Complementarity: The Impact of the ICC Prosecutor." In *The International Criminal Court and Complementarity*, edited by Carsten Stahn and Mohamed M. El Zeidy, Vol. 1, 21–32. New York: Cambridge University Press.

Moreno Ocampo, Luis. 2013. "The Place of Sexual Violence in the Strategy of the ICC Prosecutor." In *Sexual Violence as an International Crime: Interdisciplinary Approaches*, edited by Anne-Marie de Brouwer Charlotte Ku, Renne Romkens, and Lariss can den Herik, 151–156. Cambridge: Intersentia.

Moshan, Brook Sari. 1998. "Women, War, and Words: The Gender Component in the Permanent International Criminal Court's Definition of Crimes Against Humanity" *Fordham International Law Journal* 22(1): 154–184.

Mouthaan, Solange. 2011. "The Prosecution of Gender-Based Crimes at the ICC: Challenges and Opportunities." *International Criminal Law Review* 11(4): 775–802.

Muttukumaru, Christopher. 1999. "Reparations to Victims." In *The International Criminal Court: The Making of the Rome Statute*, edited by Roy S. Lee, 262–270. The Hague: Kluwer Law International.

Nesiah, Vasuki. 2011. "Missionary Zeal for a Secular Mission: Bringing Gender to Transitional Justice and Redemption Feminism." In *Feminist Perspectives on Contemporary International Law: Between Resistance and Compliance?*, edited by Sari Kouvo and Zoe Pearson, 137–158. Oxford: Hart Publishing.

Ní Aoláin, Fionnuala. 2012. "Advancing Feminist Positioning in the Field of Transitional Justice." *International Journal of Transitional Justice* 6(2): 205–228.

Ní Aoláin, Fionnuala. 2014. "Gendered Harms and their Interface with International Criminal Law: Norms, Challenges and Domestication." *International Feminist Journal of Politics* 16(4): 622–646.

Ní Aoláin, Fionnuala, Dina Francesca Haynes, and Naomi Cahn. 2011. *On the Frontlines: Gender, War, and the Post-Conflict Process*. Oxford: Oxford University Press.

North, Douglass. 1990. *Institutions, Institutional Change and Economic Performance*. Cambridge: Cambridge University Press.

Nouwen, Sarah. 2011. "Fine-Tuning Complementarity." In *Research Handbook on International Criminal Law*, edited by B. S. Brown, 206–231. Cheltenham: Edward Elgar.

Nouwen, Sarah. 2013. *Complementarity in the Line of Fire: The Catalysing Effect of the International Criminal Court in Uganda and Sudan*. Cambridge: Cambridge University Press.

Nussbaum, Martha C. 2006. *Frontiers of Justice: Disability, Nationality, Species Membership*. Cambridge, MA: Harvard University Press.

Oosterveld, Valerie. 2005. "The Definition of Gender in the Rome Statute of the International Criminal Court: A Step Forward or Back for International Criminal Justice." *Harvard Human Rights Journal* 18: 55–84.

Oosterveld, Valerie, 2013. "Prosecuting Gender-Based Persecution as an International Crime." In *Sexual Violence as an International Crime: Interdisciplinary Approaches*, edited by Anne-Marie de Brouwer, Charlotte Ku, Renne Romkens, and Lariss can den Herik, 57–78. Cambridge: Intersentia.

Oosterveld, Valerie. 2014. "Constructive Ambiguity, Legal Uncertainty and the Meaning of 'Gender' for the International Criminal Court." *International Feminist Journal of Politics* 16(4): 563–580.

Oosterveld, Valerie. 2014. Personal communication with author, May 12.

Organization of Islamic Conference (OIC). 2000. "On Slanderous Campaigns waged by certain Non-Governmental Organizations (NGOs) Against a number of OIC Member States Targeting the Islamic Shari'a under the Mantle of Human Rights Protection." 62/9-P (IS).

Ostrom, Elinor. 2005. *Understanding Institutional Diversity*. Princeton, NJ: Princeton University Press.

Pena, Mariana. 2012. "The Lubanga Case and Reparations for Victims of Sexual Violence." *International Justice Central Blog*, October 10. Accessed May 21, 2014. http://publicinternationallawandpolicygroup.org/wp-content/uploads/2012/10/WCPW_MASTER_102212.html.

Perdomo, Claudia. 2012. *Interview with the Director of the Outreach Unit, Registry, International Criminal Court*. The Hague: International Criminal Court, June 26.

Phillips, Anne. 1995. *The Politics of Presence*. Oxford: Oxford University Press.

Phillips, Anne. 1999. *Which equalities matter?* Cambridge: Polity Press.

Pierson, Paul. 2004. *Politics in Time: History, Institutions and Social Analysis*. Princeton, NJ: Princeton University Press.

Pillay, Navanethem. 2010. "Address—Interdisciplinary Colloquium on Sexual Violence as International Crime: Sexual Violence: Standing by the Victim." *Law & Social Inquiry* 35(4): 847–853.

Pritchett, Sarah. 2008. "Entrenched Hegemony, Efficient Procedure, or Selective Justice?: An Inquiry into Charges for Gender-Based Violence at the International Criminal Court." *Transnational Law & Contemporary Problems* 17: 265–305.

Puwar, Nirmal. 2004. "Thinking About Making a Difference." *British Journal of Politics and International Relations*. 6: 65–80.

Radnitz, Scott. 2011. "Informal Politics and the State." *Comparative Politics* 43(3): 351–371.

Rai, Shirin, and Georgina Waylen. 2008. *Global Governance: Feminist Perspectives*. Basingstoke: Palgrave Macmillan.

REAL Women of Canada. 1998. "The International Criminal Court—World Nightmare." Newsletter, May–June.

REDRESS. 2011. *Justice for Victims: The ICC's Reparations Mandate*. London: REDRESS.

REDRESS. 2012. "Landmark ICC Decision Recognises Reparation is a Right Owed to Victims." Press release, August 7. Accessed April 7, 2014. http://www.redress.org/downloads/Lubangareparationsdecision-070812.pdf.

REDRESS. 2015. "At long last: Reparations for Victims can now proceed in the ICC's first case." March 3. Accessed March 13, 2015. http://www.redress.org/downloads/pr-lubanga-reparations-appeals-decision030315.pdf.

Riker, William H. 1995. "The Experience of Creating Institutions: The Framing of the United States Constitution." In *Explaining Social Institutions*, edited by Jack Knight and Itai Sened, 121–144. Ann Arbor: University of Michigan Press.

Roach, Steven C. 2009. "Introduction: Global Governance in Context." In *Governance, Order and the International Criminal Court: Between Realpolitik and a Cosmopolitan Court*, edited by Steven C. Roach, 1–28. Oxford: Oxford University Press.

Robert Cryer, Hakan Friman, Darryl Robinson, and Elizabeth Wilmshurst. 2010. *An Introduction to International Criminal Law and Procedure* 2nd Edition. Cambridge: Cambridge University Press.

Rubio-Marín, Ruth, ed. 2009. *The Gender of Reparations: Unsettling Sexual Hierarchies While Redressing Human Rights Violations*. Cambridge: Cambridge University Press.

Rwelamira, Medard R. 1999. "Composition and Administration of the Court." In *The International Criminal Court: The Making of the Rome Statute*, edited by Roy S. Lee, 153–173. The Hague: Kluwer Law International.

SáCouto, Susana. 2012. "Victim Participation at the International Criminal Court and the Extraordinary Chambers in the Courts of Cambodia: A Feminist Project?" *Michigan Journal of Gender and the Law* 18(2): 297–359.

SáCouto, Susana, and Katherine A. Cleary. 2009. "The Importance of Effective Investigation of Sexual Violence and Gender-Based Crimes at the International Criminal Court." *American University Journal of Gender, Social Policy & the Law* 17(2): 337–359.

SáCouto, Susana, and Katherine Cleary. 2014. "The Adjudication Process and Reasoning at the International Criminal Court: The *Lubanga* Trial Chamber Judgment, Sentencing and Reparations." In *Human Rights and Civil Liberties in the*

21st Century, edited by Yves Haeck and Eva Brems, 131–155. Dordrecht: Springer.

Sadat, Nadya L. 2011. "Avoiding the Creation of a Gender Ghetto in International Criminal Law." *International Criminal Law Review* 11(3): 655–662.

Sara Kendall and Sarah Nouwen. 2014. "Representational practices at the International Criminal Court: The Gap Between Juridified and Abstract Victimhood". *Law and Contemporary Problems* 76: 235–262.

Schabas, William. 2011. *An Introduction to the International Criminal Court*, 4th ed. Cambridge: Cambridge University Press.

Schiff, Benjamin N. 2008. *Building the International Criminal Court*. Cambridge: Cambridge University Press.

Schiff, Benjamin N. 2010. "Evolution of ICC Legitimacy." Conference Paper for the International Studies Association Annual Meeting, New Orleans, February 19.

Senier, Amy. 2008. "The ICC Prosecutor's Appointment of a Special Advisor on Gender Crimes." *International Law Observer Blog*, May 21. Accessed January 13, 2015. http://www.internationallawobserver.eu/2008/12/05/the-icc-prosecutors-appointment-of-a-special-advisor-on-gender-crimes/.

Sharratt, Sara. 1999. "Interview with Justice Odio Benito, Justice with the International Criminal Tribunal for the Former Yugoslavia." *Women and Therapy* 22(1): 39–52.

Shepherd, Laura J. 2008. "Power and Authority in the Production of United Nations Security Council Resolution 1325." *International Studies Quarterly* 52(2): 383–404.

Shepherd, Laura J., ed. 2010. *Gender Matters in Global Politics: A Feminist Introduction to International Relations*. Abington: Routledge.

Sikkink, Kathryn. 2011. *The Justice Cascade: How Human Rights Prosecutions are Changing World Politics*. New York: W.W. Norton and Company.

Simmons, Beth A. 2009. *Mobilizing for Human Rights: International Law in Domestic Politics*. Cambridge: Cambridge University Press.

Simmons, Beth A., and Alison Danner. 2010. "Credible Commitments and the International Criminal Court." *International Organization* 64(2): 225–256.

Sivakumara, Sandesh. 2013. "Prosecuting Sexual Violence Against Men and Boys." In *Sexual Violence as an International Crime: Interdisciplinary Approaches*, edited by Anne-Marie de Brouwer, Charlotte Ku, Renne Romkens, and Lariss can den Herik, 79–100. Cambridge: Intersentia.

Sjoberg, Laura, and Caron E. Gentry. 2008. "Reduced to Bad Sex: Narratives of Violent Women from the Bible to the War on Terror." *International Relations* 22(1): 5–23.

Sluiter, Göran, and Alexander Zahar. 2008. *International Criminal Law: A Critical Introduction*. Oxford: Oxford University Press.

Slye, Ronald C., and Beth Van Schaak. 2009. *Essentials of International Criminal Law*. New York: Aspen Publishers.

Smart, Carol. 1989. *Feminism and the Power of Law*. Abingdon: Routledge.

Smith, K'Shanni O. 2011. "Prosecutor v. Lubanga: How the International Criminal Court Failed the Women and Girls of the Congo." *Howard Law Journal* 54(2): 437–500.

Smith-van Lin, Lorraine. 2013. "Victims' Participation oat the International Criminal Court: Benefit or Burden." In *The Ashgate Companion to International*

Criminal Law: Critical Perspectives, edited by William Schabas, Yvonne McDermott, and Niamh Hayes, 181–204. Farnham, UK: Ashgate.

Spees, Pam. 2003. "Women's Advocacy in the Creation of the International Criminal Court: Changing the Landscapes of Justice and Power." *Signs* 28(4): 1233–1256.

Stahn, Carsten. 2008. "Complementarity: A Tale of Two Notions." *Criminal Law Forum* 19(1): 100–112.

Stahn, Carsten. 2014. "Justice Delivered or Justice Denied? The Legacy of the Katanga Judgment." *Journal of International Criminal Justice* 12: 809–834.

Stahn, Carsten, and Mohamed M. El Zeidy, eds. 2011. *The International Criminal Court and Complementarity*, Vols. 1 and 2. New York: Cambridge University Press.

Steains, Cate. 1999. "Gender Issues." In *The International Criminal Court: The Making of the Rome Statute*, edited by Roy S. Lee, 357–398. The Hague: Kluwer Law International.

Steinmo, Sven, Kathleen Thelen, and Frank Longstreth. 1992. *Structuring Politics: Historical Institutionalism in Comparative Analysis*. Cambridge: Cambridge University Press.

Stienstra, Deborah. 1994. *Women's Movements and International Organizations*. New York: Macmillan Press.

Streeck, Wolfgang, and Kathleen Thelen. 2005. *Beyond Continuity: Institutional Change in Advanced Political Economies*. Oxford: Oxford University Press.

Struett, Michael J. 2008. *The Politics of Constructing the International Criminal Court: NGOs, Discourse, and Agency*. New York: Palgrave.

Tabak, Shana. 2011. "False Dichotomies of Transitional Justice: Gender, Conflict and Combatants in Colombia." *New York University Journal of International Law and Politics* 44(1): 103–163.

TFV (Trust Fund for Victims). n.d. "The Two Roles of the TFV: Reparations and General Assistance." The Hague: Trust Fund for Victims. Accessed April 7, 2014. http://www.trustfundforvictims.org/two-roles-tfv.

TFV (Trust Fund for Victims). 2010. *Recognizing Victims & Building Capacity in Transitional Societies: Spring 2010 Programme Progress Report*. The Hague: Trust Fund for Victims.

TFV (Trust Fund for Victims). 2011. *Situation in the Democratic Republic of the Congo in the Case of the Prosecutor v. Thomas Lubanga Dyilo: Public Redacted Version of ICC-01/04-01/06-2803-Conf-Exp-Trust Fund for Victims First Report on Reparations*. Trial Chamber 1, 1 September. ICC Doc. No. ICC-01/04-01/06.

TFV (Trust Fund for Victims). 2012. *Mobilising Resources and Supporting the Most Vulnerable Victims through Earmarked Funding: Programme Progress Report, Winter 2012*. The Hague: Trust Fund for Victims.

TFV (Trust Fund for Victims). 2013. "Financial Info." The Hague: Trust Fund for Victims. Accessed May 21, 2014. http://www.trustfundforvictims.org/financial-info.

TFV (Trust Fund for Victims). 2013. *Ferencz Family's Planethood Foundation Donates $50,000 To Trust Fund For Victims*. The Hague: Trust Fund for Victims. March 21. Accessed May 27, 2013. http://www.trustfundforvictims.org/news/ferencz-family's-planethood-foundation-donates-50000-trust-fund-victim.

TFV (Trust Fund for Victims). 2013. *G8 Leaders urge to Support TFV on Victims of Sexualised Violence*. The Hague: Trust Fund for Victims. April 11. Accessed

May 27, 2013. http://www.trustfundforvictims.org/news/g8-leaders-urge-support-tfv-victims-sexualised-violence.

TFV (Trust Fund for Victims). 2014. "Trust Fund for Victims receives over €5 million voluntary contributions in 2014." Press release, December 23. Accessed January 16, 2015. http://www.trustfundforvictims.org/news/trust-fund-victims-receives-over-%E2%82%AC5-million-voluntary-contributions-2014.

TFV (Trust Fund for Victims). 2014. *A Road to Recovery: Healing, Empowerment and Reconciliation: Programme Progress Report (Winter 2014), Support to Victim Survivors of Sexual and Gender-based Violence*. The Hague: Trust Fund for Victims.

TFV (Trust Fund for Victims). 2014. "At Global Summit to End Sexual Violence in Conflict, UK Foreign Secretary Hague announces £1 million contribution to TFV." The Hague: Trust Fund for Victims. Accessed September 20, 2014. http://www.trustfundforvictims.org/news/global-summit-end-sexual-violence-conflict-uk-foreign-secretary-hague-announces-%C2%A3-1-million-con.

Thelen, Kathleen. 2004. *How Institutions Evolve: The Political Economy of Skills in Germany, Britain, the United States, and Japan*. Cambridge: Cambridge University Press.

Tickner, J. Ann. 2001. *Gendering World Politics: Issues and Approaches in the Post-Cold War World*. New York: Columbia University Press.

Tohidi, Nayereh. 2003. "Women's Rights in the Muslim World: The Universal-Particular Interplay." *Hawwa: Journal of Women of the Middle East and the Islamic World* 1(2): 152–188.

Tomic, Alexandra. 2014. *Interview with the Chief of the Interpretation and Translation Section at the International Criminal Court*. Sydney: The University of New South Wales, April 23.

Törnquist-Chesnier, Marie. 2007. "How the International Criminal Court Came to Life: The Role of Non-governmental Organisations." *Global Society* 21(3): 449–465.

Tripp, Aili Mari, Myra Marx Ferree, and Christina Ewing, eds. 2013. *Gender, Violence and Human Security: Critical Feminist Perspectives*. New York: New York University Press.

True, Jacqui. 2010. "Mainstreaming Gender in International Relations." In *Gender Matters in Global Politics: A Feminist Introduction to International Relations*, edited by Laura J. Shepherd, 189–203. Abington: Routledge.

True, Jacqui. 2012. *The Political Economy of Violence Against Women*. Oxford: Oxford University Press.

UIA (Union Internationale des Avocats). 2012. UIA Activities at the UN-level. Paris: Union Internationale des Avocats. September 3. Accessed January 16, 2015. http://www.uianet.net/newsletter/documents/News02-2012-10-03-7-UIA-activities-on-the-UN-level.pdf.

UN (United Nations). 2005. *Basic Principles and Guidelines on the Right to a Remedy and Reparation for Victims of Gross Violations of International Human Rights Law and Serious Violations of International Humanitarian Law*. UN General Assembly Resolution 60/147. December 16.

UN GA (United Nations General Assembly). 1948. *Convention on the Prevention and Punishment of the Crime of Genocide*. Adopted by the General Assembly of the United Nations on 9 December 1949; entry into force on 12 January 1951, in accordance with Article 27(1).

UN GA (United Nations General Assembly). 1979. *Convention on the Elimination of All Forms of Discrimination against Women (CEDAW)*. Adopted and opened for signature, ratification and accession by General Assembly resolution 34/180 of 18 December 1979; entry into force 3 September 1981, in accordance with Article 27(1).

UN GA (United Nations General Assembly). 1984. *Convention against Torture and Other Cruel, Inhuman or Degrading Treatment or Punishment*. Adopted and opened for signature, ratification and accession by General Assembly resolution 39/46 of 10 December 1984; entry into force 26 June 1987, in accordance with Article 27(1).

UN GA (United Nations General Assembly). 1996. *Report of the Preparatory Committee on the Establishment of an International Criminal Court, Vol. II (Compilation of Proposals)*. Adopted by General Assembly at the 52st Session, Supplement No. 22. UN Doc A/51/22 (1996).

UN GA (United Nations General Assembly). 1998. *Rome Statute of the International Criminal Court*. Adopted by the United Nations Diplomatic Conference of Plenipotentiaries on the Establishment of an International Criminal Court on 17 July 1998, entry into Force July 1, 2002 (last amended 2010). UN Doc. A/CONF.183/9.

UN GA (United Nations General Assembly). 2005. *UN Basic Principles and Guidelines on the Right to a Remedy and Reparation for Victims of Gross Violations of International Human Rights Law and Serious Violations of International Humanitarian Law*. Adopted and proclaimed by the United Nations General Assembly resolution 60/147, 16 December. Accessed January 16, 2015. http://www.ohchr.org/EN/ProfessionalInterest/Pages/RemedyAndReparation.aspx.

United Nations News Centre. 2012. *UN Welcomes Charges Against Army Colonel Over Mass Rapes in Guinea*. February 10.

UNSC (United Nations Security Council). 1993. *Statute of the International Tribunal for the Prosecution of Persons Responsible for Serious Violations of International Humanitarian Law Committed in the Territory of the Former Yugoslavia since 1991*, U.N. Doc. S/25704 at 36, annex (1993) and S/25704/Add.1 (1993). Adopted by Security Council on 25 May, U.N. Doc. S/RES/827 (1993).

UNSC (United Nations Security Council). 1994. *Statute of the International Criminal Tribunal for the Prosecution of Persons Responsible for Genocide and Other Serious Violations of International Humanitarian Law Committed in the Territory of Rwanda and Rwandan Citizens Responsible for Genocide and Other such Violations Committed in the Territory of Neighbouring States, between January 1, 1994 and December 31, 1994*. Adopted by the Security Council on 8 November, UN Doc. S/RES/955 (1994).

UNSC (United Nations Security Council). 2005. *Resolution 1593 (2005)*. Adopted by the Security Council at its 5158th meeting, 31 March. UN Doc. S/RES/1593 (2005).

UNSC (United Nations Security Council). 2009. *Report of the International Commission of Inquiry Mandated to Establish the Facts and Circumstances of the Events of 28 September 2009 in Guinea* (S/2009/693).

UNSC (United Nations Security Council). 2013. *Resolution 2106(2013)*. Adopted by the Security Council at its 6984th meeting, 24 June. UN Doc. S/RES/2106 (2013).

UNSC (United Nations Security Council). 2013. *Resolution 2122 (2013)*. Adopted by the Security Council at its 7044th meeting, 18 October. UN Doc. S/RES/2122 (2013).

UNSC (United Nations Security Council). 2014. *Conflict-related Sexual Violence: Report of the Secretary General.* 13 March. UN Doc. S/2014/181.

UN Women. 2011. *Progress of the World's Women Report: In Pursuit of Justice.* New York: UN Women.

US Department of State. 2013. "G8 Foreign Ministers Meeting Statement." April 11, 2013. Washington, DC: US Department of State. Accessed May 27, 2013. http://iipdigital.usembassy.gov/st/english/texttrans/2013/0 4/20130411145583.html#axzz2QoECrdtY

Van den Wyngaert, Christine. 2012. "Victims Before International Criminal Courts: Some Views and Concerns of an ICC Trial Judge." *Case Western Reserve Journal of International* 44(1 and 2): 475–496.

Van Schaack, Beth. 2011. "The Crime of Aggression and Humanitarian Intervention on Behalf of Women." *International Criminal Law Review* 11(3): 477–493.

Vélez, Shiela. 2009. "Interview: Judge Odio Benito." In *The Lubanga Chronicles: The First Trial before the International Criminal Court.* August 27. Nottinghamshire: AEGIS Trust.

Vickers, Jill. 2013. "Is Federalism Gendered? Incorporating Gender into Federalism Studies." *Publius* 43(1): 1–23.

Vignoli, Maria Elena. 2015. "Reparations in Ituri: A long-awaited judgment." Beyond the Hague. March 4. Accessed March 13, 2015. http://beyondthehague.com/2015/03/04/reparations-in-ituri-a-long-awaited-judgment/

Viseur Sellers, Patricia. 2009. "Gender Strategy is Not a Luxury for International Courts." *American University Journal of Gender, Social Policy and the Law* 17(2): 301–326.

Waller, Emily, Emma Palmer, and Louise Chappell. 2014. "Strengthening Gender Justice in the Asia-Pacific through the Rome Statute." *Australian Journal of International Affairs* 68(3): 356–373.

Warbrick, Colin, Dominic McGoldrick, Christine Byron, and David Turns. 2001. "The Preparatory Commission for the International Criminal Court." *International and Comparative Law Quarterly* 50(2): 420–435.

Waylen, Georgina. 2007. *Engendering Transitions: Women's Mobilization, Institutions and Gender Outcomes.* Oxford, Oxford University Press.

Waylen, Georgina. 2011. "Gendered Institutional Analysis: Understanding Democratic Transitions." In *Gender, Politics and Institutions*, edited by Fiona Mackay and Mona L. Krook, 147–162. Basingstoke: Palgrave Macmillan.

WCGJ (Women's Caucus for Gender Justice). 1997. *Recommendations and Commentary for December 1997 PrepCom on the Establishment of an International Criminal Court, United Nations Headquarters, 1–12 December 1997.* New York: Women's Caucus for Gender Justice.

WCGJ (Women's Caucus for Gender Justice). 1997. "Action Alert International Justice for Women." Email to Caucus Members, November [original with author].

WCGJ (Women's Caucus for Gender Justice). 1998. Valerie Oosterveld—Canada, 3.

WCGJ (Women's Caucus for Gender Justice). 1998. *Gender Justice and the ICC.* United Nations Diplomatic Conference of Plenipotentiaries on the Establishment of an International Criminal Court, June 15–17 July, Rome, Italy. New York: Women's Caucus for Gender Justice.

WCGJ (Women's Caucus for Gender Justice). 1998. *Submission to the Standing Committee on Foreign Affairs and International Trade*. June 9 [original with author].
WCGJ (Women's Caucus for Gender Justice). 1998. *Recommendations and Commentary for the March 1998 PrepCom Composition and Administration of the Court*. March 18 [original with author].
WCGJ (Women's Caucus for Gender Justice). 1998. "Don't Miss this Historic Opportunity." Lobbying Document, March 10 [original with author].
WCGJ (Women's Caucus for Gender Justice). 1998b. "The Crime of Forced Pregnancy." New York: Women's Caucus for Gender Justice. Accessed October 2, 2002. http://www.iccwomen.org/icc/iccpc/rome.
WCRO (War Crimes Research Office). 2010. *The Case-Based Reparations Scheme at the International Criminal Court*. Washington, DC: War Crimes Research Office.
WCRO (War Crimes Research Office). 2010. *The Case-Based Reparations Scheme at the International Criminal Court*. Washington, DC: War Crimes Research Office. Accessed January 12, 2014. https://www.wcl.american.edu/warcrimes/icc/documents/report12.pdf.
Weldon, Laurel. 2002. *Protest, Policy and the Problem of Violence Against Women; A Cross-National Comparison*. Pittsburgh: University of Pittsburgh Press.
Whiting, Alex. 2015. "Despite Ups and Downs, the ICC is Here to Stay." *Justice in Conflict Blog*, January 8. Accessed January 9, 2015. http://justiceinconflict.org/2015/01/08/despite-ups-and-downs-the-icc-is-here-to-stay/#more-5715.
Whitworth, Sandra. 2008. "Feminism." In *The Oxford Handbook of International Relations*, edited by Christian Reus-Smit and Duncan Snidal, 391–407. Oxford: Oxford University Press.
Wierda, Marieke, and Pablo de Greiff. 2004. *Reparations and the International Criminal Court: A Prospective Role for the Trust Fund for Victims*. New York: International Center for Transitional Justice. Accessed May 27, 2013. http://ictj.org/sites/default/files/ICTJ-Global-ICC-TrustFund-2004-English.pdf.
Wiersing, Anja. 2012. "Lubanga and its Implications for Victims Seeking Reparations at the International Criminal Court." *Amsterdam Law Forum* 4(3): 21–39.
WIGJ (Women's Initiatives for Gender Justice). 2005. *Gender Report Card 2005*. The Hague: Women's Initiatives for Gender Justice.
WIGJ (Women's Initiatives for Gender Justice). 2006. *Gender Report Card 2006*. The Hague: Women's Initiatives for Gender Justice.
WIGJ (Women's Initiatives for Gender Justice). 2007. *Gender Report Card 2007*. The Hague: Women's Initiatives for Gender Justice.
WIGJ (Women's Initiatives for Gender Justice). 2008. *Gender Report Card 2008*. The Hague: Women's Initiatives for Gender Justice.
WIGJ (Women's Initiatives for Gender Justice). 2008. *Preliminary Dossier Profile of Judicial Candidates Election—January 2009*. November 10. Accessed January 14,2015.http://www.iccwomen.org/news/docs/Profile_of_Judicial_Candidates-Web_Final.pdf.
WIGJ (Women's Initiatives for Gender Justice). 2010. *Legal Filings: The Prosecutor v. Jean-Pierre Bemba Gombo and The Prosecutor v. Thomas Lubanga Dyilo*, 1st ed. February. The Hague: Women's Initiatives for Gender Justice.
WIGJ (Women's Initiatives for Gender Justice). 2010. *Report on the 10-year Review of the Rome Statue and the International Criminal Court*. 31 May–11 June. The

Hague: Women's Initiatives for Gender Justice. Accessed January 15, 2015. http://www.iccwomen.org/documents/RevConf2010-REPORT-v10.pdf.

WIGJ (Women's Initiatives for Gender Justice). 2011. *Gender Report Card 2011*. The Hague: Women's Initiatives for Gender Justice.

WIGJ (Women's Initiatives for Gender Justice). 2011. *Legal Eye on the ICC*. Newsletter, March. Accessed July 20, 2014. http://www.iccwomen.org/news/docs/LegalEye_Mar11/index.html.

WIGJ (Women's Initiatives for Gender Justice). 2012. *Legal Filings: The Prosecutor v. Jean-Pierre Bemba Gombo and The Prosecutor v. Thomas Lubanga Dyilo*, 2nd ed. August. The Hague: Women's Initiatives for Gender Justice.

WIGJ (Women's Initiatives for Gender Justice). 2012. *Gender Report Card 2012*. The Hague: Women's Initiatives for Gender Justice.

WIGJ (Women's Initiatives for Gender Justice). 2012. "Statement on the First Reparations Decision by the ICC." August 10, 2012. Accessed May 21, 2014. http://www.iccwomen.org/documents/Statement-on-Lubanga-Reparations-FINAL.pdf.

WIGJ (Women's Initiatives for Gender Justice). 2012. "First Sentencing Judgement by the ICC: The Prosecutor v. Thomas Lubanga Dyilo." Press Release, July 11. Accessed January 15, 2015. http://www.iccwomen.org/documents/Press-Statement-on-Lubanga-Sentencing.pdf.

WIGJ (Women's Initiatives for Gender Justice). 2013. *Gender Report Card 2013*. The Hague: Women's Initiatives for Gender Justice.

WIGJ (Women's Initiatives for Gender Justice). 2014. *Gender Report Card 2014*. The Hague: Women's Initiatives for Gender Justice.

WIGJ (Women's Initiatives for Gender Justice). 2014. *Statement of the Women's Initiatives for Gender Justice, Appeals Withdrawn by Prosecution and Defence, The Prosecutor v. Germain Katanga*. June 26. Accessed July 20, 2014. http://www.iccwomen.org/documents/Katanga-Appeals-Statement.pdf.

WIGJ (Women's Initiatives for Gender Justice). 2015. "ICC issues first appeal judgment on reparations *The Prosecutor v. Thomas Lubanga Dyilo*." March 3. Accessed March 13, 2015. http://www.iccwomen.org/documents/ICC-issues-first-appeal-judgment-on-reparations_Lubanga.pdf

Williams, Susan. 2012. "Customary Law, Constitutional Law, and Women's Equality." Conference paper presented at the Conference on En/Gendering Governance: From the Local to the Global, Australian National University, Canberra, Australia, August 6.

Yates, Pamela, director. 2009. *The Reckoning* [Film]. Brooklyn, NY: Skylight Pictures.

Young, Iris M. 1990. *Justice and the Politics of Difference*. Princeton, NJ: Princeton University Press.

Zwingel, Susanne. 2005. "From Intergovernmental Negotiations to (Sub)national Change." *International Feminist Journal of Politics* 7(3): 400–424.

INDEX

Abusharaf, Adila, 55
Affirmative remedies, 227n
Aggression
    definition, 217n
    Rome Statue, 220n
Akayesu case, 57
    evidence-gathering, lack, 99
    rape as genocide, 93, 94, 100–101, 110, 118, 218n, 220n
Aluoch, Judge Joyce, 67
Amann, Diane, 108
Ambos, Kai, 113, 116
Amicus curiae submissions, 60, 63, 69, 79, 81t, 112, 118
Amnesty International
    on Colombia, 173, 177, 178
    on complementarity, 169
    on Guinea, 178
    on *Lubanga*, 111
    on Rome Statute, 111, 182–183
Androcentrism, 88–91, 126
    definition, 6, 88–89
    effects, 90–91
    Fraser, Nancy on, 7–8, 37, 88–89
Arbia, Registrar Silvana, 71–72, 82, 84
Askin, Kelly, 38, 67
Atiba-Davies, Gloria, 72, 77
Azari, Julia, 12

Barnett, Michael, 20, 21, 204
Basic Principles, 133–134, 138
Bedont, Barbara, 47, 63, 87, 98
Beijing Platform for Action (1995), 97
Bemba case, 104, 117–119
    cumulative charges, 125
    gender expertise, courtroom, 69
    misrecognition, 122–123
    sexual violence against men, 122–123
    victims recognized, 219n
    victims representation, 69, 70
Bensouda, Fatou, 221n
    appointment, significant, 194
    on Boko Haram's kidnapping, 180
    as Chief Prosecutor, 82
    on complementarity, 178, 179, 188–189
    on Darfur, 200
    on gender expertise, nonjudicial, 72, 73–74
    Guinea missions, 172
    on ICC as backup system, 164
    Policy Paper on Sexual and Gender-Based Crimes, 124–126, 129, 180, 204
    on post-Westphalian state, 163
    prosecution failures, 106–107
    recommitment to gender justice, 124–125
    revision of OTP practices, 129
Bias, gender. *See* Gender bias
Blattmann, Judge Réné, on *Lubanga*, 112, 113
    majority opinion, 113–114
    reparations, 146
Bodansky, Daniel, 19, 20, 23
Boko Haram kidnappings, 180
Buchanan, Allen, 19, 20–21, 203
Buss, Doris, 89

Cahn, Naomi, 134
Campbell, John, 11
Case definition
	Appeals Chamber, 170
	pre-Trial chamber, 170
Case load, ICC 2014, 219n
Celebici case, 57
Central African Republic
	Bemba case, 117–119 (*See also* Bemba case)
	TFV assistance, 152, 224n
	victim representation, 76–77, 76f
Chappell, Louise
	on Colombia, 176
	on critical friends, 9
	on Gbagbo case, 124
	on Guinea, 227n
	on legislation, 183–185, 183f, 184f
	on preliminary examinations, OTP, 172
Charlesworth, Hilary, 9, 25, 187, 196
Circumcisions, forced male, 108, 123, 196
Cleary, Katherine, 150–151
Coalition of the ICC (CICC), 24, 35, 70
Colombia, 26
	action, ability, and willingness, 174, 176–179
	"Justice and Peace Law," 176–178
	preliminary examinations, 172–174
	Rome Statute ratification, 226n
Compensation, redistribution, 133–134. *See also* Redistribution
Complementarity (principle), 4, 40, 160–189, 193, 196
	formal rules, 161–162
	fundamentals, 160–161
	legislating for gender justice, 181–186, 183f, 184f (*See also* Legislation, gender justice)
	negotiating, 165–169
	nestedness, 161, 186–189
	post-Westhalian frame, 162–165, 186, 189, 199
	priorities, rules, and enforcement, 181t
	rebundling upward, 163–164
	Stahn and El Zeidy on, 225n
	state prosecutions, ability, 165, 168, 171, 188
	state prosecutions, invitation to ICC, 226n
	state prosecutions, responsibility, 160
	state prosecutions, unwillingness, 165–166, 168, 171, 188, 225n–226n
	two-step admissibility test, 167–168
Complementarity (principle), in practice, 169–181
	Colombia, 176–179, 226n
	fundamentals, 169–170
	jurisprudence and new avenues, 170–171
	"locking in" efforts, 179–181
	preliminary examinations, 172
	shadow side, 169–170
	silences, 169–171
Congo. *See* Democratic Republic of Congo
Constituency classifications, 202–203
Constructive ambiguity, 3, 65, 195
	definition and effect, 15
	gender definition, 47
	gender justice actors, 16
	recognition provisions, 103
	reform with, 18
	victim's participatory rights, 143
Convention on the Elimination of all Forms of Discrimination against Women (CEDAW), UN, 97, 136, 200
Copelon, Rhonda
	on crimes against humanity, 102
	on gender expertise, 59, 69–70
	on rape and sexual violence as war crime, 94–95
	on Rome Caucus, 42, 44
	on Rome Statute, 48
Côte d'Ivorie, 76f, 123–124
Court, sex- and gender-balanced, 65–81, 218n
	gender expertise, 63–65, 68–76, 194, 218n (*See also* Gender expertise)
	misrepresentation legacies, 65–66
	sex representation, judicial, 66–68, 66f, 67f, 218n

sex representation, nonjudicial,
    71–72, 71f
victim representation, 57–58, 62,
    76–81 (*See also* Victim
    representation)
Creative spaces, institutional, 15, 18
Crimes against humanity. *See also
    specific types*
  Copelon, Rhonda on, 102
  enforced pregnancy, 32
  recognition, 96–97, 102
  sexual slavery, 32, 105, 106f, 107f
  Women's Caucus for Gender Justice
    on, 96–97, 102
Criminal responsibility, 98–99
Critical friends, 9, 44
Cumulative charges, 125

Danner, Allison, 163–164
Darfur, 76f, 77, 200
De Brouwer, Anne-Marie, 132–133, 141
*Declaration on Preventing Sexual Violence
    in Conflict*, 152–153
de Gurmendi, Judge Fernández, 67
Democratic Republic of Congo, 26. *See
    also specific cases*
  Katanga, 25–26, 104, 119–121 (*See
    also* Katanga case)
  Lubanga (*See* Lubanga case)
  Mbarushimana, 122
  Open Society Foundations, 151
  reparations, Trial Chamber
    principles, 147
  reparations, Trust Fund for Victims
    assistance, 152, 153, 155
  victim gender, 219n
  victim representation, 76f, 77
Discrimination, 97–98
Distribution (resources). *See also*
    Maldistribution; Redistribution
    (gender and gender justice)
  fair, 88
Distributive injustice, 132
Dixon, Rosalind, 55
Double jeopardy, 217n
Duggan, Colleen, 55–56
Dyilo, Thomas Lubanga, 104, 143, 145,
    220n. *See also Lubanga* case
Dynamic legitimacy model, Schiff's,
    20–23, 203

Elements of Crime Annex, 31
El Zeidy, Mohamed, 225n
Enforced pregnancy
  Colombia, 176–177
  crimes against humanity, 32
  domestic legislation, states with,
    183f, 184, 184f
  recognition failure, 97, 226n
  Rome Statute, 101
Epistemic actors, external, 21
Evidence gathering, 99
  in *Akayesu*, 99
  gender-sensitive, 102
  in *Lubanga*, 112–113
  as recognition, 99
Expertise. *See specific types and cases*
External epistemic actors, 21

Facio, Alda, 45, 47
Feminist institutionalism, 17–18,
    194–201. *See also specific topics*
  formal rules, 192, 195–197
  nestedness, spatial, 199–201
  nestedness, temporal, 197–199
Ferstman, Carla, 134, 139
Finnemore, Martha, 19, 20, 21, 204
Fioretos, Orfeo, 11
Formal institutions, 12–13, 217n
Formal rules, 192, 195–197
  complementarity principle,
    161–162
  past practices and legacies, 13
  sexual violence, 93
Franke, Katherine, 30
Fraser, Nancy, 4. *See also specific topics*
  on androcentrism, 7–8, 37, 88–89
  on gender as process, 7–8
  on maldistribution, 130, 131–132
    (*See also* Maldistribution;
    Redistribution)
  on misrecognition, 87, 88–89
  on post-Westphalian state, 7, 40,
    199
  on post-Westphalian state,
    complementarity, 162–165,
    186, 189
  on representation, 88
  on resource distribution, 88
  symbolic frame, 53
  on transformative responses, 6–7

Fraser, Nancy (*continued*)
trivalent model of justice, 4, 5–8, 51, 191–194 (*See also* Trivalent model of justice)
on what *vs.* who and how of justice, 7, 53
Friend of the court (*amicus curiae*) submissions, 60, 63, 69, 79, 81t, 112, 118
Fulford, Judge Adrian, on *Lubanga*
majority opinion, 113–114
reparations, 146

Gaddafi case, 171, 188, 226n
Gatens, Moira, 8
Gbagbo, Simone, 123–124
Gender. *See also specific topics*
definition, debate, 44–47, 217n
institutional norms and practices, 18
as process, 7–8
Gender and Children's Office of the Prosecutor, 72, 77
Gender-balanced court. *See* Court, sex- and gender-balanced
Gender balance, *vs.* quota, 61–62
Gender bias, 25. *See also specific types*
international criminal law, 38, 41
law, 37–38
legal investigation and trial conduct, 39
misrecognition of substantive crimes, 36–39, 41
removing, 5
underenforcement of law, 39
Gender capture, 5, 36–37, 41, 54–55
Gender expertise, 194
Bemba, 69
Copelon, Rhonda on, 59, 69–70
courtroom, external, 69–71
gaps, 85
issues, 63–65
judicial, 63, 68–69, 68f, 199
judicial selection procedures, 61
legitimacy and value, 99
Lubanga, 114–117
Registry staff, 62, 102–103
representation, 82–83, 102–103
Gender expertise, nonjudicial, 72–76, 194

Bensouda, Fatou on, 72, 73–74
gaps, 75
Gender and Children's Office of the Prosecutor, 72–73
ICC Court Office of Public Counsel for Victims, 75
Ocampo, Luis Moreno on, 72–73
Outreach Unit, 74–75
sexual violence trauma, 74
Victims' Participation and Reparation Section, 74
Gender justice, 3, 4. *See also specific topics*
critiques of legal approach, 8–9
definition, 5–10
Fraser, Nancy on, 5–8 (*See also* Trivalent model of justice)
Goetz, Anne Marie on, 5
ICC mandate, implementation, 24
Jenkins, Rob on, 5
legitimacy, ICC, and, 47–50
Molyneux, Maxine on, 5
Nussbaum, Martha on, 5
Phillips, Anne on, 5
redistribution, 5–6, 23
representation equality, 5, 59–60
Young, Iris Marion on, 5
Gender politics, 3–4
Gender recognition. *See* Recognition
Gender Report Cards, 75, 79, 112, 196
Gender sensitivity
evidence gathering, 102
investigation, 99, 102
men, 57
procedures, 58
representation equality, 59–60
TFV assistance, 158
Geneva Conventions, gender bias, 38
Genocide, rape and sexual violence as, 93, 94, 100–101, 110, 118, 218n, 220n
Goetz, Anne Marie, 5, 37–38
Gombo, Jean-Pierre Bemba. *See Bemba* case
Goodin, Bob, 13
Grey, Rosemary, 26, 104–110, 221n
on Gbagbo case, 124
on legislation, 183–185, 183f, 184f
on preliminary examinations, 172

on prosecutorial discretion, 104–105
on prosecutor's lack of success, 105–110, 105f–107f
Grossman, Nienke, 55, 56
Guarantees of nonrepetition, 134–135
Guinea, 26
    action, ability, and willingness, 174–176
    preliminary examinations, 172–174, 227n

Hague, William, 152–153
Halley, Janet, 48–49
Hall-Martinez, Katherine, 63, 87, 98
Hayes, Niamh, 109
Haynes, Dina, 134
Heller, Kevin Jon, 170
Helmke, Gretchen, 12
Higgins, Dame Roslyn, 59
Historical institutionalism, 11
Holy See
    on enforced pregnancy, 95–96
    on gender definition, 44
    on gender rights, 97–98
    in Rome Statute negotiations, 42–43
How, gender justice, 7, 53–58
    female judges, 55, 194
    female personnel and victims, 53–57, 194
    feminist-inspired judicial officers, 56
    feminist judicial interventions, 56–57
    Fraser, Nancy on, 7, 53
    Fraser, Nancy, on representation and equal voice, 53
    gender-sensitive men, 57
    gender-sensitive procedures, 58
    Grossman, Nienke on judging, 55
    Kenney, Sally, on feminist-inspired judicial officers, 56
    Kenney, Sally, on gender capture, 54–55
    Phillips, Anne's politics of presence, 53–54
    Puwar, Nirmal's "space invaders," 54, 85
    restorative justice measures, 57–58
    Sellers, Patricia Viseur on, 56–57
    sociological legitimacy, 55–56
    underrepresentation and exclusion, 55–56
    victim representation, 57–58, 77–81, 81t, 83 (*See also* Victim representation)
How, victims, 83

Inder, Brigid, 1, 49
    on blind spots, 198
    on complementarity, 179
    dual position, 128
    on gender expertise, nonjudicial, 75
    on *Muthaura and Kenyatta*, 123
    as Prosecutor's Special Adviser on Gender Crimes, 73–74, 218n
Informal institutions, 12–13
Informal rules, 10, 11, 13, 37b, 197, 198. *See also specific rules*
    complementarity, 168–169, 187
    formal rules interaction, 13
    historical gendering, 36–37
    legacies, gender, 3, 13, 198
    power and persistence, 14
    "remembering the old," 15, 103
    reparations, 144–145
    research, 25, 36
    temporal nestedness, 197
    Waylen, Georgina on, 16, 18, 198
Institutional change, 15–16
Institutional design, 13–14
Institutionalism. *See also specific types*
    historical, 11
Institutional nestedness, 3, 13–15. *See also* Nestedness; *specific institutions*
    design, 29, 186
    design, complementarity and, 186
    feminist institutionalism, 197–201
Institutions. *See also specific types*
    Campbell, John on, 11
    hangovers, 13
    Ostrom, Elinor on, 11
International Center for Research on Women Trust Fund for Victims evaluation report, 153–154

International Criminal Court (ICC).
    *See also specific cases and topics;
    specific topics*
  design features, 30–34
  founding, 30
  gender justice constituency, 4
  historical feminist institutional
      view, 10–18
  jurisdiction, 30–31
  legacies, gender, 36–38, 37b
  legitimacy, 4, 21–22, 47–50
  Like Minded Group, 35, 36
  nestedness, 29
  nestedness, spatial, 27–29, 40–41
  organs, 31
  post–Cold War epoch, 34–35
  propio motu provision, 30–31
  prosecution record, 2
  reference materials, 24
  right to rule, 4
  Rome Statute (*See* Rome Statute)
  in time, 34–39
International criminal law
  legacies, 36–38, 37b (*See also*
      Legacies (gender))
  nonsexual violations, 39
  sexual violence, 38 (*See also* Sexual
      violence)
International Criminal Tribunal for
    Rwanda (ICTR)
  backroom deals, 64
  criminal tribunal, 2, 30, 31
  enforced pregnancy, 95, 96
  vs. national courts, primacy, 163
  problems of, averting, 59–60, 62
  senior command culpability, 98
  sexual violence, as genocide, 100,
      118, 218n, 220n
  sexual violence, as war crime, 94
  sexual violence, formal rules, 93
  sexual violence, testimony failure,
      99
  victims' experiences, response, 135
International Criminal Tribunal for
    Yugoslavia (ICTY)
  backroom deals, 64
  criminal tribunal, 2, 30, 31
  enforced pregnancy, 95, 96
  vs. national courts, primacy, 163
  problems of, averting, 59–60, 62

  senior command culpability, 98
  sexual violence, 93, 94
  victims' experiences, response, 135
International feminist legal project,
    critiques, 8–9
*International Protocol on the
    Investigation and Documentation
    of Rape and Sexual Violence in
    Conflict*, 200
Interpretation services, 63, 80

Jenkins, Rob, 5
Jolie, Angelina, 153
Judges, ICC
  female, 55, 194
  feminist, 56
  gender balance, 60–61, 218n
  gender expertise, 63
  total number, 218n
Judges, ICC elections, 208t–215t
  2003, February, 208t
  2006, January, 209t
  2007, December, 210t
  2009, January, 211t
  2009, November, 212t
  2011, December, 213t–214t
  2013, November, 214t–215t
Judicial officers, feminist-inspired, 56

Katanga case, 25–26, 104, 119–121
  guilt and acquittal, 105, 119–121
  legacies, gender, 154
  reparations, 149–150, 155
  Women's Initiatives on, 121, 128
Katanga, Germain, 105, 119
Katzenstein, Mary, 9
Kendall, Sara, 57
Kenney, Sally, 54–56
Kenya, victim gender, 219n
Keohane, Robert, 19, 20–21, 203
Keynesian-Westphalian state, 7
Kleffner, Jann, 164
Koomen, Jonneke, 80

Leach, Steve, 13
Legacies (gender), 3. *See also specific
    topics*
  formal rules, 192, 195–197
  informal rules, 198 (*See also*
      Informal rules)

[266] *Index*

international law, 36–38, 37b
Lubanga and *Katanga*, 154
maldistribution, 36
misrecognition, 36, 126–129
misrepresentation, 36, 65–66
nestedness, spatial, 199–201
nestedness, temporal, 197–199
reparations, 155–156
representation, 84
Legislation, gender justice,
    181–186
  Chappell, Louise and Grey,
    Rosemary's analysis,
    183–185, 183f, 184f
  flawed, 183
  rape crimes limitations, 184–185
  Rome Statute provisions,
    181–182
  sex and gender expertise, 82–83
  states', 182
  states' responses, 182–183
Legitimacy, 19–23
  accountability and constituencies,
    21–22
  Barnett, Michael and Finnemore,
    Martha on, 20, 21
  Bodansky, Daniel on, 19, 20, 23
  Buchanan, Allen and Keohane,
    Robert on, 19, 20–21, 203
  complementarity, 187–189
  consequential, 23, 86, 129, 131,
    158, 189
  constituency classifications,
    202–203
  definitions, 19
  design, 23
  dynamic model, 20–23, 191, 203
  external epistemic actors, 21
  feminist institutionalism, 118
  Finnemore, Martha and Toope,
    Stephen on, 19
  gender expertise in *Lubanga*,
    misrecognition, 114–117
  gender experts and women, 91, 92,
    99
  gender justice advocates'
    assessments, 203
  gender justice, ICC, and, 47–50,
    201–205, 206
  gender justice measures, 103
  gender justice record, ICC, 4, 26, 28
  importance, 19
  international organizations, 12
  international *vs.* national, 21
  vs. justice, 20
  legacies, 126–129
  male dominance, 51, 52
  misrecognition, 128–129
  nestedness, rules and, 186–189
  normative, 19
  operational, 22–23, 131, 157, 161,
    203
  perceptions, 19
  recognition, 88
  reparations mandates, 156–158
  representative gender justice, 52,
    55, 58, 61, 84–86, 91
  revisability, 16, 21
  revisions, willingness for, 202
  Rome Statute, constituencies on,
    29, 47
  Schiff, Benjamin on, 20–23, 191,
    202
  sociological, 19, 55–56
  sustainability, 204
Levitsky, Steven, 12
Liability challenge mode, 109
Liability modes, 98–99, 102
Like Minded Group, 35, 36
Locking in, 3, 14, 190
  complementarity, 179–181
  new rules, difficulties, 85
  redistribution, TFV assistance,
    156
  representation, 52
Locking out (lockout), 3, 13–14, 190
  gender reforms, 18
  redistribution claims, 156
  representation, 52
Lowndes, Vivien, 13, 14, 15
Lubanga case, 25–26, 104, 110–117
  gender expertise, courtroom, 69
  gender-inclusive approach, Trial
    Chamber, 158
  legacies, gender, 116–117, 154
  misrecognition, gender, 110–114
  misrecognition, gender expertise,
    114–117
  Ocampo, Luis Moreno on, 109, 111,
    112–113

Lubanga case (*continued*)
  Odio Benito dissent, 113, 114–115, 128
  Odio Benito on sexual violence, 114–116
  sentencing decision, 113–114
  sexual violence against men, 123
  sexual violence charges, confirmation, 222n
  summary, 110
  Women's Initiatives appeal, 112
  Women's Initiatives submissions, 69
Lubanga reparations, 144, 145–150
  appeals, 148
  Appeals Chamber, determination, 148–149
  Appeals Chamber, principles, 144
  beneficiaries, 158–159
  damage, loss and injury, 147
  decision making, delays, and TFV, 150–151
  Katanga implications, 149–150
  redistributive outcomes, 155
  Trial Chamber principles, 145–147, 150
  Trust Fund for Victims submission, 145–146, 151, 223n
  Women's Initiatives submissions, 145–146, 223n

MacKinnon, Catharine, 39, 73
Mahoney, James, 15
Maldistribution, 6, 36, 87, 129, 130–150. *See also* Redistribution (gender and gender justice)
  addressing, 130, 145, 156
  formal provisions, 187
  Fraser, Nancy on, 131–132
  gendered, 132
  legacies, gender, 36
  misrecognition and misrepresentation, 133
  post-Westphalian, 162
  reparations, 130, 145, 156
  resource, 131
  sexual violence, conflict-related, 142
  structural, 131
  transformative strategies, 191
  True, Jacqui, 132

  Trust Fund for Victims, 130, 155, 156
  violence against women, 132
Male capture, challenge to, 194
Male victims of sexual violence, 90
Manjoo, Rashida, 134
Mbarushimana, Callixte, 122
McCarthy, Conor, 137, 138, 141–142
McDonald, Judge Gabrielle Kirk, 57
McKay, Fiona, 3, 9, 11, 15–17, 28, 29, 36, 53, 71, 85, 161, 197, 217
Mégret, Frédéric, 134, 136–137, 157
Misrecognition (gender), 6, 87, 88–89. *See also* Recognition (gender, gender justice)
  aims, 89
  androcentrism, 88–91
  Bemba, 117–119 (*See also Bemba* case)
  definition, 89
  harms, 89
  Katanga, 119–121 (*See also Katanga* case)
  legacies, 36, 126–129
  legitimacy, 128–129
  Lubanga, 110–117 (*See also Lubanga* case)
  Lubanga, gender expertise legitimacy, 114–117
  prosecution and charging strategy, 103–104
  sexual violence against men, 122–123
  substantive crimes against women, 36–39, 41
Misrepresentation, 36. *See also* Representation
  conditions, 53
  legacies, 36, 65–66
Moffett, Luke, 140
Molyneux, Maxine, 5
Mouthann, Solange, 109
Muthaura and Kenyatta case
  charge confirmation, 222n
  male forced circumcisions, 108
  sexual violence against men, 123

Nairobi Declaration on Women's and Girls' Right to a Remedy and Reparation, 135, 138, 141, 146, 200

Nestedness
  complementarity, rules, and legitimacy, 186–189
  Mackay, Fiona, 161
  sovereignty, 160
Nestedness, institutional, 3, 13–15
  design, 29, 186
  feminist institutionalism, 197–201
Nestedness, spatial, 13–14, 186
  complementarity, 161
  feminist institutionalism, 199–201
  International Criminal Court, 27–29, 40–41
Nestedness, temporal, 13, 34–39
  complementarity, 161
  feminist institutionalism, 197–199
  informal rules, 197
Nested newness, 14
  Mackay, Fiona, 15–17
New institutionalism, 10–11, 13–14, 17, 40, 195
Ngudjolo Chui, Mathieu (Ngudjolo)
  acquittal, 105, 222n
Ní Aoláin, Fionnuala, 89, 134
Nonrepetition, guarantees, 134–135
Nouwen, Sarah, 57, 164
Ntaganda, Bosco, 116
Nussbaum, Martha, 5

Ocampo, Luis Moreno, 221n
  on gender expertise, nonjudicial, 72–73
  on ICC purpose, 164
  on preliminary examination phase, 172
  on prosecution failure, 106–107, 109
Odio Benito, Judge Elizabeth, 57
  on *Lubanga*, dissent from decision, 113, 114–115, 128
  on *Lubanga*, evidence gathering, 112–113
  on *Lubanga*, reparations, 146
  on *Lubanga*, sexual violence, 114–116
  on *Lubanga*, Women's Initiatives appeal, 112
  personal backlash against, 91, 198
  on rape as torture, 93
  on Rome Statute responsibilities, 115

Office of Public Counsel for Victims (OPCV), ICC, 79–80
Office of the Prosecutor (OTP)
  on Colombia, 178
  on complementarity, 160, 180, 187, 189
  gender policies, 156, 189
  Policy Paper on Sexual and Gender-Based Crimes, 2014, 124–126, 129, 180, 204
  victim representation, 77–78
Oosterveld, Valerie, 42, 44
  on *Bemba* case, 118, 119
  on complementarity negotiations, 166–167
  on constructive ambiguities, 195
  on gender balance *vs.* quota, 61
  on gender definition, 44, 47
  on gender in Rome Statute, 45
  on representation equality for gender sensitivity, 59–60
OPCV. *See* Office of Public Counsel for Victims (OPCV), ICC
Open Society Foundations, 151
Ostrom, Elinor, 11
Outreach Unit, 74–75, 78–79
Ozaki, Judge Kuniko, 67

Pena, Mariana, 147
Penile amputations, 123, 196
Perdomo, Claudia, 75, 78–79, 84
Persecution, 97
Phillips, Anne, 53–54
  on gender justice, 5
  on impartiality and judging gender justice, 91
  on inclusion of all views, 99
Pierson, Paul, 13–14
Pillay, Justice Navi, 57
  on rape as genocide, 93, 100, 218n
Policy Paper on Sexual and Gender-Based Crimes, 124–126, 129, 180, 204
Politics
  gender, 3–4
  of presence, 54
Post-Westphalian state, 7, 40, 199
  complementarity, 162–165, 186, 189
Poverty, and sexual violence against women, 132

Pregnancy, enforced
  Colombia, 176–177
  crimes against humanity, 32
  Holy See, 95–96
  opposition, 95–96
  recognition, 95–96, 101–102, 170–171
  recognition failure, 97, 226n
  Rome Statute, 101
  states with domestic legislation, 183f, 184, 184f
Prosecution, gender and sexual crimes, 104–110, 126–127, 126t. *See also* State prosecutions
  Grey, Rosemary on, 104–110, 105f–107f, 221n
  liability challenge mode, 110
  misrecognition, 104, 105f, 126–127, 126t (*See also* Misrecognition)
  prosecutorial discretion, 104–105
  range of crimes, limited, 106–107, 106f, 107f, 221n
  responsibility, 110
  reverberations, 109
  scope, 108–109
  success, lack, 105–108, 105f
Prosecutor's Special Adviser on Gender Crimes, 73
Puwar, Nirmal, 54, 85

Quota *vs.* gender balance, 61–62

Rape, 196. *See also* Sexual slavery
  as crime, limitations, 184–185
  as genocide, *Akayesu*, 93, 94, 100–101, 110, 118, 220n
  as genocide, Pillay on, 93, 100, 218n
  as torture, Odio Benito on, 93
  as war crime, 94–95
Rape victims
  as privileged subjects, 9
  prosecution failure, 107–108, 196, 201
Recognition (gender, gender justice), 2, 23, 32, 33b, 87–129, 219n. *See also* Misrecognition (gender); Trivalent model of justice
  androcentrism, 88–91, 126 (*See also* Androcentrism)
  application, 87

Bemba, 117–119 (*See also Bemba* case)
crimes against humanity, 96–97, 102
criminalization, 87
criminal responsibility, 98–99
definition, 6
designing rules, 92–103
discrimination, 97–98
enforced pregnancy, 95–96, 101–102, 170–171
evidence gathering, 99
female perpetrators, 123–124
gender experts, 99, 102–103
gender recognition rules, 100–103
genocide, rape as, 93, 94, 100–101, 110, 118, 218n, 220n
identity, 5–6
implementation, 193
investigations, gender-sensitive, 99, 102
Katanga, 119–121
legacies, 126–129
legitimacy, women, 99
liability and criminal responsibility, 98–99, 102
Lubanga misrecognition, 110–117 (*See also Lubanga* case)
male victims of sexual violence, 90
negotiations, 92–93
as path, 88–92
priorities, rules, and enforcement, 126t
prosecuting gender and sexual crimes, 104–110 (*See also* Prosecution, gender and sexual crimes)
redistribution, 193
remembering and forgetting, 103–126, 198
remembering existing legal standards, 99–100
representation, 193
revisability, 124–126, 126t
right and ability to adjudicate, 90–91
Rome Statute, 32, 33b, 87, 219n
rules, 100–103
sexual slavery, 151–152, 170–171
status subordination, 89, 90

[270] *Index*

war crimes, 94–96, 101
women as agents of war and
   conflict, 90
women judge and gender expert
   legitimacy, 91
Redistribution (gender and gender
   justice), 2, 5–6, 130–150. *See also*
   Trivalent model of justice
  complementarity, 193
  focus, 6
  at ICC, forging path, 142–143
  implementation, 193
  locked out claims and locked in
     assistance, 156
  maldistribution, 130, 131–132
  outcomes, 155–156, 158–159
  recognition, 193
  reparations, framework, 135–137
     (*See also* Reparations)
  reparations, *Lubanga*, 145–150, 158
  reparations, rules, 130, 137–145
     (*See also* Reparations rules)
  Rome Statute, 32, 33, 33b
  sexual violence, 131–135 (*See also*
     Sexual violence against
     women, redistributive gender
     justice)
  state actions, 158–159
  Trust Fund for Victims, 150–155
     (*See also* Trust Fund for
     Victims (TFV))
  victims' provisions, 135
REDRESS, 24
  on charging strategy, 149
  on *Lubanga*, 111, 157, 158, 222n
  on reparations, 139, 144, 157
  on restorative justice system, 158
  on victims, 83
  on victims' redistribution
     provisions, 135
Redress, victims', 2
Registry, 25, 31, 33b, 194
  "Call for African Women Lawyers"
     campaign, 71–72
  financial strain, 84
  gender expertise, nonjudicial, 72
  gender expertise, staff, 62, 102–103
  male and female staff percentages,
     71f, 199
  nonjudicial sex representation, 71

Office of Public Counsel for Victims
   (OPCV), ICC (*See* Office of
   Public Counsel for Victims
   (OPCV), ICC)
  Outreach Unit (*See* Outreach Unit)
  understaffing, 79
  victim protection, 194
  Victims and Witnesses Unit (*See*
     Victims and Witnesses Unit
     (VWU))
  women's representation, 71
Rehabilitation, redistribution in,
   133–134
"Remembering the old and forgetting
   the new," 15, 110, 127, 198
  Mackay, Fiona, 15, 197
Reparations, 31, 33, 223n. *See also*
   Restorative justice
  framework, 135–137
  Katanga, 149–150
  legacies, 155–156
  legitimacy, 156–158
  Lubanga, 144, 145–150 (*See also*
     Lubanga reparations)
  nonrepetition guarantees, 134–135
  recognition, 193
  sexual violence, international
     criminal law, 38
  transformative measures, 134, 136,
     138, 204–205
  victims' eligibility, 138–139
  Women's caucus priorities, 154,
     155t, 223n
Reparations rules, 130, 137–145
  interpreting, 143–145
  negotiations, 137
  principles and orders, 138–140
  Trust Fund for Victims, 140–142,
     224n
Representation (gender), 2, 5, 23. *See
   also* Trivalent model of justice
  definition, 6
  equality, 5, 88
  equality, for gender sensitivity, 59–60
  implementation, 192
  recognition, 193
  Rome Statute, 32, 33b
Representation (gender justice), 51–86
  "fair," 62, 63, 65
  gaps and counter-trend, 65

Index [271]

Representation (*continued*)
   legitimacy, 84–86
   locking in, 52
   locking out, 52
   resources and legacies, 83–84
   senior positions success, 52
   sex- and gender-balanced court, 65–81 (*See also* Court, sex- and gender-balanced)
   sex- and gender-expertise representation, 62–65, 82–83
   who and how, gender justice, 53–58
   who and how, victims, 83
Representation rules (gender), 62–65
   amicus curiae submissions, 60, 63, 69
   designing, 59–62
   interpretation and translation services, 63
   judiciary selection, 64
   successes, 64–65
   victim and witness protection, 63
   victim participation ambiguities, 64
Representation, victim. *See* Victim representation
Republic of Congo trial, 170
Resources, gender representation, 83–84
Responsibility, criminal, 98–99
Restitution, redistribution and, 133–134
Restorative justice, 57–58, 223n. *See also* Reparations
Retributive justice, 223n
Revisability, 16, 28, 86, 124–126, 191
   legitimacy, 21, 204
   Policy Paper on Sexual and Gender-Based Crimes, 124–126, 129, 180, 204
Right to rule, 4
Riker, William, 13
Roberts, Mark, 14
Robustness, 16
Rome Statute, 1. *See also specific topics*
   accountability, 30
   formal institution, 12
   Franke, Katherine on, 30
   ICC jurisdiction, 30–31

   implementation, 2, 193–194
   importance and functions, 1
   magnitude, 34
   new policies and procedures, 16
   operational phase, 48–49, 203
   origins, 1–2, 30
   propio motu provision, 30–31
   representation, recognition, and redistribution, 32, 33b
   restorative measures, 33
   Schiff, Benjamin on, 34
   Struett, Michael on, 34
   successes, 2
   victim-centered restorative justice paradigm, 31
   women in, 8
Rome Statute design
   contenders, 42–44
   contesting gender definition, 44–47
Rome Statute implementation failure, 201
   Amnesty International on, 182–183
   embeddedness, 193
   gender justice mandate, 24
   recognition/misrecognition and, 103–104, 193
   redistribution and, 193
   representation and, 192
Rule makers, male dominance, 37
Rules of Procedure and Evidence, 31
Rwanda, 133

Sá Couto, Susana, 150–151
Schiff, Benjamin
   on ICC and Rome Statute, 34
   on legitimacy, 20–23, 191, 202
   on tribunals, lessons, 35
Sellers, Patricia Viseur, 56–57, 72
   on *Bemba*, 118
   on complementarity, 188
   personal backlash against, 91
Sensitivity, gender, 57–60, 99, 102, 158. *See also* Gender sensitivity
Sex-balanced court. *See* Court, sex- and gender-balanced
Sex expertise. *See also* Gender expertise
   legislation, 82–83
   representation, 62–65, 82–83
Sex representation. *See also* Representation (gender)

judicial, 66–68, 66f, 67f
nonjudicial, 71–72, 71f
Sex representation rules
   designing, 59–62
   "fair," 62, 63, 65
   ICC, 62–65
Sexual slavery, 151–152, 170–171
   charges, brought, 106f
   charges, confirmed, 107f
   Colombia, 173–174, 176
   crimes against humanity, 32, 105, 106f, 107f
   domestic legislation, states, 183f, 184, 184f
   Guinea, 173, 175, 176
   Japan, 57
   Katanga, 105, 119, 121
   Lubanga, 111, 112
   Odio Benito and Blattmann, René on, 115
   recognition, 151–152, 170–171
   recognition failure, 97, 226n
   reparations, 151
   Rome Statute, 101
   Trial Chamber on, 120
   war crimes, 101, 105, 106f, 107f
Sexual violence. *See also specific types and cases*
   formal rules, ICTR & ICTY, 93
   as genocide, 93, 100, 218n
   judges' narrow interpretation, 195–196
   recognition failure, 97, 226n
Sexual violence against men
   Bemba, 122–123
   misrecognition, 122–123
   Muthaura and Kenyatta, 123
Sexual violence against women, redistributive gender justice, 131–135
   history, 131–132
   maldistribution, 132
   misrecognition and misrepresentation, 133
   nonrepetition guarantees, 134–135
   poverty, 132
   prosecution inadequacies, 133
   reparations, 132–134
   restitution, compensation, and rehabilitation, 133–134
   Rwanda, 133
   structural problems, 134
   unrepresentation of women, 133
Simmons, Beth, 163–164
Situation, 217n
Smart, Carol, 8
Smith, Jennifer, 12
Sociological legitimacy, 19, 55–56
Soft spots, institutional, 15, 18
Spatial nestedness, 13–14, 186
   feminist institutionalism, 199–201
   International Criminal Court, 27–29, 40–41
Spees, Pam, 36, 101
Stahn, Carsten, 120, 225n
State prosecutions
   ability, 165, 168, 171, 188
   invitation to ICC, 226n
   responsibility, 160
   unwillingness, 165–166, 168, 171, 188, 225n–226n
Status quo, gender. *See also* Legacies (gender)
   defenders, 17–18
   institutional, 17
   silences and bias, 25
Status subordination, 89, 90
Steains, Cate, 36, 46, 61–62
Struett, Michael, 34
Substance
   gender justice, 53
   justice, 53
Summons to appear, Pre-Trial Chamber, 221n
Surfacing, 8, 56
Survivor. *See* Victim
Symbolic frame, 53

Temporal nestedness, 13, 34–39
   complementarity principle, 161
   feminist institutionalism, 197–199
   informal rules, 197
Thelen, Kathleen, 9, 15
Third party enforcement, 16
Tomic, Alexandra, 80
Toope, Stephen, 19

Transformational account, 191–194. *See also* Trivalent model of justice
Transformative change, 9
Transformative remedies, 192
  reparations, 134, 136, 138, 147
  responses, 6–7
Translation services, 63, 80
Trivalent model of justice, Fraser's, 4, 5–8, 51, 191–194. *See also specific components*
  axes of social differentiation, 7
  creation, 53
  formal rules, 192, 195–197
  incremental change, 193–194
  interaction of elements, 192
  interdependence of elements, 191
  recognition, 2, 5–6, 23
  recognition implementation, 192 (*See also* Recognition (gender, gender justice))
  redistribution, 2, 5–6, 23
  redistribution implementation, 193 (*See also* Redistribution (gender and gender justice))
  representation, 2, 5, 6, 23, 51 (*See also* Representation (gender justice))
  representation implementation, 192 (*See also* Representation (gender))
  Rome Statute implementation failure, 193
  transformative remedy, 192
  what *vs.* who and how of justice, 7
True, Jacqui, 132, 226n
Trust Fund for Victims (TFV), 130, 140–142, 194
  assistance, 152–155
  financial support, recent, 152
  gender and sexual violence victims, 152–153
  gender-based perspective commitment, 152
  gender-sensitive assistance, 158
  International Center for Research on Women evaluation report, 153–154
  legacies, gender, 154
  on reparations, 150–151, 193
  on reparations, *Lubanga*, 145–146, 151, 223n
  resource issues, 151
  role, 130
  scope of programs, 153

Uganda
  Trust Fund for Victims assistance, 152, 153
  victim gender, 219n
  victim representation, 76f, 77
UN Basic Principles and Guidelines on the Right to a Remedy and Reparation for Victims of Gross Violations of International Human Rights Law and Serious Violations of International Humanitarian Law, 133–134, 138
Unwillingness to prosecute, states', 165–166, 168, 171, 188, 225n–226n

van Boven, Theo, 136
Van den Wyngaert, Judge Christine, 143, 222n
Vatican, 42–43
Victim. *See also* Redistribution; Reparations; *specific types and cases*
  definition, 138, 217n
  double status, 130
  how, 83
  redistribution, 135
  reparations eligibility, 138–139
  rights framework, 130
  who, 83
Victim-centered restorative justice paradigm, 31
Victim participation, 60, 64
Victim representation, 76–81
  gaps, 80–81
  how, 57–58, 77–81, 81t
  ICC Review criticism, 2010, 81
  negotiations, 62
  Office of Public Counsel for Victims, 79–80
  Outreach Unit, 78–79

priorities, rules, and enforcement, 81, 81t
procedures, 58
translation and interpretation, 80
Victims and Witnesses Unit, 60, 77–78
who, 76–77, 76f
Women's Caucus for Gender Justice, 60
Victims and Witnesses Unit (VWU), 60, 77–78, 135
Victims' Participation and Reparation Section (VPRS), 74
Violence
conflict-related *vs.* non–conflict-related, 226n
sexual (*See* Sexual violence)

Waller, Emily, 172
War crimes
sexual slavery as, 101, 105, 106f, 107f
sexual violence as, 94–96, 101
War Crimes Research Office (WCRO), 144
Waylen, Georgina, 10, 16, 17, 18, 41, 71, 84, 197, 198
Weber, Max, 20
What, gender justice, 7, 53
Whiting, Alex, 190
Williams, Susan, 53
Women's Caucus for Gender Justice, 35–36. *See also specific topics*
complementarity, negotiating, 165–167, 187–188
complementarity, predictions, 196–197
crimes against humanity, 96–97, 102
discrimination, 97–98
enforced pregnancy, 95–96, 101–102
establishment, motivation, 93
feminist attacks, 44
formal rules, 195 (*See also* Formal rules)
gender balance *vs.* quota, 61
gender definition, 45

gender expertise, 59
gender expertise, judicial, 68
gender experts, legitimacy and value, 99
gender experts, representation, 102–103
gender recognition rules, 100–103
genocide, 93, 94, 100–101, 218n, 220n
judicial selection procedures, expertise in, 61
legitimacy, 84–85, 99
liability modes and criminal responsibility, 98–99, 102
operational phase, ICC, 48–49
reference materials, 24
religious and conservative group attacks, 42–43, 46
reparations, 135–137, 154, 155t, 223n
representation at ICC, female, 59–61
representation, nonjudicial, 71, 71f
representation rules, gender, 62–65
Rome Statute work, 1–2, 35–36
state involvement calls, 142
state-level gender injustices, 166–167, 169
TFV mandate, 140
victim participation and representation, 60
Victims and Witnesses Unit, 60
victim's participatory rights, 143
victims' redistribution provisions, 135
war crimes, 94–96, 101
women in, 8
Women's Initiatives for Gender Justice. *See also specific topics*
accountability, 49–50
amicus curiae submissions, 60, 63, 69
complementarity, 179, 188
gender expertise, courtroom, 69–70
gender expertise, nonjudicial, 72–76, 75

Index [275]

Women's Initiatives (*continued*)
   Gender Report Cards, 75, 79, 112, 196
   on *Katanga*, 121, 128
   on *Lubanga*, 111–112, 145–146, 158
   MacKinnon appointment, 73
   on *Muthaura and Kenyatta*, 123
   reference materials, 24
   sex representation, nonjudicial, 71
   on vulnerability of sex-/gender-based violence charges, 103, 108
   women in, 8

Young, Iris Marion, 5